Backpacking and Trekking in
Peru and Bolivia

Backpacking and Trekking in
Peru and Bolivia

6th edition

Hilary Bradt

with

Petra Schepens
and
Jonathan Derksen

BRADT PUBLICATIONS, UK
THE GLOBE PEQUOT PRESS INC, USA

First published in 1974 by Bradt Enterprises. This edition published in 1995 by
Bradt Publications, 41 Nortoft Road, Chalfont St Peter, Bucks SL9 0LA, England
Published in the USA by The Globe Pequot Press Inc, 6 Business Park Road,
PO Box 833, Old Saybrook, Connecticut 06475-0833

The author and publishers have made every effort to ensure the accuracy of the information in
this book at the time of going to press. However, they cannot accept any responsibility for any
loss, injury or inconvenience resulting from the use of information contained in this guide.

British Library Cataloguing in Publication Data
A catalogue record for this book is available from the British Library
ISBN 0 946983 86 0

Library of Congress Cataloging in Publication Data
Bradt, Hilary,
    Backpacking and trekking in Peru and Bolivia / Hilary Bradt with
    Petra Schepens and Jonathan Derksen. — 6th ed.
        p. cm. — (Bradt guides)
    Includes index
    ISBN 1-56440-613-X
    1. Backpacking—Peru—Guidebooks.
    2. Backpacking—Bolivia—Guidebooks
    3. Peru—Guidebooks
    4. Bolivia—Guidebooks.
I. Schepens, Petra. II. Derksen, Jonathan. III. Title. IV. Series
GV199.44.P4B7 1995
918.4—dc20   95-14576
                                    CIP

Maps *Inside covers:* Steve Munns *Others:* Caroline Crump
Cover photographs Hilary Bradt
Front: The Inca Trail, Peru *Back:* Quechua child and alpaca
Line drawings Hilary Bradt
Typeset from the author's disc by Patti Taylor, London NW10 1JR
Printed and bound in Great Britain by The Guernsey Press Co Ltd, Guernsey,
Channel Islands

ACKNOWLEDGEMENTS

My grateful thanks to the many people whose often heroic efforts went into producing this edition. Rob Rachowiecki and Dr James Luytens managed to find time to check the natural history section at very short notice, John Pilkington came to my rescue when deadlines seemed impossible to meet, and Dr Jane Wilson Howarth succeeded in writing a comprehensive health section at the same time, it seems, as giving birth to a son.

Backpacking readers have, over the years, sent some wonderful letters updating the last edition of the guide and adding nice little touches like: 'Mrs Bradt, you would be proud of me! I am sitting under a rock in the rain...' followed by an evocative description of a hike. Others sent very helpful letters which, alas, were out of date by the time this book was prepared. If your name does not appear below please don't think your efforts were not appreciated!

Many thanks to the following travellers, residents and experts whose contributions were used to help update the text: Rick Ansell, Craig Cardon, Charles Davies, Linda Guinness & Renaye Upton, Peter Frost, Kevin Haight, Theodore Hartman and Joanne Soto, Connie Hickling, Pamela Holt, Paul Hudson, H Jenny, Bruce Kay, John Kurth, Pete Lawrence, Charles Motley, Helen O'Callaghan & Fiona Campbell, Andrew Pepper, Val Pitkethly, Richard Reiner, Sara Elliott & Paul Mosquin, Rachel Scott, Jeremy Smith & Frédérique Thiriet, Ann & Frank Spowart Taylor, and Ken Valentine.

Finally, but most importantly, my gratitude goes to my two main contributors and updaters. Petra Schepens worked tirelessly for many months updating the Peru section, bravely coping with the English language as well as sorting through the masses of information at the South American Explorers Club. Jon Derksen became my hero when he stepped in at very short notice to give me the benefit of his specialized knowledge of Bolivian hiking trails and La Paz. He kept my fax paper supplier in business. Erik Nijland, also living in Bolivia, added some good hikes.

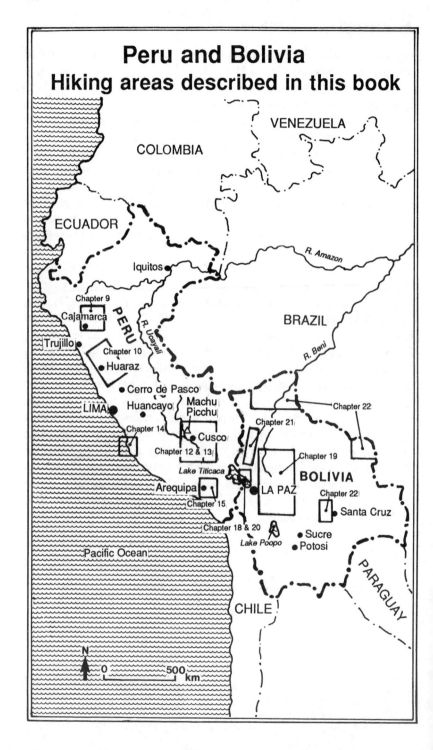

Peru and Bolivia
Hiking areas described in this book

CONTENTS

Part 1   **General Information**

Chapter 1   Preparations   3
Chapter 2   Health and Safety   15
Chapter 3   Travel in Peru and Bolivia   33
Chapter 4   The People: Past and Present   43
Chapter 5   Natural History   57
Chapter 6   Backpacking and Trekking in the Andes   77

Part 2   **Peru**

Chapter 7   Peru: General Information   93
Chapter 8   Lima   107
Chapter 9   Cajamarca and Chachapoyas Regions   113
Chapter 10   Cordilleras Blanca, Negra and Huayhuash   127
Chapter 11   The Central Andes   167
Chapter 12   Cusco and Vicinity   171
Chapter 13   The Cordilleras Vilcabamba and Vilcanota   191
Chapter 14   Paracas   225
Chapter 15   The Arequipa Area   230

Part 3   **Bolivia**

Chapter 16   Bolivia: General Information   243
Chapter 17   La Paz   257
Chapter 18   Lake Titicaca   263
Chapter 19   The Cordillera Real   267
Chapter 20   Sorata and the Tipuani Valley   292
Chapter 21   The Cordillera Apolobamba   299
Chapter 22   Central and Northern Bolivia   309

THE AUTHOR

Hilary Bradt lives in Buckinghamshire, England, with Chico the guinea pig. She has been leading treks to Peru and Bolivia for 13 years, mainly for the American company Wilderness Travel. When not trying to keep up with younger, fitter trekkers or slaving over a hot word processor writing about travel, she runs Bradt Publications.

CONTRIBUTORS

Petra Schepens (Peru) ran the South American Explorers Club in Lima for five years. Originally from Holland, she is now leading treks to Peru and Bolivia with the British company High Places.

Jonathan Derksen (Bolivia) teaches English at the American Cooperative school in La Paz. A Canadian writer and photographer, he has hiked many of Bolivia's trails accompanied by his dog, Hamlet, and wife, Tanya.

BRADT PUBLICATIONS

1995 was the 21st anniversary of our first book, *Backpacking along Ancient Ways in Peru and Bolivia*. In the intervening years we have brought out over 100 titles, specialising in off-beat destinations, hiking guides and rail guides.

Introduction

TWENTY-ONE YEARS AGO...

Working on the update of the Olleros to Chavín hike I was overwhelmed with nostalgia. It's an excuse for a little self-indulgent reminiscing.

It was this hike that started it all in 1974. George and I were staying in the Hotel Monterrey, having arrived in Huaraz via the spectacular Cañón del Pato, where we were so overcome by the views of the Cordillera Blanca that we kept asking our long-suffering bus driver to stop so we could take pictures.

Our trusty *South American Handbook* (the only guide book in those days) had brought us to Huaraz and suggested that Chavín was a worthwhile place to visit. Staying at the Monterrey to indulge our appetite for hot baths gave us time to think and plan. I can vividly remember George calling me over to look at a huge, topographical map on the wall; it filled me with foreboding. George was excited. The German map was dated 1933, he said, but look — here was Chavín and did I see the trail running from Olleros? My gloom deepened, and I started to come up with excuses. How could we go off on what looked like a two or three day hike with no map, no tent, and no information? Why not? George answered.

We had begun our journey down the length of South America on a compromise. I wanted to return to South America to continue the love affair with the country I began in 1969, and George wanted to go somewhere he could hike. I had limited experience of backpacking, had (sensibly) never camped in cold weather, and had only gym shoes since I'd never seen the point of hiking boots. But George had never been out of the United States, which offered him all the backpacking options he needed. So I agreed to bring a backpack not a suitcase, and I permitted him to bring some freeze-dried food. And that, I hoped, was that.

George won the Hotel Monterrey argument and I agreed that we should attempt the walk. After all, we had a compass, sleeping bags, and that blasted freeze-dried food that we had carried for so long. The Cordillera Blanca was already quite a popular place for climbing expeditions, but no-one hiked or trekked there as far as we could find out. All the hotel could tell us was that the trail probably still existed because it would be used by local people.

We took a truck to the turn-off to Olleros, and walked into the village. The locals stared at us in astonishment. We asked, in our limited Spanish, about the trail to Chavín and received reassurance that it was still there. Indeed, one man said, he frequently did the whole journey on horseback in a day. Do you see many gringos here, we asked? 'Nunca!' he replied.

The path was, indeed, clear and we stopped for the night near the head of the valley, having — mercifully — found a deserted shepherd's hut to sleep in. We'd brought a sheet of plastic to use in lieu of a tent, but I was happy to be under proper cover. I couldn't believe how cold it was once the sun had gone down! We collected dried dung for a fire and managed to cook some freeze-dried food, and I shivered and grumbled.

The next morning was one of glorious, warming sunshine, and I began to see the point of the whole thing. Snow-covered mountains glinted in front of us, and frost dusted the grass. My feeling of elation changed when, soon after we started walking, we had to make a barefoot crossing of a bog (I refused to get my gym shoes wet). Each little pool had its lid of ice, and I cried with the pain in my feet as we squelched across, and snivelled up much of the pass. I hated backpacking. But we reached the top, and there was the Chavín valley stretched in front of us: an easy, sunny, downhill walk and a huge sense of achievement. It was, after all, possible to walk from A to B using only a compass and commonsense. It was a wonderful way of seeing how the people lived, and experiencing the Real Peru. We did other hikes after that, and each time I enjoyed myself more. Something important had begun...

Part one

Chapter One

Preparations

GETTING TO LIMA AND LA PAZ

There are a fair numbers of airlines flying in to Lima from all parts of the world, but flights are expensive, especially when flying direct from Europe. Sometimes it works out cheaper to fly via the USA: New York/Miami to South America. Airtickets are more expensive in the high season: from April until September and around Christmas time. There is less choice for La Paz.

Your best bet is to use one of the specialist agencies for South America who offer low prices and informed advice. And check the travel sections of newspapers; many flight operators advertise special prices here.

In the USA an organization called Travel Unlimited, PO Box 1058, Allston, MA 02134, publishes a monthly newsletter ($5 each/$35 yearly subscription), giving up-to-date information about flight prices and special deals from all over the world.

It's always cheaper to buy a round-trip ticket, and anyway all countries require a return ticket for their tourist visa (though this is not always strictly checked).

From Europe

Several airlines fly from Europe to Lima: KLM, American Airlines (via the USA), Air France, Iberia, Alitalia, Viasa, Avianca, and Aeroflot. All of them have various prices, baggage allowance, ticket restrictions, special deals, etc. Use a specialist agency such as Journey Latin America in London (tel: 0181 747 8315) or South American Experience (tel: 0171 976 5511). A sample fare to Lima from London at the time of writing is with Viasa, via Caracas, for £468.

Getting from London to La Paz is much more expensive. The cheapest current price is with Aerolineas Argentinas for £633, so it would be cheaper to fly to Lima then take LAB to La Paz; or go with Avianca for £763 which enables you to stop over in Bogota and Lima.

From the USA

Several airlines serve the route Miami-Lima: American Airlines (who also go to La Paz), AeroPeru, Faucett, LanChile, Ecuatoriana and Avianca. With the exception of AeroPeru, all have direct connections with New York. In general AeroPeru and Faucett have cheaper tickets. Sometimes it works out better to pay a bit more and get an open ticket for a longer time, and most of the more expensive airlines have a better variety of flight schedules to Lima. Direct flights from Los Angeles to Lima are served by Aerolineas Argentina and Varig, but these direct flights tend to be more expensive than flying via Miami.

Flights to La Paz are more limited. In addition to American Airlines, Lloyd Aéreo Boliviano (LAB) flies from Miami which, since it can be combined with an Airpass (see below), may be worth investigating.

AIRPASSES

If you have only a limited amount of time and want to cover a lot of ground, an airpass is a good option. They are offered by some local airlines of both Peru and Bolivia, providing you also use that airline for your international flight. In Peru Faucett and AeroPeru do a 30-day 'Visit Peru' pass which offers unlimited domestic flights; the same deal is offered by Bolivia's Lloyd Aéreo Boliviana (LAB) for a 'Visit Bolivia' pass. Airpasses can only be purchased outside the country.

WHEN TO GO

Most people, if given the choice, will prefer to go in the dry season: May to October. The best months for hiking are April, May, September and October (when the rainy season is not delayed or early!). Visits to the jungle are best early in the dry season when there is still plenty of water in the rivers. The few travellers who decide to do some coastal hiking will choose the months when it is raining in the mountains but sunny along the coast: ie December to March or April.

WHAT TO BRING

Try to keep your backpack as light as possible; you will enjoy your trip much more and it is easier to look after your stuff during bus and train rides. However, you *do* need to bring all the essential equipment for your trip as it is difficult and expensive to buy it in Peru and Bolivia (although renting is an option) and the quality is poor. Select your camping equipment with care: it can make or break your trip. Keep in mind that the expensive things aren't always the best for your purposes. Consider buying second-hand equipment — you will be worrying less about things being stolen and will look less like a rich gringo.

There are some good products to be had from catalogues. In Britain Field and Trek (tel: 01277 233122) have the most comprehensive selection of outdoor gear at discounted prices. Wilderness Direct (tel: 01756 796840), the mail order department of the north of England chain Wilderness Ways, have a good catalogue. Also try SafariQuip (tel: 01433 620320) who sell a good mosquito net. Other recommended mail order companies are Oasis (tel: 01366 500466) and Nomad (tel: 0181 889 7014), especially for mosquito-related products, and Cotswold (tel: 01285 860483). Karrimor (tel: 01254 385911) puts out a beautiful and informative catalogue of their brand of hiking gear.

Americans have a much greater choice, with REI and EMS leading the field on the west and east coasts respectively.

Clothing

Remember the old travellers' maxim: 'Bring twice as much money and half as many clothes as you think you'll need'. All of your clothes should be chosen for comfort, but select one outfit which will render you respectable for that blow-out in a good restaurant, or an invitation to visit an upper-class home.

A popular saying describes a day in the Andes as including all the seasons of the year: nights are as cold as winter, mornings are spring-like, the afternoon heat can be as fierce as summer, and evenings have an autumn crispness. This means extreme temperature changes, and backpackers should be prepared accordingly. In the mountains, cold is the biggest enemy (temperatures drop to well below freezing at night). Obviously you must keep yourself warm without adding too much weight to your pack. Thermal underwear is very useful for these freezing nights, being light but very warm. A down parka (duvet jacket) is warm and light, or you may prefer a wool sweater and windbreaker. The local alpaca sweaters, scarves (mufflers), gloves, socks and hats are warm, cheap and a good way to support local labour. Since you'll warm up rapidly in the sun and through exercise, you should be able to peel off successive layers of clothing during the day. Cotton trousers (pants) over long underwear are more versatile than woollen trousers. Rohan Bags are popular and excellent, but there are other brands which are cheaper and almost as good. Corduroy (needlecord) is also light and warm. Jeans are not suitable for hiking because denim is heavy and takes ages to dry. Shorts are fine for hiking and generally acceptable in the towns. A jogging suit is very versatile and can be used as pyjamas at night, leisure wear in hotels, and worn under other clothing gives you an extra warm layer. Consider long-sleeved shirts for protection against sun and insects, and remember that T-shirts leave the base of your neck vulnerable to sunburn. Give some thought to pockets; all trousers should have deep pockets, secured with a button or zip, and they are handy in shirts as well. You may have to add them yourself.

It is likely to rain, even in the dry season. A big rain poncho which covers your backpack is very useful and doubles as a groundsheet. The warm and waterproof clothes made by Páramo (see advertisement on page 169) are excellent for high-altitude treks.

NOTE: It is dangerous to wear military-style clothing in Peru, and to a lesser extent in Bolivia. The army is not viewed with much affection by rural people.

BACKPACKING EQUIPMENT AND PROVISIONS

Experienced backpackers probably already own all the equipment necessary for a South American trip but newcomers should get expert advice. Good backpacking shops should be able to help you and climbing/hiking magazines always have good, disinterested information. It is worth looking in the classified adverts of the latter for second-hand equipment. The requirements of backpackers differ from those of trekkers who need not be so careful about weight or bulk (the long-suffering mules or porters will be carrying their stuff) so comfort becomes the primary objective.

Backpack
Be willing to spend some money on this — it will be your most important 'companion'. Spend time looking around and only settle for the best one for *you*: size, weight and capacity. Choose one that can be adjusted to your back. The leading manufacturers in Europe are Karrimor and Berghaus and in the USA, Lowe and Kelty. Backpacks with an external frame are worth considering if you are hiking at low altitudes since they are cooler and lighter in weight, as well as much cheaper. However, the frames are liable to get broken on public transport.

Trekkers need a large capacity daypack, with a hip belt, to carry all their daily needs, from camera to waterproof clothing; they will not have access to their main luggage during the day.

Boots
Together with your backpack these are the most important items for an enjoyable trip. Seek professional advice, and remember that a boot either fits or it doesn't; you should not need to break them in. Leather is preferred by many people because it is waterproof, but in the generally dry conditions of Peru and Bolivia lightweight hiking boots made from synthetic materials

are ideal, especially for women. They are always comfortable, rarely cause blisters, and with less weight to carry on your feet you will become less tired. Boots should have ankle support and Vibram soles. Trainers (running shoes) may be all right for trekking but are not suitable for backpacking, where you are at risk of turning an ankle because of the extra weight on your back.

Blisters can be avoided by wearing correctly fitting boots and woollen socks, and by not walking too far for the first few days. The most common cause of blisters is prolonged walking downhill — an unavoidable part of hiking in the Andes. When buying boots lace them firmly and stand on tiptoe, like a ballerina. Your toes should still be comfortable.

Sleeping bag
Although some very effective synthetic fillers are now on the market, you still can't beat goosedown, which is the lightest and warmest insulation available. It is virtually essential for backpackers — synthetic bags take up too much space. Backpacking or trekking in the Andes poses a problem, however, in that in the valleys the nights can be quite warm and you may be too hot in the bag which is just right for 4,000m. Your best bet is to have a sleeping bag cover or liner which gives you the versatility for moderate and freezing temperatures. A sheet sleeping bag not only keeps your down bag clean, but is perfect for jungle hiking and for use in economical hotels where sheets may not be provided. Silk is warmer and lighter than cotton. A pillow is made from a T-shirt stuffed with a sweater or duvet jacket.

Mattress/sleeping pad
It is essential to have some sort of insulation from the cold ground as well as padding. Closed-cell foam is cheap and adequate, but the best mat of all is the Thermarest, a combination of air mattress and foam pad. It's lightweight and compact, but expensive. However, if you can't afford a full length Thermarest, there's a cheaper (and lighter) three-quarter length one.

Tent
Although my first year of backpacking in the Andes was spent under a shower-curtain I concede that a good tent is necessary. It not only protects you from the elements but protects your gear from the acquisitive eyes of the locals when you are camping close to villages. In the interests of safety it is also worth choosing a colour that blends with the environment.

Good tents are expensive so try to buy a second-hand one. If you buy a cheap or used tent, be sure to bring seam sealant to block those dripping seams.

Mosquito net

This is not necessary if you are trekking or backpacking in the highlands, but overland travellers taking in the low-lying areas and staying with local people should bring a lightweight net to protect themselves from insect-borne diseases (see Chapter Two). Great advances are being made in improving the design of mosquito nets, and the most effective are now treated with permethrin which kills insects on contact.

Light

A small but powerful torch such as Magnalite, or a headlamp, should be on your list, and kept handy for hotels which are subject to power cuts, and for exploring ruins as well as for camping. Bring batteries from home, as they are of a better quality. Candles are fine for inside your tent but be very careful; quite a number of backpackers manage to burn their tent down. Slow-burning candles are useful.

Stove

A good stove is one of the most important items on your equipment list and worth spending some money on. The most practical are the MSR stoves (made in the USA) which run on any fuel. The Bleuet Camping Gaz stoves, which use gas canisters, are clean and handy, particularly for lone hikers, but can fail at altitudes higher than 4,000-4,500m. You can buy the cartridges in the bigger cities of Peru and Bolivia. It is forbidden to carry them on planes. For emergencies it's sensible to bring a tiny 'hot pot' — an aluminium cup and stand that burns tablets of solid fuel (you can buy these in Peru). Bring waterproof matches.

Making fires is strictly forbidden in national parks and reserves because of the damage caused by careless use of campfires: the National Reserve of Machu Picchu has lost many hectares of endemic forest through a hiker's carelessness, and much of the ancient Inca stonework has been permanently damaged through campers lighting fires against the walls. Even the most careful siting of fires still requires dead wood which cannot then play its part in regenerating the soil. So, cheery and warming though a campfire may be, please resist the temptation and do not allow your local guide to make a fire unless you are outside a protected area and well away from mountain villages which need the scarce fuel more than you do.

Pots and pans

If you don't already own a lightweight aluminium saucepan, buy it in Peru or Bolivia. They are cheap and available in even the smallest towns. Plastic or tin plates and mugs are both suitable, and great for warming hands as well.

Food

There is a good choice of suitable pack food available in Peru and Bolivia, so you don't need to bring food from home. You can shop in the local markets or at supermarkets in the bigger towns.

Packet soups, noodles, sugar, oatmeal and dried milk all provide a good basis for your hot meals. For lunches, cheese, fresh bread and dried fruits are excellent. Powdered fruit drinks make treated water more palatable.

Dried fruit and vegetables (sliced carrots, cabbage, onions and apples) make excellent backpacking food, and are easy to do yourself in the strong sun of the mountains.

What to bring from home? Maybe your favourite special treat, and a packet or two of dehydrated food for emergencies.

MISCELLANEOUS USEFUL ITEMS

Below is a checklist of items we have found to be indispensable: a travel alarm clock, penknife (preferably Swiss Army knife), sewing kit, safety pins, large needles and strong thread (or dental floss) for tent or other repairs, scissors, Sellotape, felt-tipped pens, pencils and ballpoint pens, a small notebook, a large notebook for diary and letters home, plastic zip-lock bags, large plastic bags for keeping your clothes dry, universal plug for baths and sinks, elastic clothesline or cord and clothes pegs, small scrubbing brush, concentrated detergent, liquid soap (non-polluting!), shampoo, small towel, dental floss, toothpaste, earplugs, insect repellent, sunscreen, handcream, lipsalve, sunglasses.

If you use glasses or contact lenses bring a spare pair. Bring a medicine kit (see *Health* chapter), compact binoculars and camera, film, a couple of paperback books, a phrasebook and Spanish dictionary, a pack of cards or other small pocket games, spare batteries, water bottle and one 2-litre container, water purifying tablets, waterproof matches, slowburning candles, compass, waterproofing for boots, large plastic dustbin liners (garbage bags) for covering packs and other equipment at night and a survival blanket.

PRESENTS

You will be the recipient of great kindness and generosity from local people and will want to show your appreciation with gifts. But be cautious with the giving of presents. Thoughtless backpackers and trekkers have created the beggars you meet in rural areas: children who demand *caramelos* or *dulces* (sweets) or *plata* (money) or simply want a present ('*Regálame*'). Gifts — even worthless things such as pens and sweets — should not be handed out indiscriminately. Instead, exchange stories, songs, games, drawings. Rural poverty is not synonymous with unhappiness, and if you examine your motives for wanting to give presents it may be that *you* feel good bringing smiles to children's faces, whereas with a bit more effort you could bring the same smile by playing a game. If you still feel guilty remember that your very presence is vastly entertaining and simply tolerating the stares as you go about your daily business is reward enough. See also pages 47-49 in Chapter Four.

MAKING DO

If you arrived in South America planning to relax but are seduced by the mountains and inspired by the tales of other backpackers, don't feel that your lack of equipment is a barrier. George and I were in the same position when much of our equipment was stolen: we used a shower curtain as a tent (rigged between trees with a cord) and a poncho as a sleeping bag (until we found a fellow-traveller in need of funds). Renting equipment is no problem in the major cities of the hiking areas, like Huaraz, Arequipa and Cusco. At the South American Explorers Club in Lima you can find some used equipment for sale, and at the popular backpackers' hostels you can put up a notice requesting equipment. When it is your turn to go home, consider selling your gear to help out other backpackers and make more space for all those Peruvian sweaters.

MONEY

The currencies of Peru and Bolivia are dealt with in the country sections. Here we cover general considerations.

The most easily exchanged currency is US dollars. You can bring your money in cash and/or travellers cheques. If you are on an organized trek and only in Peru/Bolivia for a couple of weeks you can probably manage with a combination of cash and credit cards since your expenditure will be minimal. Backpackers and long-term travellers will need to bring travellers cheques and US$100-200 in cash for emergencies and changing in small towns. The most used and accepted travellers cheques are American Express and Thomas Cook. It is easy to change travellers cheques in cities at the major banks and *casas de cambio* (the best time to change is in the mornings; open weekdays only). You cannot change travellers cheques in the smaller towns or villages. Always keep a list of the cheque numbers and note the date they are used; failure to do this will make it difficult to replace lost or stolen cheques. Never sign your cheque until the bank clerk has given the go-ahead.

Make sure that your dollar bills are not damaged (little tears or pieces missing) or they may not be accepted. Forged dollar bills are common so be wary about buying dollars in South America.

You can get cash from major banks with an American Express card and some other credit cards (but a commission is charged) and most upper-range hotels, restaurants and shops accept credit cards.

Do not take all your money with you on the hikes, only the amount you'll need and some extra. Leave the rest at a hotel that has a safe (make sure that you get a receipt).

BUDGETING

Peru and Bolivia are inexpensive by the standards of the developed world, but you will still need to assume an expenditure of around $15.00 per day although probably you will spend less. Whilst you will spend virtually nothing when hiking the trails, it's a rare backpacker who can resist the lure of a bit of luxury on hitting the cities. Keep costs down by buying food in the markets and staying in the cheap gringo hotels recommended in the popular guidebooks.

Bargaining is standard practice in Peru and Bolivia, especially with handicrafts, although personally I prefer to pay a fair price for the often painstaking work than pride myself on how little I paid for it.

NOTE: We have tried to keep prices as up-to-date as possible in this book. The Peruvian economy has been pretty stable since 1990, with an inflation rate of about 60% a year — but it is still vulnerable. Please bear with us if you find that prices have risen. The Bolivian economy is (amazingly, when you consider inflation rose to over 20,000% per year) even more stable with a rate of inflation around 10%.

PHOTOGRAPHY
Camera and lenses
You have to make a considered decision here: do you expect to take professional-quality photos on your trip or do you just want to have some memories afterwards? Serious photographers need to take more care over the safety of their equipment, give themselves time during the hikes for photography, organize a pack-animal to carry the camera equipment and have a good insurance. Others will be happy with a small, automatic camera, preferably with a built-in zoom. The comfort of carrying less weight and the security of looking less like a rich tourist is ample compensation for the poorer quality photos at the end.

Film

Kodachrome 64 is the most suitable slide film — the vivid reds seem particularly suitable for Peru and Bolivia where people and llamas wear bright clothing and decorations — but bring a few rolls of fast film for poor light or interiors. Some photographers prefer Fujichrome 100. For prints, 100 ASA will cope with bright and cloudy days. Although film is often available in Peru and Bolivia, you cannot rely on it so it is best to bring all you need from home.

Keeping the film in good condition can be a problem on longer trips where it is exposed to heat and humidity. It is worth bringing a few special bags to keep the film in. And it's probably best to wait until you get home before developing your pictures, as the quality is poor and the cost high in Peru and Bolivia.

Camera courtesy

Both countries are wonderfully photogenic, and few visitors can resist capturing as much as possible on film. However, you must bear in mind that for people living in the remote mountain areas, this can be a highly intrusive and discourteous practice. The rural people are reserved but very courteous and their initial contact with strangers has a ritualized pattern. By photographing them without establishing some sort of human contact you are being rude and insensitive. Once you have established contact you should ask permission to take a photo. If you are refused, or the person is uneasy, put your camera away.

It is a different matter for people living in the popular tourist areas. Here they can make a nice living posing for photos. This is a business and should be respected as such: if you don't want to pay don't take a photo. Try to find out the proper price beforehand — there is something obscene in paying a child posing with a llama the same fee that her father may earn working all day in the fields. If money is not demanded, don't offer it. Many people love to have their photos taken, particularly those who do not look 'ethnic'. You can get some delightful portraits of these grinning kids. Do get their address and send them a print — and honour your promise. The result will be far more treasured by the recipient than by you.

Never take photos of any military objects. If in doubt, ask someone in authority.

FURTHER INFORMATION

The best place for hiking information — and *all* information — is the South American Explorers Club (SAEC) in Lima (see page 110). And of course from the other travellers who you'll meet at the towns closest to the trails. Unfortunately many guides are unreliable sources of information, being preoccupied by the commercial side of it all. 'No' or 'I don't know' are not part of their vocabulary.

Maps

The maps in this book will give you an adequate idea of the hikes described, and the SAEC has some good detailed maps on the popular hikes in Peru. If you want to go off the beaten track and do some serious hiking and exploring by yourself (and we urge you to do this), we recommend you carry a topographical map of that area. In both countries the government-run Geographic Institute publishes appropriate maps which are available in the capital. Details are given in the relevant sections.

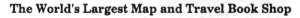

Chapter Two

Health and Safety

HEALTH

Co-written with Dr Jane Wilson Howarth

Before you go
Inoculations

South America is not the hot bed of disease you may imagine, but the following inoculations are recommended.

• Update diphtheria and polio. Also tetanus or tetanus booster.

• Yellow fever. (Not effective until ten days after inoculation; not recommended for pregnant women.)

• Anti-malarial protection (if going on a jungle trip; not needed for high-altitude treks). Peru has chloroquine-resistant strains of malaria and it is important that you follow the prophylactic regime carefully. In England phone the Malaria Reference Laboratory (tel: 0891 600 350) for the latest information. Americans should contact the Centers for Disease Control in Atlanta, tel: (404) 332 4559.

• Havrix for Hepatitis A. This is an expensive vaccine (£40) but the course of two injections protects you for ten years. If you are going on a short holiday or an organized trek the chances of contracting hepatitis are less, so you may prefer not to have the inoculation or to use the cheaper (but less effective) Gamma Globulin instead.

• Typhoid vaccine is recommended by some doctors although it will not provide total protection and being careful what you eat and drink is your best defence. It is given in two shots, four weeks apart.

• A pre-exposure rabies vaccination. Hikers are at risk from rural dogs, many of which carry rabies, and those venturing to coastal or rainforest areas could be a victim of vampire bats and other bats which are often rabid. The vaccine is essential for reseachers or naturalists who will be handling wild mammals or entering caves (see also *Rabies* on page 20).

Fitness

Being in good physical condition is an essential requirement for all hikers; lack of fitness is dangerous and will mar your enjoyment of the mountains.

However, fitness requirements are very different for independent backpackers planning a long trip compared with trekkers or others on a short holiday where daily objectives must be achieved. The former will gradually get into shape on the trail, but the latter must make considerable efforts to achieve fitness before they go.

Backpackers have the enviable advantage of being able to camp where they choose, and fatigue in the early stages of a long trip is almost an advantage since it encourages a very slow ascent, thus minimizing the danger of altitude sickness. On the other hand, the weight of your pack at the start of the trail ensures that you go slowly and there's no point in letting lack of fitness add to your suffering!

Ideally, people signing up for an organized trek or expedition must start to get fit at least a couple of months before they leave. This preparation should as closely as possible resemble what they will actually be doing: hiking in the mountains. Therefore it is much better to walk briskly in hilly country than to run along level roads. Not all potential trekkers, of course, live close to suitable countryside, but everyone has access to flights of stairs and walking, then running, up an increasing number of stairs is an excellent means of getting fit for the Andes. Cycling is also a good way of preparing for trekking, since it involves most of the same muscles.

COMMON MEDICAL PROBLEMS

This list of the most common health problems and their treatment assumes that you are not in easy reach of a local doctor. Even if the medical set-up isn't quite what you're accustomed to, remember that doctors in South America are well versed in diagnosing and treating local diseases. If you are unwilling or unable to see a doctor, pharmacists are accustomed to treating the local population for minor complaints, but check the expiry date on any medicines they prescribe. Many drugs, available only on prescription in the USA or Europe, may be bought — expensively — over the counter in South America.

'Filth-to-mouth' diseases and how to prevent them

Diarrhoea and a host of other diseases are caught by getting other people's faeces into your mouth. Contrary to popular belief, most of the diarrhoea-causing bugs get into you by way of contaminated food rather than via dirty water. Among the possible filth-to-mouth diseases that can be acquired in Peru and Bolivia is a particularly unpleasant larval tapeworm which can set up home in the brain and muscles where it is known as cystocercosis. Not surprisingly, this causes quite a serious — though curable — illness which is well worth avoiding. Cystocercosis seems to be a particular problem where uncooked foods, especially lettuce, are irrigated with untreated sewage effluent. This happens in La Paz and parts of Peru where water is very scarce. Never eat lettuce, even in expensive hotels, and try to avoid all uncooked foods including *ceviche* (marinated raw seafood) and ice-cream and farmers' cheeses. PEEL IT, BOIL IT, COOK IT, OR FORGET IT.

Take the precaution of sterilizing all water by boiling or with iodine (more effective than chlorine tablets) and be careful to wash your hands after using the toilet (this is to wash off other people's germs, not your own).

Diarrhoea

Traveller's diarrhoea is caused by enterotoxigenic forms of the bacteria which everyone has in their bowel: *Escherichia coli*. The trouble is that each geographical area has its own strains of *E. coli*, and these alien strains cause inflammation of the intestine and diarrhoea. Everyone has his favourite remedy, and it is the subject of many a gringo conversation. The most sensible way to treat the problem depends on whether you are a backpacker on a leisurely trip lasting several weeks or months or a trekker on a brief holiday. The latter needs to feel better in a hurry, and he/she is advised to bring a supply of the antibiotic ciprofloxacin. A single 500mg pill at the onset of diarrhoea is usually effective, although stubborn cases may need a course of the antibiotic. There may be side effects (and it is definitely dangerous if you are dehydrated — this medication must be taken in conjunction with lots of fluids, at least three litres per day) and in principle it is unwise to take antibiotics unnecessarily since resistant forms of the bug so quickly emerge.

If you are a backpacker and can rest up for a few days it is best to let your body expel the toxins and take no medication. 'Blockers', such as Lomotil or Imodium, will stop the diarrhoea by slowing down the action of the gut, but tend to leave you feeling ill. Drink plenty of fluids and eat bananas, papaya, mashed potatoes and boiled rice. If you don't feel like eating, don't eat. The body's ability to absorb fluids and salts is greatly improved by taking sugar at the same time, so to counteract dehydration and loss of vital minerals, sip a solution of salt (½ level teaspoon), baking soda (½ level teaspoon), potassium chloride (¼ teaspoon), and glucose, sugar or dextrose (four heaped teaspoons) dissolved in one pint (half a litre) of water. This 'electrolyte replacement' formula is effective and safe. Make up several packets before leaving home. Failing that, a pint of water containing four heaped teaspoons of sugar to half a level teaspoon of salt can be made anywhere. These rehydration solutions should taste only slightly salty — no more salty than tears. If you are travelling by public transport or are in other places where a dash to the lavatory is impractical, some sort of chemical cork is required. Codeine-phosphate (available on prescription) is a useful stopper as well as being a powerful painkiller; otherwise many people favour Lomotil. Fluid replacement is the most important part of all the diarrhoea treatments: being dehydrated will make you feel a lot worse and slows down recovery.

Diarrhoea accompanied by a fever should be treated with Ciprofloxacin. Long-term and seasoned travellers will find they gradually build up a nice collection of South American *E. coli* in their intestines and will seldom suffer diarrhoea attacks. This does not mean, however, that they should be casual over hygiene and run the risk of getting other more serious filth-to-mouth diseases such as typhoid, cholera and hepatitis E.

Dysentery

If, in addition to diarrhoea, you have severe stomach cramps, pass blood in your faeces and/or run a fever, then you probably have dysentery. A doctor or a clinical laboratory (*análisis clínico*) should confirm the diagnosis before you take medication. Flagyl is effective for amoebic dysentery, as is tinidazole. Ciprofloxacin should cure bacillary dysentery. Both antibiotics require a week-long course to be effective.

Fever

If you develop a fever for any reason you should rest and take aspirin or paracetamol. But bring a supply of amoxycillin (convenient because you only have to take it three times a day) or tetracycline with you since you could be struck by some infection in a hopelessly inconvenient place. Under these circumstances, take an antibiotic as prescribed, but not for longer than seven days without seeing a doctor.

A side effect of some medicines such as tetracycline is sensitivity to the sun resulting in sunburn on exposed parts after minimal sun exposure. This can be a problem in the Andes where the sun is strong.

Sores and skin infections

If the infection is serious (spreading redness, increasing pain, pus discharge or even fever) you will need an antibiotic, taken regularly for seven days, to clear it up. A slow healing sore can be speeded on its way by applications of honey or papaya. Athlete's foot can be a problem (see page 88). Treat it before it cripples you. Tinactin or other antifungals in powder form are effective in the early stages (shake it into your socks each morning), but I (HB) needed a course of antibiotics because a bacterial infection developed as well. (Cloxicillin, 500mg six-hourly for seven days is best — unless you are allergic to penicillin.)

Colds and coughs

Respiratory infections are very common in the Andes. Perhaps the dramatic temperature changes are largely to blame: people go sightseeing in Cusco wearing only a T-shirt, and return blue with cold when clouds or the sudden dusk puts an end to the hot sun. Colds easily turn into coughs and even bronchitis in these conditions, so bring decongestants, cough medicine and sore-throat lozenges. A soothing cough medicine can be made from equal parts of lemon or lime juice, honey, and *pisco* or other spirit in hot water.

Motion sickness

The local people are not the only ones to suffer on the rough roads in the Andes. Stugeron is recommended since it does not make you drowsy. Remember that a full stomach is more likely to empty itself than a partially full one!

Snakebite

I include this not because it is likely to happen, but because people worry that it will happen. A fatal bite from a venomous snake is rare, even in areas where the reptiles are common, for a couple of reasons: snakes are timid creatures and will get out of the way when they sense the approach of a human, and even a poisonous snake often fails to deliver the full amount of venom when it bites in self-defence.

Most of the hikes described in this book take you above the treeline where there are no snakes, but for the lowlands it is worth knowing what to do if you — or your companion — are bitten, just in case.

First forget everything you thought you knew about snakebite kits, tourniquets, sucking out the poison, etc. All are likely to cause worse problems. Snakebite experts now say that the only treatment should be to gently wash the surface of the wound to get rid of any sprayed venom which could subsequently enter the wound, and to bandage the wound itself and as much of the affected limb as possible with a crêpe bandage, tight enough to restrict — but not cut off — the blood flow. Keep the bitten part lower than the heart, and remain as calm as possible. If it is your friend that has been bitten, reassure him/her that the chances are very high that it was either a non-venomous snake or that it did not inject all or any of its venom. If you have had the presence of mind to kill the snake, keep it for identification so that an appropriate antivenin can be administered. Get to a hospital as quickly as possible.

AVOIDABLE (BUT POTENTIALLY SERIOUS) PROBLEMS
Rabies

Rabies is a viral infection of the brain transmitted by infected animals. It is invariably fatal. In the less-developed countries vaccination of domestic animals for rabies is almost non-existent so the risk of contracting rabies from dogs and other animals is high. If you have not had the rabies vaccine before you leave home but are subsequently bitten by a suspect animal, take the following course of action and forget the conventional advice about capturing the animal and keeping it for ten days to see if it dies of rabies — this is simply not practical in an Andean village:

1) Immediately *scrub* the bite for five (timed!) minutes under running water and with soap, followed by disinfection with iodine or, failing that, with *aguadiente* or other local spirit. Experiments have shown that this alone reduces the risk of contracting rabies by 90%.
2) Get an anti-rabies injection as soon as possible, but remember that the disease travels slowly along the nerves to the brain; it is only at this point, when symptoms appear, that the disease is incurable. Before that the rabies vaccine is effective, and the progress of the infection can take several weeks or even months. Make your way to a clinic in a major town as soon as you can, but reassure yourself with the knowledge that if the bite is on your lower leg or foot you have time on your side.

Cholera

In February 1991 Peru was struck with an outbreak of cholera that reached epidemic proportions. Cholera is a food- and water-borne bacterium that is spread through poor hygiene and contaminated foods. The cycle is reinforced by improper waste treatment, and the dumping of raw sewage offshore. It was predominant along the coast, though cases were reported in the highlands and jungle regions. The bacteria cause major and immediate dehydration, but for those in good health and who receive immediate care, cholera is seldom fatal. The disease has mostly affected those living in poorer conditions where fresh water and money for proper food is extremely limited. The epidemic was under control a year later, and good education has started. These days most people boil the water and you can get bottled water everywhere. Cholera is a rare disease in travellers and the vaccine is not recommended since it offers minimal protection.

Some rare Peruvian diseases

In the early part of this century large numbers of labourers were brought in to build the Lima to Huancayo railway, and accounts of the project casually mention hundreds of deaths because of accidents and disease. The main ailment was *verruga* and I (JWH) have been asked how verrucae could kill so many men. *Verruga* is also the suggested cause of the unpleasant rashes depicted on some of the pre-Inca pottery displayed in museums in Lima. So what is *verruga*? It is an unpredictable disease which occurs from time to time in the Peruvian Andes at altitudes of between 500m and 3,100m. Locals are usually immune to it, but if a large number of outsiders move into its territory it can cause outbreaks of serious disease known as **Oroya fever** or bartonellosis. The labourers who built the railway were one such group of outsiders; the Inca conquerers were, perhaps, another.

Verruga is transmitted by the bites of minute sandflies which are so small that, when hungry, they can get through mosquito netting. Once bloated on blood, however, they cannot get out. Impregnating your mosquito net with permethrin will protect you. Sandflies are mainly active in twilight so insect repellents and long clothes will protect you at dusk. If the disease strikes it is usually caught at the end of the rainy season (March to May) but the risk to travellers is small and it responds to antibiotics. The first symptoms parallel those of numerous tropical diseases, namely fever, headache, aches and pains.

It is possible that the sores depicted on those pre-Inca pots were due to another, milder sandfly-borne disease which is also peculiar to the region. This is called *uta* or **Peruvian leishmaniasis**. The painless ulcers caused by *uta* usually heal without treatment. Peruvian leishmaniasis is almost unknown in travellers but it occurs quite commonly amongst poor villagers who live between 1,200m and 3,000m in Peru and Bolivia. This form of leishmaniasis should not be confused with the more dangerous disease of the lowlands, locally called *espundia*. The sandflies that carry this leishmania are found on river banks and humid forests, especially in the rainy seasons. The resulting sores do not heal and need prompt medical attention.

Another disease that causes unnecessary alarm amongst backpackers is **Chagas disease**. This is a disease of poor lowland villages and is transmitted at night by the bite of the cone-nosed kissing or assassin bug known locally as *vinchuca*. These large insects live in the thatch and walls of wattle-and-daub type housing. Their bite is painful so you will know that you have been bitten. Some excrete the trypanosome organism in their faeces which are rubbed into the bite wound. Afterwards there may be a raised lump at the site of the bite and in some people there is swelling of the eyelids. A blood test six weeks after a bite should show if the disease is present. However, if you are likely to be staying in rural huts, you can minimize the risk by sleeping in a hammock, not on the floor, and by using a mosquito net. If you are bitten, wash the wound under running water. Untreated, the disease shows itself in fever, heart disease, and enlarged organs such as the gullet and intestines, often years after the infection. Chagas disease is the main cause of heart failure in South Americans under the age of 40, but it is extremely rare in travellers.

Emergency medical treatment and blood transfusions

HIV which causes AIDS exists in Peru and Bolivia and so does the Hepatitis B virus which is spread in the same way but is much more infectious. Although transfusing unscreened blood is a well-understood route of transferring these infections, many developing countries do not have the resources to do this screening. Nor, unfortunately, is sending safe screened blood by courier from home a real option. In most emergency situations it is unlikely to get to you quickly enough. All you can do is ask local advice (your embassy should be helpful here) on the safest hospitals.

The problem in Bolivia no doubt parallels the situation in many developing countries; only about 30% of hospitals in the country screen blood and a recent survey found that 54% of blood was contaminated with Chagas parasites, Hepatitis B, syphilis, or HIV (in that order). The prevalence (47%) of Chagas parasites in the blood samples is alarming since although easily cured in the early stages of the disease, it may not be recognized until a stage where treatment is difficult or ineffective. The good news is that the Red Cross are working to introduce a system of accreditation which will monitor hospitals which screen blood so it will be possible to pick a clinic or hospital where reliable screening is carried out. Presumably the situation is similar in Peru. (Thanks to Kate Cooper for this research.)

MOUNTAIN HEALTH

Paradoxically, backpacking in the Andes is both the healthiest and the most dangerous mode of travel. Fortunately the main killers (apart from accidents) — hypothermia, pulmonary oedema and cerebral oedema — can be avoided so read the section below carefully.

Injury

All the hikes described in this book take you well away from civilization, but most are on good and well-frequented trails. Be careful and sensible. Remember that a badly injured person cannot easily be evacuated from the Andes, and that you may or may not be able to persuade local people to assist you. All backpackers should be conversant in first aid (preferably by going on a course), and should carry an appropriate first aid booklet. There are some excellent ones specifically for mountain medicine (see *Further reading*, page 320).

Your medical kit should run the gamut from dealing with minor problems to coping with major situations like large wounds that would normally need suturing. Butterfly closures or Steristrips are suitable for these. Zinc-oxide tape is useful for holding a dressing in place (the best being non-stick Melonin dressings) and has many other uses as well. If you don't mind some funny looks bring panty-liners as multipurpose dressings: they are ideal, being sterile and water(blood)proof and the adhesive backing sticks to the bandage so they don't slip.

When compiling your medical kit (see end of section) bear in mind that medical supplies in the mountains are very poor or non-existent.

Sunburn

The combination of equatorial sun and high altitude makes sunburn a real danger to hikers in the Andes. Protect yourself with clothing and a really good suncream made for skiers or mountaineers, with a protection factor of 15. Lipsalve is essential to prevent cracked lips and should contain sunscreen, and remember how vulnerable your nose is. Wear a hat and a long-sleeved shirt, at least until you have built up a protective tan, and protect the back of your neck if wearing a T-shirt.

Hypothermia

Simply put, this means that the body loses heat faster than it can produce heat. The combination of wind and wet clothing can be lethal, even if the air temperature is well above freezing. Trekkers and those on dayhikes are more likely to have problems with hypothermia than backpackers, who, by definition, carry their requirements with them. So if you are only carrying a daypack, make sure you include a sweater or fleece, a windbreaker, and a waterproof anorak or poncho, however settled the weather looks when you set out. If you can include a survival bag or space blanket that's even better. Always carry some high-energy snacks, too. Your porters or pack animals may easily be delayed and you can get thoroughly chilled while waiting for them. Also, should you stray away from the group and become lost, the main danger to your life is taken care of. Backpackers should concentrate on keeping their warm clothes and sleeping bag dry (everything should be kept in plastic bags) and carry a space blanket or survival bag for emergencies. There are various ways of keeping warm without relying on heavy or expensive clothing. Wear a wool ski-hat, or *chullo*, to prevent heat loss from your head (although the oft-quoted statement that 40% of body heat is lost through the head is misleading since it includes heat loss through breathing!). Make sure heat can't escape from your body through the collar of your windbreaker; use a silk or wool scarf or a roll-neck sweater. Eat plenty of high-calorie trail snacks. Hot drinks have a marvellously warming effect. Have one just before going to sleep. Fill your water bottle with boiling water, put it in a sock and treat yourself to a 'hotty' at night (which also gives you sterilized, ice-free water in the morning). Always change your wet, sweaty clothes when you stop at the end of the day.

If a member of your party shows symptoms of hypothermia: uncontrolled shivering followed by drowsiness, confusion, or stumbling, he/she must be warmed up immediately. Exercise is exhausting and eventually results in worse hypothermia. Conserve energy, raise the blood sugar with food, give hot drinks, and put the person in a warmed dry sleeping bag under cover. If his condition is serious, climb (naked!) into the sleeping bag with him and use your own body heat as a radiator. And be prepared for your friend's astonishment when he regains consciousness.

Acclimatization

Acclimatization is the process of adjusting to the reduced oxygen pressure in the atmosphere at high altitude. This process differs for everyone and there are no rules as to who will suffer the effects of high altitude. Being in excellent physical condition does not aid in acclimatization, nor does it make you less prone to altitude sickness; indeed, young fit men are often the most susceptible. If you have suffered from altitude sickness in the past you are likely to suffer again, but there is a first time for everyone, sometimes after several trouble-free trips to high places. For most people it takes a week or two to become completely acclimatized, but there are some who never get there. So never compare yourself with another person, especially if travelling in a group, but respect the differing time needed for each person to be ready to proceed into the mountains.

On flying from sea-level to La Paz or Cusco everyone feels the effects of altitude to a certain degree. The symptoms are headaches, breathlessness, feelings of dizziness or lightheadedness, insomnia, and loss of appetite. You can help alleviate it by drinking lots of water (or — better — coca tea), avoiding alcohol and heavy and hard-to-digest food, and above all by resting. Spend at least three days at an altitude of no more than 3,500m, then start doing some easy day-hikes. Allow at least five days to get used to the altitude before starting your backpacking trip (reputable trekking companies build in a period of acclimatization to their itinerary). Acclimatization is achieved when the heartbeat is normal at rest, you can eat and sleep well and have no headache. If you experience any of the symptoms of altitude sickness while backpacking, try to rest for a couple of days. Then, if you don't feel better, turn back. Remember, too, that even a short visit to the coast will lose you your hard-won acclimatization.

High altitude sickness

This may be divided into three categories: acute mountain sickness (AMS), cerebral oedema and pulmonary oedema. All three are brought on by a too-hasty ascent to altitudes exceeding about 3,000m. The potentially fatal pulmonary and cerebral oedema can be prevented by acclimatizing properly before the ascent and by climbing slowly, not more than 300m daily, or even slower if a member of the hiking party shows any signs of AMS.

AMS, known locally as *soroche*, is the most common of the three variations. It is interesting to know something about the biochemistry of the problem. When there is less oxygen in the air a person needs to breathe more deeply and frequently. It is the build-up of carbon dioxide in the blood which stimulates an increase in the breathing rate, not lack of oxygen, but at altitude gas is more soluble so carbon dioxide takes longer to reach the concentration necessary to stimulate deeper and more rapid breathing. So you can help the body by remembering to take deep breaths.

The symptoms of AMS are severe headache, nausea, and sleeplessness. If the victim is only mildly active and drinks plenty of liquids for a day or two, these symptoms should moderate. Diamox (see below) can be used to treat the headache and nausea. Cheyne-Stokes respiration during sleep affects many people at high altitude. Also known as periodic breathing, it is characterized by the sleeper taking shallower and shallower breaths until he stops altogether; then comes a gasping deep breath and the cycle begins again. It is harmless, but disturbing both to the sleeper and his tent-mate.

The drug Diamox (Acetazolamide) is an effective prophylaxis for AMS. Two 250mg pills are taken each morning for three days prior to the ascent (ie: when still at sea-level or thereabouts) and continued for two more days at altitude. Diamox can also be used as treatment for AMS: take 750mg (three tablets) for small adults or 1,000mg (four tablets) for big people, then 500mg per day for four more days. Since Diamox is a diuretic, take the pills in the morning to avoid being up half the night to pee. Another side effect can be tingling of the hands and feet. Missing out one dose will solve this problem.

Cerebral oedema is a more dangerous type of altitude sickness. Fluid accumulates in the brain, and can cause permanent brain damage or death. The symptoms are intense headache or neckache, nausea, staggering gait, confusion, disorientation and hallucinations. Anyone showing signs of cerebral oedema should be taken down to a lower altitude — at least 500m lower — immediately. One of the symptoms may be denial — sometimes aggressive — of the problem so a firm hand is often needed to persuade the person to turn back.

Pulmonary oedema is more common than cerebral oedema but equally dangerous. Fluid collects in the lungs, literally drowning the person if his ill-health is not recognized. He must be taken to a lower altitude immediately. The symptoms are shortness of breath when at rest, coughing, frothy bloodstained sputum, and a crackling sound in the chest. Each year climbers die in the Andes from pulmonary oedema because they have not taken the time to acclimatize and do not recognize the symptoms in time.

Many symptoms of AMS resemble those of other diseases, but if you are at a high altitude and someone is clearly deteriorating, *descend*. If their symptoms are due to AMS their condition will improve and you will have saved a life. Do not wait overnight to see if they are better in the morning. Evacuating an uncooperative victim in the dark is no fun.

CUY CURE

Guinea pigs, *cuyes*, have always played an important part in Indian rituals to ensure health and good fortune. Recent findings suggest that the animals were sacrificed in Inca times, and no doubt the *jubeo* ceremony, practised nowadays by *curanderas* (native healers) goes back thousands of years. If a person falls seriously ill in Peru or Bolivia, his or her family are as likely to call in a *curandera* or, more specifically, a *jubeadora* as a doctor, even though the former may be more expensive.

To diagnose and cure the patient a black guinea pig is required, and these animals cost three times as much as other less potent colours. The *jubeadora* must also be paid, and since her powers are increased by good food, she is feasted as well. Her job is considered a risky one — she may catch the patient's disease or, more obliquely, her 'destiny may change', so she can command a high price.

The relatives of the patient ensure that this money is well spent by scrupulous attention to the details of *jubeo*. The ceremony should take place on a Tuesday or Friday (although in an emergency any day of the week will do). A black guinea pig of the same sex and equivalent age to the patient is selected, and a candle burns by the sick person, along with aromatic herbs. The *jubeo* begins at midnight, but preparations involving coca chewing and the consumption of *aguardiente* (a regional alcoholic beverage) begin well before that hour. At midnight the *jubeadora* picks up the guinea pig and, filling her mouth with *aguardiente*, blows the alcohol over the animal's belly, face, nose and ears. After a prayer and the sign of the cross, the guinea pig is held firmly by its fore and back legs, belly well exposed, and systematically passed over all parts of the patient's body, beginning with the chest. As the animal takes on the symptoms of the sick person, it struggles violently and — so they say — dies. (If it doesn't die the patient's illness is not considered to be serious.) Relieved of his symptoms the patient is well on the road to recovery, but diagnosis is still necessary before herbal remedies can complete the cure. The dead *cuy* is carried into the next room wrapped in a black cloth, and after further coca chewing, helped along with shots of *aguardiente*, it is opened up and its organs examined. An enlarged heart shows that the patient was suffering from a cardiac problem, an inflamed liver points to hepatitis, and so on. The animal may even be skinned so that the muscles and joints can be examined. Mission accomplished, the *jubeadora* is further fortified with food and drink, collects her fee, and goes on her way.

MEDICAL KIT

Water purifiers (best is iodine which can also be used to cleanse wounds)
Antiseptic
Vaseline (for cracked heels)
Moleskin and adhesive-backed foam rubber (for blisters and sore feet)
Butterfly closures or Steristrips, panty-liners
Crêpe/ace bandage
Fabric Elastoplast/Band-Aids (best is a dressing strip)
Ciprofloxacin and rehydration sachets; Lomotil or other diarrhoea blocker
Aspirins or Paracetamol/Tylenol
Amoxycillin or other broad-spectrum antibiotic; take tetracycline or
erythromycin if allergic to penicillin
Thermometer (with a low-reading range)
Decongestants, eg: Actifed
Cough and throat pills
Antifungal cream and powder

MEDICINAL PLANTS

You'll come across a lot of traditional medicinal plants in South America,
especially in the markets. They are the sole source of medicine for many
people, so try to learn something about them. If you decide to use them as
an alternative to Western medicine be warned that most vendors in the
markets have no idea of how to use these plants and will sell you anything
and everything. Get medical advice at one of the many local clinics where
medicinal plants are used and bear in mind that the cure will tend to be
slower than with Western medicine.

Also realise that just because it is natural does not mean that it is harmless
— several killer poisons and drugs come from 'natural, herbal' sources.
Herbal medicines have side effects and disadvantages too, and these can
be less predictable since 'dosages' are more difficult to measure.

Western medicine and local people

One of the by-products of well-equipped trekkers permeating every
mountain stronghold is that local people will beg medicines above any
other consumable. Even the most culturally sensitive trekker or backpacker
feels that to deny them this easing of the harshness of their lives would be
cruel, yet there are good reasons to say no. Apart from the risks to them of
inappropriate dosage, it adds to the belief that Western medicine is good
and traditional remedies are bad despite the advantages of the latter in
availability and cost. In short, do not dabble in other people's health!

USEFUL ADDRESSES

British Airways Travel Clinics. Phone 0171 831 5333 for the one nearest you. Inoculations, travel supplies.
Nomad Travel Pharmacy and Vaccination Centre, 3-4 Wellington Terrace, Turnpike Lane, London N8 0PX. Tel: 0181 889 7014.

Dental Projects Ltd, Blakesley Lodge, 2 Green St, Sunbury-on-Thames, Middx TW16 6RN.

Centers for Disease Control, Atlanta, GA 30333. Tel: (404) 332 4559. They annually publish the *Health Information for International Travel* bulletin which is also available from the US Government Printing Office, Washington, DC 20402, USA.

International Association for Medical Assistance to Travellers (IAMAT), 736 Center St, Lewiston, NY 14092, USA. Tel: (716) 754 4883. They provide lists of English-speaking doctors as well as health information.

SAFETY

Although the danger from the Shining Path (Sendero Luminoso) terrorists has abated, Peru is still a dangerous country for the unwary and particular attention should be paid to this section. The information here is drawn from the *Peru Packet* written by the Lima branch of the South American Explorers Club. Call or write for the most up-to-date information (see page 110).

Bolivia is much safer, but there have been incidents of robbery or even murder on some of the more popular trails so it is wise to take the same precautions as in Peru.

Peruvian police

In Peru there are three types of policemen:

1) Routine control police, who you see out in the streets controlling the traffic.

2) The private police (PIP), mostly plain clothes, who work with crime and terrorism. They are the ones most likely to check your passport and visa.

3) Tourist police whose job is to help tourists.

Of these three the routine police are the most corrupt, and street 'deals' are almost routine. The private police are usually straight and can be very tough. They are mainly concerned that tourists are travelling legally in the country (ie: that visa requirements are adhered to) and that they do not deal in drugs. The tourist police are most helpful and we recommend you to contact them when there are any problems or you need help of any kind.

Unfortunately there are also some 'fake' police around; they will flash a reasonably plausible ID card and sometimes even wear a police uniform. If stopped by the police always ask to see their ID (*'Su identificación, por favor'*). You have the right to do this so take your time. If they are not genuine police their nerve is likely to fail at this point. Providing you are not breaking the law there is no reason to be intimidated by the police. The only hassle they can give you is checking your passport and visa. Always carry your passport; if you get checked without it, the police have the right to throw you in jail for the night or even a few days.

Always be polite and friendly to the police, but put yourself on the same level and avoid giving them the feeling that they have any power over you.

Drugs

Dealing with drugs is a serious crime in both Peru and Bolivia and carries a heavy jail sentence. No one in their right mind wants to spend time in a South American jail and I am assuming my readers are sane so will say no more about voluntary drug use. There are, however, cases where drugs have been planted on tourists, especially backpackers who fit the image of 'drug-addicts'. Be suspicious of over-friendly locals and do not give the police an opportunity to plant drugs. If you feel as though you are being set up, just walk away.

There have been instances of a different sort of drug planting in Peru: occasionally one hears reports of foreigners accepting sweets or a drink from a friendly Peruvian and waking up some hours later minus all his possessions. Rare though this type of robbery is, you should be cautious about accepting food from strangers (be hospitable and offer some of your goodies instead).

Coca leaves

Someone once described coca leaves as having the same relation to cocaine as ivory has to elephants. The drug is derived from the leaves of the coca plant, which is grown in both Peru and Bolivia, but that is all. Chewing coca leaves is perfectly legal and has been part of the Indian culture for thousands of years (see page 49). Steady and prolonged chewing has a narcotic effect but few gringos have the perseverance to achieve this. Most use it to make a pleasant herb tea which seems to alleviate altitude sickness.

It is illegal to take coca leaves out of the country, but coca tea bags are usually not questioned by your customs authorities. If you are hiking in coca-growing regions be aware that whites are mistrusted because of the US coca eradication programme. If you are not American it might be sensible to advertise this fact by sewing your country's flag to your backpack.

Theft

Theft is a major problem for travellers in Peru and to a much lesser extent in Bolivia. Most theft is by deception and tricks with the thieves working in groups. One thief gets your attention, the second grabs your belongings and throws them to a third, who escapes with them. Thieves are quick and clever, and most of the time you don't even know what is happening. If you know the most popular tricks you can stay ahead of the game. The most dangerous areas for being robbed are crowded places such as markets, and bus and train stations. Basically theft falls into the three categories listed below.

Unguarded possessions

In risky situations (and that's any place where there are people around) your belongings should either be attached to your person or under lock and key. In a restaurant never hang a bag over the back of your chair, or put it on the floor without wrapping a strap around a chair leg. One minute's inattention and it's gone. Other places to be particularly careful are in the waiting areas of bus and train stations, or in the trains and buses themselves. A chain with a combination lock is an extra safeguard.

At airports make sure you lock your luggage before putting it on the plane, and strap sticky tape around the bags. Protect backpacks by putting them in a strong canvas bag or flour sack. Airport thieves are looking for easily opened luggage that looks valuable. Never ask a stranger to watch your luggage for you.

Backpack pockets are a great temptation to young or casual thieves who have a brief encounter with your unattended luggage on public transport. It is best to have detachable pockets that you can keep inside your pack when travelling.

Don't leave stuff around, even if of little value. That includes your clothes, which should not be left on the hotel washing line overnight.

Thefts from the person

Handbag snatching, slashing and pickpocketing are very common, especially in Peru. Don't carry a handbag or a daypack in cities, unless you carry it in front of your body. If, like me, you can't bear to be without a handbag, make sure it is made from tough, hard-to-cut material and that you carry it across your body. Never wear jewellery and don't keep a wallet in your pocket. When wandering around cities and towns try to carry as little as possible with you. Most people tend to carry more than they really need. When you arrive in a new place leave your camera in the hotel and take it out the next day when you have got your bearings. Keep your money and passport in a money belt, neck or leg pouch. Do not put all your money in one place.

Never carry more than you can physically handle, especially if travelling alone, and always take taxis if you have too much to carry.

If you think you are being followed, turn around, stop and walk behind the person. If someone tries to rob you and you catch them at it, shout '*ladrón!*' (thief); passers-by are likely to come to your rescue.

The best protection is not to bring belongings that are dear to you, or that are expensive. Try to shed your consumer-oriented culture. The expensive camera takes better pictures, but what's more important, the pictures or the experience?

Armed robbery

Armed robbery is not as common as ordinary theft, but it does happen. If a robber threatens you with a knife, gun or other weapon there is little you can do but hand him what he wants, just as in any other place in the world — although the small stature of most Peruvians and Bolivians has given some tourists the courage to fight back. Avoid the same sort of places in South America as you would at home: impoverished slums and poorly lit streets after dark. Sometimes an armed robbery takes place on buses or cars passing through remote mountain regions.

Tourist spots are more dangerous than areas that see few foreigners — thieves need a regular supply of victims. For this reason Cusco has become the centre for robberies in Peru, although certain parts of Lima are almost as bad. Keep alert. Generally speaking, your money and valuables are safer deep in your luggage in a locked hotel room than on your person.

Ways to protect your valuables

• Use a money belt, neck or leg pouch or inside pocket for cash and passports. Or, better, all three so your valuables are not all in one place.

• It is important always to carry your passport with you, in case you are asked to show your visa. However, a photocopy of the relevant pages of your passport will usually suffice when wandering about towns or when hiking. This photocopy will also help you replace your passport quickly should it be lost or stolen. Remember that it is illegal to be out without any form of identification.

• The safest place for valuables is in a hotel. Keep them in their safe and get a receipt, or in cheaper hotels put them deep in your luggage and lock it before going out.

• Before you leave home, write down the numbers of your passport, travellers cheques, plane ticket, credit cards and any other vital information, photocopy it and keep copies in a variety of places in your luggage.

• At most hotels you can store your unneeded luggage while you hike. Make sure it is locked, and that you are given a receipt.

- Emergency money in the form of a $100 bill is completely safe hidden under the insole of your boot. Or think of your own secret hiding place.

Remember, the point of all the above is not to make you paranoid, but to allow you to relax and enjoy the company of some of the millions of Peruvians and Bolivians who wouldn't dream of robbing you.

Safety on the trail

Mostly you will be safe on the trail, but unfortunately the number of 'rich' gringos trekking through the mountain villages have given the *campesinos* (peasant farmers) a new consumer awareness. Only a very few of the popular trails suffer from this problem. As a general rule it is safest to camp out of sight, or to stay with a family (or camp in their yard) thus gaining their protection. Keep valuables — and most of your money — at the bottom of your pack when hiking: even armed robbers are not going to rummage through your pack looking for them.

More dangerous than the people are their dogs. Most rural villages keep several underfed dogs which bark hysterically when they see a stranger, especially a strange-shaped one (with a backpack). Mostly it is just bravado, but in a continent where rabies is common, don't take the risk of being bitten. If you are planning on doing a great deal of hiking, or are cycling, it would be worth investigating one of the anti-dog sprays on the market (your postman/mailman could probably advise you!). 'Daze', an ultrasound gadget is said to frighten dogs away. Otherwise the most effective deterrent is a handful of stones. Most dogs will turn tail and flee at the very sight of you stooping to pick up a stone (if there are no real ones an imaginary one works) and actually throwing the missile — accurately — is highly effective. You can also carry a stick but dogs tend to jump at a stick, making the encounter more frightening.

Read up the section on rabies *before* you start hiking and carry the appropriate first aid items (soap, scrubbing brush) where you can easily get to them. And don't worry, although the bite of these animals is certainly worse than their bark, an attack is relatively rare.

Take care to avoid accidents. Stop walking when you are very tired, don't venture off the trail without a compass and survival equipment, avoid hypothermia and AMS, and have access to basic first aid supplies at all times.

Insurance

Be sure to get both medical and luggage insurance. Check that you are covered for mountain sports (ie: backpacking).

Chapter Three

Travel in Peru and Bolivia

TRANSPORT

In terms of availability, public transport is excellent in Peru and Bolivia. Any village served by some sort of road will have some sort of vehicle running there on some sort of irregular schedule. In terms of quality on the major routes, it's up to you whether to go for comfort or cheapness.

Buses

These come in various shapes and sizes, from luxury vehicles speeding along the intercity routes to ramshackle affairs serving the rural villages. In Peru, and to a lesser extent in Bolivia, you can get luxurious buses on the well-travelled routes (mostly along the coast and on paved roads into the mountains) with video, toilet and reclining seats. They charge about 30% more than the normal price. Make sure you buy a ticket with a well-known company where the buses mostly leave on time, stick with the route and don't stop at every corner. The smaller bus companies never leave on time and may cancel the scheduled departure altogether if there are not enough passengers.

Try to travel during the day for more comfort, safety and scenery. Try to avoid long bus rides; break your journey. You'll enjoy the trip much more, avoid problems with theft (most of which happen when you are tired), and arrive in better shape. The cheaper buses have more character, and more sights and smells. The amount of fruit peel, paper, babies' pee, and vomit that the average family can dispose of during a lengthy trip in the mountain region has to be seen to be believed.

All buses stop for meals, but not necessarily at mealtimes. Make sure you understand how long you will be stopping for, or the bus will leave without you. Better still, have your meal within sight of the driver. Plenty of snacks are available from local vendors who will pour on to the bus and crowd round the windows at every village. Remember to fill your water bottle before you leave although soft drinks are usually available from vendors.

Your luggage will be lashed to the roof or, on bus routes along the coast, be stowed away in the luggage compartment. Either way, it will be inaccessible, so bring warm clothes and something to use as a pillow during night trips (those crescent-shaped inflatable neck pillows are ideal). You'll also need games or a book for entertainment during unexpected delays or breakdowns. Keep your passport on you for police checks, and watch your luggage like a hawk. Padlock small items to the luggage rack or seat. Robbery is common on buses, but these are professional criminals not your fellow bus passengers.

Trucks

Lorries/trucks form the backbone of public transport in these two countries. Remote villages are served by trucks carrying cargo and a few passengers, but vehicles carrying only people run between the larger towns. In general, truck prices are roughly the same as cheap buses, although private *colectivos* or pick-up trucks will charge a bit more.

Although buses are more comfortable — and warmer — the views from an open truck are so fantastic that these should be your choice for short journeys through spectacular scenery. Although some trucks run to a schedule, most wait until they have collected enough passengers to make the trip worthwhile. Don't be misled by the driver telling you he is leaving *ahorita*. His and your concept of 'now' will be different; you may wait for hours before he makes a move.

Remember, it is bitterly cold riding in an open truck in the Andes. Keep all your warm clothes (including gloves, cap and even your sleeping bag) handy, and carry your foam pad to cushion those bare boards. Not all trucks have a tarpaulin, so bring protection from rain and snow. It's a good idea to strap your pack on to the side of the truck (inside) so that it's neither trampled by other passengers, nor resting in a nice pool of oil or urine during the trip. Protect it from the effluent of furred or feathered passengers by putting it in a strong bag such as a flour or rice sack (which can be purchased at any market). Bring something to eat and drink during long trips, although long-distance trucks, like buses, stop for meals.

Don't take a truck at night unless you're absolutely desperate and well prepared for freezing weather. Assume an afternoon departure will become an evening/night departure.

Colectivos

These are vans or cars which use the same routes as buses, but the long-distance ones are about double the price. This is because they are more comfortable and faster, but since they only leave when they are full there might be a long waiting time. The short-distance *colectivos*, mostly between towns, are the same price (or a little more) than the buses. They are a comfortable option (if they don't fill them up to the roof!) and very popular in Peru and Bolivia.

Taxis
There is no shortage of taxis in either Peru or Bolivia. If you can join up with other travellers to share the cost, and strike a good bargain with the driver, a taxi need cost little more than conventional transport and will save you a lot of time and effort — for example when you need to get to the trailhead and are carrying a heavy backpack. Save your energy for the hike.

Always settle on the price beforehand and make sure the taxi is reasonably likely to make the journey without breaking down. Make sure, too, that the driver knows where you want to go (in the hiking areas most know the most popular trailheads) but don't expect him to know how to read a map.

Trains
Although slower than buses, trains are a pleasant alternative — and the views are better. On the negative side, however, is the increased risk of theft. Professional teams work the most popular tourist trains and even experienced travellers can fall prey to their tricks. Thieves commonly slash bags left under the seat or take them from the rack and throw them through the open window to an accomplice. Padlock your stuff to the luggage rack and try to team up with other travellers to watch each other's luggage.

Peru   Here railways are divided into two systems:
1) From Lima to La Oroya. Here the line branches, with one line continuing on to Huancayo and Huancavelica and the other one going to Cerro de Pasco. Note, however, that at the time of writing the lima to Huancayo line is used for freight only.
2) From Arequipa to Juliaca, from where one branch continues on to Puno and then to Cusco. From Cusco there is a line to Quillabamba via Machu Picchu. Train schedules are reduced or cancelled in the rainy season. You can usually buy a ticket the day before, and reserve a seat (but this still doesn't guarantee that your seat will not be occupied!)

Even if it is against your principles it is worth going first class if you are carrying much baggage. Second class throws you into the hub of local life and conversation but it is difficult to enjoy this if you are trying to watch your luggage, and a moment's inattention may be fatal. You may also have to fight for a seat since they cannot be reserved.

On first class you are still exposed to plenty of local colour when vendors stream on to the train at stations, and some of the more well-to-do Peruvians (those that are likely to speak English) travel first class. Note, however, that first is not actually the best class. The authorities have taken notice of the gringo fear of robbers and on some lines have provided them with a carriage protected from the incursion of any but the most respectable locals. Buffet- or tourist-class carriages have locked doors and only ticket holders are allowed on. There will be no vendors so no local colour, but you *will* be safer. There is even — supposedly — a sleeping car between Arequipa and Puno.

Bolivia   In contrast with Peru, Bolivia has an extensive railway network. It is said that every time Bolivia lost a war (which happened with regularity throughout its history) the victors built a railway in compensation. As well as ordinary trains, Bolivia has the *ferrobus* which looks just as it sounds — a bus designed to run on rails.

There are two classes. On the *ferrobus* these are called *Pullman* and *Especial*, and on trains simply first and second class, although a few lines have Pullman carriages. There are no sleeping cars.

Hitchhiking
This is possible but hardly worth it as most drivers charge for the ride. There are exceptions, of course, but it is courteous to offer payment unless you are quite sure this would be offensive.

Aeroplanes
Andean roads are often in very poor condition, especially in the rainy season, so sometimes it's wise to consider taking a domestic flight. If you have an airpass (see page 4) you will be taking them frequently. Otherwise domestic airfares are fairly expensive, especially in the high season, and international flights within South America are outrageously expensive. It is far cheaper to fly from border to border, and cross the frontier by bus.

Always confirm and reconfirm your flight, and this must be from the town of departure. The tourist peak season is from June until September, with July as the busiest month, and from December until February, when Peru and Bolivia enjoy their main holiday season. Be prepared for overbooked and delayed flights, and cancellations. Flights are often cancelled in the rainy season, so allow extra time in your schedule. For security always make sure that your checked luggage is locked and put backpacks in another strong, protective bag. Most domestic airlines are pretty generous with extra luggage and don't charge excess luggage.

ACCOMMODATION

There is always a wide variety of hotels to choose from in Peru and Bolivia, from a little dark cell with a too-small bed that feels more like a hammock, to a luxury room with a king-size bed and en suite bathroom and limitless hot water. Then there are the middle range hotels. The star-rating of hotels may mislead you — few are up to European or American standards — but then they're half the price. In Peru expect to pay $US4-5 per person for a cheap *hostal*, around US$10-15 for a mid-range hotel, and US$30- 50 for most of the top-class hotels. Prices vary according to the size and tourist interest of the town, high or low season, and for groups. Prices are a little higher in Bolivia.

The hotel feature of abiding interest to gringos, most of whom have diarrhoea or are expecting to have diarrhoea, is the toilet. In the cheapest hotels this will be out in the yard and very smelly; in cheapish hotels it will be inside, but communal and probably occupied when you most need it. You may prefer to go for the upper end of the middle range to ensure that your room has its own bathroom.

Plumbing systems in Peru and Bolivia are rather half-hearted, so except in the posh hotels don't try to flush your toilet paper (yes, you must supply your own) down the lavatory, but put it in the basket or box in the corner. No, it's not nice, but a clogged toilet is nastier. South American electricians enjoy having lots of exposed wires in the shower. Be very careful when using the on/off switch for hot water. Dry hands and rubber flip-flops are a sensible precaution if the wiring looks really suspect.

All towns of interest have their backpacker hangouts. The travellers' grapevine or guidebooks will tell you where these are. The *South American Handbook* and the *Peru Travel Survival Kit* have the most up-to-date hotel listings. It is worth deciding beforehand where you will stay and taking a taxi there to avoid being hassled by hotel touts. On the other hand, finding your own, unlisted, hotel ensures lower prices and fellow guests who are not all foreigners. The cheapest hotels are almost always clustered around bus and train stations. In villages that have no obvious hotel, there is always a *señora* with a room to rent for the night, so just ask around.

Your possessions can be at risk in any hotel. The better places have safe-boxes in which you can leave your valuables (take the precaution of putting them in a sealed envelope, and make sure you get a receipt). Don't leave enticing valuables on show in your room — even an honest chambermaid can succumb to temptation. Leave them at the bottom of your backpack, in a bag that you can recognize by touch. If something goes missing, do report it to the hotel owner and if this has no effect go to the police.

Make sure you know the hotel rules: checkout times, discounts, electricity or water cuts, hot water availability and whether there is an extra charge for this, and if the price includes taxes (especially in middle- and upper-range hotels), special services, etc.

Camping

It is perfectly safe to camp well off the beaten track and usually all right in or near the smaller villages, although in remote areas you may infringe the rules of rural etiquette if you refuse offers of accommodation and then pitch a tent nearby. Avoid leaving your campsite unattended and always keep all your valuables inside the tent, which should be lockable. Never camp in, or close to, towns or cities; a hotel is much safer.

For more about camping see Chapters Four and Six.

FOOD

Eating in Peru and Bolivia is enjoyable. There are all sorts of tasty snacks sold on street corners and in cafés, and even the cheapest restaurant food is usually good, although starchy. These are meat and fish countries and vegetables are rarely served. If you don't fancy what is on the menu, most restaurants will serve eggs, potatoes and rice on request. But of course it is more fun to experiment with the local food. Bring your dictionary to the restaurant and don't be embarrassed to wander round looking at other people's choices. Sometimes that's the easiest way to select a meal — simply point to someone else's.

All the cheaper restaurants serve only set meals at lunch time, listed as *menu*, or *almuerzo* (the menu, in the English sense, is *la carta*). In a set menu you'll get soup of the day, *sopa del día*, a main dish, *la segunda*, and a dessert, *postre,* or/and a cup of herb tea, *mate*. The helpings will be substantial and the price low — US$2-5. Anything chosen from the à la carte menu will be more expensive and take longer to prepare, so save this for the evening meal.

In the mid- and upper-range hotels and restaurants a meal will cost between US$5 and $40, with an added tax (in Peru) from 18 to 31%.

Always check your bill carefully, and count your change.

Tipping is not customary in the cheaper restaurants, nor in the mid-range restaurants where it will be added to your bill. International restaurateurs expect a tip on top of the service charge and tax.

Don't get so carried away with the joys of eating that you consume risky food. Cold buffets served at up-market hotels can be particularly dangerous because it has been sitting around for a while breeding a nice variety of bacteria. Be particularly careful to avoid mayonnaise and salad, and cold meat. You'll be safer eating freshly cooked food in the market.

Do-it-yourself meals bought at markets provide a welcome change and the chance to eat fresh vegetables and fruit. It is still better not to risk salad unless you can soak it for some time in purified water.

Everywhere in Peru and Bolivia you'll find a Chinese restaurant, a *chifa*. Food here is invariably good and cheap. In tourist areas restaurants have learned to cater to gringo tastes and provide yummy chocolate cake and pizzas and so on. They also provide menu translations which can leave you more confused than ever. What, for instance, is 'Bifstek with pickpocket sauce' or 'a small locust'?

Local dishes — Peru

A classic Andean dish, guinea pig (*cuy*) is rarely served in restaurants but you will find it at street stalls during fiestas, since Indians save it for special occasions. Once pet-owning gringos see the little roasted animal lying whole on the plate and grinning at them, they tend to lose their appetite.

The typical coastal dish in Peru is *ceviche*, raw fish or shellfish marinated in lemon juice with onions and red peppers. It is delicious but most foreigners have sensibly avoided it since the cholera outbreak.

The following are the items most commonly found on the menu:

Starters

Palta rellena	Avocado filled with chicken salad
Palta reina	Avocado filled with mixed salad and mayonnaise
Papa a la huancaina	Cold potatoes with a rich egg and cheese sauce
Rocoto relleno	Stuffed green peppers (often very hot)
Tamales or humitas	Ground maize steamed in banana leaves, filled with meat or cheese; sometimes they are served sweet, with sugar instead of meat
Sopa criolla	A creamy spiced soup with noodles and a little chopped meat
Chupe de mariscos	A very rich and creamy shellfish soup
Causa	A dish made from yellow potatoes, peppers, hard-boiled eggs and other ingredients

Main dishes

Meat dishes:

Churrasco and *Lomo*	Fillet or rump steak
Apanado	Breaded meat cutlet
Chorrillana	Meat smothered in fried onions
Adobo	A Cusco speciality: chopped, marinated pork in a richly seasoned gravy, served only in the mornings
Piqueo	A very spicy stew with meat, onions and potatoes
Sancochado	Meat, vegetables and garlic
Lomo saltado	Chopped meat in a sauce containing onions, tomatoes and potatoes
Picante de ...	Meat or fish with a hot, spicy sauce
Parrillada	Barbecued beef, pork, sausage and viscera
Chicharrones	Chunks of pork fat, deep fried

CUY

In Cusco Cathedral (and in the cathedral of Ayacucho) there is a 17th century painting of the Last Supper. The scene is traditional, but the main dish is startlingly different: as befits a meal of importance in Peru, Christ and his disciples are about to dine on guinea pig.

The domestication of the native guinea pig as a source of meat for special occasions would have been noted by the priests and Spanish artists who set out to save the souls of the Inca heathens by using images they could relate to. To this day the animals, known as *cuy* in Spanish (see page 73), are kept by the Indians of the high Andes.

Cuy takes hours to prepare for the table. After the neck is broken (no blood must be shed, since this is an important ingredient in cooking), the animal is plunged into boiling water to loosen the fur, which is plucked and finally shaved with a razor blade. All organs are carefully preserved, including the intestines, from which tiny sausages, *pepián de cuy*, are made. These contain minced innards and blood.

The method of cooking *cuy* varies by region. Generally, they are grilled whole over charcoal after the skin has been rubbed with herbs and garlic (an important step, since the skin is the tastiest part). In Arequipa fried *cuy* (*chactado*) is popular: deep oil is used and the *cuy* covered by a smooth river stone to flatten it during cooking so that it resembles Peking duck. Sometimes *cuy al horno* (baked guinea pig) is offered in the Cusco area, and in other mountain villages it may be casseroled in green (herb) or red (chili and peanut) sauce.

While gringos fastidiously nibble at the scant meat on slender bones, locals crunch their way happily through head, brains and paws. One bone is carefully preserved, however. This is the *zorro*, a tiny bone from the middle ear said to resemble a fox. This is used for gambling. Wagers may be placed on the number of *zorros* collected in a given time, or the little bone is placed in a glass of beer and the drinker challenged to swallow it with the beer (surprisingly difficult, because it tends to stick to the bottom of the glass).

Foreigners more used to seeing guinea pigs as cherished pets than culinary ingredients will be relieved to hear that this role is not completely denied them in the Andes. A Peruvian friend told me his younger brothers and sisters refused to allow their pet *cuyes* to be dished up to an uncle in honour of his visit. It was three years before the uncle would speak to his family after this insult!

Chaufa	Chinese style fried rice
Cabro or *Cabrito*	Goat meat
Anticuchos	Baby beef-heart shish kebab

Fish dishes:

Corvina	Pacific sea bass
Pejerrey	Fresh water fish
A lo macho	The main fish dish comes with a shellfish sauce

Desserts

Mazamorra morada	Pudding made from purple maize and various fruits
Flan	Crème caramel
Picarones	Delicious rings of fried batter served with syrup or honey
Keke or torte	Cake

Drinks

Pisco	Grape brandy, very popular in the form of *Pisco sour* with lemon, sugar and egg-white.
Chicha	Maize beer. This is an integral part of any celebration or communal work project in rural areas. In Andean villages look out for houses with flowers or coloured plastic tied to a pole above the door: this indicates that the householder sells *chicha*.
Chicha morada	Unlike *chicha* this is not alcoholic but a soft drink made from purple maize.
Cerveza	Lager-type beer is very popular. There are several regional brands such as *Cusqueña*.
Vino	Local Peruvian wines are worth tasting, although they are very sweet by gringo standards. Tacama and Ocucaje are the best choices. *Tinto* is red wine.
Agua mineral	Mineral water is mainly drunk by foreigners so not usually available in rural areas. You will need to specify *con gas* (carbonated) or *sin gas* (non-carbonated).
Mate	Herbal tea has become very popular. The best known is *mate de coca* which is served to tourists on arrival in Cusco or La Paz to ward off symptoms of altitude sickness. Many other herbal teas such as *manzanilla* (camomile), Yerba Luisa (lemon grass), Yerba Buena (mint), and Inojo (dill) are available. *Mate* usually served after lunch.

Local dishes — Bolivia

Bolivian food lacks the variety of Peru's, most notably because the lack of a coastline means no fresh seafood. There are a few specialities, the most popular (with me) being *salteñas*. These delicious pasties are part of the Bolivian culture, being eaten in the mornings and advertised outside small restaurants that make and sell no other foods. The tough pastry casing encloses a runny mixture of meat, gravy, olives, potatoes, raisins and any other ingredients that take the cook's fancy. A good *salteña* virtually explodes at the first bite, spilling scalding gravy over your fingers and down your front. And it's worth all the mess.

Here are a few Bolivian specialities not usually found in Peru:

Main dishes

Chuños	Tiny freeze-dried potatoes prepared in the high Andes. I've never acquired the taste for them, despite the efforts of the cook to make them less revolting with the addition of egg or cheese.

Sajta de pollo	Chicken with a spicy yellow sauce and onions and *chuños*
Fricase	Stew, usually pork
Saice	Mixed vegetable and meat stew

Drinks

Singani	This is the Bolivian brand of *pisco*, also distilled from grapes. As well as being drunk on all festive occasions it is splashed around the wheels of vehicles or the hooves of donkeys to ensure a safe journey (see page 300).
Pilsener	The most popular lager
Api	A thick, hot drink made from red maize, cinnamon, cloves and lemon. It is served at dawn on street corners and makes an ideal start to the day when you have a cold truck ride ahead of you.

Chapter Four

The People:
Past and Present

INCAS AND AYMARÁS

Most sources believe that the South American 'Indian' crossed the Bering Strait from Asia to North America and gradually migrated south over thousands of years. Myths, however, are more interesting than facts, and the beliefs of the origin of Man are central to the spiritual life of both the Quechua and Aymará people. The former are by far the largest linguistic group in the Andes, being descendants of the Incas. Aymarás are a small group of tenaciously independent people living around the shores of Lake Titicaca, mainly in Bolivia. Patriotic Bolivians believe that the Aymará civilization is very old, and the Quechua much more recent, but there is little evidence to support this.

The myths and way of life of the two groups are similar, but they remain two races with different physical and psychological characteristics, different dress and agriculture and, most importantly, a different language. A Quechua tribesman cannot even understand an Aymarán: the grammar and vocabulary of the two languages are different, although they share fundamental words. This inability to communicate doubtless helps to keep the two tribes separate, even today. Some villages are half Aymará and half Quechua, and each half is recognizably different. The two groups rarely intermarry.

Quechua-speaking Indians are found throughout the old Inca empire, from the Colombian border with Ecuador to southern Bolivia and beyond. This wide dispersal of the language is due to the Inca custom of subduing newly conquered tribes by establishing Quechua-speaking settlements within their territory. They are the linguistic majority in Peru, and the minority in Bolivia where they are found in the southern part of the Altiplano, in the Department of Oruro, and around Cochabamba, Potosi and Sucre.

The Incas sought to rule by consent, not compulsion, but met fierce resistance from the Aymará, who did not submit to Inca rule until the end of the 15th century. They adopted the Inca religion, with embellishments, but kept their own language and customs.

Inca mythology has Lake Titicaca as the birthplace of Man, with the son of the sun and the daughter of the moon arising from two islands on the lake. The Aymará belief is similar: the creator, Viracocha (the name means 'creator' in Quechua and Aymará) rose out of the lake and created a world without sun, light or warmth, and peopled by giants. These creatures angered Viracocha, so were destroyed by a flood, after which Viracocha appeared from an island in the lake and created the sun, moon and stars along with men made in his own image.

Whatever the truth about the origin of the Incas, their visible monuments arguably surpass all others in the Americas. Yet it is the unseen achievements that are so awe-inspiring: their empire still stands as one of the most perfect examples of organization and administration in the history of Man.

Further reading
Further accounts of the Inca culture and conquest are found throughout this book, so check the index. However, with such a complex and fascinating subject, it is worth doing some reading before or during your trip. A selection of recommended books can be found at the end of this book in *Further Reading*.

INCA ROADS AND COMMUNICATIONS
One of the most exciting aspects of hiking in Peru is that the ancient trails linking village to village and mountain to valley were once the means whereby an empire was conquered and controlled. The Inca empire was criss-crossed with roads forming a complex administrative, transport and communications system. Roads radiated out from the centre ('navel') of the empire, Cusco, to the farthest points of its four quarters. Since horses and the wheel were unknown, relays of runners provided the speed and efficiency required. Roads were engineered to give the shortest and easiest route between two points. Steps were quicker to negotiate than a short steep slope, so steps were cut into the rock or laid as paving. Less precipitous slopes were made manageable by zig-zag paths, and tunnels were cut through the outcrops of rock obstructing the direct route.

From sea-level to 5,000 metres, and down again to the Amazon, the roads looped and curved over a distance of 5,200 kilometres. In particularly mountainous areas the footways were steep flights of steps no more than half a metre wide, but across flat open spaces the surface was often six metres wide with a fan arrangement of shallow steps going round corners.

The Inca runners, *chasqui*, relayed verbal and numeric messages to all parts of the empire from the Sun King in Cusco. The Incas had no written language, only one of several reasons we know so little about their culture, so the numeric messages consisted of knotted llama wool strings, *quipus*. With strings of different colours and thicknesses the Incas were able to keep detailed records. A *quipucamaya*, a record or account-keeper, could look at a *quipu* and learn a great deal. Gold, for example, was represented by a golden string, while the amount of gold was recorded by a series of knots along the cord. Silver was represented by white threads, while a series of red cords detailed the fighting strength of an army unit. Once the size, length and colour of a cord had been standardized throughout the empire, it was relatively easy to keep records.

The *chasqui*, sons of civil servants, were youths of great pride and physical strength. In order to fulfill their labour tax they had to run messages for two weeks in every month for about a year. Each runner was equipped with a conch-shell to blow as he approached the next *tambo* or *tampu* (resthouse) where he would pass his message to the next man. In this manner the runners could do about nine kilometres an hour, even at altitudes close to 5,000 metres. No point in the empire was more than five days' run from Cusco. From Cusco to Lima, 672 kilometres, took 72 hours. The Inca was known to send down to Acari, on the coast, for seafood. In less than two days he was eating fresh fish.

Tampus or *tambos* were built at intervals of about 20 kilometres along the roads. These also functioned as storehouses, stocked with provisions from the surrounding countryside. Some also had corrals for llamas, because not only *chasquis* made use of these roads; they were crowded with traders, tax collectors, farmers, priests, soldiers, gangs of labourers and perhaps a royal delegation off to foreign parts.

Each community was responsible for the maintenance of the road in its area, and for the construction of bridges over major rivers. These were made from twisted *manguey* fibre, and had to be remade every other year. The most famous bridge of this type, over the Apurimac river, was immortalized by Thornton Wilder in *The Bridge of San Luís Rey*. Nowadays only the supports can be seen, but the festival of San Luís Rey is still celebrated annually.

Modern travellers rather glibly refer to any stone-paved trail as 'Inca' but we know that many of the civilizations conquered by the Incas had achieved a high standard of stone masonry and it is likely that these pre-Inca people also had an interest in well-built roads to help the transport of tropical produce from the low valley to the highlands and vice versa.

Little is left of the Inca and pre-Inca roads. They have been asphalted for the motor car or lie hidden in dense jungle, but some wonderful stretches do remain, giving us glimpses of the past as impressive and tantalizing as the ruins of temples. For this reason, if no other, the Inca Trail to Machu Picchu and the Takesi Trail in Bolivia should not be missed.

MOTHER EARTH
By Robert Randall

For the Andean Indian the earth is his entire world — he exists as another plant in it and life apart from the land is inconceivable. The earth is called *Pachamama* (Mother Earth). She is alive, and during most of the year is passive and receptive, feeling nothing and leaving man free to cultivate her. There are days, however, when she is actively happy or sad, giving rewards or punishment, and it is prohibited to touch her. There is also a time (Holy Week) when she dies.

She is mother of all things, including men and women. This is meant literally, biologically. Thus offerings are made to her. At certain times there are large offerings (usually involving alcohol), and these you are more likely to witness or participate in. They are fairly simple but extremely important:

T'inka Before drinking alcohol, one allows several drops to fall from the glass on to the soil. Thus Pachamama is served first. This is done whether outside or inside the house.

Ch'ura Similar to the *t'inka* except the alcohol is scattered with the fingers. Often it is sprinkled this way on a house, animal or other object to be blessed.

Ch'alla From a small glass the alcohol is thrown to the major *apus* (spirits or gods — usually the snow peaks) of the area. The *ch'alla* is done standing up, and the person doing it completes a full circle.

These rituals may vary from place to place, but they are omnipresent in the Andes. They only begin to indicate a value system of extreme complexity and richness. From these basics, however, we should be able to glimpse the Indians' humility before, and respect for, the environment.

The Andean Indian, before first digging his *chaquitaclla* (footplough) into the soil, asks pardon and permission of Pachamama. This is an attitude which we should attempt to adopt and be constantly aware of as we walk through the Andes. The earth is alive, and we are a very small organic part of her. We should therefore approach her and the people who live with her with a profound sense of respect and humility.

We have much to learn from the Indians. Although it is impossible to generalize about so many different tribes, the people are usually honest, warm, and friendly. They have not lost the sacred connection with their environment and are aware of the spirits of the mountains, springs and rivers. If one reason we are walking through these mountains is not to re-establish some such connection, then we probably have no business there in the first place.

Robert Randall died of rabies (following a bite from a puppy) in November 1990. During his 15 years in Ollantaytambo, near Cusco, he had done more to support the local community and their culture than any other foreigner. A friend, Max Milligan, wrote in The South American Explorer: *'He held up life for us to look at while he marvelled at it... No one knew the walking routes in the locality better than he... an intimate knowledge, gained after the language and trust of the Quechua people that gave him a clearer picture of the Andean concepts of space and time, and the beliefs and myths handed down still in the highland villages'.*

At Randall's funeral in Ollanta a village elder spoke: 'Most who have come to our valley have come to take. This good man... came and gave back to us. He reminded us of who we are, of the value of our heritage and tradition'.

VILLAGE LIFE TODAY

Since the Spanish conquest the Indians of Peru and Bolivia have developed various protective mechanisms which help them cope with present-day exploitation and discrimination. They are remote not only geographically but culturally, and often seem indifferent to the modern world. This provided a fertile breeding ground for the ideology of El Sendero Luminoso (The Shining Path) terrorists. Communication is not only difficult between Indians and whites (be they Peruvian, Bolivian or European) but between Lima and the highlands, and neither side seems anxious to change the status quo. The difference between the two worlds will be very obvious to the backpacker who spends a few days in Lima before journeying up to the Andes.

In highland villages the way of life is based on structure and rituals and visiting backpackers will have much more empathy with the locals if they understand some of these. They are a hybrid of Spanish and Inca, but the Spanish influence is — at least outwardly — the most dominant.

Village land is generally owned collectively, although private ownership still prevails in some places. Each village has its headman, who may be the governor (*gobernador*), the mayor (*alcalde* or *warayo*), or council chief (*agente municipal*). He carries a ceremonial stick (*personero*) as a symbol of his position. The headman holds office for one year, and during this time is expected to sponsor traditional fiestas, paying for the musicians, and supplying food and drink for these occasions. So most headmen are wealthy when they first take office, and as poor as the other villagers when they leave it.

Rural Indians live virtually outside the money economy, and day-to-day life is organized on the basis of reciprocity or mutual help. Any big job, such as harvesting, threshing, and house building, is done with the help of neighbours who receive aid in return when they need work done. Finishing a house is an occasion for great celebration. *Safacasa*, putting the roof on, is done by a godmother or godfather who goes up on to the unfinished roof, lays the last tiles or thatch, and puts a ceramic figure or pot, or a cross, on the ridge for good luck. Ceramic bulls, to ensure fertility, are popular, as are little vessels of *aguardiente* ('firewater' brewed from sugar cane). The godparent then throws gifts of sweets, cigarettes, etc down to the family and neighbours below who have helped build the house.

You and them: village etiquette

The villages you pass through on the hikes described in this book are mostly well accustomed to backpackers and no special behaviour is needed apart from greeting people in a friendly manner, and avoiding potentially offensive behaviour or dress (men should not go shirtless, for instance).

If you explore on your own you should always remember that because you are there in the village and on their land, you will be treated as either guest or intruder. The former is much more common. Indians have a strong tradition of extending hospitality to strangers. It is not rude politely to refuse such hospitality if you want to move on; however it *is* considered rude to reject offers of accommodation and to put your tent up just outside the village and cook your own meal. Be sensitive to this: either accept the hospitality and stay with the family or move on and camp some way beyond the village.

If you are well off the beaten track, in a very remote area, the people — the women and children, at least — may flee in terror from this alien. Don't further intimidate them by approaching their house. Move on quietly, unless you want to make contact, in which case let them come to you.

On popular trails (most of the trails in this guide) you can be more relaxed. Even so, you should always ask permission to camp, both as a courtesy and for security. Don't feel you have to overdo the friendliness, and especially do not hand out sweets or other *regalos*. Your entertaining presence will be reward enough. You'll probably be surrounded by curious kids — and adults — who are fascinated by your state-of-the-art camping gear. Chat to them as you set up, explain what everything is, where you came from and where you are going to. Try to use a few words of Quechua. But be formal and polite. If the attention becomes tiresome withdraw into your tent for a while, having bid a firm goodbye.

If you accept a meal and accommodation, make sure you share some of your food with your hosts; that is what is generally expected, not money or presents. On popular routes, however, an offer of accommodation is most likely made on a commercial basis, so offer to pay.

Indians are usually both friendly and shy, polite and curious. However, there are always exceptions. If you realize that you are not welcome, or if the locals ask you to leave, then do so without fuss. It is their land and there will be a good reason for them feeling hostile, whether through fear or — more likely — because they have had a bad experience with other gringos.

Keep your distance from drunkards. As in all societies they may be aggressive or lecherous. Excessive drinking is common; indeed it is part of the culture, especially during fiestas.

Respecting a culture, warts and all, is one of the great challenges confronting travellers. It does not just mean enjoying their music, their weavings and their *chicha*, it means accepting inefficiency and poor hygiene, and turning a blind eye to cruelty to animals (unless it seems the latter is done to impress or please you, in which case explain calmly how you feel). It means trying to answer yourself the question that keeps springing to mind: 'Why don't they...?'.

Many travellers feel awkward answering the constant questions about how much they earn and how much their gear or clothing cost. Assuming you speak reasonable Spanish, try to put your enormous wealth into perspective. Tell them how much a house costs in your country, or a kilo of oranges, or a horse. Something they can relate to. Explain also about unemployment in the west. Sharing stories about your respective ways of life is an excellent way of getting to know each other providing it does not lead to envy on their side. I vividly remember my first visit to Chinchero near Cusco in 1973, when South America was part of the Hippie Trail. An American, who had chosen to live in that community as part of the process of dropping out, was deeply upset by the materialism of the villagers, who in turn were puzzled by his praise of the quality of their lives. Few of the world's unavoidably poor people view their position as enviable. Most envy our affluence. Few, come to that, share our admiration (especially if we are taking photographs) for their heavy, earthenware pots and banana-leaf wrappers. They would much prefer plastic pots and plastic bags, and would see no reason to dispose of them in an environmentally responsible manner.

If you are hiking into really remote areas, try to inform yourself about the people and their customs before you go. A local guide will do much to prevent misunderstandings as well as show you the way.

The traditional role of *coca*

For the Andean people the chewing of coca leaves heightens the significance of almost all social or ritual activities. Both Quechua and Aymará Indians view the leaves as a sacred gift from *Pachamama* (Mother Earth). The name *coca* comes from the Aymará language and means 'Food for travellers and workers' because the narcotic effect of chewing the leaves dulls the pangs of hunger and relieves fatigue. The practice has been going on for at least 2,000 years: pre-Inca Mochican ceramics show the tell-tale ball of coca leaves in one cheek. Under the Inca empire, coca was probably a privilege reserved for the royal family and priests (although historians disagree about this) and specific communities were given the job of growing it. The leaves were carried in a finely woven shoulder bag, the *chuspa* or *k'intu*.

Contrary to popular belief, the highland Indians do not use cocaine (which is extracted from the leaves through a complicated process) but the leaves themselves are used for many purposes:

Chacchar/chaccheo Quechua words for chewing coca leaves. To extract the narcotic juice the leaves are chewed until they are soft, then formed into a ball with some *llipta*, (known in Bolivia as *lejía)* a mixture of lime (the mineral not the fruit) and potash. The ball of coca and *llipta* is held in the cheek and chewed from time to time.

Social Sharing coca leaves with a stranger is the equivalent of our shaking hands.

Offerings Before entering a valley or climbing a mountain, *campesinos* will offer coca leaves to *Pachamama* asking the *Apus* of this region permission to tread on their slopes and for protection during the journey. Three nice coca leaves are put under a rock or in a ditch.

Medical Traditional healers put great value on the use of coca leaves for many curative processes (and not just as a medicine — see page 27).

Reading of the leaves The leaves are 'read' for advice on a variety of problems and for predictions. Some Quechua elders interpret the leaves by examining the form, shape and colour.

Protection The leaves are believed to protect the person carrying them.

Death When a person dies, coca leaves are given to the mourners as a sign of affection and sympathy. After three days these coca leaves and the clothes of the deceased are burnt. The belief is that his/her soul goes to heaven with the smoke.

FIESTAS (FESTIVALS)

The rich traditions of history and religion come together in local festivals. In the larger towns and cities these are often little more than an opportunity to close banks and businesses and take off for a long weekend, but in the mountain regions the people grab this chance to escape the rhythm of their daily lives and explode into an orgy of colour, music and dance. And drinking.

Most fiestas are similar in atmosphere, but are different in detail. They are common all year round throughout the Andes, but particularly in Bolivia, so you can hardly avoid being caught up in the action.

If you are a lone woman be cautious about participating in fiestas: the combination of alcohol and dancing liberates the male spirit. Your apparent availability could lead to rape. Attend in the company of a man, either local or gringo. If you feel you can handle it on your own you should expect some sexual harassment and be prepared to laugh it off or leave. Do not get angry or upset.

Never participate in a local festival unless you are invited. If you are invited, be prepared to enjoy yourself. Western inhibitions have no place here. For the locals, gringos are part of the fun.

To give a flavour of the fiesta experience, I am retaining the descriptions of three fiestas that George and I attended in the 1970s. These three towns now see plenty of tourists so the attitude to gringo participants may have changed, but not the fiestas themselves.

Chacas, Peru This village in the Cordillera Blanca is proud of its Spanish heritage, and the principal events in its week-long fiesta have a Spanish flavour. We arrived for the *carrera de caballos* (horse race). The morning was occupied by a religious procession, with the plaza full of expectant villagers as the Virgin of Chacas was carried from the church, elaborately attired for the occasion. The procession was led by the village elite with a banner-carrying horseman representing the *caballeros*. Then came the dancers, gloriously dressed and masked, some with large head-dresses of peacock feathers, and dancing to music from pipes, a fiddle and an enormous harp. After the procession had wound its way round the square and the Virgin was returned to the church, the plaza started filling up with horsemen riding magnificent Peruvian 'walking horses' (*caballos de paso*). The riders' wealth was represented by the beautiful animals they rode. We'd been expecting horse races, but in fact the afternoon contest measured the skills of the riders rather than the speed of their animals. Between two posts hung a row of sashes with a ring sewn on to the lower end. The riders had to spear this ring with a short wooden pick as they galloped between the posts. The prize for the most successful was the leadership of next year's contest. There were, perhaps, more desirable prizes; the village maidens had written their names on the sashes.

Paucartambo, Peru This is one of the finest of all Peruvian fiestas, and deservedly popular. The dancing is continuous for three days, and performed with a tribal intensity by the Indians involved. The costumes are varied and incredible: one group reminded us of agitated birds' nests, others of animated sacks. The dancers were fantastically masked and dressed. There were monsters, gringos and negroes: symbolic figures that had played a part in the Indians' history or mythology.

The procession of the Virgin of Carmen was the climax of the last day. She swayed towards us, resembling a stiff white cone of lace and jewels, smothered in flowers and with her doll's face almost hidden under an elaborate crown. Preceding her came a pure white llama, beautifully decorated. On the rooftops of the houses lining her route were dancing devils, demons and winged creatures, but before the Virgin could come under their evil influence, a flight of angels conquered them, beating them out of view.

Later, at night, we heard music. Peeping in through a doorway we saw a large room with tables laden with food, and the victors and vanquished dancing together in the middle. A friendly shout went up, we were pulled into the room, filled with food and drink, and danced with until we had to beg for mercy.

Achacachi, Bolivia Our favourite participatory fiesta was Achacachi, near Lake Titicaca, one of our 'accidental' celebrations. We were actually heading for the festival in the neighbouring town of Sorata when our bus was forced to stop by a large and noisy brass band blocking the road. We hastily gathered up our things, got out and found ourselves immediately swept into the parade. The costumes here were quite incredible. The principal dancers looked like the White Queen in *Alice through the Looking Glass*. It was hard to believe they could walk, let alone dance, in such outlandish apparel.

At the fiesta, stove alcohol was the preferred drink. Fortunately the custom of returning some of each cupful to Pachamama saved us from embarrassment. I slipped away at one point, and returned to see George dancing down the street, arm in arm with a large white bear, and hitting bystanders on the head with a banana. Later he swore that it was part of the dance; certainly the bear and the bystanders enjoyed it enormously.

Fiestas in Peru and Bolivia

Below are the main festivals in Peru. Check dates with the tourist office in the nearest large town before you go.

January 1	Año Nuevo: all Peru
January 1-6	Fiesta del Año Nuevo: Apurimac, Huancayo (Peru)
January 6	Día de los Reyes Magos: Cusco, Puno (Peru)
January 6	Niño Occe: Huancavelica (Peru)
Juanary 12	Fiesta de Negritos: Huancavelica (Peru)
January 20	San Sebastián and San Fabián: Huancayo, Cusco (Peru)
January (last week)	Alacitas: La Paz (Bolivia)
February (one week)	Carnival: throughout South America
February 2	Virgen de la Candelaria: Huancayo, Ayacucho, Cusco, Puno (Peru); Virgen de Copacabana, Lake Titicaca (Bolivia)
March 8	San Juan de Dios: Puno (Peru)
March or April	Semana Santa: throughout Peru and Bolivia
April 25	San Marcos: throughout the Andes
May (first week)	Feria de Alacitas: Puno (Peru)
May 1	Labour Day: all Peru and Bolivia
May 3	La Invención de la Santa Cruz: throughout the Andes
May 15	Fiesta de San Isidro: Moche (La Libertad), Huaraz (Peru)
End of May	Semana del Andinismo: Cordillera Blanca (Peru)
End May/early June	El Gran Poder, Calvario, La Paz (Bolivia)
Early June	Qoyllor Rit'i: Cordillera Vilcanota, Cusco (Peru)
Mid June, Thursday after Trinity Sunday	Corpus Christi: throughout Peru and Bolivia

June 15	Virgen de las Mercedes: Huancayo (Peru)
June 24	Inti Raymi: Cusco and San Juan Bautista. Día del Indio: Lima (Peru)
June 28	San Pedro and San Pablo: all Peru and Bolivia
June	Fiesta de Torre-Torre: Huancavelica (Peru)
July 6-8	Santa Elizabeth: Callejón de Huaylas (Peru)
July 16	Virgen del Carmen: throughout the Andes
July 24-28	Fiesta de Santiago: throughout the Andes
July 26	Santa Ana: Puno (Peru)
July 28	Independence Day, Peru: all Peru
August 4	Santo Domingo: throughout the Andes
August 15	Fiesta de Asunción: throughout the Andes
August 16	San Roque (patron saint of dogs): several places in Peru and Bolivia
August 25	Virgen de Copacabana, Lake Titicaca (Bolivia)
August 30	Santa Rosa de Lima: Lima (Peru)
September 8	Virgen de la Natividad: Cajamarca, Huancayo, Cusco (Peru)
September 14	Fiesta de la Exultación: Huaraz and some other mountain villages (Peru)
September 23-24	Virgen de las Mercedes: throughout the Andes
September 30	San Gerónimo: throughout the Andes
September	Fiesta de Huarachicoy: Sacsayhuaman, Cusco (Peru)
October 4	San Francisco de Asís: throughout the Andes
October 7	Fiesta de Señora Rosario and Uma Raymi (Festival of the Water): most Andean villages.
October 18	El Señor de los Milagros: Lima and San Lucas, Huancayo and some other mountain villages (Peru).
November 1-2	Todos Santos and Día de los Muertos: cemeteries all over Peru and Bolivia.
November 4-5	Festival of Manco Capac: Lake Titicaca, Puno (Peru)
December 3-13	Virgen de Guadalupe: Huancayo (Peru)
December 8	Fiesta de la Purísima Concepción: throughout the Andes
December 24	Santo Rantikuy (the buying of saints): Cusco (Peru)
December 25	Los Galos: Huancavelica (Peru)
December 28	Fiesta de los Santos Inocentes (similar to April Fools' Day): all of Peru and Bolivia

'Your Majesty, encounters have become my meditation. The moment one accosts a stranger, or is accosted by him, is above all ... a moment of drama. The eyes of the Indians who have crossed my trail have searched me to the very depths to estimate my power. It is true the world over — whoever we meet watches us intently at the quick strange moment of meeting, to see whether we are disposed to be friendly.'

From The Marvellous Adventure of Cabeza de Vaca (1528-1536), *translated by Haniel Long.*

LANGUAGE

> 'What kind of language is it when:
> *sopa* means soup not soap
> *ropa* means clothes not rope, and
> *como no* means yes?'

In fact, Spanish is not a difficult language and backpackers should make every effort to learn the essentials. Your ignorance of the language shouldn't discourage you from making the trip, but I do advise you to learn a few greetings and a basic backpacker's vocabulary, even if you don't aspire to discussing politics and philosophy.

Both a dictionary and a phrasebook are essential. The dictionary should have a Latin-American bias; avoid buying one based on the language of Spain — too many words are different.

Spanish words, given below, are incorporated into this book because their English translation is too long or doesn't convey quite the same meaning.

Campesino	Peasant, small farmer
Cerro	Hill
Cordillera	Mountain range
Hacienda; estancia	Farm; estate
Mestizo	A person of mixed Indian/European ancestry
Pasaje, portachuelo	Pass
Nevado	Snow-covered mountains
Quebrada	Ravine; narrow valley with stream
Selva	Jungle
Sierra	Highlands

'Gringo' is so common it's not even italicized. It means any white-skinned foreigner and is a term of convenience, not abuse.

Backpacker's vocabulary

You must be able to recognize these questions...

¿A dónde va(n)?	Where are you going?
(*¿va* sing, *van* plural)	
¿De dónde viene(n)?	Where are you coming from?
¿De dónde eres (son)?	Where are you from? (your country)
Paseando	Passing through, on vacation
Conociendo	Becoming acquainted (with the area)

Some other useful questions...

¿Podemos dejar esta bolsa aquí?	May we leave this bag here?

¿Podemos acampar aquí?	May we camp here?
¿Está lejos?	Is it far?
¿Puede ayudarme?	Can you help me?
¿Dónde está el camino por...?	Where is the path to...?
¿Hay una habitación?	Have you a room (hotel)?
¿Qué hay de comer?	What is there to eat?

Equipaje	Baggage
Mochila	Backpack
Pueblito; poblado	Settlement or small village
Carpa	Tent
Río	River
Puente	Bridge
Derrumbe; huayco	Landslide
Carro (Peru);	Truck or bus
Mobilidad (Bolivia)	
Trámite	Red tape; transaction
Tienda	Shop

Quechua and Aymará

Spanish is still the second language for many people in Peru and Bolivia. Quechua and Aymará are still widely spoken. Place names in the *sierra* are usually Quechua, which explains the variety of spellings: the Spanish transcribed the names as best they could.

The following list of Quechua and Aymará names is to help you to understand the Inca culture, interpret place names, and ease your travels through non-Spanish speaking communities. In addition you will find the Quechua phrasebook published by Lonely Planet a great help.

Inca words

Amanta	Royal Inca's advisors
Ayllu	The basic community, or clan, of the empire
Capac	Lord or Chief (literally, magnificent)
Capac Raimi	December fiesta in honour of the sun
Condorachi	The annual killing of a condor to ensure good crops or banish evil spirits from a town
Coya	Star; wife of the ruling Inca, often his sister
Cuntisuyu	The Inca empire
Huatana	To tie, eg *Inti Huatana*, the hitching post of the sun

Inti	Sun
Inti Raimi	Summer solstice fiesta
Tahuantinsuyu	The land of the four quarters; the Inca empire
Tambo	Warehouses or resting places along the roads

Origins of place names

Bamba	Place of	*Machay*	Crevice
Caja	Pass	*Paca*	Valley fork
Cota	Lagoon	*Pampa*	Meadow
Cucho	Corner	*Pata*	Summit, hillside
Jirca	Mountain	*Paucar*	Flowery
Huanca	Rock	*Raju*	Glacier, snow peak
Huaru	Ford	*Rucu*	Old
Huaylla	Meadow	*Rumi*	Stone
Lacta	Land	*Tambo*	Roadside resthouse
Llacta	Village	*Tingo*	Junction of two rivers
Marca	City	*Urcu*	Mountain
Yurac	White		

Quechua	English	Aymará
Maynalla	Hello	*Kamisaki*
Maypi?	Where is?	*Kaukasa*
Ari	Yes	*Jisa*
Mana	No	*Janiwar*
Walej-pacha	Good	*Walikuskiu*
Mana-walej	Bad	*Janiwa Walikiti*
Mikuna	Food	*Manka*
Yaku	Water	*Uma*
Huasi	House	*Uta*
Mayu	River	*Jawira*
Chaka	Bridge	*Chaka*
Cocha	Lake	*Cota*
Chakinan	Footpath	*Tupu*
Yanapaway	Help	*Yanaptita*

Chapter Five

Natural History

*With contributions by Tino Aucca of ECCO, Peru, and
Dr James Luytens of New York Botanical Gardens*

INTRODUCTION

The Quechua word *puna* is still used in the Andean countries to describe
the windswept grasslands between the trees and snowline on the high
plateau. The *puna* area can best be defined as above the limits of agriculture,
generally between 3,800m and 4,800m.

Puna is characterized by expanses of coarse grassland with low vegetation
and a large variety of cushion plants adapted to survive the strong daytime
sun and freezing nights. The fauna is unique, and equally well adapted to
the environment.

This is the landscape most familiar to hikers and the only biological zone
which can feasibly be described in this book. The lower regions are so rich
in flora and fauna that specialist books or information are needed. Local
conservation groups may be able to help you here, or biologists working in
local universities.

FLORA

Introduction

Although descriptions in English of the flora of the Andes are hard to find,
much research has been done in this field, mostly by local biologists and
university students. The descriptions below are not intended to be a complete
list but will help you identify and appreciate the more common flora you
will come across. The local name is given in parentheses.

Family Compositae

This is the well-known daisy family, most of which are short-stemmed.

Werneria dactylophylla (*Margarita Andina*). Also known as the *Boton Boton* it has crinkly leaves and a small white daisy flower growing in felty clumps.

Werneria nubigena (*Margarita Andina*). A common and attractive Andean daisy with large white flowers, often tinged with pink, and blue-green strap-like leaves. This daisy seems to grow directly out of the ground which it hugs closely from its long tap roots.

Family Berberidaceae
Berberis, some of which grace our gardens, exhibit spiny bluish-green evergreen leaves like miniature holly, orange and blue flowers, and blue waxy-looking fruit.

Berberis lutea (*Checche*). A shrub which fruits from April to June. They make very effective hedges to enclose farmland. The locals have a further use for the saffron-yellow wood which is used for dyeing wool.

Family Cactaceae
Opuntia floccosa (*Chapu chapu*). A spiny, hairy cactus with white flowers, typical of the cushion-forming plants of the *puna*. The hairs act as insulation in the freezing nights.

Opuntia subulata (*Cholla* or *P'atakiska*). This columnar cactus is also known as a harpoon cactus since its thorns are shaped like harpoons, so difficult — and painful — to remove from the skin.

Trichocereus cuzcoensis (*J'ahuaccollay*). A large branched cactus growing to a height of eight metres. It has creamy white flowers.

Opuntia ficus indica (*Tuna*). This is the familiar prickly pear cactus, introduced from Mexico. The fruits are eaten by many of the Indians (hence their popular name 'Indian fig'), and the large pads provide fodder for cattle. Sometimes a white powder-like substance is found on the leaves. This is excreted by the bright red cochineal beetle, which — crushed — is used as a red dye or paint base.

Family Caprifoliaceae
Sambucus peruviana (*Sauco*). This shrub is a relative of the familiar European or North American elder, *Sambucus nigra*; it fruits from March to May and the berries are used to make jams and drinks.

Family Fabaceae (Leguminosae)
The lupin family is familiar to most people. The seeds have traditionally been used as food, but the long preparation needed to get rid of the bitter

chemicals have caused them largely to be replaced by broad beans (known to the Americans as Lima beans).

Lupinus weberbaueri (*Q'uera* or *Tarwis*). A giant species of the lupin family, which grows to nearly two metres.

Lupinus mutabilis (*Q'uera* or *Tarwis*). This is the species most often used for its seeds, which must be leached in running water to remove the poison. The water is then used as a fish poison.

Family Gentianaceae
The majority of this family cultivated in British gardens are from Europe or Asia; the gentians of South America are rarely seen in cultivation yet are the most spectacular, ranging from the common blue to vivid red or yellow. The flowers vary in shape, too, being crocus or cup shaped, rather than the more familiar trumpet shape. The plants range from tiny plants to upright stems of one to two metres, clothed in gorgeous pendulous bells.

Gentiana sedifolia (*Phallcha*). These are the tiny, star-shaped flowers seen on open *puna* especially near moist areas.

Family Loasaceae
All members of this family have hairy leaves with a powerful sting. Beware!

Cajophora horrida (*Helechos* or *Otis colorada*). Most commonly seen in Bolivia, it has large orange-red scrotum-like flowers and — as its name implies — is unpleasant to touch. It stings.

Family Malvaceae
This family includes the Mallow genus, commonly grown in British gardens. They are compact rosettes of tiny grey green leaves often covered in hairs or fine wool with proportionately large flowers which may be bright yellow, white, rose or magenta, all exhibiting stamens with a prominent globose head protruding from the centre of the flower.

Family Melastomataceae
Brachyotum rostratum (*Macha macha*). It occurs more on the eastern side of the Andes, in the *queñoa* forests between the *puna* and the cloud forest. The shrub has pairs of oval, deeply parallel-veined, dark green leaves and purple or greenish flowers with pendulous furled petals. Their fruits look like little red apples.

Family Onagraceae
This is the fuchsia family. Most of the 100 or so species come from South America. They vary from scarlet tubular flowers, almost bush-like, to peach-

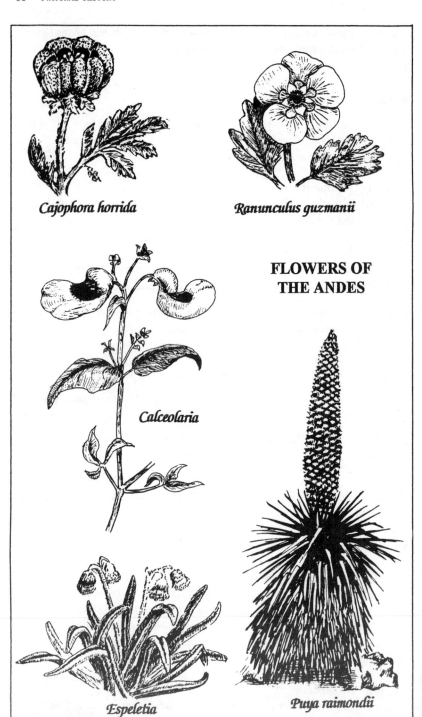

Cajophora horrida

Ranunculus guzmanii

**FLOWERS OF
THE ANDES**

Calceolaria

Espeletia

Puya raimondii

coloured downy flowers struggling to gain a foothold between ancient stone walling. The name comes from a 16th century German herbalist, Leonhart Fuchs.

Family Orchidaceae

Of the several species of terrestrial orchid found in the Andes, the purple and orange *Epidendrum* genus is the most familiar. In Peru the purple species is known as *wiñay wayna* which means 'forever young'; the ruins near Machu Picchu bear the same name.

Family Polemoniaceae

Cantua buxifolia (Kantu/Q'antu). The national flower of Peru. The red, bell-like flowers hang from bushes near rivers. The *kantu* is a popular motif in ancient weaving designs, and is still used in some religious ceremonies and fiestas. This is also the one species of the genus cultivated in British gardens, usually against south-facing walls.

Family Ranunculaceae

Ranunculus is the botanical name for buttercup, a very primitive family with many species in the Andes, some of which look more like anemones than buttercups.

Ranunculus guzmanii (Rima rima). This beautiful flower is quite common in the Cordillera Blanca. It has large, red flowers and the whole plant is covered in dense golden hairs. *Rima* means 'speak' in Quechua (as in the river Apurímac— 'The Great Speaker') and the popular name for the flower indicates its use in folk medicine: it is given to children who are slow to learn to speak.

Ranunculus weberbaurii (Chapu chapu). It resembles a turk's head or turban with its fist-sized, bulging yellow-orange flower.

Family Rosaceae

There are about 15 different *Polylepis* species; these Andean endemics grow at altitudes between 3,000m and 4,800m, just below the treeless *puna*. They have a characteristic peeling, papery, red bark, with small dark green leaves. The most common species are *Polylepis incana (Queñoa)*, and *Polylepis besseri* (also known as *Queñoa*).

Family Crassulanaceae

Escallonia are common garden shrubs in Britain with a profusion of pink blossom in the summer months.

ANDEAN VEGETATION: ENVIRONMENTAL ADAPTATION
By Jim Conrad

Plant communities in the Andes are in a state of shock; the vegetation we see today largely reflects centuries of overgrazing, burning, cultivation and firewood gathering.

If you see a lush clump of grass, gently extend the open palm of your hand into it. Probably you'll feel needlesharp blade-tips pricking your skin; this is the plant's defence against livestock poking their hungry faces into the grass's tender interior. If you see a plant without spines, probably it'll taste bitter to eat. If you see a shrub, take a good look at its stem. Probably it'll be pithy and moist-looking — hardly decent firewood material.

Andean vegetation is interesting and often downright stunning. During your passage through the Andes you'll see the following general principles expressing themselves:

• Forests seldom extend higher than 3,000-3,400m (10,000-11,000ft).

• Especially on moist eastern slopes, *puna* vegetation evolves into a soggy-soiled 'dwarf forest' or 'elfin forest' composed of gnarled trees and shrubs maybe two metres (six feet) high; tree branches are festooned with abundant mosses, lichens and other epiphytes, deriving moisture from clouds 'colliding' with the high mountain slope; this is a kind of cloudforest.

• Farther down, 'dwarf forest' develops into taller forest, similarly cloud-soaked and with the tree branches similarly festooned; this is the classic 'cloudforest'. 'Rainforest' is something else; it's found in lower elevations and derives its moisture from abundant rain, not clouds or fog.

Escallonia resinosa (*Chachacomo*). As the name implies, the resin content makes this tree suitable for kindling.

Family Scrophulariacea
Calceolaria engleriana (*Ayac Zapatilla*). This butter-yellow ladies' slipper (or slipperwort) is one of the most attractive and recognizable trailside flowers.

Family Agavaceae
Agave americana (*Pacpa*). These fleshy, thorn-tipped agaves, introduced from Mexico, are characteristic of high farming land where they are used as (very effective) hedges.

Family Alstroemeriaceae
Bomarea sp. These beautiful flowers are found in many mountain valleys. Some are cane-forming from 30 centimetres to two metres. Others are twining climbers straggling over bushes displaying vivid different colours

of tubular flowers in a terminal cluster. All flowers grow from little white tubers.

Family Amaryllidaceae
Stenomesson miniatum (*Michi michi*). Also *Zephyranthes parvula* (again known as *Michi michi*). The dark green leaves stay on the ground, while the flower grows on a long stem. It is a small crocus-like yellow flower, its reverse streaked with violet. In Britain it is grown as a pot-plant and commonly called Rainlily or Windflower.

Family Bromeliaceae
This family includes the pineapple and Spanish moss among its 2,000 or more species, but its most spectacular member in Peru is the *Puya raimondii* (see next page). Other species that are more often encountered include the smaller and more common *Puya herrerae* (*Achupalla*) and *Guzmania morreniana* which grows in trees as an epiphyte from 1,500-2,500 metres (so is not a *puna* species).

Family Labiateae
This family includes the *Salvia* genus, of which the familiar sage (used in cooking) is one species. Salvias are popular with British gardeners, and include many flowering shrubs.

Minthostachys glabrescens (*Muña*). This species smells like mint but the leaves are smaller, growing on little bushes in the higher altitudes. When made into a tea this is a popular natural remedy for high altitude sickness. The Incas used this herb to cover their potato harvest, preventing it from sprouting and repelling insects. Potatoes stored this way were said to keep up to a year.

Family Liliaceae
Nothoscordum andicola (*Chullcus*). This lily is often found in the ruins of Sacsayhuaman. It resembles an onion flower, but is delicately scented and coloured a white-tinted mauve.

Family Poaceae (Gramineae)
Stipa sp. (*Ichu*). This is the spiky, tough grass commonly found in the *puna*, and the cause of many a resting trekker rising hastily to his feet. It is used for thatching houses.

PUYA RAIMONDII

The monster of the Andes, this *puya* is the tallest flower spike in the world, sometimes topping 10 metres. It is said to live 100 years and flower once before it dies. And how it flowers! An estimated 8,000 greenish-white blossoms grow on one stalk between October and December, and attract the hummingbirds and moths which pollinate it. Other birds nest among the spiky leaves and some stab themselves to death on their doorstep. The sharp spikes are also a danger to livestock. *Puya raimondii* are found only in Peru and Bolivia where they are protected in Andean national parks. In the north the local name is *Llacuash* and in the south, *Titanca*. There is an easily accessible group in Parque Nacional Huascarán, in the Cordillera Blanca (see page 130).

FAUNA
Birds
Given the scarcity of large mammals in the high Andes, birds are, for most hikers, the most interesting fauna. They are also easy to see and quite easy to identify.

The polylepis forest holds 57% of Peru's endemic birds, and 65% of those are classified as endangered. Deforestation is a major problem in the Andes, and this habitat destruction is threatening the survival of many species. Trekkers have a particular responsibility not to disturb the fauna, particularly nesting birds.

The list below covers all the species you are most likely to see while hiking in the mountains, classified by size (largest first). The local name is in parentheses.

Caracaras, hawks, eagles, vultures and falcons
Being the largest, these are at least easy to see, although telling them all apart takes some practice.

The Andean condor; *Vultur gryphus* (Quechua, *Kuntur*). The largest and heaviest flying bird in the world. A male can weigh 12 kilogrammes and has a wingspan of three metres. He differs from the female by his crinkly comb. You may be fortunate enough to see an Andean condor circling below you as you rest at the top of a high pass. From this vantage point they are unmistakable, with broad white bands on the top of their wings, and you'll probably pick out the neck ring of fluffy white feathers. Seen high above you, against a bright sky, they are harder to identify, but the 'fingering' on the end of the wings is a distinctive feature. Despite their name, Andean condors are more often seen on the coast of Peru scavenging the sealion colonies; carrion is harder to find in the high places.

A condor's feet are not designed for grasping prey, so the occasional stories you hear about them carrying off babies are untrue. Their legs often hang down as these birds glide on air thermals, rarely flapping their wings.

Mountain caracara; *Phalcoboenus megalopterus* (Quechua, *Alkamari, Acchi*, Spanish *China linda*). These scavengers have a wingspan of 100 centimetres. They are very common throughout the Andes, and there's no mistaking them with their black and white plumage, bare red faces and orange legs. Caracaras find roadkills a particularly good source of food and often follow vehicles. You will see them solo or in groups of two or three.

Black-chested buzzard eagle; *Geranoaetus melanoleucus* (Quechua *Ank'a*, Spanish *Aguila*). In the air they look like a flying triangle, with tail and

Andean lapwing

Andean condor

Torrent duck

**BIRDS OF
THE PUNA**

Tinamou

Andean cara cara

wings as one. They are always seen alone. The plumage is grey and white, with a conspicuous dark grey breast, white belly and black tail.

Puna (or variable) hawk; *Buteo poecilochrous* (Quechua *Hat'um hua-mancha*, Spanish *Aguilucho*). A white, grey and brown hawk seen at high altitudes: 3,000m-5,000m. The altitude and the white tail with a black bar aid identification.

Red-backed hawk; *Buteo polyosoma* (Quechua *H'uchuy hua-mancha*, Spanish *Aguilucho común*). Very similar to the puna hawk but smaller, and with a larger tail relative to its size. Found below 3,500m.

Aplomado falcon; *Falco femoralis* (Spanish *Halcón perdiguero*). An elegant falcon with long wings and tail, easily seen and recognized by its light eyebrow, thin but distinct moustache, and dark 'vest'.

American kestrel; *Falco sparverius* (Quechua *Quillichu*, Spanish *Cernícalo*). A small ruddy-coloured raptor often seen hovering. It has a characteristic pattern on its head: two vertical black stripes, and a rufous-coloured tail tipped with black. Widespread in all kinds of open country at all altitudes.

Waterfowl (grebes, ducks, geese and others)
Puna lakes are excellent places for bird-watching, especially the shallow reedy ones which support a large number of waterfowl. The ones you are most likely to see are given below.

Silvery grebe; *Podiceps occipitalis* (Spanish *Zambullidor blanquillo*). Recognizable by its grey back and grey plumes behind the eyes. Back of neck black.

Crested duck; *Lophonetta specularoides* (Spanish *Pato cordillerano*). A large, handsome duck with a blue bill and brown crest and back: the largest of the ducks likely to be found on a mountain lake.

Andean duck or **ruddy duck**; *Oxyura jamaicensis*. Recognized by the blue bill and black head and tail of the male, it may be mistaken for the much smaller puna teal.

Puna teal; *Anas versicolor* (Spanish *Pato de puna*). This small duck has a conspicuous blue bill, which is yellow at the base, creamy-white sides of head and throat and a black cap.

Speckled (yellow-billed) teal; *Anas flavirostris* (Spanish *pato sutro*). Recognized by its yellow bill and brown head, and speckled black and brown head and neck.

Torrent duck; *Merganetta armata*. This fascinating little duck is found not in lakes but on boulders in the middle of fast-flowing rivers. They dive into the torrent in search of larvae and insects and can swim against almost any current using their very large, powerful feet for propulsion and long, stiff tail as a rudder. They are found in pairs up to about 4,000m. The male is very conspicuous with a black-and-white patterned head and bright red bill. The female is a more subdued reddish brown.

Andean goose; *Chloephaga melanoptera* (Spanish *Ganso de los Andes*, Quechua *Huallata*). These handsome and very common birds feed in pairs or in large groups on marshy ground near lakes or on the open *puna* in boggy areas. Its white head and body and black wings are instantly recognizable.

Andean lapwing; *Vanellus resplendens* (Quechua *Lek'echo*). Another very common bird which is found on the *puna* even in quite dry areas, as well as around lakes. Its black and white V-shaped markings on the wings as it flies off with a noisy alarm call makes it unmistakable.

Andean gull; *Larus serranus* (Spanish *Gaviota de los Andes*). This is a species of the familiar black-headed gull of the Old World but it spends the summers (and some of the winter) in the high *puna*. In the winter its black head turns white.

Puna ibis; *Plegadis ridgwayi*. This handsome bird has a greeny-blue sheen to its black feathers.

Buff-necked ibis; *Theristicus caudatus* (Spanish *Bandurria*). Another ibis found in flocks on marshy ground, with grey wings and a fawn-coloured neck.

Giant coot; *Fulica gigantea*. Identification is easy: a goose-sized coot with a dark red bill tipped with white, white frontal shield, and enormous feet. It builds a huge floating nest of weeds, nearly two metres in diameter.

Slate-coloured coot; *Fulica ardesiaca*, and **Common gallinule**; *Gallinula chloropas*. These familiar water birds are similar to their North American counterparts, with a black body and white (coot) or red (gallinule) 'shield' above the bill.

Tinamous

These chunky birds look a bit like a small chicken and hide in the long grass, to fly off with a great commotion when nearly stepped on. It scares the hell out of most hikers! The locals call them *los perdizes de los Andes* or Andean partridges, a misnomer although superficially they do look and behave like partridges. Their speckled colouring offers perfect camouflage. There are many species; all are ground-nesting, laying olive-green or purple eggs which have a beautiful porcelain-like sheen.

Ornate tinamou; *Nothoprocta ornata* (Quechua *Llut'u)* Spanish *Falsa perdiz*). They are a speckled greyish ochre, with a grey breast and a whitish head spotted with black.

Swifts and swallows

Andean swift; *Aeronautes andecolus* (Spanish *Bencejo Andino*). White collar, rump and underparts, including vent.

Brown-bellied swallow; *Notiochelidon murina* (Spanish *Golondrina plomiza*). Dark smoky grey below. Found between 2,100m and 4,300m, mostly in humid and semi-humid regions.

Andean swallow; *Petrochelidon andecola* (Spanish *Golondrina andina*). A chunky bird with triangular wings and only slightly forked tail. The throat is grey-brown, with a whitish belly. It is found between 2,500m and 4,600m in open arid country.

Woodpeckers

Those found in the *puna* have hardly seen a tree in their lives. They live in holes in rocky areas and are extremely well camouflaged.

Andean flicker; *Colaptes rupicola* (Quechua *Jac'acho*, Spanish *Carpintero de las piedras*). An attractive bird with a speckled brownish back, yellowbuff breast, and a telltale yellow rump which shows when it flies away whistling its loud alarm call.

Sparrows, finches and siskins

Rufous-collared sparrow; *Zonotrichia capensis* (Spanish *Gorrion americano*, Quechua *Pichingo*). It has a distinct rufous half-collar and blackish spot on the sides of its breast. A very common bird.

Ash-breasted sierra finch; *Phrygilus plebejus*. (Quechua *Pichitankas*). These very common little birds live in large groups, feeding in the open fields or on farmland. They are greyish with a white belly and a large bill.

HUMMINGBIRDS

These little birds, widespread throughout the Americas, elicit many superlatives: the smallest, the most brightly coloured... and the most interesting of the birds found in the Andes. The local name for these tiny nectar-feeders is *picaflor* and the Quechua name is *Q'entes*. Surprisingly, many species of hummingbird live on the chilly slopes of the Andes, and they show a remarkable adaptation to their habitat and food source. About half of the flowering plants of the *puna* are pollinated by hummingbirds, and these have evolved trumpet-shaped flowers, so the nectar can only be reached by the hummingbird's long bill and even longer tongue, and long stamens which dust the bird's forehead with pollen. An example of this mutual dependency is the white, trumpet-shaped *datura* flower which is pollinated by the swordbill hummingbird whose bill is actually longer than its body. Such flowers generally have little scent because hummingbirds have no keen sense of smell. Cross pollination is ensured by providing the bird with just enough nectar to allow it to reach the next plant. Hummingbirds need to feed every 12 minutes or so; they use energy faster than any other animal. Their wings beat 70 times a second (one third of their body weight is wing muscle), and in flight their heartbeat may reach 1,200 per minute!

The Andean hillstar, a hummingbird that lives just below the snowline, shows a special adaptation which allows it to survive the freezing nights. It saves energy by perching on, rather than hovering over, the flowers (usually the *chuquiagua*), and at night goes into a state of torpor. Its body temperature may drop to 15°C (from its normal daytime 39.5°C) and its heart slows down to 36 beats per minute. Thus the bird is able to conserve energy. The large, well-insulated nests of the Andean hillstar are usually built on the eastern face of rocky cliffs to catch the morning sun.

Siskin; *Spinus* sp. (Spanish *Jilguero*). Another common Andean bird with several similar species. Like the finches, they feed in large groups in open fields. They are identified by their black and yellow colouring.

Thrushes

Chiguanco thrush; *Turdus chiguanco* (Spanish *Tordo*, Quechua *Chihuaco*). They are woodland birds but are common in open areas, feeding on a large variety of seeds and fruits. Recognized by their brown colour with a yellow bill and legs and a great variety of calls: this bird is said to produce 14 different sounds.

Hummingbirds

General information on the Trochilidae family is given in the Box above; the following species are most likely to be seen by hikers.

Giant hummingbird; *Patagona gigas* (Quechua *Huascar q'ente*, Spanish

Picaflor gigante). A very large hummingbird, the size of a small dove, with a whitish rump and cinnamon below. It flies with erratic wingbeats interspersed with gliding, and does not hover over the flower like other hummingbirds.

Great sapphirewing; *Pterophanes cyanopterus* (Quechua *Sihuar q'ente*). A very large hummingbird, dark green with blue wings, with a thinner and straighter bill than the giant hummingbird, and with a more typical hummingbird flight pattern, though it still has some erratic wingbeats and glides.

Greentailed trainbearer; *Lesbia nuna*. The tail is deeply forked, about the length of the bird's body, and the tips of feathers are a glittering emerald green. The bill is generally small and straight. Common.

Sparkling violet-ear; *Colibri coruscans* (Spanish *Picaflor vientre azul*). Quite a large shining green hummingbird with a dark, subterminal bar on its tail. The blue of its ear-plumes continues as a chinstrap.

Field guides to birds
An expensive but extremely beautiful book, *Birds of the High Andes* by Jon Fjeldså and Niels Krabbe, has been published in Denmark (Apollo books, Lundbyvej 36, DK-5700 Svendborg, Denmark) price DKK 700. There is no other similarly comprehensive guide to the birds of the Andes but *South American Birds* by John Dunning is very useful and has some good colour photos (Harrowood Books, USA).

Among the specialist books listed in the extensive catalogue of the Natural History Book Service (Britain, tel: 01803 865913) are *A Birder's Guide to Travel in Peru*, *Birds of South America* in four volumes, and *The Birds of the Department of Lima*.

Mammals
In post-conquest Peru and Bolivia the wildlife suffered the same depredations as gold and silver artefacts: it was squandered for immediate gain. Whereas during Inca times hunting was controlled and restricted, now it was available to anyone and the Spaniards' superior weapons must have decimated the edible mammals. As always, however, destruction of habitat played, and still plays, a more serious role in the extinction of species. The widespread cutting down of forests, particularly the slow-growing native woodlands of the *sierra*, has resulted in wildlife being scarce and timid.

That said, however, an alert hiker will see quite a few animals in the *puna*, especially in remote areas where they inhabit small groves of trees or seek protection among rocks.

Carnivores

Puma *Felis concolor*. The name is Quechuan (one of the few Quechua words to join the English language); the animal was the symbol of power in Inca and pre-Inca cultures in Peru. This elegant tawny cat is now an endangered species, having been hunted as an enemy of farmers.

Colpeo fox; *Dusicyon culpaeus* (Quechua *At'oc*). A grey fox seen throughout the Andes and regarded as a predator of livestock, so killed whenever possible. It is also a useful scavenger.

Andes skunk; *Conepatus rex* (Spanish *Zorillo*). Rarely seen, but often smelled! An attractive black and white animal.

Weasel; *Mustela frenata* (Spanish *Comadreja*). A common animal in the *puna* but seldom seen, living in rocky crevasses. They are about 50cm long.

Herbivores

White-tailed deer; *Odocoileus virginianus* (Spanish *Venado de cola blanca*, Quechua *Luychu*). Despite being heavily hunted this animal is still common in the more remote areas. Very adaptable, it occurs from the coastal plain to 4,000m, and on the humid eastern slopes of the Andes.

Andean Guemal; *Hippocamelus antisensis* (Spanish *Taruca*). This is an endangered species, less adaptable than the white-tailed deer so more affected by loss of its favourite habitat, small isolated patches of woodland at high altitudes. It is recognized by its location (just under the snowline), its greyish brown colour and no white tail.

The mountain viscacha; *Lagidium peruvianum inca*. The wild mammal you are most likely to see is this member of the chinchilla family. It looks like a cross between a squirrel and a rabbit, and whistles when alarmed. Groups of viscachas live at the foot of scree slopes where they can take refuge among the rocks. If you see one you'll see 20, bounding from rock to rock, or standing upright to see you better. At rest they are hard to spot, their yellow-grey colouring providing perfect camouflage.

DOMESTICATED ANIMALS
Guinea pig

The South American guinea pig, *Cavia cobayo,* has been domesticated in Peru for thousands of years. Archaeologists investigating Culebras, in the north of the country, found the remains of hundreds of the animals. Those ruins date from 2500 BC, and *cuy* housing was already part of the architecture. The Paracas culture, too, evidently raised guinea pigs, and by Inca times they were well established: excavations in Pisac have revealed *cuy* 'cages' beneath the classical niches of Inca buildings. Indians in the *sierra* still raise guinea pigs in much the same way, and the animals are one of the main sources of meat in the central Andes.

One explanation for their continuing popularity is that they are so easy to raise. Even city dwellers keep them, and every rural house has a horde of squeaking *cuyes* — the name is onomatopoeic, since the animals seem to chirrup 'cuy cuy cuy' — scuttling around in the kitchen. Sometimes they are confined in cages or boxes, but they usually run free, making full use of the thoughtfully provided holes in adobe 'furniture'. I once visited a house in a remove part of the Cordillera Blanca and questioned the householder about a row of tortoise shells ranged neatly by the wall. She lifted one up and out popped a *cuy*! A fiesta was starting the next day...

Guinea pigs eat household scraps, with an occasional supplement of alfalfa or green barley, and are remarkably clean, producing small dry droppings that are easily swept up. Like all rodents, the animals are prolific breeders: litters of three or four are born every three months. Adults usually weigh about one kilo (two pounds) — not much meat considering the time taken to prepare them. Various research projects in Peru have produced super-*cuyes* weighing in at about two kilos (about four and a half pounds), but the benefit of higher meat production is counter-balanced by the extra work involved in selected rather than haphazard breeding, and in keeping the animals separated in cages.

Guinea pigs are usually raised for home consumption or sold within the village. You may sometimes come across a *cuy* transaction taking place in the market: a squeaking sack on the ground and the potential buyer expertly testing the animals for plumpness.

The cameloid family: llamas, alpacas, guanacos and vicuñas

Llamas and their relatives were the only animals domesticated by the Incas, and have been associated with man for at least 7,000 years. They were described appreciatively by Augustín de Zarate, a Spaniard, in 1544: 'These sheep of Peru are large enough to serve as beasts of burden... their wool is very good and fine ... and they can go for four or five days without water.

Their flesh is as good as that of the fat sheep of Castile'. De Zarate also noted that the Spanish used to ride the llamas — something unknown to the Indians past and present. Not surprisingly a tired llama 'turns his head around and discharges his saliva, which has an unpleasant odour, into the rider's face'. Llamas and their relatives do spit (the contents of their stomach, not saliva!) but rarely at humans. They prefer to get the message across to other llamas.

These are the New World camels, as perfectly suited to the harsh environment of the *altiplano* as the humped camel is adapted to the deserts of the Old World. These cameloids show a special adaptation to the altitude. They have more red cells in their blood than lowland mammals, thus increasing the amount of oxygen-carrying haemoglobin available, and a higher respiratory rate. Special water cells in the stomach rumen enable them to survive long periods without drinking.

There are two wild cameloids, the guanaco (which is common in the southern part of South America but seldom seen in Peru or Bolivia) and the vicuña. Their two domesticated descendants (almost certainly the result of a vicuña/guanaco cross), are llamas and alpacas.

Llamas. Bred as beasts of burden and for meat, llamas are willing to carry only about 25kg of cargo, so large herds are necessary for efficiency. Llamas can be distinguished from alpacas by their long ears (curved like parentheses), long legs and necks, and the cocky angle of their tails.

Alpacas. These are bred for their wool, and consequently have a much heavier fleece than llamas, with a characteristic 'apron' of wool bushing out from their chests. Their noses, legs and ears are shorter and more sheep-like than those of llamas. Ideally, alpacas should be sheared every three years, but if their owner needs money, he may do it more often. Just as frequently, however, the animals are not sheared at all, but slaughtered with a full coat of wool which is sold with the hide.

Owners of llamas and alpacas will put colourful ear tassels in the animals' ears around June 23 at the celebration of the festival of San Juan Pastor, the *fiesta de campesinos*. Large herds of llamas and alpacas are easily driven over the mountains since each group has a leader, so the herdsmen only need to control one animal.

Vicuña. Reputed to have the finest wool of any animal, the vicuña was reserved for the Inca emperor himself. The animals were captured, shorn and then released. But after the conquest vicuñas were killed for their wool, and the numbers declined to near-extinction. After careful protection the species has recovered and they are not uncommon in southern Peru and in Bolivia. It is a singularly beautiful little animal, slim and graceful with a golden coat and white underparts.

Guanaco. Not often seen but unmistakable since it looks like a llama but with an orangey-brown coat shading to white on the underbelly.

GEOLOGY

The Andes are young mountains formed during the late Secondary and early Tertiary periods, at about the same time as the Alps. On the geological time scale ' young' is a relative term; before the Andes were born some 50 to 60 million years ago, the South American continent was a going concern with the Amazon flowing into the Pacific!

Continental drift, resisted by the earth's crust beneath the Pacific, created intense compression and crumpled the land's surface, releasing igneous rocks which form most of the high peaks and folding the original strata into grotesque shapes. You will see evidence of this in many of the high valleys.

The effects of glaciation, volcanic action and water erosion have completed this process and helped form the deep gorges and sheer mountainsides that we see today.

Glaciers are still shaping the Andes. As the ice moves down a mountain, its snout forms a cutting edge and glacial debris piles up on each side, forming lateral moraines. The maximum extent of the ice is marked by a terminal moraine. This glacial footprint remains long after the glacier retreats, and can be seen far below the treeline on the eastern slopes of the Andes of Peru. Those flat, rock-strewn, grassy areas so commonly found at the base of mountains were once lakes, dammed by boulders or ice, into which the rocks and silt carried down from the mountains were deposited. Gradually the lakes dried up and meadows were created.

CUY ROULETTE

One of the charms of travelling to out-of-the-way places in South America is the home-made entertainments devised by the locals. At a small fiesta I once watched a most effective form roulette.

A circle was made of up-ended cardboard boxes with holes cut in the sides and numbers chalked on the tops. Onlookers bought numbered tickets and a guinea pig was released into the centre of the circle. It scurried into one of the boxes, and the holder of the corresponding ticket won a prize. Simple and fun!

APACHETA

On every high pass of the Andes you'll see piles of stones, *apacheta*. These are built gradually through the custom of each traveller carrying a stone from the valley to place at the highest point as an offering to the *Apus* (gods of the *nevados* or snow-peaks). This has been going on since pre-Hispanic times.

When the pass is a major one, connecting two important valleys or villages, or overlooked by a mighty snow-peak and its *Apu*, the pile may be enormous and is sometimes topped by a cross. The ritual thanks the *Apu* for leading the traveller safely up to the pass; when the stone is deposited the *Apu* will give you protection for the rest of your journey.

Chapter Six

Backpacking and Trekking in the Andes

WHERE TO GO: AN OVERVIEW OF THE REGIONS

Although some readers will be familiar with South America and can plan their itinerary from an informed position, the majority will have no idea what to expect and where to go. This summary will help you select areas that suit your interests and physical capabilities.

The Cordilleras Blanca and Huayhuash, Peru

This region in the north has attracted mountain climbers for over a hundred years and organized trekking since the late 1970s — one of the first places in South America to compete with the popular Himalayan routes. The appeal is the magnificent scenery with tightly clustered snow-peaks, many over 6,000 metres, numerous turquoise-blue glacial lakes and a large choice of trails. Distances are not great, and the variety of lowland scenery is an added bonus, with green, flower-filled valleys grazed by cattle providing contrast to the high, cold passes. Always there are stunning close-up views of the *nevados*, the snow-peaks.

This area, however, is not the Peru of tourist literature since the local people are *mestizo* (mixed blood) rather than Indian so you do not see the wonderful costumes and hats of the more traditional areas, nor do you see llamas and alpacas, nor Inca remains.

The Cordilleras Blanca and Huayhuash, therefore, are for lovers of mountain scenery. The advantage of the Blanca is that it can be enjoyed by walkers of any age or level of ability (see *Geriatrekking*, page 79). Several roads built by an over-enthusiastic government in the 1980s lead over the *cordillera* providing access to vehicles. The Cordillera Huayhuash, by contrast, is the most challenging range in this book, and only suitable for fit, experienced hikers.

The Cordilleras Vilcabamba and Vilcanota, Peru

The two mountain ranges near Cusco, provide, between them, something of everything: Inca ruins, Inca roads, colourful Indians tending llamas and alpacas, thermal springs, snow-peaks and sub-tropical jungle — and plenty of other hikers.

The Cordillera Vilcabamba
The world famous Inca Trail runs through this range, but there are several other choices, many of which descend into the densely forested valleys and along river gorges. Because the countryside is less open, there are not many opportunities to get off the beaten track and find your own route. This area is also unsuitable for llamas and alpacas so once you are hiking you are unlikely to see these animals. The chief attraction is the greenness of the scenery contrasting with the rugged snow-peaks, and the marvellous Inca remains that form the focus for many of the routes.

The Cordillera Vilcanota
This is an austere, challenging area of high, cold *altiplano* (the high plain) with low rainfall, sparse vegetation and mountain passes that test the fittest walker. Here the lives of the Quechua people can have changed little since the days of the Incas as they scratch a living from land that no-one else wants. Brightly coloured, hand-woven garments are worn by the women and some of the men, and in each community the women sport a different style hat. The people can be remote and seemingly unfriendly — the consequence of isolation. The grass is nibbled to its roots by large herds of llamas and alpacas. The Vilcanota is the 'real' Peru, and worth the effort for the stunning mountain views in the most remote areas. You cannot drive to these views, as in the Cordillera Blanca and, to a lesser extent, in the Vilcabamba. You must walk there.

The Cordillera Real, Bolivia
This is a super area for backpacking for two reasons: most of the trailheads are within a few hours' drive of La Paz, with plenty of llamas and alpacas in the high meadows and splendid views of snow-peaks, and most hikes end up in the Yungas (eastern slopes of the Amazon), a semi-tropical region with comfortable hotels; a deserved reward after all that effort. If you find going downhill difficult, however, this is not the region for you!

The Cordillera Apolobamba, Bolivia
This is the mountain range for adventurers and experienced hikers. Even getting there is a challenge and with no good maps available you are left largely to your own resources. The Apolobamba is wonderfully rewarding for those who dare, with dramatic scenery, high passes, and a fascinating local Indian culture.

GERIATREKKING

When I decided to introduce my 77-year-old parents to the Andes I chose the Cordillera Blanca. For a couple who had been avid walkers all their lives but now looked for an adequate level of comfort and only a few miles of walking per day, this was an excellent choice. Huaraz has some good hotels (we stayed at the Hostal Andino which could not have been better) and enough reliable tour companies to ensure a driver and sturdy vehicle could be hired. Then it was just a question of selecting the most scenic of the new roads leading into the Cordillera.

Each day our driver took us high into the mountains, then drove back down the road to wait for us at a preselected place. We would walk downhill for a couple of miles, eat our picnic in meadows full of wild flowers and surrounded by the mighty peaks of the Cordillera Blanca, then continue walking down to the car. Thus were we able to see some of the finest scenery described in Chapter 9.

We also took an organized trip to the glacier of Pastoruri. The day tour first stopped at the grove of *puya raimondii* then continued on to the glacier, which, at almost 17,000ft, is probably as high as you can get by vehicle anywhere in the world. You can climb on to the glacier (the tour company provides a rope for assistance) which my father managed despite his artificial hip. It was 51 years since he had been on a glacier — well worth the US$8 tour fee.

BACKPACKING OR TREKKING?

Broadly speaking, trekking differs from backpacking in that your gear is carried by pack animals (or, in the case of the Inca Trail, porters) and that some local organization is involved in supplying tents, food, transport, etc. In effect, a trek is a package tour which leaves you free to enjoy the mountains without worrying about any of the logistics.

There are many advantages of trekking over backpacking, not least that all the hassle and anxiety of travel in rural Peru and Bolivia are taken out of your hands. For most trekkers there is no choice: for those with only three weeks' holiday a year, or who are disinclined to heave a 20kg/45lb pack around, or cope with the uncertainties of arranging their own porters or pack animals, the only way they will set foot in the Andes is with an organized group. Furthermore, it is only with pack animals that really long distances can be covered: most backpackers find a week's supply of food is all they can carry. Finally, with transport laid on, an organized trek can reach areas that are inaccessible to backpackers using public transport. Besides, it's often more fun (if you are with a compatible group) than doing it on your own.

In spite of this, the ultimate hiking experience, for most people, will be with one or two chosen companions, and all the effort and hassle of backpacking. For this is what exploring the wilderness is all about. Whatever the brochures say, with an organized group you are not exploring; on your own, even with a guidebook, you are. You are open to serendipitous events, you can stop when you are tired, go as far as you want, and choose the route that most appeals to you. And it will cost you about half the price of a packaged trek.

Organized trekking: choosing the right company

Trekking companies advertise in all the usual places: travel sections of daily or Sunday newspapers, travel magazines and walking and climbing magazines. An alternative source is *Adventure Holidays* published annually by Vacation Work of Oxford (England) and *Guide to Study, Travel and Adventure* published by the St Martins Press in New York for the Council on International Educational Exchange (USA).

Care must be taken when selecting a tour operator. Read between the lines of the brochure to be sure that you can cope physically and mentally with the trek. Check the altitude gain each day, find out the height of the highest passes and the number of rest days. Do not be beguiled by talk of 'verdant rainforests and glistening peaks'; the former will be hot and wet, and the latter cold and exhausting. You can only enjoy the beauty if you can cope with the terrain. Check whether riding horses are available in emergency. A good tour operator will put you in touch with someone who has done the trip, so you can get an unbiased account of what it's like. Remember that costs usually reflect the quality of the tour operator and the comforts lavished on you, so unless you are very tough and adventurous, be wary of just going for the cheapest.

There is a considerable difference between trekking in Peru and trekking in Bolivia. In Peru it is now well established, with excellent local operators in Huaraz and Cusco. In Bolivia, trekking is limited to a very few operators, and is much less comfortable and more adventurous. Equipment tends to be basic, there are no emergency riding horses and a more flexible attitude is needed. But the rewards in scenery and solitude are great.

Trekking: the experience

If the trek is organized from your home country, the pampering should start shortly after you sign up, with pre-departure information giving you a good idea of what this particular company provides. Most likely they will deal with your air ticket, send you an equipment and reading list, and generally prepare you for what is in store.

In South America you will be met by your trip leader (or he/she may travel out with you) and will not have to think for yourself until you pass through passport control on your way out of the country! It's a wonderful chance for high-powered people to regress into complete dependency, and the happiest trekkers are often those who do just that.

All well-organized treks will have a built-in period of acclimatization. In Peru, this is usually a few days' sightseeing in the Cusco area, or perhaps some gentle hiking around Huaraz. You will probably be agreeably surprised at how comfortable and well fed you are during this period. Then the tough part starts. Often you must travel in an open truck to the trailhead, because these are the only vehicles which can cope with the rough roads, and you will have to learn how to put up your own tent (or rather, the tent supplied by the local operator). With some of the very classy trekking companies your tent is put up for you, but the *arrieros* have so much to do anyway this only delays more important jobs — like preparing your supper.

You will be surprised at how many pack animals are needed — an average of one donkey per person. And you may likewise be surprised at the number of people taking care of your needs. A typical camp crew is led by a representative of the local tour operator who is both the guide and organizer. It is he who hires the *arrieros* or porters, buys the food, supplies the tents, decides where each night will be spent (pasture for the animals being the deciding factor) and deals with any crisis of a local nature.

Your own Fearless Leader's role is to keep you happy, healthy and well informed. Often there is a trip doctor who takes care of the healthy part, although his/her job is almost always limited to treating colds and diarrhoea (in the score or so treks I've led, there has been no case of serious illness or injury). All treks provide an impressive medical kit. Subordinate to the guide are the cook (and his helper) and the *arrieros* or porters. The cook generally works exclusively for that particular operator, whilst the *arrieros* are contracted locally, near the trailhead.

A typical day begins at dawn (about 6:00) with a wake-up call, although those sleeping near the camp crew (something you learn not to do) will have been woken long before by sounds of chattering and laughter as breakfast is prepared (the cook gets up at about 4.30 to start this chore). The concept of 'I'm not a morning person' seems to be exclusively Western: *all* South Americans are morning people! Some pampered trekkers find a bowl of hot water outside their tent. Otherwise, few take washing very seriously. With outside temperatures below freezing it's a question of putting on even more clothes and staggering out to the tea tent. The tea tent is one of the joys of trekking. It's big enough to stand and walk around in, and with fifteen tightly packed bodies can become quite cosy. Breakfast is a substantial meal. You will usually get porridge, eggs and bread, and sometimes even pancakes. The quality of food on a trek often comes as an unexpected pleasure.

While you are eating breakfast, the *arrieros* are rounding up the animals and starting to pack up. This is a long procedure, and you will get a head start, leaving camp at about 8.00 for the day's walk. In your daypack you will carry your picnic lunch, camera, sweater, raingear (however bright the day looks) and any other goodies you need. Your main luggage will not be accessible during the day. Lunches tend to be rather dreary — there's not much that can be done with week-old bread — and most trekkers bring their own trail snacks. The group will spread out on the trail but assemble at lunchtime, generally at a pre-arranged spot.

The day ends around 3.30 when the first walkers march into camp. There is a distinct advantage in not walking too fast. If you arrive before the pack animals and camp crew, you will have a chilly wait. If you struggle in at dusk, sobbing, at least someone will have put up your tent and tea will be almost ready. And tea is the most welcome 'meal' of the day; a chance to take your boots off and ease your aching limbs, and warm your hands round a mug of hot liquid while discussing the day. Supper comes at around 6.30 to 7.00. Meanwhile there is desultory or lively conversation, cards, Scrabble, jokes, boozing, reading, complaining... depending on the disposition of the group. The evening meal is usually ample: three courses, often with fresh meat (chickens ride on donkeys, along with the luggage, and sometimes sheep join the trek — for a while), although vegetarian are catered for. Most people are in their sleeping bags by 8 o'clock.

Some miscellaneous points

Most trek operators provide riding horses for emergencies, and these are often in use for ill or tired trekkers. If there are no horses (as in Bolivia), there is generally a rest day built into the itinerary which can be used as a sick day. Professional evacuation, with helicopter, etc, is very rarely possible.

Some outfitters supply toilet tents, which allows for a pit latrine to be dug, thus dealing with one of the major environmental problems caused by trekkers.

Washing soon becomes a non-priority. Even shower-twice-a-day Americans settle down to a quick dab every day or so when it's freezing outside and the shower comes from a glacier. In fact, hot water for washing yourself, your hair, or your clothes is often available on request. A plastic collapsible bucket is very useful for this. You soon get in the habit, on ordinary walking days, of bringing soap, etc for a noontime bath when the sun is hot.

Backpacking: the experience

Backpackers from North America, where areas of wilderness are set aside for recreation, are often surprised at the lack of solitude in the Andes. They tend to forget that the indigenous people cultivate fields and tend their animals at extraordinarily high altitudes, and some live just below the snowline. There are communities several days' walk from the nearest motorable road. The trails here are foot-roads, made and maintained by the *campesinos* who use them, and there is a constant traffic of people and their pack animals moving along them. Only in very remote areas will you be alone in the mountains.

The reception you receive in small villages depends a lot on how popular the trail is with gringos (see Chapter 4), but mostly the locals will be friendly and curious, and your chance to observe their way of life and make temporary friends without being obtrusive is one of the highlights of walking in the Andes.

Backpacking: practical considerations
Camping

Where to camp is governed by water supplies. The most idyllic camping places are near lakes or at the upper end of a *quebrada* (ravine, or narrow valley) where the water is unpolluted and the views exceptional. Often, however, you will need to set up camp near a village or small community, since houses are also built near available water (see *Village etiquette* on page 47 for advice on appropriate behaviour). The route descriptions in this book always indicate water supplies, but towards the end of the dry season some may dry up so it is wise always to carry water.

Except in remote areas do not leave your campsite unattended. Theft is common near villages on popular trails. If you can lock your tent it will protect your belongings from being pilfered.

Never leave food outside your tent; animals will be attracted to it.

Livestock

Cattle and horses All the valleys are used as grazing land, and mostly for cattle and horses. You will find them as high as 4,500m. The cattle, even virile-looking bulls, are almost never aggressive and usually flee as people approach. Be wary, however, of approaching cows with newborn calves.

If you encounter cattle being driven along a trail, stand well back, preferably on the down-side of the track so if the animals spook they will run uphill (slowly), not down.

Llamas It's a great treat for hikers to encounter a herd of ear-tasselled and laden llamas coming towards them on the trail. Everyone gets his camera out and waits for the animals to get within photographic range. And the llamas stop dead or scatter. For the sake of their *campesino* herder get well off the trail so the herd can pass uninterrupted on their way.

Dogs See page 32 for advice on dealing with vicious dogs. Most families in the Andes have at least one dog for guarding the property or livestock.

Insects

They are not much of a problem at higher altitudes (above 4,500m), but in the low valleys small biting midges or blackflies can be a real pest. They tend to be near streams, damp green meadows and around cattle. Keep your tent closed and always carry insect repellent. At least they are not mosquitoes so are unlikely to carry diseases, but the bites itch like crazy. There are also horseflies (deerflies) which bite painfully. Some solace comes with the fact that they are slow and easily killed.

FINDING YOUR OWN ROUTE

This is the most exciting sort of backpacking, and one which I hope all readers with sufficient time will adopt. Apart from the thrill of stepping into the unknown with only your map, compass and passing *campesino* to guide you, finding your own trails will help prevent over-use of the popular ones. There are thousands upon thousands of footpaths in the Andes, well used and passing through beautiful scenery, and only a very few of them have been trodden by gringos.

As well as the anticipation generated by not knowing what is over the next hill, you have the wonderful bonus of never being lost, because you never knew where you were anyway.

The methods George and I used to find the trails described in our first books published in the 1970s can be easily adopted by other fit and adventurous people. First we selected an area known for its natural beauty, or recommended by the locals, and with a population large enough to maintain trails between villages. No problem in the Andes. Then we tried to find a topographical map covering the area, preferably 1:100,000 or 1:50,000 scale. Again, usually no problem with the geographical institutes in Peru and Bolivia. Even with only a road map you can pick a likely looking area above the treeline, between two towns, and be fairly confident that there will be a trail. Then we packed enough food to last the estimated number of days, plus two more, and additional emergency rations. And that was it...

Here are a few do's and don'ts for Andean explorers:

• **Do** carry a compass and know how to use it.

• **Do** carry and know how to read a topographical map.

• **Do** turn back if the route becomes dangerous.

• **Do** ask the locals for advice and directions.

• **Do** carry extra food.

• **Don't** plan a jungle trip without a guide.

• **Don't** underestimate time, distance, or weather conditions.

GUIDES, PORTERS AND PACK ANIMALS

For independent travellers the reverse of finding your own route is to use local expertise to ensure a trouble-free trek. Guides, cooks, porters, muleteers (*arrieros*) and their pack animals — either donkeys (*burros*), mules (*mulas*) or horses (*caballos*) — are often hired by hikers to take the donkey work out of backpacking. You will not be allowed to hire the animal without its owner. Nor are llamas ever available.

Arrieros and porters can be hired in most towns and villages next to the trailhead of popular routes. The charge in mid-1994 was US$6 a day for the man and US$3 for his donkey, but this is likely to have gone up so check at the South American Explorers Club in Lima or at the tourist office in the trekking area. A porter (*portador*) charges about US$6 a day (necessary on certain routes, such as the Inca Trail, where pack animals are not permitted).

In most well-known trekking areas, the *arrieros* have formed an association, and control the prices and conditions. This has done much to avoid exploitation by unscrupulous tour operators or individual hikers. Always go through the association, if there is one, not only to provide local employment and to encourage the maintenance of standards, but to iron out any misunderstandings or problems that may arise.

Most *arrieros* are trustworthy, but you need to make your requirements clear, and to keep your valuables with you. When choosing an *arriero* try to get a recommendation from another traveller. That way excellence is rewarded. Take time to draw up a contract in writing. Discuss the price (only pay half up front, and the other half at the end of the trip), the duration of the trip, side trips, whether cooking is part of the deal, and whether you need to provide his food and/or sleeping equipment as well. *Arrieros* will have their own idea of how long a trip will take and it is almost impossible to shift them. Part of this seeming obstinacy is the necessity of camping where there is good pasture for the donkeys. Despite what may appear to us as frequent cruelty to animals, *campesinos* are very solicitous over their general welfare: they need fit, healthy animals. So ask them how many days it will be, and agree on a total price for that time period.

Hiring local people is an important way for tourists to help the rural areas and bridge the cultural gap. However, for many hikers the freedom of walking alone outweighs the moral and practical advantages of using *arrieros*. A compromise is to hire someone for the first day to take your packs to the top of the first pass, and then continue on your own.

MINIMUM IMPACT

As backpacking and trekking become increasingly popular in Peru and Bolivia, hikers must develop an awareness of their effect on the environment. Even the problems besetting the national parks in developed countries, such as erosion caused by over-use, are now seen here! Inca ruins that have withstood hundreds of years of the forces of nature have been damaged by the campfires of tourists, and the flights of Inca stairs built for the light tread of bare feet have been worn down by the heavy tramp of hiking boots.

Environmental abuse, however, takes on a wider meaning since the foreign hiker is making his mark not just on the landscape, but on the local people. Ironically, of the two major problems, litter and begging, one is caused by imitating local customs and the other by ignoring them.

Litter

We should be truthful about litter. It offends the eye (and sometimes the nose) but does no permanent harm to the environment. However, it is so easy to put right, and so unpleasant when left, that we should do everything in our power to ease the problem. The quantity of litter and rubbish left on the popular hiking trails in Peru and Bolivia is horrifying, and compounded by the fact that local people are the worst culprits. Waste matter of all sorts: paper, fruit peel, plastic, etc, is dropped on the highways and byways, rivers and creeks, and visitors soon follow suit. Tourists, both gringo and South American (perhaps mostly the latter) drop more litter in rural areas because the *campesinos* have so little to throw away: cigarette packets, sardine tins and plastic bottles mostly. Tourist litter is so much more conspicuous: brightly coloured toilet paper, cans, dried food packets, film cartons, Band-Aids, aluminium foil. It's hard enough to understand why visitors blow their noses on pink toilet paper and then drop it on the wayside, but why they also shit beside the trail, leaving a pile of turds and toilet paper is almost beyond belief! The culprits are unlikely to be readers of this book so it is a waste of space to preach about it. All I can say is try to clear up other people's mess as well as your own, unpleasant though it may be. And remember that orange peel is just as unsightly and alien as toilet paper, even though it is biodegradable.

Carry several roomy plastic bags and collect rubbish as you walk. It's tedious and tiring, but you'll feel noble (and if you do stoop to shit-paper you'll feel hypernoble) and will be doing something positive. Later you can burn or bury your collection. People are much more likely to throw rubbish in an area that's already littered.

Tell your porters or *arrieros* that you will pay them extra if they carry all the rubbish back to the main town, and help you clear up littered areas. This is a case where interfering with their culture *is* a good thing!

The preservation of the beauty of Peruvian and Bolivian hiking trails is up to you. Here are a few recommendations:

• Leave the trail and campsite cleaner than you found them. If you can't carry out other people's tin cans, bury them away from the trail.

• Defaecate well away from the trail and water supply; dig a hole, or cover your faeces with a rock, and burn the paper.

• Don't burn firewood needed by the local population, nor create a fire risk. Cook on a stove. If you are in a remote area where there is plenty of wood, no local people and no other hikers, you may make a fire (you will do so whether I say you may or not!) but be very careful to extinguish it completely before retiring for the night. Uncontrolled fires cause major damage each year in Peru and Bolivia; don't become part of the problem.

• Don't contaminate streams. Pans and dishes can be cleaned quite adequately without soap or detergent, or use one of the biodegradable liquid soaps sold in tubes.

Begging

Another indication that a trail is a popular gringo route is that children rush up to you and demand sweets or money. Before you offer a child such presents, reflect on the consequences of your action. You are giving him tooth decay in an area with no dentists, or you are teaching him that begging is rewarding and that he can, after all, get something for nothing. His increasingly insistent demands will irritate future trekkers and help widen the gap between gringo and *campesino*. (This subject is covered in more depth in Chapter 4.)

Adults, too, have been taught to beg. They usually ask for cigarettes or money and one's attempts at conversation or normal social interaction are thwarted.

This cultural erosion is reversible. If all trekkers and hikers stopped handing out unearned presents the begging would cease in a few years, and the *campesinos* would return to their traditional system of reciprocity, where presents and labour are exchanged, not given. So give a smile and a greeting instead.

If you are sick of straining your eyes trying to read by 40 watts, buy a 100-watt light bulb and use it in those dingy hotels.

BROTHER CAN YOU SPARE SOME RICE?

By George Bradt

I went to Cajamarca for a vacation, Hilary went to do some hiking. I slumped around eating and sleeping while Hilary scurried about organizing a hike.

After two days of frantic activity, Hilary broke the bad news. 'George, you won't believe the wonderful hike I've plotted out for us. Out of bed, lace up your boots, put on your backpack and let's go.'

'Isn't it too late to start walking this afternoon?' I suggested hopefully.

'Isn't it too late still to be in bed?' she countered.

'OK. Where are we going, and how long is this gem of a walk?'

'Well, I must admit we really should have bought a map in Lima. I've tried all over town to get something but the best I could do was the library. I asked a nice man there if we could walk from Cumbe Mayo to San Pablo and he said it would only take a few hours. There's quite a big village on the way so we can stock up with more food there.' I became suspicious.

'You have bought enough food for this trip, right?' Hilary goes in for slimming during our walks, and doesn't mind reduced rations. I'm slim enough and the very idea of reduced rations brings on a feeling of weakness about the knees.

'No problem, I've already got cheese, rolls, soup and lots more.'

By this time we'd reached the outskirts of town and I'd had the chance to admire Hilary's new hiking style: she was walking on her heels like a penguin.

'What's this, the new Bradt Ergonomic Propulsion Technique?'

'No, it's athlete's foot, and I don't want to hear any jokes about it.'

Before we could pursue the subject further we heard the welcome sound of a vehicle climbing the hill behind us. A lift to Cumbe Mayo would save us a lot of walking. Sure enough, the jeep stopped and a young archaeologist offered us a ride all the way to the site. We had plenty of time to look around the area with him before finding a camping place and eating a lavish supper.

The next day in the village of Chetilla we met the mayor, a very gracious gentleman, sitting outside a house. When he saw us he bustled over and asked our business: we were missionaries perhaps? Or selling veterinary supplies? We told him about our walk and asked if we'd reach San Pablo that evening. He wasn't at all encouraging and added 'Maybe you are fast walkers'. Hilary looked nervous, but recovered her composure and asked directions to the village shops.

'There is only one, and it's closed because the owners have gone to San Pablo.' We thanked him and walked on. As we continued through the village Hilary kept nipping off down side streets and asking for eggs or bread. No one had any, and this was the only village along our route. We ate our lunch in some fields. I was just reaching for a third roll when Hilary said 'George, two are plenty, why not save the rest for tomorrow?'

'OK, just fill me in on your supper plans then; you know, kind of give me something to look forward to.' Just as I was beginning to suspect, there would be no supper. In icy silence we put away our picnic supplies and walked down to the river valley. On the way, Hilary's search for some sort of local food became more vigorous. Braving the hysterically barking dogs, she asked at every hut we passed. The few people we saw looked apprehensive about the two hungry gringos on their doorstep, and none admitted to having any spare food.

We crossed the river at the bottom of the valley and had started up the other side when we met a man milking cows. We asked to buy a litre, and to our relief he agreed readily. After he had filled our water bottle with warm milk he refused to accept payment. 'Why should you pay me for the milk when it has no value?' he asked. We continued in better spirits, but lunch was beginning to wear off, and after four hours of climbing our legs felt like jelly.

We climbed, slower and slower, until just before sunset. 'After all, there's nothing to cook, so there's no point in stopping early.' said Hilary philosophically. Finally we found a good campsite, set up the tent, and tucked into 'supper'. Hilary, gallantly pretending that a litre of fresh milk was all she needed, swapped four peanuts for my share of the milk.

'If you're still hungry, George, you could walk over that rise and see if there's a village. I think I saw a soccer field up there from across the valley.'

'Me? Hungry? After hogging an entire roll and four peanuts? I'm full to bursting!'

'I'd go myself, but I don't think I can walk.' She'd taken off her boots and socks to reveal ten swollen, oozing toes with great raw areas where the skin had come off. Thinking that we were lucky to have survived this far, I sped up the hill, hoping to see a road. There was no village at the top of the ridge, not even a house, and certainly no road and therefore no transport.

It was rather depressing to wake up to no breakfast, and even more depressing to climb uphill all morning and find how quickly we were drained of the energy we had accumulated overnight. Our food-finding efforts continued unsuccessfully. We began naming specific vegetables: squash, corn, potatoes. By this time Hilary was hobbling along like an old crone, her feet wrapped in an assortment of colourful rags. Eventually we came across a woman weaving, with lots of hens scratching about in the dust.

'Have you got any eggs?' we asked as we casually waved a fair-sized bank note.

'Yes, I've got two', she said. Bliss, our salvation was at hand. Two eggs weren't much, but they'd help. She began weaving all the harder. Better check. Yes, we'd heard correctly, but she wasn't interested in getting them.

'You know, we're very hungry.' More weaving. 'We haven't eaten anything for three days.' Completely unmoved, even with my exaggeration. A day or two without food means nothing to these people. Then she saw someone hurrying towards us, and unhitched her backstrap loom immediately. She lifted a sitting hen, gave us the eggs, and took the money. The youth running towards us stopped and motioned us towards him. 'Why don't I cook those for you, and give you some rice as well?' We couldn't think of any particular reason why not, so followed him to a nearby house. Very soon we were ploughing through two bowls of rice topped with a fried egg.

After watching us satisfy our initial hunger, he asked us about our trip: where we'd come from, where we were going. We told him all the details, then he asked the obvious question: 'But why didn't you bring any food with you?' We told him and he laughed. He kindly suggested we take extra rice with us in case we didn't reach San Pablo until the next day. But he assured us that even walking slowly, 'like fat ladies', we'd reach the town before sundown.

We'd stuffed ourselves so full of rice we could hardly get up, let alone carry our backpacks. But we liked the stuffed feeling better than the empty feeling. And we liked our arrival in San Pablo better than the journey.

This piece first appeared in the 1980 edition of this guide. Obviously things have changed in the Cajamarca region but as a reminder of what can happen to unfit, unprepared hikers it is worth keeping. Anyway, I like it!

BRIBERY

Corruption is a way of life in South America, especially in Peru. It is particularly common in government-run offices and among employees of the government, most of whom are grossly underpaid and expected to augment their incomes with bribes. In some respects it works quite well, with those who can afford it supporting the less affluent.

Visitors who avoid giving bribes, or refuse to do so, are easing the way for those who follow, but there may be times when a few dollars and a lapse of high principles are necessary.

Part two

PERU

Peru

COLOMBIA

ECUADOR

R.Amazon

BRAZIL

● Cajamarca

Cordilleras
Blanca &
Huayhuash

● Huaráz

● Cerro de Pasco

● Lima

Cordillera
Vilcabamba

Cusco ●
Cordillera
Vilcanota

B O L I V I A

● Paracas

Puno ●
L.Titicaca

● Arequipa

Chapter Seven

Peru:
General Information

Introduction

Peru was named by Francisco Pizarro who first landed in South America on a beach in southern Colombia. Nearby flowed the Birú creek, and this became the name of his newly discovered country. Or so legend has it. Peru is a country of contrasts, a place of extremes: desert and jungle, snow-peaks and sand-dunes, great wealth and grinding poverty.

Tourism here is based on special interests and adventure travel. This is not the country for someone who simply wants to lie on a beach: despite the long coastline there are few beaches one would want to spend any time on and no seaside resorts as such. What Peru does have is mountain scenery and trekking to rival the Himalayas, rainforest reserves full of animals and birds, the most impressive Inca ruins and arguably the best museums in South America, and the Andean people, descendants of the Incas, with their dignity, colour and ancient customs.

Peru suffers all the problems of infrastructure and reliability that you would expect in a country emerging from economic catastrophe and more than a decade of terrorism. Visitors who expect everything to run like clockwork will not be happy here. What surprises those who love Peru is how much *does* run smoothly.

Physical and social geography

A cross-section of the country, from west to east, would reveal the following picture.

First the Pacific Ocean, teeming with fish and their predators, and bringing the cold Humboldt Current close to shore. The strong sun and cold water create a mist, *garúa,* which blankets the entire coastal strip for part of the year. This strip is desert, some 500km wide, but some sections are watered by streams from the mountains. Cotton, fruit and sugar crops are grown, and most of the nation's industrial sector is located along the coast including Lima, the capital.

Crops don't really begin to grow without irrigation until a height of about 2,000m is reached on the western slope of the Andes. Corn, potatoes and sun-loving vegetables flourish up to about 4,000m, then cattle and general livestock take over, with mining the only activity in the very high altitudes around 5,000m.

Crossing the continental divide, with peaks ranging from 2,500m to 6,768m, the descent begins to the Amazon basin. The change is noticeable immediately. Warm, moist air rising up from the jungle makes these slopes greener and wetter. At a height of about 3,000m dense rainforests begin, and continue uninterrupted to the Atlantic Ocean.

The population of Peru (at the last census, 1993) is 22.5 million, nine million of whom are in Lima. Of the remaining population 50% live in the Andes at an average altitude of 3,000m. The rainforest, covering 60% of Peru, contains only about 10% of the population.

Climate

With three distinct geographical regions you have three distinct climates.

The coastal desert (*la costa*) The Austral winter runs from April until November when the coastal region is mostly cloudy, with daytime temperatures around 10-18°C, and a cold wind sweeps over the desert. It rarely rains but *garua* hangs over the region from time to time. Lima has this mist throughout the winter, which, since it coincides with the sunny — and thus the tourist — season in the highlands, adds to the negative view of the capital.

Summer is from December to April. It's very hot with temperatures between 20° and 36°C — sometimes more — and a warm breeze.

The mountain region (*la sierra*) In the Andean highlands there is a dry season and a rainy season. In contrast to the coast, it is dry and sunny from April to the end of October. At 3,500m or over it is very cold (around or below freezing) at night and in the early morning and evening. It is cool on cloudy days — even the dry season is no guarantee of sunshine. Daytime temperatures range from 10° to 18°C.

The rainy season runs from November to April (when it is sunny on the coast). The mornings are mostly clear, but it starts raining in the afternoons and sometimes continues during the nights. It doesn't get as cold as in the winter dry season: daytime temperatures vary between 10° and 13°C and at night they drop to around 8°C.

The jungle (*la selva*) The weather pattern is the same as the highlands. In the dry season it gets very hot in the rainforest (23° to 32°C during the day), and is not much cooler at night. There is an exception, however. During June, July and August a cold front, *el fraije*, may pass through from the south, pushing temperatures down to 8°-10°C which can come as a nasty shock to the unprepared traveller. It only lasts for a few days, however.

As you would expect, the rainy season in the rainforest is very wet indeed. The rivers rise — some are not navigable during this season — and road connections with the *sierra* can be closed by mud slides. Temperatures only drop about 5°C, but it feels chilly in the constant rain. During the fine spells it is very humid with lots of mosquitoes.

El Niño

A warm current flows south along the Pacific Ocean. Since it arrives around Christmas, fishermen call it *El Niño* (the Christ-child). Every four years or so, a catastrophic version of *El Niño* hits Peru and Ecuador, bringing drastic changes to the climate and the water temperature. The effects of a severe *El Niño* year are disastrous for wildlife. The rise in sea temperature drives the small fish and other marine creatures to deeper, cooler water, and the numerous species further up the food chain starve to death. Literally. In *El Niño* of 1982 an estimated six million seabirds died. The whole balance of nature is upset, with land animal species profiting from the burst of lush vegetation caused by the unseasonable rains, and marine animals perishing. The last, not very severe, *El Niño* was in 1992.

A brief history
Pre-conquest

The earliest cultures of any significance emerged around 900BC: Chavín de Huántar in what is now known as the Cordillera Blanca, and Sechín Alto, inland from Casma on the north coast. During the 700 years of their prominence they achieved some remarkable works of architecture, ceramics, textiles and metalwork, including gold, silver and copper. Around 500BC their powers declined and the Nazca culture emerged in southern Peru, lasting until about AD500. The textiles excavated from the tombs of Paracas, preserved by the dry desert, are arguably the finest ever found, and the Nazca ceramics are their equals in intricate and imaginative design. The famous Nazca Lines — vast 'line drawings' cut into the desert and easily visible only from the air — add weight to the awesome achievements of this culture, though little is known of the Nazca beliefs and way of life.

The Moche, on the other hand, left us a perfect record of their day-to-day concerns in the form of their wonderfully realistic pottery vessels depicting scenes from everyday life (including sexual activities). Many Moche achievements were echoed some 500 years later by the Incas: roads and other engineering feats, and irrigation canals. Their desert kingdom stretched from Piura to Casma, with Chan-Chán, later a Chumú city, their capital.

Around AD600 the power shifted from the north coast to the Andes and the Huari-Tiwanaku cultures. The Huari dominated the central highlands

THE GOVERNMENT AND THE TERRORISTS
By Bruce Kay

Since the early 1980s, two guerrilla groups have been active in parts of Peru, the Maoist *Sendero Luminoso* (Shining Path) movement and, to a much lesser extent, the *Movimiento Revolucionario Tupac Amaru* (MRTA). By far the stronger and more violent of the two is Sendero Luminoso, which launched its armed conflict on election day in 1980 in the central highland department of Ayacucho. Since the early 1980s, Sendero has left its original base of operations in Ayacucho and spread to diffuse regions of Peru, from the upper Huallaga valley, where half the world's supply of cocaine is produced, to the sprawling shanty towns nestled in the hills ringing the capital city, Lima. Although it is impossible to determine the extent of Sendero Luminoso's following in Peru, there is no question that the bulk of its supporters are drawn from these two areas. The bloodshed from the conflict has cost the lives of many thousands of Peruvians (by 1992 an estimated 26,000) as well as a few foreign journalists and workers in non-governmental aid organizations.

After nearly a decade of failure to combat the spread of terrorism, the Fujimori government now seems to be succeeding in bringing the problem under control. Perhaps the most significant victory against the guerrillas came in October 1992, when Sendero Luminoso's founder and leader, Abimael Guzman, whose *nom de guerre* is 'Presidente Gonzalo', was captured in a Lima suburb along with several key Sendero leaders and sentenced to life imprisonment. By most reliable accounts, Guzman's capture has badly weakened the organization and caused a serious rift in its leadership; although the bombings perpetrated by Sendero's militants continued to plague Lima and its surrounding areas, the number of attacks has significantly diminished over the last year or so. Sendero is itself divided between the 'doves' who, along with their imprisoned leader, favour a truce with the government and hardliners who want the continuation of the armed struggle. Unfortunately the government's success in controlling terrorism has not completely eliminated the violations of human rights in areas under military control.

Considerably smaller and less significant as an opposition group is the MRTA which began armed operations in Lima in 1984. The group is less fanatical than Sendero Luminoso and more in line with the traditional Latin American guerrilla movements of the 1960s and 1970s. Nevertheless, the MRTA managed to gain control over territory in some parts of the central highlands before being eradicated by its main competitor, Sendero Luminoso. Its founder and leader Victor Polay Campos, a leader in the APRA youth movement along with Alán García, was captured in 1989 and imprisoned for life. Although the group still carries out the occasional act of sabotage, its significance has dwindled to the point of non-existence.

An estimated 80% of Peruvians are unemployed or underemployed. Of the nine million inhabitants of Lima, one million are street vendors.

and the Tiwanaku had their religious centre around Lake Titicaca, but there was apparently friendly communication between the two. What we now think of as Inca achievements were further developed by these cultures with road-building, land terracing and irrigation being perfected, along with efficient administration and a labour tax.

When these civilizations collapsed, the Incas stepped in and completed what is widely considered the model of successful socialist government. The Inca dominance was short compared with its predecessors: about 300 years, from around the year 1200 to the Spanish conquest in 1533. In this period they developed from a small tribe in Cusco to the largest empire ever known in the Americas, stretching from the present-day Ecuador-Colombia border to the Río Maule in central Chile, and east to the Amazon. The story of its decline through civil war and its destruction by the Spanish conqueror Pizarro is told in the Cajamarca and Cusco chapters.

The impression is often given that Pizarro's conquest was the end of the Incas, but in fact they struggled to regain power through uprisings, with the last reigning Inca, Tupac Amaru, killed in 1572, and the last Inca noble, Tupac Amaru II, meeting his death in 1780.

Post-conquest
The Spanish also had to defeat groups that had largely resisted Inca domination. These included the Chimú in the north, whose capital, Chan-Chán, had fallen to the Incas a century earlier, and the Chachapoyas culture, with their main fortress at Kuelap (see Chapter 8).

A sea-going nation like Spain needed a port as its New World capital and Francisco Pizarro founded Lima in 1535. For the next 200 years the viceroys ruled throughout the Andean countries, retaining much of the old Inca system with Indian chiefs controlling large groups of natives. Quarrels among the *conquistadores* led to Pizarro's assassination in 1541, and constant uprisings by the Incas and later the Peru-born Spaniards made government of this valuable acquisition an unrewarding task. Finally, in 1821, José de San Martín proclaimed Peru's independence, even though the country was still in the hands of the viceroys. The great liberator Simon Bolívar came to San Martín's assistance three years later, and the decisive battle of Ayacucho in 1824 led to full independence in 1826.

Independent Peru was as turbulent as in the colonial era. In the 1830s Peru and Bolivia briefly united in a confederation, and in 1883 the two countries went to war with Chile; as a result Bolivia lost its sea coast and Peru lost much of its southern territory.

Peru was under military rule from 1968 until 1980, but, most unusually, the junta in power in the early part of that era was socialist and instigated the agrarian reforms and redistribution of wealth that the country so sorely needed on moral grounds. Economically the reforms were a disaster, however, and the subsequent military rulers were right-wing. Peru was one of the first South American countries to move away from military rule towards democracy, and in 1980 presidential and congressional elections were held and Fernando Belaunde Terry was elected president. His successor was Alán García who was elected with enormous enthusiasm in 1985, and rejected with equal enthusiasm in 1990, having failed to deal with the rising economic problems and increasing terrorism. Alberto Fujimori was elected as president, entering national politics for the first time. Two years later, in April 1992, Fujimori 'interrupted' democratic rule in his controversial *autogolpe* (or self-inflicted coup) in which Congress was shut down and the constitution suspended. Since then, the government has drifted in a more authoritarian direction with Fujimori firmly in command, though it is still very far from the repressive Argentine or Chilean regimes of the 1970s. National and municipal elections are still held on a regular basis and there is considerable freedom of the press. On the other hand, with the election of a 'rubber stamp' Congress in 1992, an absolute majority of which came from the president's *Cambio 90* party, and the narrow approval of a more conservative constitution in October 1993, more power has been ceded to President Fujimori while the strength of Peru's political parties has been undermined in the process. He was re-elected in 1995 — a landslide victory.

EXITS AND ENTRANCES

Visas are at present not required by western Europeans or North Americans, but rules change so check if you need one. Australians and New Zealanders do need a visa.

All nationalities are given a tourist card by the immigration authorities on arrival: a stamp and a little white slip of paper. Don't lose it, as you need it when leaving the country, and you may be asked to show it to prove you are in the country legally (attach it to your passport, and make a photocopy for extra security). If you do lose it, get a new one at the Immigration Department in Lima. All nationalities are automatically given a 90-day stay, although 30- and 60-day permits are also given so if you are staying for three months make sure you tell the authorities on arrival. You can renew this permit for a further 90 days (although you may only be given 30 days at a time) at the Immigration Department in the bigger cities for US$20 for each 30 days. After that you need to leave the country before you can get another visa (spending one day across the border is enough).

Legally, you need to show a ticket out of the country when you enter. This, however, is not strictly adhered to and the authorities seldom check.

Usually an explanation that you are travelling overland by bus will satisfy them, but failing that buy the cheapest bus ticket from one border town across the frontier to the next town (for example, Tacna to Arica).

Make sure you get an exit stamp when leaving Peru or the next country may not grant you entry. At most borders the departure/entry procedure goes very smoothly, but at some remote border crossings you will need to get your exit stamp in the last town that has an immigration office (for example, leaving Peru via the Amazon river into Brazil, you need to get an exit stamp in Iquitos).

Don't let your visa expire.

CURRENCY

The currency in Peru is called the *sol* but has changed a few times over the years. Due to the high rate of inflation, from time to time the authorities lop off a few zeros and change the name. It went from the (old) *sol* to the *inti* in 1986 and to the new *sol* again in 1991. In August 1990 inflation was stopped in its tracks when Fujimori came up with the solution: hyper-inflation for one day! This shocked Peruvians, but has brought the inflation rate down to about 60% a year, instead of the 3,000% and more the year before.

Local currency exists in the following units:
Coins: 0.01, 0.05, 0.10, 0.20, 0.50, 1 *sol,* 2 *soles* and 5 *soles.*
Notes: 10, 20, 50, 100 and 500 *soles.*

It is easy to change travellers cheques in the large towns, and Banco de Crédito is probably the best bank. When changing into *soles* there is no charge, changing into cash dollars will incur about 2-3%.

If you are changing cash dollars it is best (and safest) to do it in a *Casa de Cambio*. Unfortunately, you'll only see them in the bigger towns; in the smaller towns you have to trust the street money-changers. In smaller places it's hard (or impossible) to change dollars, so plan ahead when heading off into the more remote areas of the mountains and take enough *soles*. Try to bring small denominations: no-one ever has change.

Due to inflation, prices are often published in dollars in the upper-range hotels, restaurants, and shops. Most of these places will accept credit cards, or you can pay with local currency using the exchange rate of the day, which is lower than that offered by the *Casas de Cambio* and banks.

Never accept damaged dollar bills, you won't be able to change them back again. And beware of forged dollars or *soles*.

NOTE: Controlling inflation means that Peru is no longer a very cheap country. Prices in this book (given in dollars) may have risen by the time you travel. Be sure to travel with adequate funds!

USEFUL INFORMATION

Telephones

Peru's telephone company is called Telefonica and operates all over the country, even in the smallest villages. They handle local, national and international calls using a token, *rin*, which can be bought at their offices or from street vendors. Recently they have introduced public phones which accept coins or phone cards, so *rins* may be phased out. You can call via the operator, but this is more expensive; a deposit is required and you may be in for a long wait.

Recently a phonecard has been introduced which can also be bought at Telefonica offices. AT&T cards (and some others) are accepted all over Peru. Dial 19 to get an AT&T operator (check on the number, it will be different if you hold another card) except in Lima where you have to go through the international operator.

Lima, tiresomely, has its own telephone company called CPT. There are only two offices, one in the centre of Lima (Plaza San Martin) and one in Miraflores (corner Diez Canseco and La Paz). You'll also find Telefonica offices in Lima, offering the same services as anywhere else in the country, but no telephone operators.

You can send faxes and telexes from most Telefonica offices.

Holidays

At least once a month a saint has his or her birthday which is lots of fun for the saint since they get to leave the church for a parade around town. It's an excuse for a fiesta (see page 50) and a national holiday. If the day falls in the middle of the week, it is automatically moved to the next Monday to make a long weekend. Remember that banks, shops and offices are closed on these days.

The national school holidays run from the end of December until the end of February. As at home — but worse — everyone wants to get out of town for Christmas so prices of hotels and transport double and all tickets on all means of transport are sold out days before. Avoid travelling at this time. The same problem occurs around Independence Day (July 28), bang in the middle of the tourist season, when school holidays start one or two weeks before the holiday and continue until mid August.

Business hours

Siesta is rigidly observed all over Peru throughout the year, except in Lima. You might as well join them since everything is closed from 12:30 until 16:00. Business hours run from 10:00 to 12:30 and 16:00 until 19:00. Shops are open from 09:30 to 12:30 and 16:00 until 20:00.

Lima has the normal business hours, 09:00 to 17:00, closed one hour at lunch time. Government-run offices are mostly only open in the mornings. Some tourist shops stay open at lunch time.

Mail

Receiving If you want mail to be sent to you, American Express is more reliable than the post office, but you need to be a customer, with either Amex travellers cheques or a credit card. For the post office, letters should be addressed to *Lista de Correo* or *Poste Restante*, followed by the town. Ask your correspondents to write your last name in capitals or underline it to avoid letters being filed under your first name (but when you call for your mail check your first name anyway). Letters are held for up to two or three months. A small collection fee is charged. Never risk having any money or valuables sent by mail unless they are registered.

Letters sent from the USA or Europe to Peru can take anywhere between eight days and three weeks.

Tell your nearest and dearest not to send you a parcel. Getting it through customs is an unbelievable hassle (at least a day is needed) and extortionate taxes are charged. For this reason you will be doing no great service to your Peruvian friends if you send them a parcel.

NOTE: In a Peruvian address, *Casilla* or *Apartado Postal* are not street names, they are the equivalent of 'PO Box ...'.

Sending Surprisingly, most letters sent from Peru reach their destination. To USA or Europe can take between five days and three weeks. Letters sent within South America always take longer than six days, and the post office is sometimes on strike...

Parcels sent home do get there, but set aside a day to do it and a fair amount of money for the postage. The post office requirements are exacting. Some shops will mail purchases for you.

If you are desperate to get a parcel home you could use a courier such as UPS or DHL.

Air-freight

This is a good alternative to the post office or couriers, particularly if you have more that 30kg of stuff to send home. The price is then about US$3-4 per kilo, plus about $100 on paperwork and a day at the airport. It's reliable and they will deliver to your home address (though it's cheaper to have it picked up at the airport). Receiving an air-freight parcel is a different matter — there is as much hassle, time and bureacracy as receiving a mailed parcel. If this is unavoidable, for instance for a large expedition, set aside several days and expect to hire a 'fixer' at the airport.

At the airport

When you choose your airline ask about the baggage allowance both to and from Peru. Some airlines allow two bags of 30kg each going out but only 25kg coming back. Others allow two bags (unlimited weight) each way or only 25kg in total.

The international departure tax is US$18, payable in dollars. The national tax is about US$3 payable in *soles*. This is not always adhered to at the smaller national airports. A US$1 security tax, paid in *soles* or dollars, is charged by the major airports in Peru, including Lima.

When arriving in Lima on international flights, the luggage hall can be a complete shambles. It can take ages to clear customs particularly if you are behind a Peruvian family who have been on a shopping spree to Miami. Every purchase will be examined and argued over. Tourists rarely have their luggage searched, so try to get in a queue with other travellers.

Never pay a bribe at the airport.

On departure, customs officers frequently check travellers. If they pick you out after you have checked in, you'll be taken to the back where they look through your luggage. This is a normal security procedure, so don't be alarmed. Body searches are very rare.

Laundry

Laundries in posh hotels are very expensive, charging as much as US$3 per item. Fortunately the public *lavanderías* charge by the kilo: about US$2. You bring your laundry to the laundromat in the morning and it is ready in the evening.

Handicrafts

Peru has a wide variety of beautiful handicrafts and the artisans are proud of their work and its origin in their *tierra* (hometown): handwoven alpaca products from Huancavelica and Puno, ceramics from Cajamarca, Ayacucho and Cusco, carved gourds, silver work and weavings from Huancayo, tapestries from Ayacucho, wooden articles from Piura, and so on.

Lima is the main outlet for the sale and export of handicrafts, and it's also the refuge for many artisans of the *sierra* escaping poverty or terrorism. So the range and quality is likely to be better in Lima than in the place of origin. The prices are also better.

The biggest and best craft market in Lima is situated along Avenida La Marina (from the 9th until the 12th block) in the suburb of Pueblo Libre. Spend some time looking around and examining the quality, and feel free to bargain. For top quality goods it is better to go to a shop which only buys the best. Of course you will pay more, but it will be money well spent. The best shops in Lima are where the money is: Miraflores and San Isidro.

If Lima has the selection and quality, the tourist centres such as Cusco, Puno and Huancayo have the fun. You are probably buying direct from the maker here and, since handicraft sellers are part of the town scenery, you will not have to set out purposely to shop. Shopping for hand-made items is one of the ways that travellers can make a positive contribution to the local economy and well-being of the people and their culture. It encourages the continuation of traditional crafts and the development of new ones, and it helps prevent the drift to the cities. For this reason try to rethink the cliché that it is somehow shameful for a traveller to pay a little too much for an article. If it's not too much for you it certainly won't be too much for the vendor!

Strikes

During military rule strikes became a popular way for an aggrieved population to show their feelings. These days disruptive strikes are rarer, but you do still see *¡Huelga!* painted on some walls. It has a more defiant ring to it than 'industrial action'. When strikes affect transport they can be quite tiresome, but fortunately even general strikes are usually uncoordinated and poorly run.

PROTECTED AREAS OF PERU

Peru is one of the most biologically rich countries in the world, ranking second in bird diversity, third for mammals and fifth for plants. Of the world's 114 life zones, 83 are found within Peru's borders.

Conservation of this unique natural heritage was officially begun in 1961 when Peru's first National Park was established: Cutervo, in the Department of Cajamarca. Just over 7% of the country is now officially protected — 17 million hectares in 45 protected areas. Conservation is under the control of the Instituto Areas Naturales Protegidos de Flora y Fauna Silvestre, a section of the Instituto Nacional de Recursos Naturales. Their address is Calle 17, no 355, Urb Palmar, San Isidro, Lima. Tel: (014) 410425/414606. Open Monday to Friday, 08:30-12:00, 13:00-17:00.

There are four categories of protected area:

Parques nacionales (national parks)

Areas with complete protection and preservation of fauna, flora and nature. Special entry permits are required for visitors but the local people have the right to use resources if part of their culture.

The national parks, their size, department and date established are given on the following page:

Cerros de Amotape (91,300 hectares)	Tumbes	1975
Cutervo (2,500 hectares)	Cajamarca	1961
Huascarán (340,000 hectares)	Ancash	1975
Manu (1,532,806 hectares)	Madre de Dios	1973
Tingo María (18,000 hectares)	Huánuco	1965
Río Abiseo (274,520 hectares)	San Martín	1983

Reservas nacionales (national reserves)

Areas set aside for wildlife protection, but government-controlled culling is allowed, and the local people have the right to use the resources.

Calipuy (64,000 hectares)	La Libertad	1981
Junín (53,000 hectares)	Junín and Cerro de Pasco	1974
Lachay de Lomas (5,070 hectares)	Lima	1977
Pacayá Samiria (2,080,000 hectares)	Loreto	1982
Pampas Galeras (6,500 hectares)	Ayacucho	1967
Paracas (335,000 hectares)	Ica	1975
Salinas y Aguada Blanca (366,936 hectares)	Moquegua	1979
Tambopata-Candamo (1,500,000 hectares)	Madre de Dios	1990
Titicaca (36,180 hectares)	Puno	1978

Santuarios nacionales (national sanctuaries)

Here there is complete protection of fauna, flora and nature. Special entry permits are required and no one is allowed to use resources.

Calipuy (4,500 hectares)	La Libertad	1981
Huayllay (6,815 hectares)	Cerro de Pasco	1974
Pampas de Heath (102,109 hectares)	Madre de Dios	1983
Lagunas de Mejía (69,060 hectares)	Arequipa	1984

Santuarios históricos (historical sanctuaries)

Areas of historical or archaeological importance, receiving complete protection, including fauna and flora. No use of resources is permitted.

Chacamarca (2,500 hectares)	Junín	1974
Machu Picchu (32,592 hectares)	Cusco	1981
Pampa de Ayacucho (300 hectares)	Ayacucho	1980

These are the best-known protected areas but this list is not complete. Also important are the **Bosques nacionales** (national forests). There are many, but unfortunately they receive very little protection.

Conservation in the 1990s

By John Forrest

In February 1992 President Fujimori addressed an audience at Kew Gardens in the third Kew Environmental lecture. He highlighted poverty levels within Peru and argued that the Government could only prioritize environmental issues once the basic standard of living of the vast majority of people had been upgraded. His other main proposal was that international cooperation could be stimulated through environmental initiatives.

The rapid economic growth experienced by Peru in the early 1990s has improved living conditions for many but widespread poverty will remain for the foreseeable future. In the meantime, there is a danger of severe environmental degradation on a large scale in the name of rapid economic expansion. Many periphery regions now being sucked in to the economic regeneration programme are those that are most environmentally valuable and fragile. Over-fishing around the Paracas peninsula, incursions by loggers into Manu National Park and pollution affecting the lagoons of Mejia are just some examples.

The concept of international cooperation through environmental projects has yet to be realised. The establishment of a national park in the Cordillera del Condor close to the Ecuadorian border may help to resolve the 40 year old frontier disagreements in this area, which flared up again in early 1995, but these plans are not far advanced. A proposal to establish a national park in the Tambopata area of south-east Peru linked to the adjoining Madidi region of Bolivia is on long-term hold while explorations for oil and natural gas are undertaken in both areas. In 1992 the Pacaya-Samiri National Reserve, near Iquitos, came under threat from oil exploration but, in a notable turnaround, permission to prospect within the reserve was withdrawn after local and international protests.

Virtually all protected areas in Peru are severely underfunded and rely heavily on international aid to enable them to carry out at least part of their mandates. However, Manu National Park, arguably the most well-known protected area in Peru, is still without an effective management plan despite receiving significant funding for several years from organisations such as WWF. A national management plan for all protected areas is now being prepared and it must be hoped that this will bring about some concrete conservation actions in the near future.

Ecotourism
Ecotourism by responsible visitors who will respect the rules and pay the required fee will help conserve threatened habitats in Peru, so do inform yourselves about the protected areas and make a point of visiting them. If you wish to help further, any of the organizations below would be pleased to hear from you.

Conservation organizations
Fundación Peruana para la Conservación de la Naturaleza (FPCN)
The Peruvian Foundation for the Conservation of Nature works closely with many foreign agencies such as the WWF, The Audubon Society, the

IUCN, and the Nature Conservancy of the USA to protect viable, representative examples of each natural community or ecosystem in Peru and the biological diversity it contains. This is being achieved through the establishment and management of protected areas, by promoting the sustainable use of natural resources and by building environmental awareness.

You can become a member of the FPCN's 'Friends of the Foundation' and help finance conservation projects in Peru. Write to FPCN, General Recavarren 446, Miraflores, Lima 18. Tel: 463801; fax: + 511 4 469178. Membership enquiries also to PO Box 02-5645, Miami, FL 33102, USA.

Asociación Peruana para la Conservación de la Naturaleza (APECO)
One project that The Peruvian Association for the Conservation of Nature is working on is to map the Cordillera de Colán in the Amazonas Department. Following a preliminary study by a team of British and Peruvian ornithologists, APECO is hoping to raise £10,000 towards improving the protection of this dwindling cloudforest. For more information write to APECO, Parque José da Acosta 187, Magdalena del Mar, Lima 17. Tel: 616316.

Sociedad Peruana de Derecho Ambiental (SPDA) This organization investigates the legal implications and formulates Peru's standing in relation to intellectual property rights, pharmaceutical and gene prospecting, and the rights of indigenous peoples with respect to conservation initiatives. Plaza Arrospide 9, San Isidro, Lima 27. Tel: 400549; fax: +511 4 424365.

Britons who would like to support the people of Peru (non-political affiliation) should contact the Peru Support Group, Fenner Brockway House, 37-39 Great Guilford St, London SE1 0ES. Tel: 0171 620 1103. The organization publishes a bi-monthly news letter and an annual workshop.

Chapter Eight

Lima

Introduction

Most people arrive in Lima by air. The drive from the airport to the suburbs provides their first glimpse of the city and they must wonder why on earth they came. Brown adobe slums on brown rubbish-strewn earth, and the occasional stiff body of a dead dog line this scenic drive. Add to this the chaotic traffic which, with horns blaring, only marginally slows down for red lights. And all shrouded in the grey pall of Lima's winter *garúa*.

Actually it's not that bad. If you stay in one of the suburbs such as Miraflores, and indulge in some seafood eating, shopping and museums, you will not regret your time there. Each district has its own character: the centre with its Spanish-colonial buildings; Miraflores, the affluent commercial centre; Barranco with a Colonial Spanish flavour and attractive bars and little restaurants; and the fishing 'village' of Chorillos.

Tourist information is available at the *Infotur* offices in the city centre and in Miraflores (see *Useful addresses*), and *real* information from the South American Explorers Club (see page 110).

There are some useful publications, too. A free booklet, *Peru Guide,* is available from many hotels and the tourist office and contains much useful information on Lima and other tourist cities in Peru. The monthly English-language magazine *The Lima Times* is well worth buying; in addition to events around town it will give you a very good insight into the political and economic situation in Peru.

TRANSPORT

Airport arrival

This is a chaotic airport. You emerge from the relative haven of the customs area to a mayhem of 'porters', taxi touts, hotel touts, and other Limeños intent on getting an early look in on your dollars. Change some of your money into *soles* in the luggage claim area so, on emerging, you can walk decisively to your chosen means of transport into town (16km away).

The cheapest, and perhaps the easiest for the first-time traveller, is the Trans-Hotel minibus. You buy a ticket from a kiosk near the bank, either to Miraflores or to Lima, and for a bit more can be taken to your hotel or a private address. You may have to wait a while for the bus to fill with passengers — it won't leave until it is full.

If you prefer a taxi, ignore the expensive black ones which wait by the door of *Arrivals*, and walk into the parking area where you will find a taxi which will cost about US$8. It saves money to get together with other arriving travellers to share the ride.

The best hotels provide their own private buses so look out for the drivers holding up a sign with the name of the hotel.

City transport

Lima has an extensive bus, *colectivo* and taxi service. It needs it — the distances are huge. They run even on public holidays.

Buses Fortunately the buses all list the main streets on their route on the front window. And they are very cheap. There are two types: private buses, painted different colours according to their route and usually in very bad condition, and the yellow, government-run buses, which are mostly new. Buses run between 06:00 and 24:00 daily, although some routes run throughout the night, costing an extra 50% after midnight.

Colectivos Private cars or minibuses running the same routes as the buses and with routes also listed on the front window. As a further aid the helper/money-collector will scream the main destination out from the window. They stop wherever the passenger wants to get off, or when they are hailed, so are more convenient than buses, and only a little more expensive. They run between 06:00 and 01:00 daily, although some routes run throughout the night, costing an extra 50% after midnight..

Taxis Taxis are ubiquitous and usually Volkswagens. Settle on the price before you get in; they rarely have meters. You should pay US$3-5 for most trips. All taxis carry a taxi sign, but they do not need any legal documents to operate, and anybody can be a taxi driver. Be wary late at night. Radio cars can be ordered by phone and are punctual and secure, but double the price of the normal 'street' taxis.

SLEEPING AND EATING
Accommodation

There are several good guidebooks which keep an up-to-date listing of hotels and *hostales*. For a complete list see *Further Reading* at the back of this book, but the *South American Handbook*, updated anually, probably has the most recent information. Prices range from about US$5 per night to US$150.

The list below gives you the recommended backpackers' places, and a few mid-range hotels. Most backpackers stay in the centre of Lima because it has the cheapest accommodation and bus stations are close. Others prefer Miraflores, which is cleaner, safer and quieter. Watch the safety aspect in the centre, take taxis if you need to move around with your luggage, and avoid walking around at night.

NOTE: In 1995 phone numbers in Lima changed to seven digits, with previous six digit numbers having a 4 in front. However the code for Lima changed from 14 to 1, so if dialling from outside Peru, the number will not appear to have changed.

Accommodation in the city centre
Recommended budget hotels with basic rooms, mostly without private bathrooms, or dormitory style. Prices range between US$5 and US$10 per person.

Hostal Roma Jiron Ica 326. Tel: 277576.

Hostal España Calle Azangaro/Ancash. Tel: 285546.

Familia Rodriguez Calle Nicolas de Pierola 730. Tel: 236465.

Mid-range hotels, rooms have ensuite bathrooms and sometimes include breakfast. Prices from US$10 to US$20 per person.

Hostal Renacimiento Parque Hernán Verlarde 52. Tel: 332806.

Hostal San Martín Av Nicolás de Piérola 882, 2nd floor, Plaza San Martín. Tel: 285337.

Hotel Granada Calle Huancavelica 323. Tel: 279033.

Accommodation in the suburbs
Miraflores is the most popular place to stay. There are two cheap options:

Albergue Juvenil Internacional (youth hostel), Calle Casmiro Ulloa 328 (a side street off Av Benavides). Tel: 465488. You do not have to be a YHA member. $10 for non-members, $9 for members. Recommended.

Hostal Larco Av Larco 1247. About US$8.

Mid-range hotels in Miraflores, rooms with private bathroom. Prices between US$10 and US$15.

Pensión San Antonio Paseo de la República 5809. Tel: 475830.

Pensión Yolanda Escobar Domingo Elias 230. Tel: 457565.

Residencial El Castillo Diez Canseco 580. Tel: 469501.

In Sta Beatriz

Hostal Mont Blanc Jr Emilio Fernández 640. Tel: 247762. Comfortable, quiet, convenient, recommended.

Restaurants

There are some excellent restaurants in Lima; seafood is particularly recommended. Be warned that an 18% government tax and a 13% service charge will be added to the bill in posh restaurants. For that final-day splurge the following are recommended.

La Rosa Náutica at the end of the pier at Miraflores. The most expensive and probably the best restaurant in town. Very popular with groups. Tel: 470057.

Carlín La Paz 646, Miraflores. Tel: 444134. Cosy, international food. Pricey.

L'Eau Vive Ucayali 370. Opposite the Torre Tagle palace in central Lima. Good food and the profits go towards helping the poor.

Entertainment

The best source of information (if you read Spanish) are the local papers, *El Commercio* or *La República*. Look under the cultural section, and you will find a list of cinemas (English-language films are usually subtitled, not dubbed), music, and so on. *The Lima Times* lists (and reviews) English-language theatre or special film showings and concerts. For folklore shows or *peña* try the tourist office or the *Peru Guide*.

Peña is typical Peruvian entertainment: a restaurant with live folk music and dance shows in traditional costumes. Not to be missed.

Maps

While in Lima take the opportunity to purchase all the hiking maps you need. The government-run Instituto Geográfico Nacional is on Avenida Aramburu 1190, in the suburb of Surquillo. Open from Monday to Friday, 08:30-16:00 (January to March 08:30-13:00). The area covered by the IGN 1:100,000 topographical maps runs from the coast to the highest point of the Andes, with some exceptions (most annoyingly in the Cusco area). Eventually the IGN plans to map the whole country, but they've been saying that for 21 years.

The IGN also publishes a good road map of Peru, departmental maps, satellite maps and satellite photos, a political map, a geographical map and others. It's worth a visit but check at the South American Explorers Club first. They sell some IGN maps and can tell you — in English — what's available at the IGN.

THE SOUTH AMERICAN EXPLORERS CLUB

This is a non-profit organization for travellers, business people, hikers, scientists, mountaineers, armchair explorers — indeed for anyone interested in South America. The club's administration office is in Ithaca, New York, but its clubhouse in Lima has been a flourishing concern since 1977.

First and foremost, the club is an information centre. Every year travellers from all over the world turn to it for specialized information on trip planning, scientific expeditions, travel to out of the way places, safe areas, or more mundane matters like finding a good hotel, travel and seasonal conditions, currency exchange and so on. The club has a good selection of books and maps on South and Central American for sale.

The SAEC is entirely member supported. The tax-deductible membership fee is currently (1995) US$40 per year (US$60 for a couple) and includes a subscription to the quarterly magazine, the *South American Explorer*. Club membership entitles you to use the club's extensive library, information files, trip reports and map collections. If you are travelling north there is also a clubhouse in Quito which offers the same facilities. Other membership services include equipment storage, mail pick-up and forwarding, notification of expedition opportunities, introductions to other travellers and much more. Members receive discounts on maps and books, from a complete list in the club catalogue.

Remember, to get all these benefits you need to be a member. The hard-pressed volunteers who work there do not have time to answer enquiries from non-members (except briefly by phone) so even if you are only planning a short trip it is worth joining. You can sign up at the club, or through Bradt Publications in England (tel: 01494 873478 — an administrative fee is charged on top of the membership fee) or at the Ithaca office.

The club postal address in Lima is Casilla 3714, Lima 100. The street address is Av Republica de Portugal 146, Breña, (off the 13th block of Av Alfonso Ugarte) Lima. Tel: 250142. Hours are 09:30 to 17:00, weekdays. It would be best to phone before going to check the address: they are talking about moving...

The headquarters address in the USA is 126 Indian Creek Rd, Ithaca, NY 14850. Tel: 607 277 0488.

USEFUL ADDRESSES IN LIMA

Tourist Police Museo de la Nacion building, Javier Prado y Aviacion, tel: 378171/ 351342/378262. Open 08:00 to 20:00.

Tourist hotline If you have a complaint or problem to do with hotels, restaurants, tour agencies, airlines or theft, phone 712994/712809. English-speaking, helpful. The hotline functions day and night.

Peruvian Touring and Automobile Club Av Cesar Vallejo 699, Lince; tel: 403270/225957; fax: 419652. Open Monday to Friday, 09:00 to 17:00.

Infotur (tourist office) Calle Belen (La Unión) 1066, central Lima; tel: 323559. Also a tourism booth in Parque Kennedy, Miraflores, open 09:00 to 20:00.

Club Andino Peruano Av Paseo de La República 932, Santa Beatriz. Meetings take place on Thursdays from 19:00 to 22:00. The president (1994) is Lucho Serpela, tel: 637319.

Dirección General de Migraciones (Immigration), Paseo de la República 585, central Lima. Open Monday to Friday, 09:30 to 13:00.

Banco de Crédito Jiron Lampa 499, central Lima; also the corner of Av Larco and Shell, in Miraflores. Open Mondays to Fridays, 09:00 to 16:00. The best bank for changing travellers cheques.

Interbank Jiron de la Union 600 is also good for changing travellers cheques.

CPT (the Lima telephone company), Plaza San Martin; also Calle La Paz and Diez Canseco, Miraflores. Open daily from 09:00 to 22:00.

Post office The main one (for *Lista de Correos* is next to the Plaza de Armas in the centre of Lima.

24-hour supermarket MASS, Calle Benavides/Calle La Paz, Miraflores.

National airlines

Americana Av Larco 345 (5th floor), Miraflores. Tel: 4440202/4471902.

AeroPeru Av José Pardo 605, Miraflores, tel: 4478900; also underneath the Sheraton Hotel, central Lima, tel: 4331341.

Faucett Garcilaso de la Vega 865, central Lima. Tel: 4643322.

Aero Continente Av Francisco Masias 544 (8th floor), San Isidro. Tel: 518280/428770/225063; fax: 303531; also Av. Garcilazo de la Vega 949. Tel: 4333069.

Medical attention

Clínica Anglo-American Calle Salazar (3rd block), San Isidro. Tel: 403570.

Clínica Internacional Calle Washington 1475, central Lima. Tel: 288060.

Clínica San Borja Av del Aire 333, San Borja. Tel: 753141.

AN EXCURSION FROM LIMA

Lachay de Lomas

A day trip to this national park is recommended by Charles Davies who spent several months in Peru studying the cloud forest on the Cordillera de Colán.

The park is very rarely visited by foreigners though popular with Peruvians. This protected area of fog-desert lies 110km north of Lima, just before you reach Huacho. The bus will drop you off at the entrance. The park has good visitor facilities and footpaths.

The best time for a visit is from August to October, when the desert is in spring bloom, but any time of year is rewarding. The landscape has an other-worldliness about it, with gnarled trees and cacti, and you can see a variety of rare birds and mammals including the endangered desert fox.

Chapter Nine

Cajamarca and Chachapoyas Regions

THE CAJAMARCA REGION

Introduction

Cajamarca is one of Peru's gems. Situated at only 2,650m in the northern highlands of Peru, it nestles in a quiet, green valley surrounded by low mountain peaks.

The town has a colonial charm with lovely churches, and to this day the Indians have kept their traditions, fiestas and to a large extent their traditional costumes. It has a relaxing atmosphere, with open hospitality and excellent Andean food, and the surrounding green countryside is steeped in history. One attraction of Cajamarca is the *Baños del Inca* 6km outside the town. Thermal springs are channelled into a pool and private baths. A real treat, especially after a few days hiking.

If you happen to be in this area around February (therefore in the wrong season for hiking) you will be able to take part in Carnival, one of the most colourful celebrations in Peru. In Cajamarca there is a marvellous display of costumes, music and dancing. The downside is that throwing water — and worse — at passers-by is a traditional carnival activity. Watch out for buckets containing the 'and worse' part.

History

Cajamarca was important long before the Incas established themselves here. Various pre-Inca sites have been found in the area and archaeologists are still making new discoveries. Any visitor who has read about the Incas will associate Cajamarca with one of history's great turning points: the conflict between Inca and Spaniard. The Incas had not been long in the area before the Spanish arrived: the estimated date of the Inca conquest of the local tribes is 1460. Cajamarca became an important place on the main Inca highway between Quito and Cusco. In November 1532 the victorious Inca, Atahualpa, rested for a few days in Cajamarca before marching down to Cusco to take control of the empire after defeating his half-brother in the civil war. At the same time, the Spaniards, under the command of Francisco Pizarro, landed on the coast of Peru.

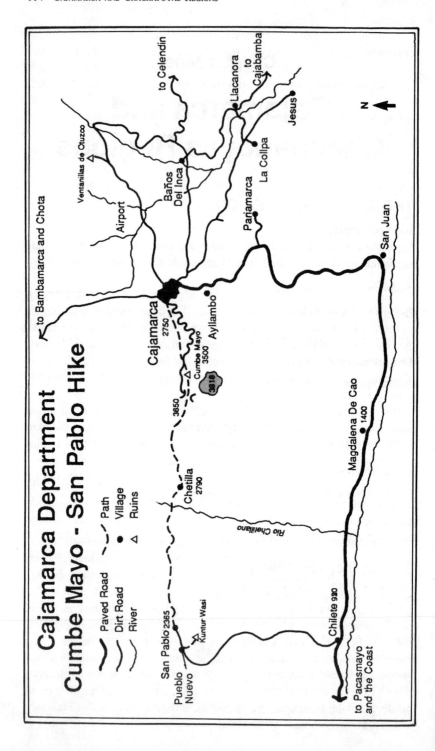

Atahualpa agreed to a meeting with the Spaniards, was ambushed, and taken prisoner by Pizarro. In an attempt to secure his release his followers agreed to fill a room once with gold and twice with silver. But to no avail. Their supreme ruler, the Sun God, was garotted and the empire died with him. Thus were 179 tired Europeans able to defeat an army of 6,000 or so and destroy one of the largest and best-organized empires the world has ever known.

Today little remains from the Inca period and these grim events are best held in the imagination. A visit to *El Cuarto de Rescate* (the Ransom Room) is worse than uninspiring; it cancels out your own mental picture.

Sleeping and eating
Accommodation
The following are cheap backpackers' hotels, mostly with communal bathroom and cold water and costing around US$8 per person.

Hostal Sucre Calle Amalia Puga 815.

Hostal Plaza On the Plaza de Armas.

Mid- and upper-range hotels, mostly with private bath and hot water.

Hostal Amazonas Calle Apurimac. About US$8.

Hotel Cajamarca Calle Dos de Mayo. About US$12.

Hotel Turistas corner Calle Lima/Calle Cajamarca. About US$28 single.

Hotel Lago Seco a country resort style hotel next to the Baños del Inca, 6km outside town. US$30 single.

Restaurants
There's plenty of choice and good local food. Try the market on Calle Amazonas for fresh bread, fruit and vegetables. At the many *Tiendas de productos lacteos* you can buy the famous Cajamarca cheese, also *manjar blanca* (sweet caramel spread) and *galletas de maíz* (puffed corn biscuits).

Getting there and away
From Lima (via Trujillo) — 856km:
By bus About 17 hours, US$16. Daily buses.

By air About 2 hours, US$70 one way. The schedule is unreliable, but normally there are one or two flights a week. No flights in the rainy season.

From Tumbes (via Chiclayo) — 812km:
By bus Tumbes to Chiclayo about 10 hours, US$9. From Chiclayo to Cajamarca, about 7 hours, US$6. Daily buses.

By air No direct flights, but daily flights from Tumbes to Chiclayo, one hour, US$30 one way.

Short hikes around Cajamarca
Half-day hikes

To Ayllambo, 3½km, 1½ hours.
A pleasant walk to the pottery village of Ayllambo. Leave from Av Independencia and walk south. Along the way you'll pass several craft shops selling the typical ceramics of Cajamarca. In Ayllambo there is a workshop, Escuela Taller, where pottery is taught.

To Cerro Santa Apollonia, the hill overlooking Cajamarca with a statue of Atahualpa on top. Leave from Calle Dos de Mayo, up the endless steps to the top.

To the Baños del Inca, 6km, 1½ hours. Follow Calle Inca from town.

A day hike through the countryside
Take a bus or walk 7km to Ventanillas de Otuzco from Av Arequipa. Visit this interesting pre-Inca cemetery which consists of hundreds of funerary niches. From here you can walk 6km to the Baños del Inca. Ask the locals to show you the path which runs south to the river. It can be very muddy in the rainy season. Cross the river and follow the river-bank to your right. The local people are very friendly and often stop to have a chat.

Once at the Baños enjoy yourself! A huge private bath with all the hot water you want costs about US$1. Bring a towel. Clean and relaxed, continue your walk 7km along a dirt road to Llacanora, a typical country village, with an old colonial church on its little plaza. A walk up the valley from the plaza for 15 to 20 minutes brings you to a nice little waterfall. Another 15 minutes and you arrive at a larger one. Ask the locals for directions.

Continue the hike from Llacanora to La Collpa, about 7km. A dirt road connects these two places, running through flat farmland, but there are shortcuts. Corn, wheat and barley are grown. La Collpa itself is a co-operative for cattle farming, and you can visit the Centro Ganadero and purchase cheese and *manjar blanca*.

From La Collpa it's a 2½ hour walk (11km) back to Cajamarca.

Cumbe Mayo
This is an extraordinary site, so even if you do not want to do the hike described below it is well worth taking a tour here. Even without the pre-Inca remains the area would be worth a visit for the 'forest of rocks' covering the bare hilltops. There are tall, thin rocks, enormous limestone faces cut deep by erosion, and isolated goblets. There is a cave decorated by pictographs showing influence of the Chavín culture, and a remarkable aqueduct channelling water down to Cajamarca, carved into the rock with

geometric precision. There are many perfect right angles, and dead straight stretches, as well as tunnels. It serves as a reminder that the Incas didn't invent the art of stone cutting. No-one knows the exact purpose of this aqueduct, but it certainly wasn't purely for agricultural purposes. It doesn't carry enough water and there are plenty of streams watering the valley anyway. Most likely it — and the cave with the pictographs — featured in some sort of water ritual.

CUMBE MAYO TO SAN PABLO

This three- or four-day hike takes you through some lovely scenery and rural villages, beginning at one of the area's most important pre-Inca sites.

Practical information

Distance	About 95km
Altitude	From 2,750m to 3,650m, descending to 2,365m
Rating	A comparatively easy walk, but with some steep ascents and descents.
Timing	4 days. One day less if you get transport up to Cumbe Mayo.
In reverse	Possible, but a long ascent
Start of the trail	Plaza de Armas in Cajamarca or Cumbe Mayo
Transport at the end	From San Pablo to Chilete, ½hr, pick-ups, buses and trucks, mostly in the morning. From Chilete to Cajamarca, 3 hrs, buses and trucks.
Maps	IGN sheet *Cajamarca* (15-f)

Route description

You may not want to walk all the way up to Cumbe Mayo. Sometimes you can catch a lift with a tour bus or private car going up to the site, or it may be worth organizing a taxi. Another possibility is to sign up for a tour for the advantage of the lift up there and guidance round Cumbe Mayo (explain that you will not be coming back and check that they don't mind taking your luggage). It takes one hour by car.

Starting from the Plaza in Cajamarca, pass Cerro Santa Apollonia to your right. There is a short cut, a path well used by the locals which goes straight up, from time to time crossing the road which curves its way up to Cumbe Mayo. It takes about 3 to 4 hours to get to the Cumbe Mayo pass (3,500m) where there are a few houses. The main footpath continues down into the valley, but you continue along the dirt road to your right, which works its way up the valley side to the second pass. After about one hour's hike (3km), you see a road going down into the valley to your left, with steep, rock-crowned slopes and a river below. Descend into the valley. The aqueduct lies in front of you at the foot of the narrow valley. It's still in a very good state, and is followed by a stone path that runs into the valley for about 500m.

The area is beautiful, with steep green hillsides, incredible rock formations and deep valleys. The locals who graze their sheep here are friendly, curious and anxious to have a chat with you. There are some great camping spots, but it gets cold and windy as soon as the sun disappears, so put your tent up in good time.

The easiest way to Chetilla, the next community, is to follow the dirt road up to the pass (3,900m). You can take a short cut by following the path up the mountain range to your left (ask a local to direct you as the path is not very clear). At the pass you get a great view over the valley.

Follow the dirt road for about 2 hours, descending into the valley, passing a few hilltops with crosses and the little *casario* of Jancate to your left. On the third hilltop (with three crosses), which you can reach via short cuts, you'll enjoy a good view into the valley in front of you. Descend into this steep valley, following the road for about an hour until you see a well-used stone path to your right. This leads to Chetilla (which the road bypasses). The walk takes about 3 hours through beautiful countryside.

Chetilla (2,790m) is an attractive little village — a few houses and a school — and about 800 friendly inhabitants who keep to their traditional way of life. Please respect that.

Continuing to San Pablo, the trail is part stone, part sand and part steps which descend steeply down to the river. Cross this via the bridge and climb the steep hill on the other side until you reach green pastures with a few houses and a school, about 3 hours from the river. Sometimes the path fades away in the pasture but look ahead and you'll see the continuation; also ask the locals.

The path contours along the right slope of valley, giving great views and past sub-tropical vegetation splashed with little waterfalls. Then the path finally climbs up the mountainside, through pastures with a few houses, to the pass which is about 7 hours from the school. Here there's a little house with a gate on its left. Enjoy the view, it's the last one before you descend to San Pablo.

From the pass the path follows the mountainside, descending slowly, passing through the *casario* of Tamincha. From here it goes up hill, then descends to the river. Cross the bridge and take the steep short cut up the hill on your right. From here you can see the little picturesque village of San Pablo surrounded by green *pampa*. It's about a 5 hour hike from the pass/gate.

San Pablo is a typical colonial village, with its small streets and carved wooden balconies. The people are friendly and their culture intact. By the plaza at the lower end of the village is an attractive church with no less than three bell-towers. On Sunday there is a market on the main street and the locals from the surrounding villages come to barter or sell their produce. The village has one simple hotel and several well-stocked shops. You'll find a few basic restaurants so can indulge in the usual post-hike eating orgy.

The ruins of Kuntur Wasi

This was once an impressive pre-Inca site showing strong Chavín influence: the remains of a triple-terraced pyramid which once supported a temple. Unfortunately the ruins are now completely overgrown and anything of value has been removed. The entrance is marked by steps and you can still see the remains of a monolith carved with feline/human features. The area has been well explored by a Chinese expedition which studied the ruins for about two years, taking away some objects for further investigation.

The ruins are not really worth visiting unless you are a passionate enthusiast. To get there walk down the main road from San Pablo to Pueblo Nuevo (about 45 minutes). Here you'll find on the hill to your right a small path and a sign 'Kuntur Wasi'. Follow the path up to the top of the hill, where you'll see the ruins.

THE CHACHAPOYAS REGION

Introduction

This area in the northern high-altitude rainforest/cloud forest region in the department of Amazonas is scattered with ruins dating from pre-Inca times (800BC to AD1100). Many are hidden under the thick vegetation and hung with epiphytes, but some have been studied by national and international archaeologists, including such well-known names as Henri and Paula Reichlen from Switzerland, the American Gene Savoy, and the Peruvian archaeologist Federico Kaufmann-Doig, director of the Instituto de Arqueología Amazónica in Lima, who is still working periodically on the site. Many of the ruins are situated on or near the trails which still give the only access into this area.

The local farmers know the ruins pretty well and are a good source of information, supplies, guides and mules. The area is rarely visited by tourists, who require more comfort that the place can provide. Adventurous backpackers with the desire to feel like Real Explorers will have a good time: the area is not easy to reach, and the paths and ruins are hard to find. Known as *La Ceja,* or eyebrow of the jungle, the cloudforest here is particularly rich in bromeliads and other epiphytes, making it a rewarding area for botanists and natural history enthusiasts.

Chachapoyas Region

Dirt Road
River
Trail
● Village
△ Ruins

Pedro Ruiz Gallo

Olto

Luya Viejo • Lamud
Santa Catauna • Luya

• Tactama
Ingumpata **Chachapoyas** 1834
• Calli
Colcamar
Vista Hermosa
Congon
Santa Maria
Pueblo Nuevo
Kuelap Levanto
Tribulon 3500 Tingo • Magda
Choctamal 1800
Longuita

to Mendoza

Río Utcubamba

• Ocumal

Leimebamba 2280

Río Marañon

3678

N

Balsas 1065

to Celendin

The ruins of Kuelap

Kuelap was first discovered in 1843. It is said to have been the last outpost of a white race, known as the Sachupoyans or the Chachas, who were retreating from the advancing Incas around the years 1450 to 1470. Rumours of fair-skinned people living in remote areas of South America are not uncommon, and the Inca chronicler Garcilaso de la Vega mentions the Cloud People, a race of tall, white warriors in the Amazon region.

In its heyday, before the conquest of the Incas, Kuelap must have supported at least a million people. Charles Motley, who owns a guesthouse in the area, writes: 'How spectacular is it? Let's compare it with one of the seven wonders of the world, and Napolean's often-quoted calculation that the stones of Egypt's Pyramid of Cyclops would make a wall, ten foot high and a foot thick, around France. But the pyramid's 16 million cubic metres of material seem small compared with the 40 million which went into the making of Kuelap!'

Kuelap is situated at about 3,100m, on a ridge high above the left bank of the Utcubamba river overlooking the little village of Tingo. It lies about 37km from Chachapoyas and 189km from Celendín and the roads are poor. It is an oval-shaped city about 600m metres across, and entirely surrounded by a massive defensive wall 6 to 8m high. The small entrance amid the huge walls must have made it virtually impregnable. Inside the walls can be seen the remains of many round buildings. Charles Motley considers that 'Kuelap was designed to be a death trap. Its walls were so high and backfilled to prevent any chance of breeching. However, its three doors leading inward were open and laid out to give an optical illusion to the approaching enemy that they could storm inside. However, inside was a killing corridor with huge walls on the sides and a steep climb as the corridor got narrower and narrower to a final point where only one man at a time could squeeze through.' Perhaps, Charles speculates, the Sachupoyans thus succeeded in wiping out all the Huari leaders (the Huari preceded the Incas) and precipitated the collapse of that empire and the emergence of the Incas.

Tingo 1,800m

A small village with little to offer except its position as gateway to Kuelap.

Sleeping and eating

There are some very basic and cheap places to stay in town, costing about US$5. Possibilities are **El Viajero**, on the main road, and **Hotalito Tingo**, at the entrance of the village.

Chachapoyas 2,400m

The region's main town is a friendly place. Nevertheless on arrival you must register with the PIP (police). Useful archaeological and some hiking information is provided at the Instituto Nacional de la Cultura, Calle Libertad, block 12.

Sleeping and eating

There are some basic hotels in town, all charging about US$5. Some recommended ones are **Hotel el Danubio**, Junín 572; **Hotel el Dorado**, Ayacucho 1062; **Hostal Kuelap**, Jr Chincha Alta 631. More upmarket is **Hacienda Santa Isabel**, situated on the outskirts: a beautiful lodge built by US engineer Charles Motley, who is married to a Chachapoyan. Charles is a good source of information and conversation if he is not in the USA. He has also built a lodge in Choctamal, and plans to build more lodges in the Kuelap area.

There are several basic restaurants, serving typical, local food. And there's a market for hiking provisions.

Information

Tourist office: Jirón Ayacucho, 2½ blocks from the Plaza in the Ministry of Tourism building.

Those wishing to continue to improve their knowledge of the area can try the following:

The Instituto National de la Cultura in Chachapoyas

Local archaeologist Martín Antonio Oliva, Calle San Juan de la Libertad 361, Chachapoyas

Charles Motley, Hacienda Santa Isabel, on the outskirts of Chachapoyas (see *Sleeping and eating*)

Peruvian archaeologist Federico Kaufmann-Doig, director of the Instituto de Arqueología Amazónica in Lima (tel: 490243) who is still working on sites in this area.

Getting there

By air Expreso Aereo and Aerocondor fly Lima-Cajamarca-Chachapoyas daily. Flights are not reliable and are often cancelled (especially in the rainy season).

By road From Cajamarca to Celendín, 112km/5 hours, US$4. 2 to 3 buses daily. From Celendín to Chachapoyas, 227km/12-14 hours (more in the rainy season), US$12. Two buses (both only on Sundays), trucks on Thursdays (when lucky) and Sundays. The road is in a very poor condition, and breakdowns are common. Wait for the direct buses from Celendín to Chachapoyas, even though there is transport between Celendín and Balsas, and Leimebamba and Tingo, then on to Chachapoyas; it is almost impossible to make the connections in Balsas and Leimebamba.

From Chiclayo to Chachapoyas, via Bagua and Jaén, 430km, 13-16 hours (longer in the rainy season), US$11. The road is in bad condition and is next to impassable in the rainy season. Even so, this is still a better route than via Celendín. A recommended guide for the Chachapoyas area is Martin Chumbe who lives in Chachapoyas.

Hiking and exploring the ruins
Climate
The only hiking time is in the dry season (April to November). In the rainy season the paths are too slippery and muddy. Always be prepared for rain in the dry season. Don't forget you are walking in the cloudforest most of the time, which means dense vegetation, lots of insects and difficult paths (if any).

Food and supplies
Bring everything you need with you, there is nothing for sale or to rent in the towns. Chachapoyas is the best place to stock up on food supplies. The local *campesinos* may trade some potatoes with you for bread, coca leaves, sugar, salt, and other food, but don't rely on it. Bring plenty of insect repellent and a well-stocked first-aid kit, and take anti-malarial tablets.

Guides/*arrieros* and mules
Ask in Chachapoyas for recommended guides (who will charge anything between US$15 and $30 a day). *Arrieros* and mules you can find in almost any small village where you start your hike. An *arriero* will charge about US$8-10 a day for him and his mule.

Maps and books
No topographical maps are available of this area; in fact it's hard to find any kind of map.

The book *Antisuyo* by Gene Savoy, is a great source of information if you can get hold of it (it is out of print). Useful, if you can read Spanish, is *Historia del Peru* by Federico Kaufmann-Doig, in two volumes. A number of works published by local archaeologists can sometimes be found at universities, the Instituto de Arqueología Amazónica in Lima, and the Instituto de la Cultura in both Chachapoyas and Lima.

Visiting the ruins of Kuelap
Timing	3-4 hours hike from Tingo to the ruins
Altitude	From 1,800m to 3,100m
Rating	Steep ascent, often muddy trails
Starting point	Tingo, 2 hours from Chachapoyas on the Celendín-Chachapoyas road.

Entry requirements   The fee to the ruins is about US$5. Open 08:00-
                          18:00. The gatekeeper lives in the last house before
                          you get to the ruins, which also functions as a
                          hostal (about US$3). You can get a guided tour
                          around Kuelap which includes the entrance fee.

Route description and information The obvious trail starts at Tingo and
works its way up to the ruins, short-cutting the new road (constructed in
1990). The guardian to the ruins has the key, and is a great source of
information.

Ruins and hikes beyond Kuelap

Various interesting ruins and hikes are situated beyond Kuelap, including
the ruins of Gran Vilaya discovered by Gene Savoy and his *campesino*
helpers in 1985. The area is remote and isolated, though some *campesinos*
cultivate land around here. They are a good source of information, and if
you do one of these hikes you are recommended to take a guide. Always
carry enough food and be prepared for rain. See map for more details on
the hikes, and back this up with information from the Instituto National de
la Cultura in Chachapoyas.

From Kuelap to Choctamal, 5-6 hours' walk. Follow the road behind
Kuelap to the village of Choctamal. Here you can stay with a family or
there is a basic hotel; local families will cook you a meal. Some *campesinos*
will work as guides, so ask around. You will need a guide to see the many
ruins in the Choctamal area; there are no paths.

From Choctamal to the top of Mount Shubert (3,700m). 5-6 hours there
and back. Follow the main trail out of the village (west) until the junction.
The right-hand path goes up the mountain and the left-hand one goes up to
the pass of Abra Yumal. There are some ruins on top of the mountain, but
it is the view that makes the climb worthwhile. It gets cold at the top, so
take a jacket and some water.

From Choctamal to the pass of Abra Yumal (3,500m). 2 hours' climb,
with good views toward Choctamal and Kuelap.

From the pass to Tribulon. 4-5 hours' walk downhill through the valley.
Tribulon is a small community, with friendly people. Here you can stay
with a family who will supply you with basic meals and guide you round
the several ruins from Tribulon. All of them are hard to get to, through
dense cloudforest with no paths. Don't risk going without a guide. The
following are the main ruins:

- Las Pilas. A small site with an unusual water system.

- Machu Llaqta. 1½-2 hours' walk. A large and impressive site.

- Santa Cruz. 30 minutes from Machu Llaqta. These ruins are situated on top of a ridge with great views down to the valley.

- Pueblo Alto. Ruins from an unknown culture.

- Ojilcho.

- Santa María. An impressive fortress.

The return route from Tribulon to Choctamal takes 6-7 hours.

Other hikes and ruins near Chachapoyas
From the pass of Abra Yumal to Vista Hermosa, 7-8 hours. A steep, difficult path through cloudforest. The small community of Vista Hermosa offers basic accommodation and meals with a family. Nearby are the ruins of La Plazuela, a steep climb up from Vista Hermosa, and a bit further on are the ruins of La Mesa and La Pirquilla. You also pass an impressive Inca staircase. You need a guide to visit these sites. The return to Tribulon will take 4-5 hours.

From Vista Hermosa to Chachapoyas. Allow two days for this hike. You'll be passing through the community of Shipata, where you can admire the *sarcófagas* situated on the mountain slope called Karajia, outside Shipata. Just before getting to Chachapoyas, at the village of Luya (1½ hours away from Chachpoyas by truck), you can hike for 1½ hours to the ruins of Wangli. Here there are impressive tombs, petroglyphs and funeral niches.

And further afield
Yalape, near Levanto. César Torres Rojas, of the Instituto Nacional de la Cultura in Chachapoyas, recently supervised the clearing of these ruins. The site was probably a residential complex and includes many well-preserved examples of typical Sachupoyan architecture. Some beautiful friezes have survived. The scale of this site is similar to Kuelap.

To get there take a truck early in the morning from Chachapoyas to Levanto, which takes about 2 hours, or — better — do it on foot, 3-4 hours along a pleasant but steep path. Take plenty of water. Leave from the plaza in Chachapoyas, down Jirón Amazonas for two blocks and then turn left down Santo Domingo. Generally speaking, for the first 2½ hours take each left fork you come to. After you cross a small field, near the end of the walk, you'll see a stone path leading off to the right. Take it and continue turning right until you arrive at Levanto. Ask for directions frequently from the *campesinos* because it is easy to get lost.

Levanto is a small, friendly mountain village. There are no hotels, but you can get accommodation with a family if you ask around, or you can camp. Some basic meals are available at the small shops or with a family, but it is best to bring your own food.

Lamud This is situated 37km northwest of Chachapoyas, a 2-hour ride along a very poor road. There is basic accommodation here, and a worthwhile hike to *chulpas* some 5km from Lamud, 45 minutes' walk each way.

Pueblos de los Muertos South of the community of Tingorbamba, a 3-hour climb from the valley at 750m to 2,250m. This is an impressive site with mummy casings, caves and cliff-dwellings.

Purún Llacta This site was named Monte Peruvia by Gene Savoy. It is 40km east of Chachapoyas on the road to Mendoza, and a 2½-hour walk from any public transport. Here are hundreds of stone houses with staircases, temples and palaces. The site is pre-Inca but was probably also used by the Incas.

Puente de Conica, 8km from Purun Llacta, has some pre-Columbian burial figures in niches on the cliff side, known as the Purumachus de Aispachaca.

La Congona, near Leimebamba Buses and trucks run to Leimebamba from Chachapoyas, taking about 4 hours. A 2½-hour hike from Leimabamba are the ruins of La Congona, a Sachupoyan site. There are three sites here, originally on hills or mounds, two of which have now been levelled. A conical mound remains, with 30 decorated round stone houses and a watchtower. The ruins are covered in brambles and thick undergrowth, but the views are wonderful.

Get clear directions before setting out from Leimabamba. The trail starts next to the police station, levels out and contours the mountain before dropping down into a little valley. The ruins are above the cliff, but to reach them you have to climb the adjoining, higher hill which rises above the cliff. There is no trail here; head straight up for 20 minutes. At the very top the ruins are clustered in a small area, impossible to see until you are right above them.

Chapter Ten

The Cordilleras Blanca, Negra and Huayhuash

Introduction

This is an incredible hiking and climbing area, with fascinating flora and fauna and the remains of a pre-Inca culture. The focal point — or rather line — of the area is the Callejón de Huaylas, the name given to the Río Santa valley which separates the Cordillera Negra (west) from the Cordillera Blanca (east) in the department of Ancash in Peru's northern highlands. The department capital, Huaraz, is at the southern end. A paved road runs through the length of this valley, linking the villages and providing spectacular views of the Nevados Huandoy and Huascarán.

THE CORDILLERAS

There are three *cordilleras* (mountain ranges) in Ancash: the Cordillera Negra, the Cordillera Blanca and the Cordillera Huayhuash. The Cordilleras Negra and Blanca face each other across the Río Santa, and the Cordillera Huayhuash lies about 50km to the southeast of the Cordillera Blanca. All three are excellent for hiking and draw enthusiasts from all over the world.

As its name implies, the Cordillera Negra is not snow-covered (although 'black' is an exaggeration). Nevertheless it is still a good area for hiking, if only for the stunning views of the Cordilleras Blanca and Huayhuash.

Cordilleras Blanca and Huayhuash are the highest of the country's astonishing total of 20 glaciated mountain ranges. The largest concentration of tropical-zone glaciers in the world is found in the Cordillera Blanca, including Peru's highest mountain, Huascarán, at 6,768m/22,206ft. The second highest mountain, Yerupajá (6,634m/21,759ft), is in the Huayhuash.

The *campesinos*, who cultivate land up to about 4,000m and graze cattle and sheep almost to the snowline, are mainly *mestizos*. The Indian culture is still alive, but less than in the Cusco area, perhaps because this was never an Inca stronghold. No Inca ruins of importance are found in this area, but the pre-Inca site from the Chavín culture more than compensates for this lack.

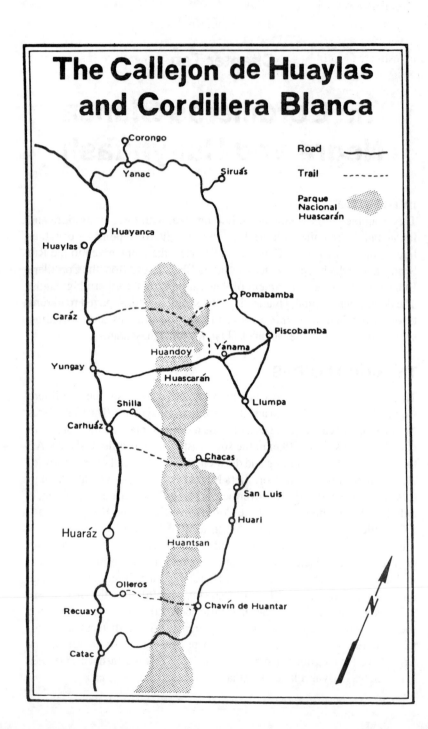

The Callejon de Huaylas and Cordillera Blanca

Cordillera Negra

Because few hikers want to spend much time in this snowless range we have given it short shrift. This doesn't mean, however, that you should not investigate the trails yourself. All the hikes are fairly easy, the highest pass being around 4,500m and the highest peak 5,187m (Rocarre, in the northern part of the range).

If you hike in this area be sure to carry plenty of water; there are few streams.

Cordillera Blanca

This is Peru's best-known mountain region. Only 100km from the Pacific Ocean, and 180km long, it provides a barrier between the desert coast and the wet Amazon basin. If you count the multi-peaked mountains, 33 peaks rise above 6,000m/19,686ft. The range is quite narrow so all hiking areas are easily accessed from the road. The glaciers are retreating and rarely extend much below 4,800m; the valleys below are grasslands, *puna*, usually grazed by cattle. There are no llamas in this region. Most hiking routes run from west to east, crossing the *cordillera* at a high pass and descending to a road. These trails were created centuries before the arrival of recreational hikers, being the main thoroughfare for the Andean inhabitants. Some of the trails have recently been made into roads for vehicular traffic.

We have described the most well-known hikes in the Cordillera Blanca, but of course there are plenty more. You can discover your own personal trek or follow in the footsteps of Val Pitkethly and Mark Klassen who walked the complete length of the Cordillera Blanca from north to south.

Cordillera Huayhuash

This compact range is only 30km in length from north to south, and yet it has seven peaks over 6,000m. Many hikers consider it even more spectacular than the Cordillera Blanca, and it is certainly more remote and challenging. The peaks all seem to have towering, vertical ice-covered faces on all sides! The major town and starting point for hiking is Chiquián. The classic hike here is a complete circuit of 164km around the Cordillera Huayhuash.

Parque Nacional Huascarán

Huascarán National Park was established in July 1975, rewarding the efforts of Peruvian journalist and mountaineering expert Cesar Morales and Huaraz politician Augusto Guzman Robles. These men had been urging the government to declare this exceptional area a national park since 1960, but it was only after the attention of the world was drawn to the area by a catastrophic earthquake in 1970 that the authorities took notice.

The park includes the whole area of the Cordillera Blanca above 4,000m, with the exception of Nevado Champará at the extreme northern end of the range, and covers in total 3,400km².

Conservation and development are the main goals of the park administration; it sometimes seems that development is winning, with roads being constructed through some of the most beautiful areas.

The park office is on Av Raimondi, block 13, in the building of the Ministerio de Agricultura (tel: 722086); open Monday to Friday, 08:00-13:00. All visitors to the park have to register at the office and pay the entrance fee of US$1 per person/per day. Unfortunately, there is little or no control at the park entrances so most visitors don't bother. This is a shame; the fee would — or should — help with conservation projects.

In common with national parks throughout the world, there are regulations to stop tourists damaging the place they've come to enjoy. Sadly, these are often ignored:

• Don't leave garbage; carry it all out.

• Don't make fires.

• Don't harm the flora or fauna.

• Don't pollute the streams and lakes.

• Don't fish in the lakes during the spawning season from May to September.

Even if you do not plan to go hiking, try to visit the park's most spectacular living thing: the *Puya raimondii* (see page 64). These incredible plants grow in the valley of Pachacoto, 57km south of Huaraz. You may not be lucky enough to see them in flower, but even so they are an unforgettable sight. Get transport to the village of Pachacoto (see *Getting there and away*) and hike up the valley to the park station (2½ hours). You'll find the puyas up the road from there, to your right. Organized day tours go to this area, then on to the glacier of Pastorurí.

Safety
There have been some scare stories about the safety of hikers in this area. Yes, there have been robberies and even deaths, and because of the terrorist threat the Cordillera Huayhuash was closed to tourism between 1990 and 1992, with many people staying away from the Blanca as well. The danger from the Shining Path terrorists seems now to have disappeared, which leaves only the occasional robbery to worry about. This happens from time to time on the most popular trails, but robbery can happen from time to time anywhere. Be sensitive to the attitude of the locals, ask permission to put up your tent, and if people seem hostile do not camp near their village.

HUARAZ

Situated at 3,050m/10,007ft, this thriving small town has a lovely climate and lively atmosphere. It exudes energy: there's a bustling market, some discos, and all the gringos you meet here are either planning a hike or have just returned from a hike, so it is easy to get information. There are lots of travel agencies, shops, hotels, restaurants, night-life, and all the attractions designed to persuade the visitor to stay as long as possible.

History

The problem with Huaraz is that visible historical remains keep disappearing under landslides. From time to time the water levels build up in the high mountain lakes, causing them to breach. When an avalanche lands in a lake, or rather when an earthquake dumps half the glacier there, a huge wall of water, mixed with snow, ice, mud, rocks and other matter, flows down the mountain taking everything with it. There have been three disasters this century: in 1941, an avalanche in the Cojup valley landed in Laguna Palcacocha, broke its banks, and inundated Huaraz; in 1962, a huge avalanche came down from Huascarán and destroyed the town of Ranrahirca; the last and worst catastrophe was in 1970, when a massive earthquake devastated much of central Peru and the town of Yungay in the Santa valley was completely buried. Evidence of this disaster is still to be seen throughout the valley.

A government organization, INGEMMET (Instituto Geológico Minero y Metalúrgico), has been formed to control the lakes and to try to avoid future disasters of this kind.

Sleeping and eating
Accommodation

The following are cheap, backpackers' places, all for about US$5-8 per person:

El Albergue de Casa de Guias, Parque Ginebra. Tel: 721811.

Hostal Copa, Calle Bolívar 615. Tel: 722619.

Edward's Inn, Calle Bolognesi 121. Tel: 722692.

Casa de Señora Lopez, near the Estadio, just off Calle Bolognesi.

A little more comfortable, about US$10-12 for a single room with private bathroom.

Hostal Montañero, Parque Ginebra (next to Casa de Guías). Tel: 721811.

Hostal Colombo, Francisco de Zela 210. Tel: 721501.

Hostal Yanett, Av Centenario 106. Tel: 721466.

Hostal Santa Victoria, Av Gamarra 690. Tel: 722422.

And as a treat:

Hotel Andino, Pedro Cochachin 357. Tel: 721662. Terrific ambience and service. US$50-90 per person, depending on the room.

Hotel de Turistas de Monterrey. A few kilometres out of town, next to the (public) hot thermal baths. An old and characterful hotel with all comforts. Double: about US$40.

El Patio, on the main road. Expensive bungalows. Double: about US$32.

Accommodation in other towns:

Carhuaz: La Casa de Poncha, $18 including meals; Hostal La Merced, on the Plaza. Single: about US$6; and Hostal Residencial Carhuaz.

Yungay: Hostal Gledel, along the main road. A friendly, family run place. Single: about US$8.

Caraz: Some basic *hostales* around the Plaza and market place. The better ones are Hostal Chavín and Hostal La Suiza Peruana, Calle San Martán 1135 and 1133 (one block from the Plaza). Rooms with private bathroom and hot water. Single: US$6.

Restaurants
Chalet Suisse, at the Hotel Andino. The best (and most expensive) place in town, with Swiss cuisine. About US$25 per meal.

Créperie Patrick, Av Luzuriaga 424. French cuisine, good crépes and desserts. Moderate to expensive prices.

Monta Rosa, Av Luzuriaga, block 4. A good pizzeria, moderate to expensive prices.

Casa de Guías, Parque Ginebra. Good muesli, yoghurt, pizzas, soups and salads. Moderate prices. Open for breakfast and dinner.

Chifa Min Hua, Av Luzuriaga 424b. Great Chinese food, cheap and lavish helpings.

Local restaurants open for lunch and dinner include:

Tumi, Calle San Martín 1121.

La Familia, Av Luzuriaga 431.

Samuels, Calle La Mar, block 6.

Entertainment
El Tambo, Calle La Mar, block 7. A popular gringo disco.

Amadeus, Parque Ginebra. Local disco.

El Pub, Calle La Mar 661. A gringo hangout, as you'd expect from the name, but deserves its popularity.

Tourist police
Just off the Plaza de Armas, in Pasaje Tiburios. Open 08:00-13:00 and

16:00-19:00 daily. Friendly and helpful. Some English spoken. Contact them if you are robbed or in the event of an accident in the mountains.

Tour operators
The reliable ones have been there for years; others come and go. Recommended tour companies include:

Pablo Tours, Av Luzuriaga 501. Tel: 721145.

Chavín Tours, Av Luzuriaga 508. Tel: 721578.

Milla Tours, Av Luzuriaga 528. Tel: 721742.

Andes, Jirón Victor Cordero 854. Tel: 721195. For organized trekking groups.

Pyramid Adventures, Av Luzuriaga 530. Fax: +51 44 722525. Work with UK and US tour operators; highly recommended.

Day tours tend to be cancelled if not enough people sign up, so it's best to get your own group together.

Casa de Guías
Parque Ginebra 28-G. Tel/fax: (044) 721811. Open 09:00-13:00, 16:00-20:00. This is the best place in Huaraz for information on trekking and climbing, local or private transportation, prices, guides/*arrieros* and mules/*burros*. They can also advise you on organized trips, weather conditions, and a place to meet up with other hikers. They rent equipment, have a rescue team and their qualified mountain and trekking guides are registered members of the association. They have a small library of hiking books for reference. Don't head for the mountains without visiting them.

Getting there and away
The information below is comprehensive enough to get you from Lima to Huaraz, and to the surrounding villages and trailheads.

From Lima to Huaraz (400km)
By road The journey takes 8 hours by bus and costs about US$8. The road is paved all the way, though landslides may be a problem. Recommended bus companies are Ancash (part of the Ormeño bus chain), Rodríguez, Cruz del Sur and Móvil (more luxurous and a bit more expensive). Also Comite 14 (a small van) runs this route whenever they can fill up the vehicle; price US$10. Try to travel during the day in order to enjoy the beautiful scenery.

By air One small airline flies in to Huaraz's little airport in the tourist season between April and September a few times a week (the schedule often changes). A 2-hour flight (via Chimbote) for about US$60 one way.

From Chavín to Lima (438km)

14 hours/US$12. One or two buses daily and some trucks.

From Chiquián to Lima (353km)

10-14 hours/US$8. Several buses a week.

From the north of Peru

Huaraz may be reached from the northern coast via three routes. They are all rough and time-consuming, but the visual impact of approaching the *cordilleras* this way, particularly in an open truck, is unforgettable.

Casma to Huaraz, 150km. 6-7 hours (longer/impossible in the rainy season).

Chimbote — Río Santa Valley — Huallanca — Cañón del Pato — Caraz — Huaraz (185km). 10 hours (longer/impossible in the rainy season). The worst road, the best views.

Local transport through the Río Santa valley

Colectivos run the 66km between Huaraz and Caraz daily, between 07:00 and 20:00. They leave whenever they fill up, every 15 minutes or so, from Av Fitzcarrald on the first and second block. The full journey takes about 2 hours, but they stop at every village along the way: Monterrey (20 minutes), Marcará (45 minutes), Carhuaz (1 hour), Mancos (1½ hours) and Yungay (1½ hours).

Going south

From Huaraz to Recuay (27km), 1 hour; **on to Catac** (11km), 20 minutes; **on to Pachacoto** (9km), 15 minutes.

From Huaraz to Chiquián (120km). 4 hours. A daily, afternoon bus, 'El Rápido', leaves from between Calle Raimondi and Tarapaca in Huaraz. Occasional trucks leave from the market.

Routes to the eastern side of the Cordillera Blanca

These are all dirt roads going over the high passes of the *cordillera*. In the dry season trucks and some buses run daily. In the rainy season, road conditions are poor and there's little transport.

From Macará to Vicos (7km). 1½ hours.

From Carhuaz, up the Ulta valley and down to Chacas (75km). 7 hours. Trucks daily in the morning. Occasional buses from Huaraz. The road is closed in the rainy season.

Huaraz to Chavín (99km). 5 hours.

Huaraz to Piscobamba (62km), 3 hours; **on to Pomabamba** (22km), 1 hour.

From Yungay, up the Llanganuco valley and down to Yánama (58km). 4 hours. Daily vehicles in the morning. Most transport continues on to **San Luís** (61km). 3 hours.

Huaraz to Chavín and Huari (61km). 3-6 hours.

Huaraz to Piscobamba (62km) and **Pomabamba** (22km).

There are also pick-ups from Yungay, that run to the **Lakes of Llanganuco** in the tourist season; 1½ hours.

From Caraz to Cashapampa (22km). 2-3 hours. Daily trucks (mornings).

From Huaraz to Pitec Pick-ups leave from the corner of Calle Caraz/Comercio, Mondays and Thursdays, whenever they fill up (about every 30 minutes), between 06:00 and 18:00 and the other days about 4 times a day between 10:00 and 17:00. They go as far as **Llupa**; 30 minutes. Ask the driver to drop you off at the footpath up to Pitec, just before Llupa. From there it's a 2-hour walk.

From Huaraz to Olleros, 7km before Recuay. Either get off at the junction on the main road and walk the 2km up a dirt road, or catch a truck from Calle Frigorífico in Huaraz, going all the way to Olleros, 29km. 45 minutes.

From Catac to Chavín (98km). 3½ hours. Buses and trucks daily. **On to Huari** (38km), 2 hours, and on to **San Luís** (61km), 3 hours. Several trucks and buses a day serve this route.

From Huaraz to Chavín Three bus companies (Chavín Express, Lanzon de Chavín and Huascarán) go in the early morning, 4-5 hours.

From Pachacoto to Huallanca (140km). 4 hours. Few trucks and buses do this route. From here there is transport on to La Unión and Huánuco.

HIKING
Weather
Although the dry/wet season pattern is more reliable than the weather in temperate climates, you should not be surprised to have rain, hail or snow in the dry season, nor some bright, clear weather in the rainy season. Bear in mind that in bad weather it is unrewarding and even dangerous crossing the high passes which will be cloud-covered and you may get caught in a blizzard. Even in the dry season always carry good quality, waterproof camping equipment, warm clothing and extra food just in case you need to wait out the bad weather somewhere in the mountains.

Acclimatization
Read the section on this subject in the *Health* chapter carefully, and spend two or three days in Huaraz before doing any hiking trips, then do a few practice day hikes.

Guides
There is no shortage of guides in Huaraz, but only a few are really experienced and reliable. The Casa de Guías will advise you or, better still, get recommendations from other hikers. A set price of US$30 per day is charged. However, you do not need a guide for the hikes described in this

chapter. The trails are clear, and if you do get lost it's no great disaster assuming you are carrying sufficient food. You are not lost, you are exploring, and after a while you'll meet a *campesino* who will put you right.

Arrieros and their animals

Many hikers use mules or *burros* (donkeys) to carry their camping equipment and food. They are ideal for groups, who can get one or two animals to carry the heavier stuff. *Burros* and mules may only be hired with their owners, the *arrieros*, who lie in wait for hikers at the trailheads, so don't worry about finding one before you leave Huaraz. The *arrieros* have organized themselves into an association, and the prices are set: at the time of writing an *arriero* costs US$6 per day and a *burro* US$3 per day. Plus you are responsible for providing all meals for the *arrieros* and their helpers, and should check that they have shelter for the nights, otherwise you may need to provide that as well. Settle all conditions beforehand (in writing if both you and they can read/write Spanish) and pay half at the start of the trip and the other half at the end.

Entrance to the valleys

The *campesinos* who farm the land at the foot of the trails operate a sort of toll system so that hikers with *burros* have to pay for the gate at the start of the trail to be opened. If you have an *arriero* with you he will deal with this. The fee is expensive — from US$5 to US$15 — but does not apply to backpackers who can climb over the gate. For further information check at the Casa de Guias.

Renting equipment

All camping equipment, boots, clothing, tents, stoves, etc can be rented in Huaraz, at reasonable prices, eg: sleeping bag US$2.50, stove US$1 per day. However, the equipment is rarely of a good quality, being mostly the discarded gear of other hikers, so it's still preferable to bring everything you need from home.

The best rental places are: Casa de Guías, Plaza Ginebra; MonTrek, Av Luzuriaga 646; Andes Tours, Av Luzuriaga 538.

Food and supplies

Huaraz is the best place to buy food for your trip. In the smaller towns in the valley you can usually get fresh food from the market, but the choice is limited. Up in the mountains, you might be lucky to find a Señora who wants to cook a meal for you, or you might find very basic food at some tiny shop. You cannot rely on this, however — mostly the *campesinos* have barely enough to feed themselves — so bring enough for the whole trip, plus some extra. The market in Huaraz has a good selection of trail food, and on the corner of Av Luzuriaga and Calle Raimondi there is a pretty good supermarket.

The local fuel is what Americans call white gas, and Brits know as stove alcohol. The *bencina* may not be top quality, but it burns and is widely available in hardware stores and pharmacies for about US$2 per litre. Kerosene/paraffin (*kerosina*) is sold at the petrol/gas stations and hardware stores. And the butane canisters (Camping Gaz) are for sale at some equipment rental places and travel agencies.

Maps

You are advised to take a map if you are hiking independently. Fortunately there is a good selection:

Cordilleras Blanca y Huayhuash by Felipe Diaz. Available in Lima and Huaraz. This useful map shows the routes and roads in the valleys, giving you an overview of the whole area with enough information for the popular hiking trails.

Topographical maps of the Cordilleras Blanca, Negra and Huayhuash, at a scale of 1:100,000, are published by the Instituto Geográfico Militar (IGN), but these are only available in Lima. They are useful and interesting, but only really necessary if you are finding your own route. The entire Cordillera Blanca is published in six sheets (so you need to have decided beforehand which areas you are visiting) and the Cordillera Huayhuash in two. When planning a new route bear in mind that the glaciers have receded a lot since the area was surveyed.

The South American Explorers Club has published some useful black and white maps of the most popular treks: Llanganuco to Santa Cruz, Honda Valley, and Huayhuash. These cost US$2 or so — much cheaper than the US$6 needed for the IGN maps.

HIKING ROUTES IN THE CORDILLERA BLANCA

The following hikes have been selected for their views, their variety, or because they are relatively easy. We begin with an acclimatization hike near Huaraz, and then describe the longer treks beginning at the northern end of the range and working south:

A day-hike outside Huaraz
Cashapampa to Pomabamba
Cashapampa to Vaqueria or Colcabamba
The Lagunas Llanganuco and 69

Quebrada Ulta to Colcabamba
Quebrada Honda to Chacas
Huari to Chacas
Quebrada Ishinca
Quebradas Churup, Quilcayhuanca, Shallap and Rajucolta
Olleros to Chavin

A day hike outside Huaraz
By H Jenny

This is an easy hike outside Huaraz, so ideal for acclimatization and to
enjoy the views of the city, the Cordilleras Blanca and Negra and the
Cordillera Huayhuash.

Practical information

Distance	6km
Altitude	Between 3,150m and 3,650m
Rating	Easy
Timing	3-4 hours
In reverse	Possible
Start of the trail	Plaza de Armas in Huaraz
Map	IGN sheet *Huaraz* (20-h)

Route description
Head south from the Plaza de Armas on Av Luzuriaga until the intersection
with Av Villón. Turn left and walk up Av Villón until the cemetery, then
right and left again and follow the obvious dirt road uphill then curving to
the right. Follow this road all the way to the pass, taking shortcuts where
possible. The road drops into the valley on the other side of the pass, with
some spectacular views. Stay on this side of the valley, following the
footpath which goes along the mountain ridge and finally drops down in
the direction Huaraz again. The path meets up with the start of the trail at
the cemetery.

Cashapampa to Pomabamba
By Val Pitkethly

This is perhaps the toughest and longest hike of the Cordillera Blanca, so
don't attempt it unless you are fit and properly acclimatized. The rewards
are awesome scenery, varied hiking conditions, and a great feeling of
accomplishment.

Practical information

Distance	About 83km

Altitude	Between 2,800m and 4,850m
Rating	Difficult, only for the well-acclimatized hiker
Timing	9-12 days (depending on side treks)
In reverse	Possible
Start of the trail	Cashapampa at 2,900m; transport available early morning from Caraz or Yungay
Maps	IGN sheets *Corongo* (18-h) and *Pomabamba* (18-i)

Route description

The starting point, Cashapampa, has a small shop. *Arrieros* and *burros* are available for hire if you want to take the donkey-work out of the long trudge up to the pass. The first destination is Cholín, 8km north of Cashapampa. Many paths lead in that direction, so check with the locals to find the main trail. Follow it for 3-4km, passing the Baños de Huancarhuas (disappointingly more like a footbath). From here the trail continues to Cholín, 2,850m. Camping spots are available, with a good water supply nearby, although it is hard to find a level area. Ask permission to camp at the small house nearby. This is the last place with water for 12km. Beware of the dogs!

After Cholín, the long, hard climb to Laguna Cullicocha begins, with an altitude gain of about 1,800m (5,904ft)! This will take 5 or 6 hours. Follow the red dirt trail that climbs steeply north from Cholín to the top of the Inca terraces. After passing through a flat area, you'll come to the start of a long series of switchbacks which you think will never end. The trail crosses the remains of a 1970 earthquake landslide, then climbs slowly past two dry (most of the time) creeks, and comes to a meadow atop a little hill. This is a possible camping place, with great views, but if there is no water you will need to continue. It is another 7km of moderate climbing to Laguna Cullicocha. Continue up the switchbacks, passing a creek, before the trail goes up a ridge where you get the first glimpses of the *nevados* (snowfields). The trail climbs to the right and comes to a fork. Here you're at about 4,450m and 14.5km from Cholín.

The trail to the left goes to Laguna Cullicocha and the one straight ahead to Laguna Yuraccocha. If you want to take a side trip to Laguna Yuraccocha, it is 9km with little change in altitude.

The trail to Laguna Cullicocha continues climbing to 4,650m, about 3.5km from the trail fork. There is another, higher, lake, Rajucocha, but it is difficult to reach. The best campsites are found at the little Laguna Azulcocha, just north of the outlet from Laguna Cullicocha.

Now head towards the village of Alpamayo. The trail starts about 40m below Laguna Cullicocha, crosses some granite rock, and climbs up to the pass of Los Cedros at 4,800m, about 3km from the lake. A long descent begins into the Quebrada de los Cedros, via a series of switchbacks. Near

Cordillera Blanca: North Huascaran National Park

Paved Road	) (Pass	Nevado Glaciers
Dirt Road	• Village	
River	Limits of the Huascaran National Park	
Lake		
Trail		

Piscobamba

Pomabamba 2950

Palo Seco

Yeguacorral

Yanacollpa

to Pasacancha

Yánama 3400

Huilca

Taulliraju

Colcabamba

Pucajirca 6050

Contrahierbas 6036

Vaquería

Paria 5510

Piramide 5885

Alpamayo 5947

Pisco 5752

Q. Ulta

Santa Cruz 6259

Huandoy 6395

Huascaran 5655

Q. Alpamayo

L. Cuillicocha

Q. Santa Cruz

Q. Llanganuco

Huallayan

Cholín

Cashapampa

Musho

Huaripampa

Santa Cruz

Huallanca 1820

2290 Caraz

Yungay 2500

Tingra

Sucre

Rio Santa

Mancos

Huaylas

Huata 2740

Cordillera Negra

to Chimbote

N

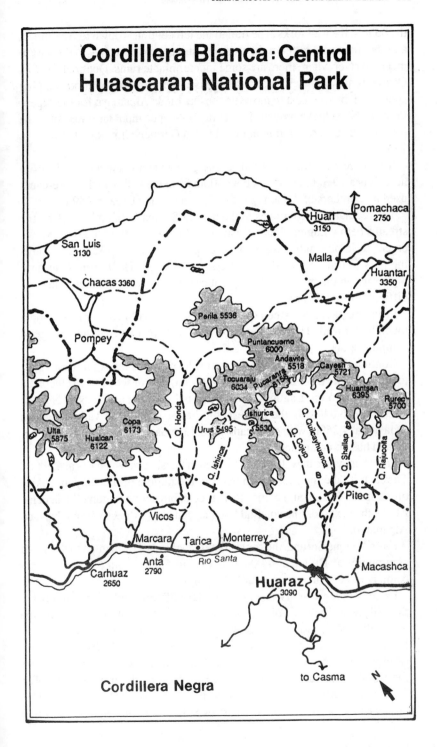

the bottom the trail forks. The trail to the left continues down to Alpamayo, and the main trail to the right crosses a stream and descends to the east to meet the river where there are some indeterminate ruins. Quebrada de Los Cedros is at 4,000m, 10km from the pass. There are lots of good camping spots here, but it's best to move up the Quebrada Alpamayo for the superb views of Nevado Alpamayo. This pyramid-shaped mountain was voted the most beautiful mountain in the world by a German climbing club back in 1966.

If you are still full of boundless energy you can made a side trip from here. It is a 10.5km climb of about 500m from the valley to the base-camp used by climbers of Alpamayo (5,947m) and Santa Cruz (6,259m).

The regular trail continues to the pass of Safuna (4,830m), crossing the streams below Laguna Jancarurish, and climbing north to the right of two creeks to some small lakes. Continue up the slopes of loose rock towards the pass (on the right side of the crag at the top). The trail is faint until higher up on the moraine. Take great care in bad weather when it may be difficult to find this route.

From the pass it's a steep descent into Quebrada Mayobamba, but on a much better trail. This is a beautiful *quebrada* (canyon) with many good camping spots.

Continue towards a ridge on the east side of the valley. A faint path goes to the top of the ridge at a small pass (4,600m) then descends into Quebrada Tayapampa, to the Lagunas Safuna just below the multi-peaked Nevado Pucahirca (6,040m is the highest) on the far side of the valley. Laguna Baja lies at 4,250m with good campsites. Laguna Alta is a kilometre further on and has no campsites.

From here you can walk 5.5km to Laguna Pucacocha which lies at 4,500m. To reach it take the trail which leads to the middle of the canyon, passes tiny Laguna Kaiko, and comes to a crude cabin above Laguna Pucacocha. Above the next moraine you find Laguna Quitaracsa, directly below Nevado Alpamayo.

From Laguna Safuna, the trail follows Quebrada Tayapampa to the small community of Huilca at 4,000m. It's about 5.5km from the lake. If you camp here keep an eye on your belongings.

From here there are two possible routes to Pomabamba. The first is via the village of Laurel. Follow the road, with several shortcuts, along the Río Collota down to the valley which runs to the northeast of the village. It's about 3km. From here the road climbs up to a small pass at 4,300m. Coming down the other side you'll see some small lakes, about 12km from the Río Collota valley. At this point the road and the trail separate. The road continues to Palo Seco and the trail goes southeast to Laurel. The trail descends about 6km through a narrow valley to Laurel at 3,500m. From

Laurel you can find buses to Pomabamba, or continue to the north and return to Huaraz via the Cañón del Pato.

The second choice is longer, via Yanacollpa, but goes direct to Pomabamba. The trail climbs steeply from Huilca, heading northeast, to the first pass at 4,280m. You'll see Laguna Shuitococha ahead. The trail continues east to the second pass at 4,350m. It's about 6.5km from Huilca. From here it drops down into Quebrada Yanacollpa, passing a few small lakes. Here you are faced with another choice of two routes. If you decide to go to the village of Yanacollpa, continue down through the meadows to the stream. Follow this on its left bank until a bridge where you can cross the stream, and descend to Yanacollpa (3,700m). It's about 8km from the pass. To continue to Pomabamba you then drop down to the river and up the other side of the valley to the community of Anpucru. From here it's downhill until the end of Quebrada Yanacollpa, passing a small village. Cross the bridge over the Río Shiulla, and reach the main road. Pomabamba lies 2km to the right. The distance from Yanacollpa to Pomabamba is about 12km.

The alternative route from the small lakes is via Quebrada Jancapampa. At the small lakes you can see a path going up the slopes to the south; follow it until the pass at 4,350m, from where it goes steeply downhill on a faint path until the upper end of Quebrada Jancapampa, just below the Nevados Taulliraju and Picahirca. From here it's an easy descent (10-12km) over the meadows to the start of the *quebrada*, following an aqueduct. Continue down to the Río Shiulla and thence to Pomabamba.

Pomabamba is a nice little town with friendly people. You can stock up on some supplies here, find accommodation, and give yourself a good feed in one of the basic restaurants before returning to Huaraz.

Cashapampa to Vaquería or Colcabamba

This is deservedly the most popular trail of the Cordillera Blanca. The views as you follow the Quebrada Santa Cruz are quite breathtaking. Giant, snow-covered peaks tower above you on both sides of the valley as the trail leads gently upwards.

Most trekkers do the route from Llanganuco to Santa Cruz (indeed, that's always the way I've done it) but Petra and her friends from the South American Explorers Club put an excellent case for the approach from Santa Cruz described here.

Practical information

Distance	45km
Altitude	Between 2,900m and 4,750m
Rating	Moderate

Timing   3-4 days (without the side trips)
In reverse   Possible, and popular
Start of the trail   Cashapampa (2,900m), accessible by morning
                      truck from Caraz or Yungay
Maps   IGN sheets *Corongo* (18-h) and *Carhuaz* (19-h);
                      trekking map *Llanganuco to Santa Cruz* from the
                      SAEC

Route description

The trail starts just outside the village of Cashapampa where you can hire *arrieros* and *burros* if you need them. If you need accommodation in this village, Achilles and Lydia have been recommended.

It is a steep, slippery climb up the Quebrada Santa Cruz, following the right bank of the river along a narrow path, crossing some landsides higher up. The path is pretty obvious, but not easy, taking you all the way up to the first *pampa* (meadow), about 6km from the village which makes a suitable camping place for the first night, being 5-6 hours from Cashapampa.

Next day continue up the Santa Cruz valley, with spectacular mountain views on both sides, until you reach Laguna Chica and, a bit further up, Laguna Grande at 3,900m. This lake is about 11km from Cashapampa, and some 3-4 hours from the *pampa*. The trail continues up the valley, crossing the swampy meadow of Tayapampa to the right (south). Good campsites may be found at the start of the Quebrada Artizon beyond. More swampy meadows follow, until you reach a stream where you need to look for a crossing place. From here it's a steep and long climb up to the pass of Punta Union at 4,750m, about 15km from Laguna Grande and a 7-8 hour walk. The view from the pass, looking back at the Santa Cruz valley, is one of the finest in Peru. The majestic peak of Taulliraju guards the pass, its glaciers calving into the turquoise lake of Taullicocha. Opposite are the snows of Chacraraju, while Huandoy and Huascarán form the backdrop of the valley ahead.

After gazing at the view, prepare yourself for the steep, slippery descent into the valley on the other side, keeping to the right and passing the Lagunas Morococha on your right, with the peak of Nevado Pucaraju (5,028m) ahead of you. The trail makes a right turn, descending into Quebrada Huaripampa, a lovely valley of meadows and small lakes. Keep to your right, following the river, until you reach the junction of Quebrada Paría, about 11km (3-4 hours) from the pass. There are plenty of excellent camping places here, with the glaciers of Artesonraju (6,025m) providing a spectacular backdrop.

The energetic can take a side trip up Quebrada Paría and, further down, up Quebrada Ranincuray. Both are on your right, and get you closer to those magnificent mountains.

From Quebrada Ranincuray it's only a short hike to the village of Colcabamba. Here there are all the rewards of a small town: basic accommodation, meals, and transport back to Yungay and Huaraz or to Yánama and San Luís.

An alternative is to miss Colcabamba and cross the Quebrada Huaripampa at the bridge south of Quebrada Ranincuray, to follow the trail to Vaquería. Here you join the road and can find transport back to Huaraz, providing you get there by 9:00. After that hour there is unlikely to be any buses or trucks.

The Lagunas Llanganuco and Laguna 69
By John Kurth

The valley of Llanganuco is spectacular for the views on Chopicalqui (6,354m), Huascarán (6,768m and 6,655m) and Huandoy (6,395m). A dirt road runs up and over the pass to Yánama on the eastern side. This carries very little traffic and it does give access to the valley for less-fit hikers who are not able to manage the long walk up. In addition to this wimpish advantage, there is a semi-derelict hut near the unromantically named Laguna 69, so you can spend one night in this beautiful area without carrying a tent.

Practical information

Distance	About 7km (one way) from the lakes
Altitude	Between 3,840m and 4,450m
Rating	An easy hike, not steep, with beautiful scenery
Timing	2-3 days
Start of the trail	At Yungay, get transport up the Quebrada Llanganuco until the park control point: about 2 hours
Maps	IGN sheet *Carhuas* (19-h)

Route description

Below the lakes there is a check point of the park office; you can camp here if you made a late start in Yungay. It is also possible to get transport to the lakes and beyond.

The trail climbs up to the lakes from the park control. Take the shortcuts along a footpath, not the dirt road. It's about 6km, 2 hours to the lakes. First you'll pass the smaller Laguna Chinan Cocha, and then the bigger Laguna Orcan Cocha. It's best to cross the stream at the upper end of the Lagunas Llanganuco where the path continues up the valley, crossing the road several times. Don't forget to look back on the superb views. After about 3km, the path descends to the meadows beside the stream in the Quebrada

Yanapaccha at about 4,200m. There are good camping spots here.

This is the start of the trails up to Pisco base camp and Laguna 69. Follow the trail up Quebrada Yanapaccha. The path is fairly obvious and the scenery is pleasant. You will pass some huts and then the trail peters out. Stay on the left side of the valley toward the stream. The valley ends in open pasture and you are confronted by five waterfalls. Head toward the furthest of the two cataracts on the right (east) and follow the trail up and then to the left. The trail takes you above the group of three waterfalls and continues in the same general direction up Quebrada Yanapaccha, passing a small lake before dropping into an open meadow. There are cows here and it can be wet in places, but there are places to camp.

Continuing across the plain you should find a sign indicating that Laguna 69 is 3km away toward the left (north) and that the Cabaña Glacier Broggi is 2km ahead (east). Both trails are fairly obvious.

To reach the *cabaña* continue up Quebrada Yanapaccha. The hut is located in the shadow of Chacraraju (6,112m), the summit off toward the left (northeast), above Laguna 69. Sadly, the hut is dirty, trash is strewn about and the doors have been removed as has the glass in the windows. However, it has a good roof, offers protection from the wind, and if you don't have a tent but want to do an overnight hike, this is a great option. You are serenaded to sleep by avalanches breaking off the mountain face. If everyone takes away some rubbish and tries to keep it clean, it will be a nicer place for the next hiker. Little lakes near the *cabaña* provide water, but it should be purified: there is plenty of human waste in the area.

After a night in the hut you can walk back to the junction in the meadow, then hike the 3km up to Laguna 69. Returning to the road you have several options: continue over the pass (Portachuelo de Llanganuco, 4,767m) and head for Colcabamba or Yánama (there is a morning truck to Yánama if you don't want to walk); complete the Quebrada Santa Cruz circuit by swinging north at Colcabamba and up to Punta Union; or return the way you came to Yungay.

Quebrada Ulta to Colcabamba

This isn't a popular hike, which is one of its advantages. It has plenty of other things going for it: marvellous views of the snow peaks peeping above the valley on either side of the *quebrada* and some great side trips. There's also the opportunity to be terrified as you come over one of the Cordillera's most dramatic, nerve-racking passes. If you are scared of heights don't do this one — there's an alternative (and less stressful) route to Chaças.

This trek provides one of the best opportunities in the Cordillera Blanca for seeing condors.

Practical information

Distance	About 42km
Altitude	Between 3,050m and 4,900m
Rating	Generally easy, except for the passes, which are tough-going
Timing	4 days (excluding side trips)
In reverse	Possible, but difficult coming over the pass
Start of the trail	From Carhuaz, get a truck to the little village of Shilla (3,050m) or Llipta, although there is not always transport available
Maps	IGN sheet *Carhuas* (19-h)

Route description

There is a road all the way up the Quebrada Ulta and down the other side to Chacas, but it carries few vehicles because of the difficulty in getting over the pass. Sadly, the newish road does interfere with the path going up the valley, but it does nothing to destroy the superb views. There are plenty of camping possibilities in the valley, but be careful never to leave your belongings unattended.

From Shilla follow the main footpath to Llipta; it crosses the road several times. After about 7km of path and road beyond Llipta, you come to the entrance of the Quebrada Auquiscocha to the right. There is a possible side trip up this *quebrada* to its lake at 4,300m, about 3km walk from the entrance of the valley. There are not a lot of camping possibilities at the lake, but a large cave hidden behind the underbrush just to the right of the outlet stream will give you shelter.

The main trail continues climbing up the valley, until the Portada de Ulta (the entrance of the valley) at 3,600m, about 3.5km from Quebrada Auquiscocha. Quebrada Huallcacocha leads off to your right, and there's another possible side trip up this to Laguna Huallcacocha, 4,350m, about 3.5km from the *portada*.

The main route splits into several trails running from the *portada*, through the meadow and up the valley. The snow-covered summit of Chopicalqui appears to the left and on your right you'll see the Quebrada Matará. There are some super campsites in the meadows of the Quebrada Matará at 4,350m about 4km from the entrance of the *quebrada*. The massive cliffs of Nevados Huascarán (6,768m) and Chopicalqui (6,354m) loom above.

You have a choice here: if you can't face the drama of the Yanayacu pass, there is an easier route which follows the road to the right up to the pass of Pasaje de Ulta. It climbs to the right of a little ridge, crosses the pass, and brings you down to Pompey and then Chacas.

The more adventurous trail to Yánama continues east towards Nevado Contrahierbas (6,036m) at the head of the *quebrada* at 4,100m, just under

2km from the Quebrada Matará. It passes above the shallow Laguna Yanayacu (possible campsites, and the last water for 8km), turns up the valley to the east, and climbs to the pass of Punta Yanayacu at 4,850m, about 8km from the start of the *quebrada*. This is the dramatic one. The narrow path is cut into the side of the mountain, with a rock cliff on one side and a sheer drop on the other. Having survived this, you descend to a very high and cold lake full of icebergs, below the glaciers of Contrahierbas. If you are well equipped for freezing conditions, this is a marvellous campsite, with rumbling avalanches during the evening and night. The path continues down the valley and soon reaches the valley floor and good campsites.

Keep to the left side of the stream, crossing it near the lower end of the valley, and you have reached the junction of the Colcabamba trail and the Yánama road at 3,350m, about 10km from the pass. Take the left trail to

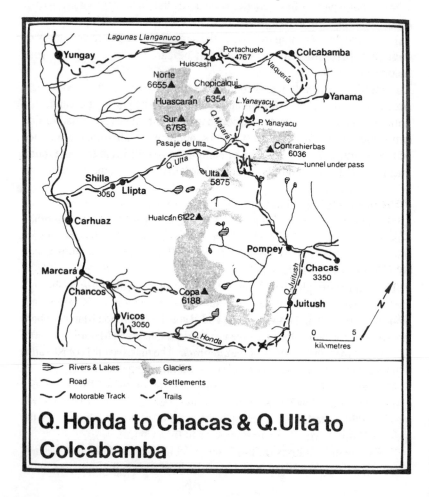

Q. Honda to Chacas & Q. Ulta to Colcabamba

Colcabamba, which climbs steeply for about 500m. Then it levels out and traverses the ridge before dropping to the village of Chaullua. Here it meets the Colcabamba-Yánama trail. Take this to the left, making a short climb to where the trail splits; the upper trail leads to Quebrada Morococha and the Portachuelo de Llanganuco, and the lower trail to Colcabamba, about 6km.

Note: Don't camp close to the villages in this area, and watch your belongings.

Quebrada Honda to Chacas

This is a nice easy walk up the Honda valley. Even though a new dirt road has been constructed here, it is still a great hike with some very interesting side trips. Locals are very friendly and eager to have a chat with you. The pass gives excellent views and good possibilities to see condors, the valley on the other side is green and beautiful, and Chacas is still an unspoiled, picturesque mountain village.

Practical information

Distance	47km
Altitude	Between 3,050m and 4,750m
Rating	Moderate, with a steep pass
Timing	4 days (excluding side trips)
In reverse	Possible and interesting
Start of the trail	From Marcará get transport to Chancos and Vicos
Maps	IGN sheet *Huari* (19-i)

Route description

From the little village of Vicos at 3,050m, a dirt road has been constructed all the way to the end of the Quebrada Honda. Follow the footpath, which provides a shortcut and is more interesting than the road. First you'll pass the Portada de Honda, the gate to the entrance of the valley at 3,600m, about 9km from Vicos. There are good campsites just after the gate.

The first side trip is shortly after the *portada*. A road branches off to the left, and runs to about half way up Quebrada Paccharuri. Then a path continues to Laguna Paccharuri (4,450m), which is situated below the majestic bulks of Nevados Copa (6,188m) and Paccharaju (5,751m) at the head of the canyon, about 9km from the entrance of the valley.

The main hike continues up the Quebrada Honda and is pleasant and easy, following the dirt road along the river, passing through farming land, steep canyons, and green meadows, until the end of the valley; this area is called the *rinconada*, and if you left Vicos in the morning you should reach it by the end of the day. The route is well travelled and you'll probably be accompanied by local *campesinos*. These friendly people love to chat to gringos if your Spanish is good enough. It's about 10km from the *portada* to the *rinconada* which lies at 3,850m.

From here there is a possible side trip to Laguna Pucaranracocha: a trail leads southeast up the Quebrada Minoyo or Pucaranra, crossing a bridge, and climbing past a mighty waterfall. 2km past the falls you'll see the Quebrada Escalón on your right. Continue along the river, across the meadows and up the moraine at the head of the canyon. A short, faint spur to the right leads to Laguna Pucaranracocha at 4,400m, about 9km from the *rinconada*. A trail beyond the lake continues to a mine (which is the reason for the Quebrada Honda road).

Back to the main trail. Leaving the valley floor at the *rinconada*, you have to look for the start of the trail climbing up the left side of the valley; it is not easy to see.

The climb to the pass is steep, but the views are great (the surrounding peaks are Chinchey (6,222m), Palcaraju (6,274m) and Pucaranra (6,156m)) and this is a well-known spot to see condors. The Portachuelo de Honda pass is 4,750m, about 7km (3 hours) from the *rinconada*.

A steep descent brings you into the Quebrada Juitush, and meets the dirt road on the left-hand side of the valley, after passing through lush green meadows and farmland with good campsites everywhere. The little settlement of Juitush lies about 9km from the pass (3 hours) at 3,800m. After Juitush, the trail forks as it approaches a bridge. The left-hand trail crosses the bridge and runs up the other side of the valley, which is the route to the village of Pompey, about 9km away. There you could get a truck or hike over the Pasaje de Ulta and back to Huaraz. The right-hand trail continues to Chacas, 12km (3 hours) from Juitush.

Chacas is a little village at 3,350m. There are some basic shops, a market and trucks leaving in the morning and early afternoon to San Luís.

Huari to Chacas
By John and Christine Myerscough

We discovered this trek after waiting in vain for transport up the eastern side of the cordillera to Pomabamba. The route passes through two beautiful, peaceful and mainly uninhabited green upland valleys, crossing a pass of 4,500m from where there are good, though brief views of the peaks north and west of Chacas. More impressive though, besides the tranquillity, are the contorted bands of rock.

Practical information
Distance	About 34km
Altitude	From 2,700m (Huari) to 4,500m
Rating	Moderate; some steep sections

Timing	2-3 days
In reverse	Possible (see page 154)
Start of the trail	Huari (served by bus) or Chacas
Maps	IGN sheet *Huari* (19-i)

Route description

From Huari Leave the lower (cathedral) plaza by the steps climbing from the lower left hand corner, to meet the higher of two roads which leave Huari to the north. Follow the road round for 2km to the town of Ulia. Just after passing through Ulia plaza with its church, you cross a river. Immediately afterwards take the path which climbs steeply up to your left. This is the most direct route up to Laguna Purhuay, which you will reach in about 1½ hours.

Alternatively you may prefer to follow the rough road which zigzags up along the bottom of the Río Purhuay valley, and forks left a little further on. Both road and track join before you reach the tranquil Laguna Purhuay. Here you may like to pause and catch a few trout for your supper — the lake seems well stocked with them. Rest at least: from here your route is steep and ever upwards.

As soon as you reach the southern end of the lake, look for a fork to the left. This is not very clear in its lower part, but from the lake shore it is clearly visible higher up where it passes a small group of eucalyptus trees. Whatever happens, don't follow the lake shore beyond the first small valley and stream to enter the lake from its western side. Once on the path, you'll find it easy to follow, taking you up and round into Quebrada Asnoragra. There's a good picnic spot where you cross the stream which is a rare source of water.

Once across the stream the path continues steeply up through the scrub and bush, eventually emerging in open *puna*. On the crest, the path forks, the main route continuing left and upwards whilst a smaller path goes straight on. Less than 100m more of climbing, at a more gentle angle now, brings you round on to a high level path above and to the south of a deep *quebrada* unnamed on the IGN map. It will take 3-4 hours from the lake to here.

The next 3 or 4km are a pleasant high traverse, with several camping possibilities and plenty of side streams for water. If it has been a long hot day and you want a private pool and jacuzzi, continue until the path drops down the valley, running along the left-hand side close to the main stream. There are plenty of camping opportunities here.

The path now remains in the valley bottom and climbs steadily, crossing the stream from left to right where the main valley bends to the right. Little water is available once you leave the valley bottom until you drop well down the other side of the pass, so it's a good idea to fill up your water bottle when you cross the main stream. As you round the bend in the valley the top of the pass comes into sight some 3km ahead. The cross on its summit cairn is clearly visible. Unlike most routes in the *cordillera* the climb to the pass is gentle and relatively painless, and another hour or so will see you crossing the ridge between rock bands, and traversing around the top of a high valley dotted with small lakes.

From the summit the path drops steeply down, entering the valley of the Río Arma via a side valley. Your may decide to camp at the junction of these two valleys. If not there are one or two small sites amongst the trees before the path crosses the side stream in Quebrada Tayanchocha, some 2.5-3km further on, otherwise you will be forced to continue all the way down to Chacas (another 4-5 hours walk) or pitch in a farmer's field lower down the valley.

There is only one obvious path down the left hand side of the Río Arma. This climbs up and to the left to cross the tributary stream coming from Laguna Patarcocha by a splendid little bridge. Turn right across the bridge and continue along the path high up on the left hand side of the valley. Eventually this will bring you to the small group of houses which comprise the village of Cochas, and, beyond these over a slight rise, the town of Chacas.

From Chacas To do the route in reverse (which has the advantage of a higher starting point: Chacas is at 3,350m), go out of Chacas at the top end of the plaza and, after two blocks, take the track leading to the left, up over a low ridge, to the village of Cochas. Passing through Cochas keep on the main, high track which leads round to the right and will bring you out high above the Río Arma on the right-hand side of the valley. Follow this up to the bridge over the side stream from Laguna Patarcocha. Cross the bridge and take the path to the left which curves around the end of the spur between this tributary valley and the main valley of the Río Alma. Continue along the path up the right side of the Río Alma, crossing the Río Tayancocha by an earth bridge. The path leaves the valley of the Río Alma by the next *quebrada* up, and is then the only obvious path to lead up and over the pass.

Similarly the descent at the other side is by the only path along the valley bottom. After the valley bends to the left, cross the main stream and keep to the path down the right hand side of the valley bottom, traversing round to the right and staying high as the valley falls away more steeply. The route from here should be obvious and needs no further description.

Quebrada Ishinca
By Val Pitkethly

This is a beautiful one-way hike up the valley of Ishinca, with an interesting side trip to the Ishinca glacier. There are great views all the way, and the hiking is easy. A popular trip with climbers going up to Ishinca peak.

Practical information

Distance	19km
Altitude	From 3,200m to 4,950m
Rating	Easy to the *quebrada*, a steep climb to the lake
Timing	2 days from Colón to Ishinca base camp
Start of the trail	Get transport from Huaraz to Puente Paltay, the entrance of the dirt road to Colón. If you're lucky a truck will take you up to the village (3,200m) or you can hike there in 2-3 hours (6km).
Map	IGN sheet *Huari* (19-i)

Route description

The trail begins from the road end at the school in Colón. After 200m the trail forks: take the lower trail, crossing the stream over the second bridge, climb steeply over a good trail that heads east, and continue across the hill and through farmland. The locals are friendly, but may not be very helpful with directions. Follow the trail for about 3 hours through *queñoa* forest to the *portada*, the entrance of the Quebrada Ishinca, at 3,850m, about 7.5km from Colón. Campsites can be found here.

The trail continues through a series of meadows to the head of the valley. Good campsites abound. A clear path passes by a waterfall on the south wall, and after an easy climb of 2km it crosses the stream and reaches the Ishinca climbers' base camp, at 4,400m, about 8km (4 hours) from the entrance of the valley. There is a little hut here, but camping is better.

Beyond the base camp the trail begins to climb the south wall, at times quite steeply, before passing a swampy meadow and making the final climb to Laguna Ishinca, at 4,950m. This is about 3.5km (2 hours) from base camp.

From here it takes about an hour to the Ishinca glacier, following the moraine on the right side of the lake.

There is a possible 1½-hour side trek up to Laguna Toclla, below Nevado Tocllaraju (6,034m). An alternative side trip is to the base camp for Nevado Urus: a trail climbs up from the head of Quebrada Ishinca to this small base camp at 4,980m, about 2½ hours. There are a few small camping spaces and beautiful views of the Nevados Ishinca (5,530m), Ranrapalca (6,162m) and Ocshapalca (5,888m).

Return the way you came.

Quebradas Churup, Quilcayhuanca, Shallap and Rajucolta

All these routes are close to Huaraz, making them ideal warm-up hikes for something more ambitious. Some are short hikes from Huaraz, like Churup, and some are spectacular valleys where you can spend a few days and do some side trips.

The start of all the hikes is Pitec (3,850m), east of Huaraz. You may be able to get transport all the way there, or just part way and then walk along the obvious path. Pitec is not a village, just a low pass with a few farmhouses.

The IGN *Recuay* map (20-i) covers these hikes.

To Laguna Churup

Distance	3.5km
Altitude	From 3,850m to 4,600m
Rating	A steep climb, sometimes off the trail
Timing	3 hours from Pitec to the lake

Route description There are several ways to climb from Pitec to the lake. Probably the simplest and most direct route is to start climbing from the end of the road at Pitec, along the left side of the long ridge (moraine) beside the creek. You'll come to some trail markers showing where a trail crosses to the right. Follow this trail across the ridge, past a small pond, and over the granite rock to the lake. This is a jewel of a lake, deep blue in colour and half encircled by Nevado Churup (5,495m).

Up the Quebrada Quilcayhuanca to the Lagunas Tullpacocha and Cuchillacocha and Quebrada Cayesh

Distance	19.5km to the lakes
Altitude	From 3,850m to 4,650m
Rating	Easy to moderate
Timing	4 days

Route description The dirt road from Pitec continues to the Portada de Quilcayhuanca, at 3,850m, about 3km from Pitec. Go through the gate or climb over it and follow the trail up the valley on the left hand side. This is an easy hike to the head of the valley, through green, marshy meadows with lots of cattle, ascending slowly up various plateaux. The distance is about 8.5km, 3½ hours, to 4,050m. There are plenty of camping places.

The *nevado* in front of you is Andavite (5,518m), the valley to your right is Quebrada Cayesh and the one to your left is the continuation of Quebrada Quilcayhuanca which brings you to the two Lagunas Tullpacocha and Cuchillacocha.

If you want to go up Quebrada Cayesh — and you should, for a closer view of the dramatic *nevados* — look for the little natural bridge over the stream, hidden to your right. Cross and climb up the small ridge to the meadow. Across the meadow is another stream. Look for a shallow place to cross, and enter Quebrada Cayesh. The first part is green meadow; it's best to cross to your left, where you'll find a path bringing you all the way up to the head of the valley, passing through *queñoa* forest. Distance: 8km, 2½ hours. Good campsites (but look for a dry place) and great views of the needle-like Nevado Cayesh (5,721m) to the left, Maparaju (5,326m) in front of you, and San Juan (5,843m) and Tumarinaraju (5,668m) to your right. For an even better view climb up the mountain slope to your right, which takes about an hour. First climb over the moraine as far as the little bushes next to a huge boulder. Then it's best to climb up the boulder, finding the easiest route.

To reach the lakes in the Quebrada Quilcayhuanca, leave the valley floor and head left. You'll see a well-marked path climbing up the ridge to the meadow. The path runs across the meadow on the right-hand side, crossing a few streams. The trail starts climbing up the ridge, following the right side of the valley. The river, flowing from Laguna Tullpacocha, comes down on your right. Follow the path until you have reached a little open area between the bushes, just before you cross the stream again on your left. This is about 3km from the valley floor.

There are two lakes to be reached from here: Laguna Tullpacocha and Laguna Cuchillacocha. To get to the former look for the trail to your right, curving around the mountain, passing the old INGEMMET hut, and continue up the small canyon until you reach Laguna Tullpacocha, at 4,300m, about a half hour's walk from the start of the trail. The lake is right underneath Nevado Tullparaju (5,787m).

To reach Laguna Cuchillacocha from the point where you cross the stream on your left, look for the path crossing the valley on the opposite side and climbing up the mountain slope in a series of switchbacks to the top of the ridge, where there is a meadow. The path was once used by workers from INGEMMET (the government agency responsible for the glacial lakes) so is well worn but is now overgrown. It crosses a stream and continues to the head of the valley in about 4km (1½ hours). If you look to your right you'll see a path climbing up the slope, making a few switchbacks, until it reaches a little meadow with the old INGEMMET camp. From here follow the trail to your left, contouring the mountain side, to Laguna Cuchillacocha at 4,650m, about a half kilometre from the start of the trail.

The head of the valley provides good campsites and super views of Nevados Huapi (5,530m) and Pucaranra (6,156m) in front of you, with Chinchey (6,222m), Tullparaju (5,787m) and Cayesh (5,721m) to your right.

For even better views, climb up the mountain slope to your left (as you face the mountains) until you reach Laguna Paqsacocha in about 1½ hours.

To Laguna Shallap

Distance	10.5km
Altitude	From 3,800m to 4,300m
Rating	Easy to moderate
Timing	About 5 hours from Pitec to the lake

Route description   From Pitec, you'll see the valley of Shallap to your right. It first descends to the Quilcayhuanca bridge, and then climbs the opposite bank, crosses a plateau, turns left, passes the community of Cahuide, and starts up the Quebrada Shallap. The Shallap bridge is down a path to the right of the corrals, just past Cahuide. Another bridge is 400m further and the trail ascends through the boulders and thick brush, to the *portada* marking the entrance of the Quebrada Shallap at 4,000m and about 4.5km (2 hours) from Pitec.

The path ascends the valley, through some pleasant meadows and past waterfalls, until the lake's moraine. Pass the old INGEMMET hut and you reach Laguna Shallap at 4,300m. This is 6km (3 hours) from the *portada*. It lies just below Nevado San Juan (5,843m). There are some exposed campsites at the lake; better camping is found in the *quebrada*.

To Laguna Rajucolta

Distance	17km
Altitude	From 3,800m to 4,250m
Rating	Moderate
Timing	8 hours from Pitec to the lake

Route description   This is an exceptional hike because of the way Nevado Huantsán dominates the view so you hardly notice the cliffs and waterfalls en route.

Pick up the trail at the Shallap bridge, at Quebrada Shallap. Cross the bridge and continue up the trail along the stream until you are out of the ravine. You can see a trail to your right, working its way up the mountain slope. Follow it to an open meadow. Another 2km brings you to the community of Janco. Follow the path up the ridge toward Quebrada Rajucolta (south) to the pass at 4,300m which lies below Nevado Huamashraju (5,434m); about 7km (3-4 hours). Descend to the valley below until you reach the entrance of Quebrada Rajucolta, at 4,050m, about 3km from the pass. Go through the gate, and on to a second gate. Continue through grazing land and a boulder-strewn area with many trees, along the left bank of the stream. The best and last campsites are found at the foot of the slope that leads to the lake. Follow the trail to a large field of boulders, knocked there by the landslides following the 1970 earthquake. Continue to the base of the canyon wall, where you follow the path along the stream and up to the lake. Laguna Rajucolta lies at 4,250m, a perfect glacial lake backed by the majestic Nevado Huantsán (6,395m). It is about 6.5km (2-3 hours) from the *portada* to the lake.

Olleros to Chavín

Compared with others in the Cordillera Blanca, this is not a very spectacular hike, lacking views of amazing snow peaks, but it is easy and takes you to one of Peru's most interesting archaeological sites, Chavín de Huantar. Some people attribute this trail to the Incas, because of the stretches of fine stone paving, but it almost certainly pre-dates the Inca empire. The trip is made much more exciting and dramatic by taking two extra days and visiting Laguna Tararhua, tucked in between three glaciated peaks.

Practical information

Distance	37km
Altitude	Between 3,200m and 4,700m
Rating	Moderate
Timing	2-3 days
In reverse	Possible, but a more difficult, steeper climb from Chavín
Start of the trail	Truck to Olleros or hike in from the main road
Map	IGN sheet *Recuay* (21i)

Route description

From Olleros (3,420m) go past the plaza and after 100m take a clear track (actually a dirt road) downhill to the right and across the river. The trail goes straight up the valley to the right of the Río Negro for about 5 hours. Look out for the entrance to Quebrada Rurec on your left after about 9km (3 hours). The dirt road crosses the river at this point, and so should you if you want to do the side trip up Quebrada Rurec (described later). Otherwise stay high on the trail as it continues along the right side of the river (although the trail leaves the river at one point) until it drops down to a wide marshy area with some good campsites about 8 hours from Olleros. Here you will be faced by three valleys; take the left-hand one, best reached by following the trail up the ridge between the middle and left-hand valleys.

The trail rises sharply with good views starting to open up in front of you. There are two 'false' passes before you reach Punta Yanashallash at 4,700m, about 14km (4-5 hours) from the marsh. There are some nice, but cold, campsites near the lakes. From the top of the pass the trail drops down to Chavín, following the Quebrada Huachecsa on its left, and passing the community of Jato at 3,900m, about 6km from Punta Yanashallash. From Jato to Chavín (3,200m) takes about 3 hours.

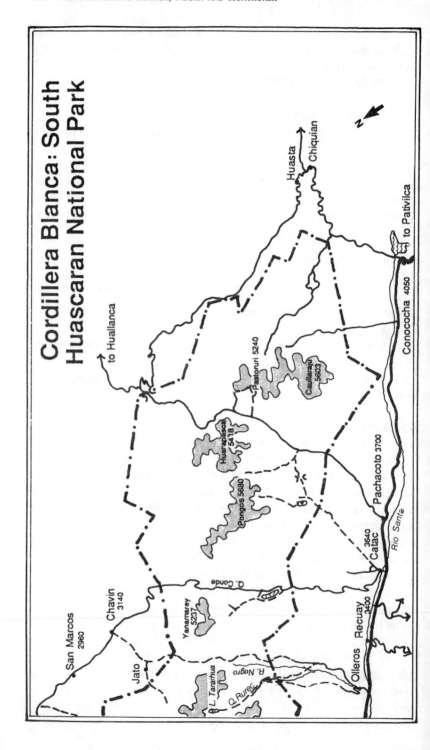

Cordillera Blanca: South Huascaran National Park

To Laguna Tararhua

Quebrada Rurec, about 9km from Olleros, is easy to find because that's where the road crosses the river. The 25km, full day trip, to Laguna Tararhua takes you up the *quebrada* on a good trail. Follow the right bank of Río Rurec to the *pampa* and the entrance of the valley where there are a few houses. Beware of dogs! Continue along the path to Laguna Tararhua at 4,500m, set below the glaciers of Nevados Rurec (5,700m) and Uruashraju (5,722m), about 3 hours from the entrance to the valley.

To return to the eastern section of the mail trail (at the marshy area) it should be possible to skirt the sides of Uruashraju, and hike due south across country. However, I don't know anyone who's tried it.

Chavín

This is a rather dreary small town, made exciting by its ruins. It has four basic *hostales* around the plaza, the best being Hostal el Inca, about US$5 per person, with a bathroom and sometimes hot water. The restaurants all serve a very basic meal, and there's a little market.

The ruins

The ruins and museum are open from 08:00 to 17:00, with an entrance fee of about US$2. The guard is knowledgeable and will usually act as a guide. Bring a torch for exploring the dark underground chambers.

Experts vary in their estimate of the age of the Chavín culture, but most agree that it flourished between 1300 and 400BC, spreading from the coastal areas to the northern highlands, and reached its zenith around 500BC, when the temple at Chavín de Huantar was built. Chavín appears to have been a predominantly religious culture with various animalistic deities. Highly stylized feline forms are a common feature of the sculptures and carvings, along with eagles or condors, and snakes. It's a fascinating place. The enormous and enigmatic stone heads and finely carved reliefs have a strength and beauty unrivalled by the Incas, who left little in the way of representational art. The seven underground chambers have the finest stone work and an impressive sacrificial stone placed in the middle of the complex. There is electric lighting, but your torch will help pick out the details.

See page 319 for an excellent book on the Chavín civilization.

Chavín monolith

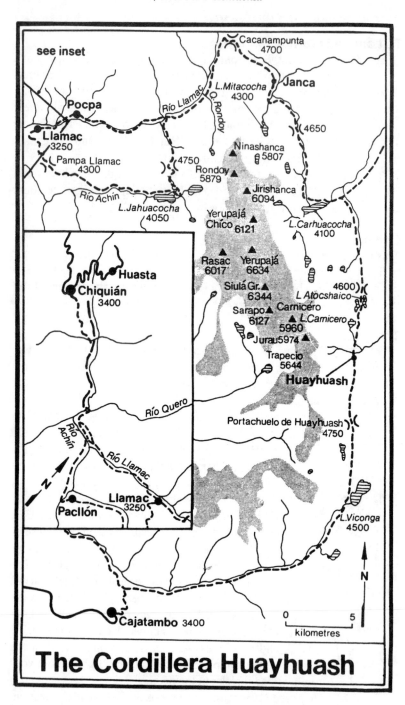

The Cordillera Huayhuash

THE CORDILLERA HUAYHUASH
Hiking the Huayhuash circuit
Updated by Andrew Pepper, and Kate and Mathew Heal

This hike circles the entire range, and is probably the most scenically exciting hike in Peru. The most dramatic scenery of the walk is around the east side of the *cordillera*, where a chain of trout-filled lakes reflect the towering white peaks. The whole circuit involves 160km of walking between altitudes of 2,750m (9,020ft) and 5,000m (16,400ft), which represents a serious and difficult endeavour, so this is only recommended for hikers in excellent physical condition or who plan to take at least 12 days to complete the circuit. Of course it is not necessary to do the whole thing: you can hike for a few days and backtrack, or leave the trail at Cajatambo (a 7-day hike) from where there is transport to Lima. Side trips are mentioned in the route description.

The route is fairly obvious most of the way, although a well-worn trail is not always present. Because of the popularity of this circuit, garbage is beginning to mar the enjoyment of some camping areas. Don't add to it, and better still help clean up!

Practical information

Distance	164-186km for the full circuit (depending on whether you do side treks)
Altitude	Between 2,750m and 5,000m
Rating	Difficult, with more than 6,000m (19,680ft) of climbing
Timing	7 days (if you leave at Cajatambo), 12 days for the circuit (without side trips)
In reverse	Possible
Start of the trail	Chiquián. You can also start at Cajatambo, when coming from Lima, but most hikers want to stop over in Huaraz first to get organized, acclimatized and to see the Cordillera Blanca.
Chiquián	A little mountain village (at 3,400m) with some basic accommodation, restaurants and a pretty good food supply, but more expensive than in Huaraz. You can easily arrange to hire *burros* here for about US$2.50 per day with US$8 per day for the *arriero*.
Maps	IGN sheets *Chiquian* and *Yanahuanca* or *The Cordillera Huayhuash* from the SAEC.

Route description

The construction of a road has been started from Chiquián in the direction of Llamac, but so far only a few kilometres has been completed. Follow the footpath which shortcuts from the north side of the cemetery in Chiquián, eventually descending to the Río Pativilca where you meet the road; about 1½ hours. Stay on the right side of Río Pativilca for 1-1¼ hours, crossing on a bridge above Río Quero. Continue down the left-hand side, crossing the Río Achin. The path then curves round a spur and turns left up the Achin valley. The path follows the Achin valley and crosses the river after about 1½ hours, continuing on to Llamac. This lies at 3,250m and is about 21km from Chiquian — about 9 hours of hot walking. There are good campsites along the way, better perhaps than in Llamac, where your large audience may get on your nerves.

Llamac is a small community where you can make a refreshments stop even if you don't camp; the shops sell some soft drinks and very basic food. If needed you could probably find some basic accommodation and meals with a local family.

If you are leaving the Cordillera at Cajatambo it is well worth taking the longer route via Laguna Jahuacocha, the epicentre of the Huayhuash as far as most visitors are concerned. Take the path south from Llamac. About 10 minutes from the edge of the village the path rounds a spur and doublebacks to the left, climbing diagonally to the left, towards an obvious cleft in the mountain horizon. Climb up the eroded mountainside to a false pass, then for a further hour (enlivened somewhat by an Inca wall) to the real pass, Pampa Llamac (4,300m) which is on the right of a round, loaf-shaped hill. The ascent is a real struggle, but it really *is* worth it. I experienced one of my moments of purest exhilaration here. In front lies the western face of the Cordillera: giant dragon's teeth of glistening white — Rasac, Yerupajá, Jirishjanka. As a further reward, the trail turns into a proper Andean path, winding gently through *queñoa* trees and lupins, past waterfalls and rocky overhangs to the valley below. In another 2 to 3 hours (if you haven't decided to camp on the way) you will arrive at Laguna Jahuacocha. A local family may offer to cook you trout and potatoes, or to sell you Coca-Cola.

When you are ready to leave the lake and rejoin the main trail, take the path along the left (south) side of the lake, which swings to the left and begins to go uphill. Fill up with water before you start on the pass — there are no streams for several hours. It should take 2 to 3 hours to reach the top, but it took our group 4 hours; not because it was so difficult, but because it was so beautiful. We had to keep stopping to gaze. You seem to be almost on top of Rondoy's glacier, and look down into a milky, blue lake full of little icebergs. The serious business starts below a long, scree slope: the pass is to the right of a set of jagged, grey teeth. The path goes directly to the left of the teeth, then traverses across to the 4,750m pass. To descend, it is probably best to go down to a small lake at the foot of Rondoy/Ninashanka, and follow the *quebrada* to the valley floor. Or traverse the hillside on the left, but keep low. In all events, you will reach Río Llamac, at the bottom of the valley, and turn right on to the main trail.

Hikers taking the direct route from Llamac will continue along the trail running east from that town, heading for an hour up the valley to the smaller community of Pocpa, at 3,450m. This is a steep ascent, with good camping spots before Pocpa. The climb continues up the valley, passing another small community called Pallca, and finally you arrive at the entrance of Quebrada Rondoy at 4,000m, about 11km (4-5 hours) from Pocpa. From here you get the first glimpse of snow-capped mountains, and there are some good camping spots.

Side trip: if you want to get closer to those snow-peaks, an enjoyable hike can be made to the lake at the end of Quebrada Rondoy, below Nevados Rondoy (5,870m) and Ninashanca (5,607m).

The main trail passes a trail junction to the left (which goes up to the north, leaving the Cordillera). Follow the right trail, climbing steeply up the valley to the first pass of Cacanampunta at 4,700m, about 6km (3 hours) from the entrance of Quebrada Rondoy. From the pass, the trail drops down through a wide marshy valley to the junction of two rivers. The main path goes straight ahead, but you are strongly recommended to take the diversion to Laguna Mitacocha: continue to the right, up the Río Janca for about 1½ hours to Laguna Mitacocha (4,300m), where there are fantastic views and plenty of camping places.

Side trip: from Mitacocha you can continue up the valley to Laguna Ninacocha, at the foot of Jirishanka Chico (5,446m). It's a steep climb, but not difficult, over a moraine. It takes about 1½ hours.

The route continues from the river crossing, up the valley (south), passing the corrals of Mayas, to the pass of Punta Carhuac, at 4,650m, 7km (2-3 hours) from the river crossing. On the descent follow the river to the Laguna Carhuacocha (2 hours) at 4,100m. This is a gorgeous place with some marvellously scenic campsites, the best being above the lake on the *pampa* with fantastic views. There is a little community situated below the lake. Mitacocha to Carhuacocha takes 4-5 hours.

Side trip: Up to the Lagunas Siula, at 4,300m (4km/2 hours) and Quesillacocha, which lie nestled below the towering east face of Nevado Siulá Grande (6,344m).

Continuing the main route you will need to find a fording place across the river below Laguna Carhuacocha since there is no bridge. The easiest places are a few hundred metres below the lake. Climb steeply up the valley to your right (south), passing dry lakes and a good chance to see vicuñas, to the pass of Carnicero, at 4,600m, about 8km (3 hours) from Laguna Carhuacocha. The trail (definite now) comes down between the two Lagunas Atocshaico, at 4,500m. Good campsites but cold nights. The trail continues its descent, passing a little settlement, to the community of Huayhuash, at 4,350m, 4km from the lakes. The village is situated on the bottom of the valley, with a junction of another valley to the right. This is a popular camping spot.

The trail continues up the valley (south), with good camping places and some small lakes at the right, to the pass of Portachuelo de Huayhuash, 4,750m, 5km (3-4 hours) from Huayhuash. Ahead are spectacular views of the Cordillera Raura. The trail drops down from the pass to Laguna Viconga, 4,500m, 5km (1 hour) from the pass. If you decide to stop the night here, camp above the lake. The path goes to the lower end of the lake, where there is a dam and a building for a hydro-electric project.

This is the point where you can leave the Cordillera via Cajatambo; the town lies at 3,400m, about 22km (8-9 hours) from the lake. On this trail, after about an hour, you'll come to small thermal pools. Not the best hot springs in Peru, but after six nights camped above 4,000m you are not going to be fussy! There is basic accommodation in Cajatambo and transport to Lima. Bella Tours run 3 buses a week, on Tuesdays, Fridays and Sundays, leaving the Plaza de Armas at 06:00. There is little alternative transport.

The main route continues from the dam and climbs up the valley to your right to the pass of Punta Cuyoc at 5,000m (making it the highest pass on this hike), a good 4 hours from Laguna Viconga. The pass lies quite a bit above and to the left of the ridge's low point below Nevados Cuyoc (5,530m) and Puscanturpa Sur (5,442m). A steep, slippery trail descends to the *pampa* where there are good campsites, then down the narrow valley of Quebrada Guanacpatay to Río Huayllapa, 4,000m, about 12km (4-5 hours) from the pass. If you are planning to go directly to the village of Huayllapa, the left bank of the river is better (not passable for *burros*). If you wish to take the side trip to Lagunas Jurau and Sarapococha, stay to the right of the river. There is a dramatic (300m) waterfall just before Quebrada Guanacpatay meets the Río Huayllapa, which makes a wonderful shower.

Side trip: up to the Lagunas Jurau (4,350m, 7km, 3-4 hours) and Sarapococha. Take the trail heading up the right bank of the Río Huayllapa to the base of the moraine in front of Laguna Jurau. Some steep, rocky trails climb to the right of the outlet stream to the barren, beautiful lake lying below Nevados Jurau (5,600m) and Carnicero (5,960m). It is easy to cross the stream near the lake and take the path across the moraine heading toward Sarapococha. Another small lake, Ruricoltau, lies to the right directly below the face of Nevado Sarapo (6,127m). You can descend back to Río Huayllapa from Laguna Sarapococha. This side trek will take one day.

The main trail descends down from Río Huayllapa, passing the entrance of the long Quebrada Segya which leads to Laguna Caramarca below Nevados Rasac (6,017m) and Tsacra (5,548m), which can be another side trip, to the small village of Huayllapa, at 3,600m. In the village you can find accommodation and meals and even stock up on some basic foods.

From Huayllapa you have another chance to leave the Cordillera via Cajatambo.

The main route continues north up the valley to your left (when coming from Quebrada Huayllapa and a 10-minute hike from the village), climbing up to the *pampa* where there are good campsites in about 2 hours. Stay on the left-hand side until a high valley appears to your left after about an hour. That's the route up to the next pass of Punta Tapush, 4,800m, 8km (5 hours) from Huayllapa. The trail descends past two small lakes to the valley junction to your right, about one hour from the pass.

The trail straight ahead goes to the village of Pacllón, but most people want to make the diversion to Laguna Jahuacocha. This trail climbs east up the right-hand valley for about 2½ hours to the obvious pass of Yaucha at 4,800m. From the pass the trail descends to the left (north) into the Río Huacrish, and along the river to its junction with Río Achín, just below the southern shore of Laguna Jahuacocha, 4,050m (12km, 4 hours) from Punta Tapush. If you are brave enough to swim, there is a lovely pool here. It's a 10-minute hike up to the lake from the river junction. The lake is the focal point of the Cordillera Huayhuash, and the many visitors have left far more than footprints. If you can clean up their garbage as well as your own, you will have earned the meal a local family is likely to offer to cook for you.

The trail back to Llamac and Chiquián goes down the north bank of the Río Achín below the lake. It's not a clear path, but stay on the right, passing the settlement of Juhuacocha (where another trail climbs up to the right — north — but very steeply) to the small community of Huayan, about 2 hours from the lake. From here you climb up the valley to your right for about 2 hours until you reach the pass. There are lots of trails coming down from the pass; stay on your left until you reach Llamac in about 2 hours.

It's another 6 hours' hike from Llamac to Chiquián.

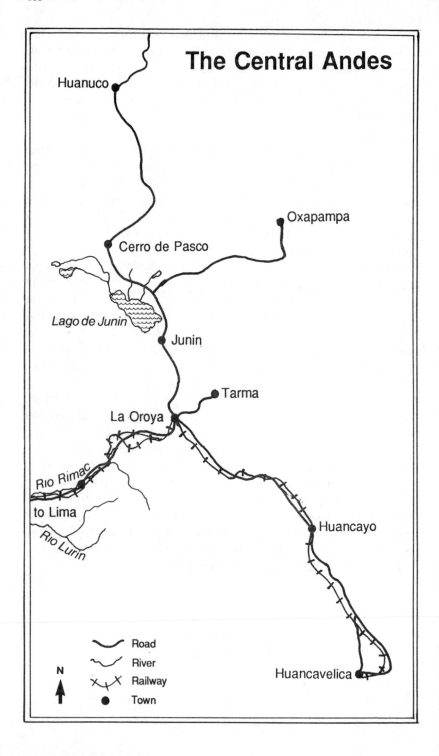

The Central Andes

Huanuco

Oxapampa

Cerro de Pasco

Lago de Junin

Junin

Tarma

La Oroya

Rio Rimac

to Lima

Rio Lurin

Huancayo

Huancavelica

Road
River
Railway
Town

N

Chapter Eleven

The Central Andes

Introduction
This part of Peru covers the departments of Huánuco, Cerro de Pasco, Junín, Huancavelica, and Ayacucho. This is a beautiful and remote mountain region, scattered with small towns and villages, and inhabited by a Quechua-speaking population holding on to the remains of the Inca culture. Their lives centre round subsistence farming and their animals — mainly llamas and alpacas. Poor communication with Lima and the coastal region maintains the isolation, allowing the traditional way of life to survive.

Hiking possibilities
There are no established hiking trails, no organized trekking, no towns geared to backpackers. This is the place to come if you want to find your own routes, learn more about the Quechua culture, and experience the Real Peru. The choice of hikes is limitless, since the area is networked with paths linking village to village, but there are some high mountain ranges as well. Some little-known but spectacular Inca ruins are also found here, such as Huánuco Viejo, and long stretches of the Inca Road which once ran unbroken from Quito to Cusco.

Safety
This region was the apex of terrorist activity between 1989 and 1992, when the Sendero Luminoso virtually controlled most of the towns and villages. During those years the area was unsafe for foreign travellers. However, since 1992 the army has regained control and terrorism has gradually disappeared. Even so, there is still some tension, and you should seek information on the current situation before venturing into the area. The best source of up-to-date information is the South American Explorers Club in Lima; their advice is informed and objective.

When planning your hikes talk to the local people and get their views on your safety before wandering off into the mountains. Schoolteachers are often an excellent source of information and will speak Spanish. It is essential that your own Spanish is reasonably good so you do not get into trouble through lack of communication.

Road conditions

The whole area is networked with dirt roads and paths. Every village has a road connection to the next village for vehicles and a more direct footpath for pedestrians. There is regular traffic between the major towns, but little traffic between the villages, and hardly any traffic between the small communities. In the rainy season, road travel is virtually impossible with the dirt roads churned into axle-deep mud and periodically blocked by landslides. Only visit this region if you have a flexible travel schedule.

Maps

The Instituto Geográfico Nacional in Lima publishes topographical maps of this Andean region. You will need them if you explore off the beaten track.

Guides

In such a little-known and possibly risky region it would be sensible to take a guide. A local person will give you a better feel for the culture and can show you remote ruins and mountain areas. By taking a guide you can play a small part in helping this impoverished district. A recommended guide is Lucho Hurtado.

PLACES OF INTEREST

Huánuco

A remote mountain area, with some interesting ruins.

Cerro de Pasco

A chilly, high town with some interesting hikes in the surrounding mountain areas.

Tarma

A typical mountain village, situated in a beautiful valley. There are some exceptional hiking possibilities in the surrounding mountains, with ruins, lakes and caves.

Huancayo

Quite a large town, functioning as an important communications centre between the Central Andes and Lima. This is the best place to learn about typical crafts and festivals. It is a good base for day hikes into the Mantaro valley.

Huancavelica

A very pretty mountain town with good crafts and local festivals, and some interesting hiking possibilities in the surrounding mountains.

Ayacucho

Until recently this was more famous as the birthplace of the Sendero Luminoso. Now it is regaining its prominence as an important centre with notable crafts and festivals. There are plenty of hiking possibilities in the surrounding mountains, with some interesting ruins.

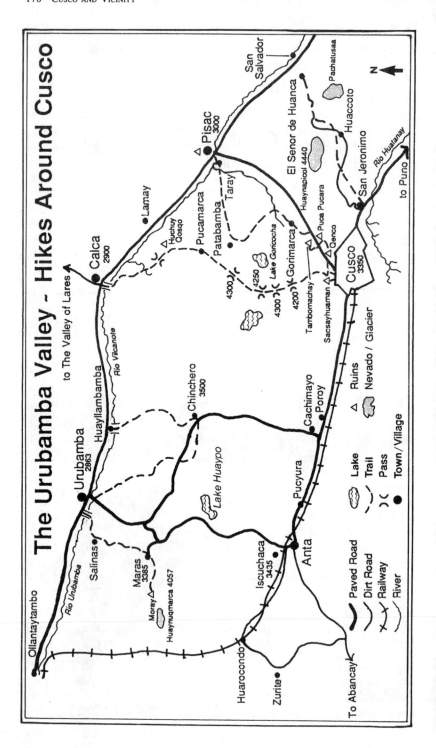

The Urubamba Valley - Hikes Around Cusco

Chapter Twelve

Cusco and Vicinity

Introduction

Cusco lays claim to being the oldest continuously inhabited city in the Americas. It was the religious and administrative capital of the far-flung Inca empire, and the equivalent of Mecca for the Inca's subjects: every person of importance throughout the empire tried to visit Cusco once in his lifetime.

Tourists feel the same way. Cusco is indisputably the most beautiful and interesting town in Peru, and one of the finest on the whole continent. Nowhere else do you find the combination of splendid Inca stonework and elegant Spanish colonial architecture, Quechua and *mestizo*, traditional and modern. The tourist boom in the 1980s ensured that homesick gringos could munch their way through chocolate cake and pizza as well as *cuy* and *papas*, and luxuriate in top-quality hotels as well as backpacker *hostales*. And as one who remembers Cusco from 1969 I cannot say the town has been spoiled by tourism. For one thing it smells a lot better!

HISTORY OF THE INCAS

The Inca legend tells us that Cusco was founded by the son of the sun, Manco Capac, and the daughter of the moon, Mama Occllo, who materialized on the Islands of the Sun and Moon in Lake Titicaca and journeyed together to Cusco, 'the navel of the earth'. The Incas built their empire on the achievements of earlier cultures: the coastal peoples that they conquered have left an artistic legacy richer than that of the Incas. It was in the field of conquest and social organization that the Incas excelled. At the time of the conquest the empire stretched from the present-day Ecuador/Colombia border to the River Maule in southern Chile, bounded in the east by the Amazon jungle and in the west by the Pacific Ocean.

Expansion began around 1438 with the Inca ruler Pachacuti (Pachacuti Inca Yupanqui), who was largely instrumental in defeating the Chanca, long-time enemies inhabiting the region northwest of Cusco. His son Topa Inca continued to extend the empire and his efforts were consolidated in the next generation by Huayna Capac. The Inca conquered and ruled by a combination of conciliation and force. Nobles of the conquered groups were given important positions, and officials from the Cusco area settled in the remote reaches of the empire to teach the Quechua language and customs.

The empire was in decline before Pizarro reached Cajamarca. Before Huayna Capac died he divided the unwieldy empire in two: his son Atahualpa was to rule the north, whilst the south was under the control of Huáscar. Rivalry between the two half-brothers exploded into a civil war which Atahualpa eventually won around the time that the Spaniards reached the Peruvian coast. The story of what happened when they arrived in Cajamarca is told in that chapter.

The Inca empire was called Tawantinsuyo, meaning the four quarters of the earth. Cusco was the heart of it, and its exact centre was considered to be the main plaza of the city. To the north lay the Chinchaysuyo, to the west the Condesuyo, to the south the Collasuyo and east lay the Antisuyo. The name Andes comes from the original inhabitants of this region, the Antis.

The victorious Spaniards marched into Cusco and began to destroy it although, according to the chroniclers, they marvelled as they smashed. Gold was stripped from the walls and the great stones broken up to be used for Spanish buildings. What the *conquistadores* began, rebellion and natural disasters completed. An insurrection by Manco II left much of colonial Cusco in ruins, and a devastating earthquake in 1650 finished the job. The combined forces of man and nature, however, could not destroy the great Inca stone walls which stand to this day.

Subsequent centuries were punctuated with uprisings against Spanish rule, the most important one being led by the *mestizo* rebel Túpac Amaru II in 1780. Peru gained independence in 1826.

With the discovery, in 1911, of Machu Picchu by Hiram Bingham, Cusco was back in the limelight again and overseas visitors began to arrive to admire the mysterious ruins. Cusco was added to the list of the world's cultural heritage by UNESCO, which has been instrumental in conserving the visible remains of that great empire.

FESTIVALS

The area is well-known for its traditional celebrations, with most of them having an Inca/Spanish mix. It is well worth visiting one if you happen to be in the area.

- January 6, Ollantaytambo. Festival of the Magi, with dancing and parades.

- January 14, Pampamarca. Festival and market.
- January 20, Cusco. Procession of saint effigies in San Sebastián district.
- Easter Monday, Cusco. Parade of the Lord of the Earthquakes.
- May 2 and 3, at all mountaintops with a cross on them. The Vigil of the Cross.
- June, the Thursday after Trinity Sunday, Cusco. Corpus Christi. Saint effigies from all the churches of Cusco are brought to the cathedral to 'sleep' with the other saints, and paraded the following day.
- Early June, Qoyorití. The 'Star of the Snow' festival at a remote mountain site near Tinqui, north of Auzangate.
- June 17, Raqchi. The festival of Viracocha.
- June 24 and several days on either side, Cusco. Inti Raymi, the Inca festival of the winter solstice, celebrated at Sacsayhuamán.
- July 28. Independence Day.
- August 14, Tinta. Festival of San Bartolomé.
- September (date changes every year), Cusco. Huarachicoy festival at Sacsayhuamán. A re-enactment of the Inca manhood rite, performed in dancing and Inca games by the boys of the local schools.
- September 8, Chumbivilcas. Bullfights and horse races.
- September 14, Huanca. Religious pilgrimage to the shrine of El Señor de Huanca.
- November 1, All Saints' Day, celebrated everywhere with bread dolls and traditional cooking.
- November 4, Combapata. Local festival.
- December 24, Cusco. Santo Rantikuy, 'the buying of saints', a massive celebration of Christmas shopping in Cusco style.

CUSCO

You will see various spellings: Cusco, Cuzco or Qosqo (the Quechua spelling) but they all mean 'navel of the earth' or — more prosaically — centre of the empire. Some historians say that the Incas built Cusco in the shape of a puma, with the River Tullumayo (which now runs underground) forming its spine, Sacsayhuamán the head, and the main city centre the body.

Visitors should spend at least two days here getting used to the altitude (3,350m). Make the most of it — there is something for everyone: excellent shopping for handicrafts, the best Andean music, good food, fine colonial buildings, and of course the awe-inspiring Inca stonework. The crisp air, hot sun and clear blue sky of the winter dry season make it an ideal town for pottering around and there are plenty of coffee shops and juice bars to collapse into when you get tired.

Accommodation

You are spoilt for choice in Cusco, from luxury hotels to the basic backpackers' places. Prices are lower outside the tourist season and good deals can be expected at the upper-and mid-range hotels around that time. Most prices include taxes, but always check, and remember that prices given here are a guide only; they are likely to have gone up.

Top of the range

Libertador-Marriot, in a colonial building on Calle San Agustín 400. Tel: 231961. Single US$75/double $95.

Royal Inca I and II, Plaza Regocijo. Tel: 231067/234221. Single US$40/double $60.

El Dorado Inn, Av Sol 395. Tel: 231232. Single US$40/double $50.

Mid-range

Hostal Kristina, Av Sol 341. Tel: 227251. Single US$18/double $22.

Hostal Loreto, Pasaje Loreto 115, one block off the Plaza de Armas. Tel: 226352. Single US$12/double $18.

Hostal del Solar, Plaza San Francisco. Tel: 232451. Single US$12/double $20.

Hostal Corihuasi, Calle Suecia, block 4. Tel: 232233. Single US$15/double $23.

Budget

Hostal Suecia II, Calle Tecsecocha, block 2. Tel: 239757. Single US$9/double $12 (cheaper without bathroom).

Hostal Inca World, Calle Tecsecocha (opposite Suecia II). Single US$10/double $15.

Hostal Residencial Las Rojas, Calle Tigre 129. Single US$7/double $10.

Hostal Familiar, Calle Saphi 661. Single US$6/double $8.

Albergue Juvenil (youth hostel), Av Huarupata, in the suburb of Huanchac (20 minutes' ride from the Plaza de Armas). Tel: 223320. US$6 per person.

Restaurants

Most backpackers will want to try typical Andean dishes rather than international fare although the taste of home is welcome after a long trek.

Mesón de los Espaderos, off the Plaza de Armas on Espaderos and Plateros. Parrillada. *Cuy* sometimes on the menu.

Roma, Plaza de Armas. One of the original Cusco restaurants. Varied menu. Reliable. Folk music.

El Truco, Plaza de Cabildo. Popular with groups because of the good folk music, so quite expensive. Good food.

Pizzeria Morengo, Plaza Regocijo. For the homesick.

Govinda, Espaderos. Hare Krishna vegetarian restaurant. Excellent and cheap.

Quinta Eulalia, Choquechaca 384. Popular with the locals, a nice courtyard so best for lunch. *Cuy* is usually available.

Entertainment

As you'd expect in the tourist capital of Peru, there is plenty of choice. Peñas (nightclubs with folk music) include **Peña Do Re Mi** and **Los Incas**, both on the Plaza de Armas, and nightly folklore shows at **Centro Qosqo** de Arte Nativo, Av Sol 604 and Teatro Inti Raymi, Calle Saphi 605. The Teatro Municipal, Calle Mesón de la Estrella 149, shows plays, music and dancing on most nights.

The English-run Cross Keys Pub, on the Plaza de Armas, is a popular hang-out for travellers and a great meeting place.

Tourist information and useful addresses
Empresa Turística Regional Inka (Emturin), Portal Belén 115, on the Plaza de Armas. Tel: 223339. Open: Mon-Sat 09:30-13:00/15:00-18:00.

Ministry of Tourism, Av Manco Capac, 1020 4th floor, Huanchac. Tel: 233701-232347. Open: Mon-Fri 08:00-13:00.

Automóvil Club del Perú, Calle Pavitos 527. Tel: 224561.

The Universidad Nacional San Antonio, Av de la Cultura.

Tourist Police, Portal Belén 115, first floor, on the Plaza de Armas. Tel: 221961.

Immigration office, Av Sol, block 5. Open: Mon-Fri 08:00-13:00.

Telefonica (telephone company), Av Sol 386. Open: Mon-Sat 07:00-20:00, Sun and holidays 07:00-12:00. For local, national and international calls.

Post office, Av Sol, block 5. Open: Mon-Sat 08:00-19:00.

Medical help
Hospital Regional, Av de la Cultura.

Private doctors: Dr Oscar Tejada Ramírez; Tel: 233836, or Dr Jaime Triveño; Tel: 225513.

Tour operators
The first three are reliable and long-established. The others are cheaper but could be more risky, and there are many others.

Lima Tours, Portal de Harinos 177, Plaza de Armas. Tel: 238857.

Milla Tours, Av Pardo 675. Tel: 231710.

Explorandes, Avendia Sol, block 5. Tel: 238380.

Luzma Tours, Portal Confituría 241, Plaza de Armas. Tel: 226041.

Kantu Tours, Portal Carrizos 258, Plaza de Armas. Tel: 221381.

Snow Tours, Portal de Panes 109, oficina 204. Tel: 241313.

Instinct, Procuradores 50. Tel: 233451. For river trips.

Visitor's ticket
This ticket covers entrance fees to the main (but not all) churches, museums and ruins for US$10 (half price for students) with a validity of 10 days. It

can be bought at Emturin, Portal Belén, on the Plaza de Armas. It is possible, but more expensive, to purchase individual entrance tickets.

Getting there and away
By air
Flights are heavily booked and more expensive around school holidays (January/February and July/August) and national holidays, especially around Independence Day and Christmas.

The airport tax is US$3.50 and security tax US$1. Airport information, tel: 222611/222601. Always reconfirm flights.

To Lima. 1 hour. Prices always change, so check. Daily flights with Americana, Faucett, Aero Continente and AeroPerú.

To Arequipa. Half hour. Daily flights with Americana and a few weekly with Faucett, AeroPerú and Aero Continente. Some flights continue to Tacna.

To Juliaca. Half hour. Once a week with Faucett.

To La Paz. 1 hour. Lloyd Aéreo Boliviano has two flights a week; AeroPerú also flies there — check their schedule.

By road
To Juliaca (344km). 12 hours (longer in the rainy season). Daily buses and trucks, mostly at night. Poor road conditions. **On to Puno** (44km) 45 minutes. There is a good *colectivo* system between the two towns.

On to La Paz (Bolivia). 8 hours. *Colectivos* leave daily in the morning.

To Arequipa (521km). 18 hours (longer in the rainy season). Several buses and trucks a day. Poor road conditions.

To Abancay (195km). 6 hours (longer in the rainy season). Several buses and trucks a day. **On to Andahuaylas** (135km), 6 hours (longer in the rainy season).

On to Ayacucho (252km). 16 hours (longer in the rainy season. Poor road conditions.

NOTE: Always check the political situation in the Central Andes before travelling by road through these areas. The Abancay to Nazca route, in particular, has had security problems recently but may be safe by the time you read this.

By train
To Juliaca At Juliaca the line splits, one part going to Puno and the other to Arequipa. The train station is at the end of Avenida Sol, opposite the Hotel Savoy. There are daily trains in the dry season and a few a week in the rainy season (complete cancellation after heavy rainfalls) leaving at 07:45 and arriving in Juliaca at around 19:00. This station is frequented by

thieves, and changing trains here can be chaotic and time-consuming. One part of the train goes on to Puno and takes about an hour. The other goes to Arequipa, arriving at about 07:00 the next day.

Pullman/tourist class costs US$15 (only ticket holders are allowed on the train), first class $20 (reserved seats) and second class $15 (no reserved seats). Tickets are sold out quickly, especially before school and national holidays. You can get tickets from travel agencies, but always check the date and seat number and pay only when receiving the ticket.

To Machu Picchu Everyone takes the train since the site is not accessible by road. The station is next to the San Pedro church and market, in an area which used to have a bad reputation for theft. Security has been much improved recently. There is a local train (*tren local*) with three classes (buffet, first and second), which continues on to Quillabamba, and also an *auto-wagon* (tourist train) which terminates at Machu Picchu. Both have two departures daily.

The first train leaves Cusco at 06:20, arriving at Machu Picchu around 10:00. The second one leaves Cusco at 13:00, arriving at Machu Picchu around 17:00.

The first *auto-wagon* leaves Cusco at 06:00 and arrives at Machu Picchu around 09:00, and the second leaves Cusco at 12:45 and arrives at Machu Picchu around 15:45.

The *auto-wagon* costs US$20, buffet class $12, first class $5, second class $4. You can also buy tourist tickets which include transport by train and bus up to the ruins, entrance fee, guide service and food, for about $85.

NOTE: Time schedules change, so check.

HIKING INFORMATION
Climate
The weather here is typical for the Central Andes, with a dry season (April to October) and rainy season (November to March). If you can only visit in the rainy season don't be downhearted. Apart from the really wet months of January and February you are likely to have some sunny days, and mornings are often fine. Most days are clear and sunny in the dry season but you should still be prepared for rain or — more likely on the high passes — snow.

Acclimatization
Adjusting to the altitude is no hardship here. Take time to see the marvels of Cusco and the Urubamba valley before you set off for the mountains.

Guides, *arrieros* and pack animals

You do not need a guide for most of the trails described here and in Chapter Thirteen (they are popular and quite easy to follow) but if you are venturing off the beaten path you would do well to hire one, as much for security reasons as to find the way. There is plenty of choice, so try to get a recommendation from a reliable local person or another traveller. Clarify all details before you set out, pay half the money in advance, and sign an agreement.

Pack animals can be organized in Cusco through a trekking agency, but if you speak Spanish it will be cheaper to do it yourself in the village at the trailhead. Around Cusco, as elsewhere, most *arrieros* are members of an organization and there are set prices: *arrieros* US$6 a day and *burros* $3. But these can vary from area to area and may well have gone up by the time you read this. For the Inca Trail, which is not suitable for animals, you can hire porters (see Chapter Thirteen).

Renting equipment

Several trekking agencies in Cusco rent out camping equipment. There are also some equipment rental shops. The quality is poor, so check all items carefully before paying your deposit. Prices per day: tent US$3, sleeping bag $2, stove $3.

Food and supplies

Buy all your trail food in Cusco. Between the markets and supermarkets the selection is good. Start your search down Avenida Sol. Buy extra food for your *arriero* if you are hiring pack animals or using porters.

Maps and books

Unfortunately the Instituto Geográfico Nacional, that normally reliable source of hiking maps, has not yet got round to mapping the most popular trekking areas in the Cordillera Vilcabamba. There is a map of the Department of Cusco (scale 1:400,000) which is some help in planning, and topographical maps (1:100,000) for the area from Calca, Cusco and to the south.

Many tour operators sell a small map of the Inca Trail, but the best map of this trail is from the South American Explorers Club in Lima. The club also publishes a good map of the Auzangate circuit.

Cusco has a couple of good bookshops where you should be able to purchase the most informative and best-written guide to the area: *Exploring Cusco*, by Peter Frost. Other books which include sections relevant to Cusco are listed in *Further reading* at the back.

HIKING ROUTES AROUND CUSCO

The area around Cusco is a delight for hikers. Here you can step back in time and see a rural way of life that has hardly changed for four hundred years: women spin as they walk along the trails, carrying babies in their brightly coloured woven *mantas*; herds of llamas and alpacas peer at you curiously, donkeys and mules are driven round and round over the freshly cut wheat or barley to separate the grain from the chaff, and the earth is still dug using the ancient Inca foot plough.

In the valleys near the thatched huts of the descendants of the Incas, and high on the hills far from human habitation, are the marvellous remains of that mighty empire: stone walls and temples of a grace and strength unique in the Americas and backed by a range of snow-covered mountains.

The hikes detailed are just a beginning and there are lots of other possibilities. If you do go out exploring by yourself, please respect the culture, make contact with the local people and ask permission when you want to camp on their land. Do not be the instrument of change, environmental or social. Your responsibility is to keep these places as they are. The following hikes are described.

Inca ruins around Cusco
Tambomachay to Pisac
San Jerónimo to Huanca
Cusco-Huchuy-Qosqo-Calca hike
Chinchero-Urubamba Valley hikes
From Chinchero to Huayllabamba
From Chinchero to Urubamba
From Chinchero to Maras (ruins of Moray), Salinas and the Urubamba River
The Valley of Lares

Inca ruins around Cusco

For most people Sacsayhuamán and the nearby ruins are their first introduction to Cusco's Inca past — and the breath-taking effects of its altitude. To do the full distance would be too much for a new arrival: until you are fit and acclimatized, limit yourself to sections and take it slowly, both to appreciate the ruins and to ease your breathing. Bring your visitor's ticket (see page 177).

Practical information

Distance	20km (10km if you find transport back to Cusco)
Altitude	Between 3,500m and 3,900m
Rating	Easy
Timing	One day

In reverse	Possible, and easier (downhill)
Start of the trail	Plaza de Armas, Cusco
Safety	Robberies have happened in and around the ruins. Try to go in a small group. If alone, don't carry any valuables.

Route description

Sacsayhuamán is a massive Inca temple-fortress overlooking Cusco. It's a steep half hour's walk to the site, beginning at Calle Suecia which runs from the upper corner of the Plaza de Armas by the cathedral. Keep going uphill, taking the track rather than the road, until you reach the gigantic walls that are Sacsayhuamán.

Everything that is 'known' about the origin and purpose of Sacsayhuamán is pure speculation. Every tourist guide has a different story. Some claim that it is pre-Inca, others that it is very early Inca. As in all matters pertaining to Cusco, I find Peter Frost's *Exploring Cusco* the best short account, though serious students of the Incas should read one of the experts, such as John Hemming. To the casual visitor, it scarcely matters why the massive zig-zag walls (attributed to defence — in the event of an attack the enemy would expose his flank — or to the deities of lightning or the puma) were built. They are one of the wonders of Peru, and the most accessible example of massive Inca stone masonry. Climb to the top of the mound to see the 'reservoir' or astrological structure, built in a circle with 12 radiating 'spokes'. Most likely this was the foundation of a tower, with an underground system of water channels. Opposite the giant walls, across the 'parade ground' which is now used for the spectacle of Inti Raymi on June 24, are naturally eroded rocks, some with Inca carvings. This is popularly known as the Inca's Throne, and the rocks make good slides for young Inca descendants and gringos alike.

Women bring their llamas for a highly profitable graze in the Parade Ground. They are extremely photogenic and well aware of their current worth. Bring plenty of change, and don't be conned into paying more than the equivalent of 50 cents or so for a photograph.

From Sacsayhuamán hike up the hill (east) to the statue of Jesus, and then follow the road to the sign for Qenco (Kenko). A path to the right will bring you to this unusual site. Qenco is a huge limestone rock, naturally eroded, and skilfully carved both on top and within its caves. It is full of enigmas, too. The rock monolith in front could have had a phallic significance (unlikely, the Incas seem not too impressed with the phallus as a symbol of power), or could be a desecrated carving of a puma ... or what you will. The delicate zig-zag carvings on top of the rock were probably ceremonial channels for *chicha*, and the beautifully carved cave must surely have been associated with Pachamama, Mother Earth.

From Qenco continue east along the trail for about 15 minutes and you'll reach Cusillyuioc (Temple of the Monkeys) although you will be puzzled by the name as you explore the caves and tunnels. Continue east for another 15 minutes to Salumpunku, another carved rock. There are usually children around who'll be delighted to show you the main features: a carved cave and altar, a very eroded puma shape and a sundial. Salumpunku lies about 1.5km from the road to Pisac (to the east) via a dirt road.

Follow the road to the ruins of Puca Pucara, about 6km from the junction with the dirt road; you'll see the sign to your right. This site is unimpressive, but across the road lie the Inca Baths of Tambomachay which are well worth seeing. Inca 'Baths' were to do with ritual bathing rather than washing, and this is an excellent example of the Inca fascination with water and their ability to direct it where they wanted. Water is channelled through three stone outlets and is pure enough to drink.

If you are tired, there should be buses or *colectivos* to take you back to Cusco. Otherwise you can return the way you came.

Tambomachay to Pisac

Tambomachay marks the end of one hike but the beginning of another. You cross the mountain range behind Cusco, dropping down the other side to Calca in the Urubamba Valley. The varied sights and scenery include an Inca ruin, typical villages and traditional agriculture.

Practical information

Distance	25km
Altitude	From 3,500m to 3,900m, then down to 2,930m
Rating	Long in distance but fairly easy hiking apart from the steep descent to Pisac
Timing	1-2 days
In reverse	Possible, but more difficult, with a steep climb up from Calca
Start of the trail	Tambomachay. Take a tour which culminates in Tambomachay, or the bus or *colectivo* towards Pisac, leaving from Cusco's Avenida Tacna. Get off at the ruins — about 45 minutes from Cusco.

Route description

The trail starts about 100m down the road from the ruins. Take the well-marked trail up the hill, then through farmland passing a few farmhouses, and climb the slope to the pass, admiring the views of Cusco from the top. This should take you about 1 hour.

Follow the path to the right, along the mountain slope, passing through two valleys and climbing to a ridge above the little village of Qorimarca below — about 45 minutes. The path descends into the valley, with an aqueduct to your right. Pass through Qorimarca and continue down the valley, following the main road until you reach a concrete bridge over the stream to your left in 45 minutes or so. The main road continues down the valley and connects with the paved road from Cusco to Pisac.

Cross the concrete bridge. Your goal from here is the top of the mountain range. You have several options, so get your bearings:

1) Up the left-hand valley: A road has been constructed all the way to the pass to service the pipeline that supplies Cusco with water from Laguna Qoricocha up in the mountains. Take the direct route to the top, following the footpath which crosses the road several times until you reach the edge of the lake. Pass the lake to your right and continue climbing to the highest point of the mountain range in front of you. From here you can see the village of Patabamba on the edge of the *pampa*. It will take about 4-5 hours from the bridge to here.

2) Up the middle valley: Start up the left-hand valley following the road and taking shortcuts, until a smaller valley, with a stream, opens up to your right. Follow the path up to the highest point of the mountain range in front of you, keeping first to your right and then up the mountain ridge to your left. At the top you get a great view over Laguna Qoricocha, and can see Patabamba below. It takes about 4 hours from the bridge to the top.

3) Up the right-hand valley: Make a right turn after the bridge and hike up through the village to the valley furthest to the right, which has the advantage of leading to the lowest pass. Start climbing to the top of the ridge, keeping to the right of the stream. At the top the area flattens out and you'll walk through farmland. Hike up to the highest point of the mountain range, where you can enjoy a great view and the sight of Patabamba below you.

From this point there is only one possibility. Descend to Patabamba and continue through the village to the edge of the ridge (stay to the right and ask the locals for the path to Taray and Pisac). You'll see the Urubamba Valley far below you. Give your knees a pep-talk and start the descent. To add to your misery fine sand from the soft white rock of the mountainside covers the trail and makes it slippery. Learn from the crab: sideways may be safer. At some point stop to admire one of the Inca's most amazing feats: canalizing the Río Vilcanota so it runs dead straight for over 3,000m, probably to conserve the farmland on the sides. Once the trail levels out, continue up the valley towards Pisac, passing through the small village of Taray. It takes about 2 hours from Patabamba to Pisac.

From San Jerónimo to Huanca

The destination for this hike is one of the landmarks of the Sacred Valley. Tour groups from Cusco often ask their guides about the large, red-roofed church which stands, seemingly alone, on the mountainside. This is the Sanctuary of El Señor de Huanca, and pilgrims have been coming here since 1674 when Our Lord made a miraculous appearance before an Indian miner. For good measure He appeared again in 1713, this time shrewdly choosing a rich landowner as witness, hence the handsome church that commemorates the event.

This is a long day-hike (if you don't want to bother with camping gear) or two days if you want to be more leisurely and are getting acclimatized for trekking. The trail is clear, but steep and rough in places. It's best to stay the night at Huanca since transport back to Cusco is erratic. Always carry plenty of water.

Practical information

Distance	15km
Altitude	From 3,300m to 4,250m and down to 2,950m
Rating	Easy
Timing	7-8 hours
In reverse	Possible
Start of the trail	San Jerónimo, a town to the east of Cusco. *Colectivos* run there from Plaza San Francisco in Cusco every 10 minutes. The journey takes an hour. A taxi will cost around US$3.

Route description

Leave early if you want to do this hike in one day. A road has been constructed from San Jerónimo all the way to the pass (eventually it will run all the way to Huanca) so if you are in a taxi and want to cheat a bit, have the driver take you to the top. The road does take away some of the beauty and remoteness in this mountain area, but mostly you will be following the footpath, which only crosses the road a few times.

If you are hiking up from San Jerónimo, start from the plaza on the right-hand side of the church, following the street and turning left at the first opportunity. Follow this road to the end of the village, making a right turn at the end, and continue on the footpath which goes slowly uphill through eucalyptus groves. Ask the locals if you're not sure. The path is an old Inca road, passing some *tambos* (Inca rest places) and following an Inca aqueduct up the mountain ridge. It takes about 2-2½ hours to the top of this plateau. You can see a few farmhouses to the right, and the road winds its way up the mountain to the right. After the houses on your left the footpath climbs up in the same direction as the road, but passes the highest point on the left.

At the first pass at 3,700m, which you will reach in about half an hour, you can see the village of Huaccoto on the other side of the valley. Descend down into the valley and towards the village; this a further half hour. Walk through this small, typical Quechua village, taking the well-marked path (with loose stones) up the hill to your right. The path makes a left turn, winding around the mountainside above the village. Soon you reach the top, which has a cross on it. An open *pampa* stretches in front of you. Continue up the *pampa*, keeping left, until you reach the pass and the highest point on this hike at 4,250m — about 2½ hours from Huaccoto. The pass gives a spectacular view over the Urubamba Valley. The mountain to your right is called Pachatusan (4,950m). Just a few metres below the pass on the other side, on top of a cliff, you'll see the remains of an Inca building which probably served as a guard post overlooking the Sacred Valley.

As you descend you'll see the church roof below you on the right. A well-marked path descends down along the steep slope. The descent takes about 1-1½ hours. Take time to visit the church and its painted rock which commemorates the first miracle and is now part of the altar.

From the sanctuary to the village of Huanca it's a half-hour walk with a further half hour to go to San Salvador. From here you can get transport back to Cusco via Pisac — a 2-hour journey.

Cusco-Huchuy Qosqo-Calca

This is a treat of a walk, taking you through lovely countryside and over the mountains just outside Cusco, with spectacular views, interesting and seldom-visited Inca ruins, then down the Urubamba Valley.

Practical information

Distance	31km
Altitude	From 3,350m to 4,350m and down to 2,930m
Rating	Moderate, with four high passes
Timing	Two days
In reverse	Possible
Start of the trail	Cusco or Sacsayhuamán

Route description

Hike or take a taxi up to the ruins of Sacsayhuamán, passing the site on your left and following the path up to the road where you turn right. After about 150m, just before the house, turn left following a small footpath up the valley. This widens as you climb. Continue up, passing a radio mast, until you come to a dirt road. You can see the Cusco-Pisac road to your right. Cross the dirt road and continue hiking up the hill along the fairly obvious trail which parallels with the Cusco-Pisac road for a while.

Follow this trail all the way up to the first pass at 4,200m — 3 hours. Go down the valley along the left-hand slope until you come to the stream at the bottom. The path splits going up on the other side: it doesn't matter which one you choose, they both lead to the second pass at 4,300m, from where you'll see the small Laguna Quellacocha lying in the valley in front of you. Descend on the high trail round the north end of the lake, ignoring the path that leads off to the left. Climb east to the third pass at 4,250m (about 3-4 hours). From the top you can see Laguna Qoricocha to your right. There are campsites in both this valley and the next one.

Continue along the trail leading northeast over the next ridge and on to the fourth pass at 4,300m. Descend into the valley ahead of you, keeping to the right. Get directions from the *campesinos* whenever possible — the trail disappears in places.

After a while you'll see the village of Pucamarca. Below it the valley forms a steep ravine, and on the right is a platform with Inca walls. Cross this and find a steep, well-preserved Inca stairway descending into the ravine. At the narrowest part of the ravine, cross to the left bank. The trail traverses around the mountainside (west) for a spectacular view of the Urubamba Valley. The path leads through an Inca gateway: the entrance to the ruins of Huchuy Qosqo.

Huchuy Qosqo means 'Small Cusco' in Quechua. Little is known about this extensive and mysterious site, although Charles Brod in his book *Apus and Incas* quotes John Hemming's theory that these buildings may have been built as a tribute to the conquering Inca Viracocha by the local tribe, and could have been used by the Inca lord as a 'country retreat' from Cusco. Brod writes:

> 'As you enter into the ruins you can see a small reservoir that is choked with weeds but still functions... The main buildings are grouped around a walled-in, sunken area that may have served as a swimming pool, though no water channel is apparent. Located in a far upper corner of the complex, a stone enclosed by high walls and large niches is reminiscent of the pinnacle at Qenco, but its sacred function has been lost to time.
>
> 'At the main plaza, a long building with six doorways stands above the terrace wall. This is a *kallanka*, a large building that once had a peaked roof covering it. These structures were constructed around the main plazas in the principal towns of the empire to house soldiers, labourers and other transient people. It was from buildings like this one that Pizarro and his men made their desperate charge on the Inca Atahualpa at Cajamarca, capturing him and massacring thousands of his Indian troops.'

To continue on to Calca, cross the stream to the left of the ruins when facing the Urubamba Valley (ask the caretaker at the ruins for directions). Follow the path up to the mountain ridge, passing a farmhouse. From the ridge it's an obvious, but steep and tiring zig-zag path down into the Urubamba Valley. Be careful; it can be slippery on the loose gravel. On the valley floor the trail turns left along the base of the cliffs to the dirt road. It follows the river, passes a small building (the mineral-water baths of Minas Mocco) and continues to a bridge which you cross to reach Calca.

Chinchero-Urubamba Valley hikes

Chinchero is on the tourist route, but a perfect example of the resilience of the Andean Indian to outside influences. The Sunday market is still amazingly colourful, full of traditionally dressed women in the regional cartwheel hats, and geared as much to the villagers' needs as to those of the milling tourists. Women sit in groups by their produce, fry fish, or serve *chicha* from earthenware pots. Others sell handicrafts.

Chinchero is well worth visiting, even on a weekday, for the impressive Inca stone wall forming one side of the plaza, and some wonderful terracing with very fine stonework. The town used to be an important Inca centre and there are many examples of their stone carving. If you walk down the Inca stairs which start behind and below the church to the left of the terraces, you'll come to the main trail going down the valley. There are two large rocks near the path, with carved stairs, seats and water channels.

These walks are three of several which take you into the Urubamba valley with its many Inca sites and transport back to Cusco. At the high point there are lovely views over the Cordilleras Vilcabamba and Vilcanota.

Leave Chinchero by noon at the latest (preferably earlier) to be sure of reaching the valley floor before dark. Always carry water on these hikes; the valley is pretty dry and hot, especially in the dry season.

Chinchero to Huayllabamba

This trail is a fine example of an Inca road, with the ruins of a *tambo*, an Inca posthouse, half way.

Distance	8km
Altitude	From 3,500m down to 2,760m
Rating	Easy
Timing	4 hours
In reverse	Possible, but a steep climb from the valley so it will take longer
Start of route	Chinchero

Route description From the plaza of Chinchero you can see the trail on the opposite hill, climbing up to the right (north). Follow the trail up the slope, heading northeast. It makes a turn around the slope and starts descending, staying to the left of the Quebrada Urquillos and dropping steeply to the small village at the bottom. From here continue along the road leading down the valley to the village of Huayllabamba, a few kilometres away (note this is not the same Huayllabamba as on the Inca Trail). At Huayllabamba a bridge crosses the river and puts you on the main road through the Urubamba Valley.

Chinchero to Urubamba
A pleasant hike through a patchwork quilt of farmland, with good views of the *cordilleras*.

Distance	10km
Altitude	From 3,500m down to 2,865m
Rating	Easy
Timing	3-4 hours
In reverse	Possible, but hard work and longer
Start of the trail	Chinchero

Route description Follow the old Chinchero-Urubamba dirt road, which leads off to the left when leaving Chinchero. Ask the *campesinos* if you're not sure. The dirt road makes its way over the *pampa*, crossing the paved road, and continues until the edge of the valley. From here the route drops into the valley, following a pretty obvious trail, although it does fade away in places. It's hard to get lost, however, as you just need to head down the valley until you reach the river. Here you join up with the paved road again, which crosses the Urubamba River by a bridge and takes you into Urubamba.

Urubamba is a pleasant place to spend the night (there are several hotels) and is a good base for exploring the Sacred Valley where there are numerous walks.

Chinchero to Maras (ruins of Moray), Salinas and the Urubamba River
This is a longer hike than the others. It takes you through interesting countryside and Quechua villages, but its outstanding feature is the three very different but equally impressive ancient sites visited en route.

Chinchero has already been described: a classic of traditional imperial Inca stone walls and terraced farmland, with a small colonial church thrown in for good measure. Moray is quite different: unique, in fact. It is not the ruins of a city or a fortress, but an earthwork. The ancient peoples of the region took four huge natural depressions in the landscape and sculpted them into agricultural terraces that served, hundreds of years ago, as an experimental agricultural station for the development of different crop strains. Much of the terracing survives intact, leaving regular concentric layers flowing harmoniously into the land. The interest here is more subtle than the massive walls of the Inca sites, it is a place more for contemplation than admiration.

Salinas, as the name suggests, is a village of salt. A salt river runs down the mountainside, partly underground, and since pre-Hispanic times salt has been collected here in hundreds of artificial salt pans, using a natural process of evaporation.

Distance	27km
Altitude	From 3,760m up to 4,057m and down to 2,865m
Rating	Easy walking, but a long day unless you take a car for the first part
Timing	8-9 hours
In reverse	Possible if you find transport for the last stretch into Chinchero; otherwise not feasible in one day because of the steep climb.
Start of the trail	Chinchero

Route description Leave Chinchero in the direction of Urubamba and follow the paved road until the turn-off to Maras in about 11km. If you want to avoid the long road-walk, catch a ride with one of the many buses or *colectivos* on this route. From the turn-off follow the gravel road to Maras (3,760m), about 4km. This is a colonial town, which used to thrive on mining the salt deposits in the cliffs to the north. Now it is smaller and you can only expect to buy basic supplies here.

The trail to Moray (Huaynuymarca) leads westwards, away from the town in roughly the same direction you followed from the paved road, at right angles to the main street. Ask the locals for directions as the path is hard to find.

Follow the path until you reach the first ravine (6-8m deep), cross it on a log bridge, and continue until the second ravine (about 30m deep). Cross the bridge again. Don't continue along this main trail up the slope to the right. Take, instead, the path that climbs to the left, almost straight up the slope, passing a farmhouse and two small ponds; you'll be able to see a large signboard in the distance bearing the name of the site. Aim for that, crossing the third ravine (about 15m deep), to arrive at Moray, about 7km/ 1½ hours from Maras. Here, as well as the earthwork and terraces described earlier, there are the remains of an irrigation system.

A dirt road connects Moray to Salinas (3,385m), about 5km/1½ hours away. Approaching Salinas from above like this is ideal: it is an astonishing and extremely photogenic site. The pans look like a giant white honeycomb, with the small bee-like figures of Indians bustling around the rims harvesting their 'crop'.

To finish the hike follow the trail down the left side of the valley from Salinas to the Urubamba River. If you turn left when you reach the river you'll come to the picturesque village of Pichinjoto. Turn right here and you'll soon reach a footbridge over the river. Cross it and follow the trail another 500m to the main road of the Urubamba Valley about 5km from Salinas. Turn right to reach Urubamba in about 6km.

Thanks to Peter Frost for information from his book Exploring Cusco.

The valley of Lares

The valley of Lares is the place for explorers who want to get away from popular trails. To add to the adventure there are no IGN maps and the information we have is only sufficient to tell you whether you are lost or not — but not how to avoid getting lost. Good luck!

A dirt road runs into the Lares Valley from Calca, so you can catch a truck in and out. The whole region is scattered with impressive Inca and pre-Inca remains. Little is known about these ruins and paths are hard to find. If you are looking for a local guide, Paulino Mamani is recommended. You can contact him in Calca at Calle Cahuide 325.

Practical Information

Altitude	From 3,000m to 4,000m
Rating	Easy to moderate
Timing	4-8 days
Start of the trail	Calca, about 2 hours from Cusco. From Calca you can usually find a truck into the Lares Valley, leaving around 07:00-08:00. Get off at Paucarpata. The ride takes about 3 hours.

Route suggestions

We can give you approximate times: beyond that you're on your own.

From Paucarpata, hike up the valley on your right (northeast) to Laguna Alojohuay — about 2½ hours. From this lake you can continue 1½ hours to Laguna Pumacocha, and go on from here to the ruins of Umapata in about 5 hours. From Umapata to the ruins of Tambo Cancha is a further 3½ hours, and you can continue to the ruins of Torre Moro in 3 hours. The route returns the same way to Paucarpata, taking 2 days.

From Paucarpata to the ruins of Choquecancha is about 3 hours, with another 1½ hours needed to reach the ruins of Aucani. Further ruins at Lucamarca lie about an hour away. From Lucamarca to the ruins of Chachin will take 4 hours or so, and on to the ruins of Ancasmarca a further 5 hours. Callispujio ruins are some 2 hours away, and then back to base in Calca in about an hour.

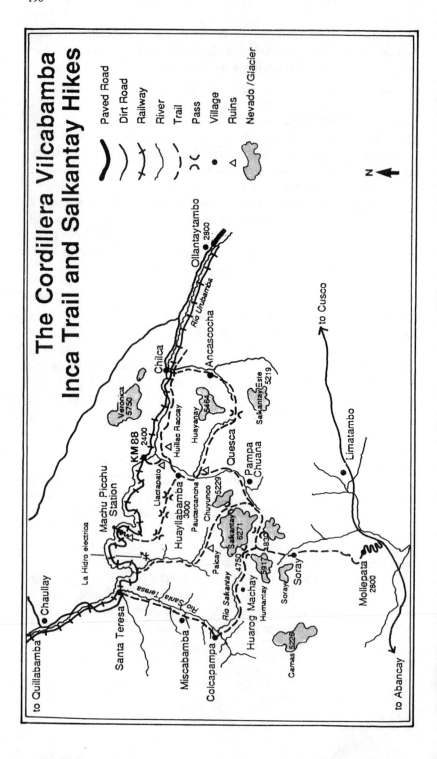

The Cordillera Vilcabamba
Inca Trail and Salkantay Hikes

Paved Road
Dirt Road
Railway
River
Trail
Pass
Village
Ruins
Nevado / Glacier

N

to Quillabamba

Chaullay

Santa Teresa

La Hidro electrica

Miscabamba

Colcapampa

Machu Picchu Station

KM88
2400

Veronica
5750

Chilca

Ollantaytambo
2800

Rio Urubamba

Ancascocha

Huillac Raccay

Huayanay
5464

Llactapato

Huayllabamba
3000

Paucarcancha

Chuyunco
5229

Quesca

Pampa Chuana

Sakantay Este
5219

Rio Santa Teresa

Rio Salkantay

Pakay

Salkantay
6271

Huarog Machay

Humantay
5917

Soray
2830

Soray

Soray

Camas
5226

Mollepata
2800

Limatambo

to Cusco

to Abancay

£76.50

Perry Thorton
0893
£1
3/6 - Bell - 01252 -346099
1

Emma Rolf? - Curchods
HORSLEY
01483-281010

Richard Morgan

Ask if they

want

all

the

curtains?

1. ½
1
2
_____
5

1
_____
8 h.

Chapter Thirteen

The Cordilleras
Vilcabamba and Vilcanota

Introduction

Now you are acclimatized, you are ready to tackle some of the longer walks
that are the goal of most of the hikers who come to Cusco. The Cordilleras
Vilcabamba and Vilcanota offer some of the best hiking on the continent;
not only snow covered mountains, but sub-tropical valleys and outstanding
Inca ruins, along with the traditional way of life unchanged for so many
centuries.

Below is a list of hikes covered in this chapter.

THE INCA TRAIL
From Kilometre 88
From Ollantaytambo or Chilca to Llactapata
From Chilca to Huayllabamba

SALKANTAY HIKES
From Mollepata to Soray
From Soray to Huayllabamba
From Soray to Santa Teresa
From Soray to La Hidroeléctrica

VILCABAMBA HIKE

AUZANGATE HIKES
The Auzangate Circuit
From Pitumarca to Laguna Sibinacocha
From Pitumarca to Tinqui, via Chillca
From Raqchi to Pitumarca or Tinqui via Chilca

THE INCA TRAIL

This is deservedly the most famous footpath in South America. It has everything: gorgeous mountain scenery, cloudforest and lush sub-tropical vegetation with numerous species of flowers, a stunning destination (Machu Picchu) and, above all, the Inca remains that give the trail its name. There are Inca paving stones, Inca stairways, an Inca tunnel, and of course the ruins: Runkuracay, Sayacmarca, Phuyupatamarca, Huiñay Huayna (Wiñay Wayna) and Machu Picchu itself.

Getting organized

You do not need a guide for the Inca Trail — the way is clear — but many people opt for porters so they can fully enjoy the hiking. If you only want to hire porters but do not want any of the other trimmings of an organized trek, you'd do best to hire your porters in Ollantaytambo. If you don't want to backpack it is probably easier to sign up on an organized trek in Cusco. This way all the logistics are taken care of, including food and equipment. Be very selective about choosing a tour company or guide. Discuss and write down all details beforehand. There have been problems with cheap and consequently poor-quality tours which don't fulfil their promises, supply poor camping equipment and food, leave garbage behind and don't pay the porters. Be wary of choosing the cheapest, and if you are not happy with the organization take time to report it to one of the conservation groups in Cusco (see page 196).

The price of an organized trip ranges from about US$60 to $300 per person for four days. It all depends on how informed and comfortable you want to be: the quality of the equipment, food and guide, if the local or the tourist train is used, the number of porters and the experience of the guide. Make a list of the services you'd like on the trail before choosing a tour company.

If you arrive in Cusco alone and want to backpack the Inca Trail in company, ask around at the backpacker *hostales*. Within a few days you will have got a group together.

What to bring

Because so many people with no previous hiking experience do this trail it is worth emphasizing the importance of careful preparations. Remember that tinned food is heavy and you will be tempted to leave the cans behind: bring packaged, dehydrated foods such as dried soup, thin noodles (which cook quickly), cheese, some fruit, and chocolate and raisins for energy. Rice takes a long time to cook so uses up your valuable fuel supplies. Oatmeal (*avena*) cooks quickly, and is filling and energy-producing. You will be drinking purified water so bring something to hide the taste of iodine.

Lemons are good value for weight.

Be prepared for hot days and freezing nights. An alpaca sweater is light and warm so ideal for the Inca Trail. Longjohns will help keep you warm at night and weigh very little. A woollen Cusco hat will make a big difference on the cold nights as will fingerless gloves or mittens. A scarf (muffler) takes up almost no room and keeps your neck and chest cosy.

Be prepared for rain.

Don't forget a good supply of plastic bags for carrying out your rubbish, toilet roll and matches (so you can burn it), and 'Wet-Ones' or equivalent for washing when water is scarce.

Bring insect repellent against the very persistent midges in the lower areas.

Safety

It is not dangerous to hike the Inca Trail. During the worst of the Sendero Luminoso era horror stories abounded, but they were mostly just that: stories. Yes, a couple of Dutch hikers were murdered, but by their German and Norwegian travelling companions (no one knows why). Robbery (armed) has happened on the Inca Trail, but only on the first part, close to the village. This opportunist sort of attack is still very rare, given the number of hikers who do the trail each year (about 5,000). Camp only in the designated campsites. There is no problem with hiking alone, because the truth is that you won't be alone on this trail; there will always be other hikers starting off with you at Kilometre 88.

Another, perhaps more important, safety consideration is the slippery state of some of the Inca stairways in the rainy season. During these months (December to March/April) the trail can be very muddy, and the passes covered in clouds and/or snow. Be careful.

Conservation

The Inca Trail has been abused by hikers for over 20 years. Litter is the main problem, but this is mainly aesthetic. Pollution of water supplies by human faeces is more serious, and worst of all is the destruction of Inca stonework by lighting fires. Damage done here is irreversible.

Most readers of this book will be only too aware of the need and importance of leaving no trace of their passing. They should try to encourage the local people — the worst culprits because their needs and values are different — to protect their heritage. A little money goes a long way in persuading porters to clean up an area.

Small organizations have always been the most effective in taking care of the Inca Trail. The first clean-up was done by the South American Explorers Club along with the Peruvian Andean Club in 1980. It took years to get permission to remove the rubbish. The team collected 400kg of tin cans along with a mini-mountain of other trash. Other organizations, such as the Earth Preservation Fund, continued the job. They picked up 700kg of rubbish.

The impetus needs to come from local people, however. The organizations below are involved in conservation. Your encouragement may help them to be more involved.

Instituto National de la Cultura (INC), Calle San Bernardo, Cusco. They collect the entrance fees to the Inca Trail and Machu Picchu. In theory this money is used to conserve the area.

Instituto Regional del Inca, next door to the Hospital Seguro on Av de la Cultura, Cusco.

National Parks Department, Av Sol, between blocks 5 and 6, Cusco.

Ministry of Tourism, Av Manco Capac, 1020, 4th floor, Huanchac, Cusco.

Starting points
All routes end in Machu Picchu (it is forbidden to do the trail in reverse) but there are various starting points. The most popular starts at Kilometre 88 (inaccessible by road, but the train stops here). Organized groups usually start in Ollantaytambo because they can drive there with all the equipment and meet the porters there.

From Kilometre 88
Getting to the trailhead
Take the *tren local* (see page 179) from Cusco or Ollantaytambo. It's a 3-hour journey from Cusco to Kilometre 88 which is immediately after the first tunnel, about 22km beyond Ollantaytambo. You can't miss it: a surge of hikers with backpacks will make for the train door. If you can't see any other backpackers ask the conductor or keep an eye out of the right-side window for the kilometre markers.

Practical information
Distance	49.5km
Altitude	Between 2,400m and 4,198m
Rating	Moderate
Timing	3 to 4 days (note: the hiking times given below are for trekkers rather than backpackers who should add at least a half hour to the times).
In reverse	Not permitted
Entrance fee	It costs US$20 per person (in *soles*) to hike the Inca Trail. The price includes the entrance to the ruins of Machu Picchu, so save your ticket until the end.

Route description

At Kilometre 88 (2,400m) you walk down to the entrance, pay your fee and sign in, cross the bridge and make a left turn following the trail gently uphill through a eucalyptus grove to Llactapata and the first major ruins on the route. Vast retaining walls have converted the steeply sloping hillside into agricultural terraces: an amazing sight. There is a campsite here, and it is a suitable stop for the first night for those who have arrived on the afternoon train.

Just below Llactapata the Río Cusichaca, a tributary of the Urubamba, takes a spectacular plunge into the ground and runs through a subterranean channel for some way. The trail climbs steeply out of the ruins over a low pass, and the hike up the valley begins. After about an hour you'll reach a bridge, putting you on the other side of the valley, and will continue on to the village of Huayllabamba (3,000m). You will reach it in a further half hour. By this time it is likely to be very hot and you will welcome the soft drinks at the village which makes its living out of Inca Trail hikers.

At Huayllabamba the trail turns right (northwest) up the Llullucha valley. After slogging and sweating upwards for about 1½ hours you will drop down to a grassy clearing, popularly known as The Forks. There is a designated campsite here. The path then enters woods — first scrub, then very beautiful cloud forest where the trees are hung with moss. These fairy-tale woods will help keep your mind off the fact that you are still going steeply uphill with no sign of respite. Eventually, however, the trees become more stunted and you emerge into a meadow, Llulluchapampa. From The Forks to the meadow is about 2 hours. This is the last campsite before the pass, aptly named Abra de Huarmihuañusqa, 'Dead Woman's Pass' (4,198m), which you can see ahead of you.

It will take you about 1½ hours to climb to the top of the pass. This is the highest point on the trail, so take heart — if you survive this, you'll survive the other passes. Take time to look around you. You should be able to pick out the circular ruins of Runkuracay ahead, just below the next pass. The descent is steep but not difficult. Just follow the trail on the left side of the valley to the valley floor and the next designated campsite at Pacamayo (3,600m). From the valley floor it will take you about an hour to reach Runkuracay, a ruin not, perhaps, very impressive in itself, but occupying a commanding position overlooking the valley, and at the end of a series of rock-hewn steps that at last give you a feeling that you are on the trail of the Incas. There is another campsite here.

From Runkuracay the path is clear over the second pass (Abre de Runkuracay, 4,000m) and, excitingly, much of the time you are on Inca steps. The descent down the steps is steep, so take care. Just before the trail turns right, you'll see the sign for Sayacmarca. These ruins lie about an hour from the top of the pass and the name, which means 'the Secret City', is apt. You approach Sayacmarca up a superbly designed stone staircase. This is a diversion (the main trail continues its gradual descent to the right) but don't let fatigue persuade you to miss it.

Like so many Inca ruins, no one really knows the purpose of Sayacmarca, but these are the visible facts: it was built on a precipice commanding a spacious view; there are no agricultural terraces so the complex could not have supported many inhabitants; ritual baths and an aqueduct run round the outside of the main wall; there are curious stone rings set in the wall by trapezoid openings. For me the mystery adds to the beauty, and it is beauty all the way from here — if you are fortunate with the weather.

The trail continues down to the valley floor. From here it becomes a glorious Inca Road, being on a raised causeway over marshy ground that then rises up through cloudforest (the photo on the cover of this book was taken on this stretch). Stone paving on raised stone foundations, steps and a gentle gradient make for easy walking, and even if it is raining (and it often is) you will marvel at the Inca workmanship. Before the climb to the third pass there is a campsite. During the ascent you climb through two Inca tunnels, and if it is a clear day you will have the added bonus of a view of Salkantay over to your left. The pass (4,000m) is used as a campsite, but it gets crowded and water is some way below. Below the pass, about 2 hours from Sayacmarca, are the impressive ruins of Phuyupatamarca. Access is down a steep flight of stairs. Clear water runs through the channels cut into the rock that feed five baths, leading one from the other down the hill. Backpackers are advised to camp near Phuyupatamarca for the final night. Beyond here the only camping place is the crowded and unscenic area near the hostel; in the peak season you are likely to find it full of groups.

Leave early in the morning with a full canteen. An Inca staircase leads from the west side of the ruins (the far end from the baths) and disappears into the jungle, leading you down a thousand steps. Literally. You'll think that your knees will never feel the same again.

The end comes in the form of the hostel which marks the beginning of the trail to the ruins of Huiñay Huayna (Wiñay Wayna). Camping is permitted here and floor space is usually available as well as accommodation. There is a small restaurant. Beer! This is also the last place to fill up with water before Machu Picchu itself.

If you still have a thirst for ruins there are some newly excavated ones to the west of the main trail, just before you reach the hostel. Allow an hour for this side trip.

Huiñay Huayna lies just below the hostel to the right, and is the most extensive of the ruins so far. It has some beautiful stonework, a fantastic location, and an air of mystery often lacking in the crowded Machu Picchu ruins.

The trail from the hostel to Machu Picchu (2 hours away) is clearly marked. It contours a mountainside and disappears into cloudforest full of begonias, bromeliads and tree ferns, before coming to a steep flight of stairs leading up to the first Inca gate. The path continues to the main gate, Intipunku — 'the Gateway of the Sun' — and suddenly the whole of Machu Picchu is spread out before you. A magical moment.

After drinking in the scene, you can stroll down to the hotel, radiating smugness amongst the groups of tourists who arrived by train, and have a slap-up meal in the outdoor cafeteria. You might even take a look at the ruins! There is a place for storing your luggage near the entrance (a small fee is charged).

Try to arrive at Machu Picchu several hours before closing time. Your ticket will be stamped on arrival so leave yourself enough time to look around. You will be charged for re-admission if you return the next day.

You will need to decide where to sleep. Few backpackers stay in this hotel (it is expensive and usually fully booked) but for the incomparable experience of sleeping near the ruins (and I speak as one of the lucky ones who slept *in* the ruins during my first visit in 1969) the less impecunious might see if there has been a cancellation. Otherwise you can camp down by the river or, if you feel like a bed, walk down the railway to Aguas Calientes which has a choice of budget accommodation.

Ollantaytambo or Chilca to Llactapata

These two towns are on the Urubamba River, providing a gentle day's walk before the strenuous part, and removing the hassle of the train journey. From Ollantaytambo to Chilca (not really a village, just a few houses) is a 3-4 hour hike — about 7km. If you start out from Chilca on Saturday, you will arrive at Llactapata on Sunday, when there are no local trains so very few other hikers on the trail at the same time as you. Unless you are a strong walker, you will need two days to reach Llactapata from Ollantaytambo — 8 hours is fast time for this stretch; from Chilca it is a one-day hike.

Route description

Cross the road bridge in Ollantaytambo and follow the dirt road along the south side of the river to the Chilca bridge, about 7km away (you may catch a ride on this stretch). You will pass some fine Inca terraces and ruins before reaching a very arid region of dry tropical vegetation. After Chilca the trail passes the interesting remains of a Spanish *estancia*. Note the ruined church and the beautiful courtyard; both buildings are still used, but no attempt has been made to restore them to their former elegance.

From Chilca it will take 3 or 4 hours to reach Llactapata. The trail is always easy to follow, and more or less level until the last section where it climbs to the rim of a spectacular canyon full of tropical vegetation. The descent and ascent up the other side are very steep. You can camp in the gorge and Llactapata is less than an hour away.

Chilca to Huayllabamba

This trail also starts at Chilca but is a dramatic, not easy option. It adds another two or three days to the Inca Trail and includes a steep pass and the lovely *nevados* (snow-peaks) Huayanay and Salkantay Este, sister to the region's highest mountain, Salkantay, to the west.

Practical information

Distance	30km
Altitude	Between 2,800m and 4,600m
Rating	Moderate/tough
Timing	2-3 days
In reverse	Inadvisable since you would have to pay the Inca Trail fee

Route description

From Chilca, head due south up the valley opposite the bridge across the Urubamba River, and follow the trail, which keeps close to the *quebrada*, west and northwest. After about 5 hours you reach the small village of Ancascocha. Turn right here, southwest, and head up the valley to your right. There are waterfalls here and some good camping spots. The trail continues towards a pass, skirting left of a small lake and reaching the top at 4,600m, some 2-3 hours of strenuous climbing from Ancascocha. The two snow peaks on your right are Salkantay Este and Huayanay.

The trail now drops down towards the village of Quesca, 2-3 hours away, going to the right of the broad *pampa*, and down to Quebrada Cusichaca and some Inca remains (probably a *tambo*). Follow the left slope of the valley to Quesca. From the village to Huayllabamba is 3 hours. En route is the Inca fortress of Paucarcancha, an almost unknown semi-circular ruin in an inspiring position at the junction of two rivers, about 2 hours from Quesca. From here to Huayllabamba is about an hour. Cross the Cusichaca river and follow its left bank downstream.

Paucarcancha is the focal point of several alternatives. If you continue to Huayllabamba you have the choice of doing the Inca Trail or hiking to Kilometre 88 and taking the train to Machu Picchu or Cusco, or you can head south up the Cusichaca and do the Salkantay hike (see below) in reverse.

SALKANTAY HIKES

The *cordillera*'s highest mountain, Salkantay (6,271m), provides an awesome backdrop for these hikes. You then have a choice of keeping high or dropping down to the sub-tropical regions. The area is seldom crowded — this is Peru at its most perfect.

All three treks share the same route from Mollepata to Soray — a beautiful walk with the added bonus of the chance to visit the lovely Inca site of Tarahuasi before arriving at Mollepata.

Mollepata is at a sub-tropical 2,803m. It overlooks a citrus growing area where flocks of parakeets screech overhead. The gradual ascent towards Salkantay is made up a valley full of flowering shrubs buzzing with hummingbirds, across streams and past isolated grass-thatched houses, while ahead of you the snow-covered flanks of Salkantay and Humantay gleam in the afternoon sun. At the head of the valley, in the tiny settlement of Soray, you have the choice of three treks: the sub-tropical delights and thermal baths of the trail to Santa Teresa, the icy, breathless, but stunningly beautiful Salkantay trek to Huayllabamba, or the middle route, combining elements of both: Inca ruins, ice and snow, and sub-tropical forests.

Mollepata to Soray
Getting to the trailhead
Get transport from Cusco to Mollepata by bus or truck, leaving from Avenida Arcopata early in the morning. The 06:00 bus is recommended if you want to reach Soray that day. The ride of 76km takes 3-5 hours.

Limatambo and Tarahuasi
Unless you're in a great hurry I strongly recommend you spend the first night in Limatambo. It is a pleasant, low-lying little town with basic accommodation or camping possibilities. Nearby, at Tarahuasi, is an Inca temple with one of the finest examples anywhere of Inca polygonal masonry in a long retaining wall. On the upper level are 28 tall niches, thought by John Hemming to have been for liveried attendants or for mummies. The stonework, in roseate patterns, is orange-coloured through its covering of lichen. This amazing place sees few tourists.

Tarahuasi was the site of a battle between the Spanish and Incas. Hernando de Soto and his soldiers were resting here on their way to Cusco when they were attacked by 4,000 Inca warriors; four Spaniards were killed and many injured.

Arrieros and pack animals
Horses and mules are available in Mollepata. Juan Castillo, who lives at the upper end of the village, has been recommended, also the Perez family

(with Marcelino particularly recommended). Craig Cardon suggests hiring pack animals to take your luggage to Soray only. A sensible suggestion which will give you a good start on that long, uphill first day.

Practical information

Distance	About 16km
Altitude	Between 2,800m and about 3,500m
Timing	1 day
Maps	None available

Route description

Mollepata has improved from the days, a century ago, when George Squier described it as a 'place unsurpassed in evil repute by any in Peru'. There is an attractive green plaza, some pretty houses, and even basic accommodation. There is a dirt road from Mollepata to Soray now, but the short cut via the footpath is much more scenic and you don't even cross the road.

The path heads steeply uphill just outside Mollepata, in the direction of the mountains. Ask locals if you're not sure, but it's a pretty obvious trail, going up the left side of the valley (northwest). After about 2-3 hours you'll be nearing the top of the pass called Marcaccasa, distinguished from afar by two trees silhouetted on the horizon. There are good campsites here. Or continue to the cross on the hill where the last possible campsites are. Below the cross, a difficult to follow trail bears round to the right, keeping on high ground, heading northeast through shrubs and bushes. There are many paths through the bushes, all leading to the same main trail, about 45 minutes from the cross.

Once you join the main trail the way is clear (and uphill) and you will shortly come to a stream. Fill your water bottle here — the next water is about 3 hours away. The trail continues round a corner and a splendid view of Humantay (5,917m) comes into sight. The path climbs up the long Humantay valley to Soray, reached in about 4 hours of easy and beautiful hiking. The view of Salkantay appears just before Soray. Campsites are found just above the village, across the river, or — even better — an hour higher up.

From Soray to Huayllabamba
Updated by Craig Cardon

This is the spectacular option, but also the toughest, passing high around the flank of Salkantay and visiting some interesting Inca remains. You may then link up with the Inca Trail to complete an Inca-saturated trek.

Practical information

Distance	About 40km
Altitude	Between 2,800m and 4,880m
Rating	Difficult
Timing	2-3 days
In reverse	Yes, if you start from Chilca (see *Chilca to Huayllabamba* hike, page 198)

Route description

An hour beyond Soray is the giant V of a moraine spreading down from Salkantay. The trail, not very clear, runs northeast up the right side of the moraine, crossing some streams which run from the moraine. After some steep climbing, the terrain levels out and the trail turns sharply to the right and uphill, near a big boulder, and continues along the right-hand bank of a small stream for about an hour (the stream may be dry). Before reaching a flat, boggy meadow, you'll see a low cliff (about 5m) hung with icicles formed by the dripping water. Cross the stream below the cliff and climb straight up to the meadow. The trail seems to disappear in this boggy stretch, but you can pick it up where the meadow starts to dry out towards the centre and follow the path a little to the left. It's worth making a detour to the glacier. You can see the layers of ice representing annual precipitation, rather like the annual rings on a tree-stump. Notice, too, the quality of the ice: the old, compact ice is blue and almost clear, while new ice is frosty-looking with trapped air.

Above the plateau the path zig-zags up the reddish coloured scree slope, becoming more conspicuous as it nears the top of the pass of Incachillasca which lies at the top of the scree in the saddle of two minor ridges. This is an impressive 4,880m (over 16,000ft) and it will take you 5-6 hours to climb here from Soray. The view makes it all worthwhile. The path descending on the other side is quite clear as it traverses the right-hand (east) side of the mountain. There are some good camping places (about 1½ hours from the pass) at the point that the river and trail make a sharp left turn down the valley.

The trail continues down the right bank of the stream to some stone corrals, about 3 hours from the pass, then crosses the *quebrada* and follows it down the valley. Keep to the left-hand bank of the river as it turns northeast, picks up speed, and descends through a small gorge. About an hour past the moraine, just past a *campesino* settlement (Pampachuana) on the right-hand bank, the river — astonishingly — becomes a canal. Shortly after the end of the canal, cross to the right bank via a footbridge and follow a good path along the right-hand side of the river down the narrow, steep valley to a river junction and settlement some 1-1½ blister-making hours away.

The Inca fortress Paucarcancha stands here. From the foot of the fortress you'll see the trail leading to Chilca, one day's hike away. To reach Huayllabamba, cross the river and follow the left-hand bank down to the Río Cusichaca, about 20 minutes beyond the crossing. From Huayllabamba you can join the Inca Trail for the 3 day hike to Machu Picchu, or hike out to Chillca in 4-5 hours, or to Kilometre 88 in 2 hours.

From Soray to Santa Teresa

This lovely and varied hike is the 'soft option' from Soray since the pass is lower (though still a tough 4,750m (15,580ft) and then it is mostly downhill through forested valleys, above deep ravines, past (or in) a wonderful thermal spring, until you end up in the citrus groves of Santa Teresa which is linked by rail to Machu Picchu.

Practical information

Distance	About 50km
Altitude	Between 1,500m and 4,750m
Rating	Moderate to difficult
Timing	3-4 days
In reverse	Possible — but you'd better like walking uphill!
Getting to Machu Picchu	Check train times from Santa Teresa to Machu Picchu or Aguas Calientes before you leave Cusco.

Route description

Go up the left side of the moraine at the head of the valley, crossing to the left bank of a stream to pick up a path leading up the side of the mountain. It goes steeply uphill for half an hour, then comes to a series of zig-zags (Siete Culebras is the local name of this stretch). At the top of the seventh switchback the terrain levels out under Salkantay's lateral moraine, and drops gently down to the small Laguna Soirococha. The pass you see above is, alas, a false one; the main pass is a little further on, but the view of Salkantay looming above you more than compensates for the effort. The real pass at 4,750m is reached after 3-4 hours from the moraine, and is marked by a pile of stones, *apacheta*, which grows daily as each traveller adds his pebble to thank the *apus* for a safe trip (see box, page 76). A few cattle skulls add a macabre touch.

The trail descends to the left-hand side of the valley, becoming indistinct in swampy areas. If the weather is bad there are caves providing shelter about 20 minutes below the pass. Once the valley narrows there is only one obvious trail on the left of the river. Some 2-3 hours from the pass you'll reach a small hut and a level area which is a popular camping spot. This place is called Huayrajmachay ('Eye of the Wind').

You'll leave the beautiful pyramid-shaped peak of Humantay behind as you drop below the treeline, known as *la ceja de selva* ('eyebrow of the jungle'), and walk through groves of bamboo with many orchids and other flowers and lots of hummingbirds. Don't forget to keep looking back at the snow-peaks behind you, framed by bamboo fronds. After about 2 hours the trail crosses an old landslide and in another 2 hours you'll drop steeply down to the bridge across the Río Chalhuay. This is a beautiful camping area, but there's an even better one an hour further on. Twenty minutes beyond the tiny settlement of Colpapampa are the hot springs: turn right at the trail junction by the river. Just before the bridge a single stream of hot water is piped into a semi-natural pool on the right-hand side of the trail.

You are now at the confluence of two rivers, the Totota and the Santa Teresa, and you'll be following the latter all the way down to the town of the same name. The best campsite is the other side of the turf bridge, and the best mineral deposits from the thermal springs are a short way below the campsite, following the river bank (scramble over the rocks).

After the bridge the trail stays close to the river (ignore a fork to your left) and then, surprisingly (because you were expecting 'downhill all the way'), climbs up to contour round the mountainside through bamboo groves. Soon you will come to a stream which disrupts the trail. Go up this for about 8m to pick up the trail again on the other side. Carry on uphill to a spectacular waterfall. This cascade drops some 300m and the trail crosses it midway! A perfect shower, and the water/air temperature is now warm enough for you to welcome a bath. Following the trail up and down, you come to a second waterfall, with swimming in the pool above. This is an incredibly beautiful stretch, with begonias, purple and orange orchids and strawberries lining the path.

Some 5 hours after the hot springs you'll come to the hamlet of Miscabamba. Some basic provisions and drinks are available here. Camping in Miscabamba is not recommended, however, because of problems with theft, so it is better to camp well outside the village. From Miscabamba to the small village of Paltachayoc and the start of the dirt road will take 2-3 hours. There are good campsites near the bridge. From the bridge it's another hot 2-3 hours through citrus, banana and coffee plantations to Santa Teresa which has basic accommodation and food. As you approach Santa Teresa (1,510m) ignore the road that leads off to the left to a *hacienda*. Continue to the river, crossing the suspension bridge that leads to the station.

You can take the train to Machu Picchu (45 minutes) or Cusco (4-5 hours), or a truck or bus to Cusco (6-7 hours).

Male fertility is drastically reduced during the first few days at high altitudes. Those spare condoms make excellent water carriers!

Soray to La Hidroeléctrica

From Apus and Incas *by Charles Brod*

This is the inner of the three routes around Salkantay. It combines several distinct features of the two outer routes. Like the trek to Santa Teresa, it winds through the montane forest regions above the Río Urubamba and, like the trek to Huayllabamba, passes an Inca ruin and the remains of an Inca road. It terminates at the power station on the Río Urubamba, with the ruins of Machu Picchu lying just a short train journey away.

Practical information

Distance	About 50km
Altitude	Between 1,650m and 4,880m
Rating	The most difficult of the three options, passing over two high passes.
Timing	4-5 days
In reverse	Possible

Route description

From Soray follow the directions for the Salkantay hike (see page 203), over the Incachillasca Pass and down to the *campesino* shelter and stone corrals.

From the shelter you need to climb to the pass between Salkantay and Chuyunco. The trailhead is just below the moraines, and climbs along the grassy slope parallel to Salkantay. The grass thins and becomes loose stone as the trail begins to switchback to the pass at 4,830m, which you'll reach after climbing beyond a narrow slot in the ridge, about 2 hours from the moraine. From the pass, the trail leads off to the right, making switchbacks down to the pasture, where it fades away; you can pick it up again at the far end. It then descends along the left slope of the valley. Here the valley curves to the left and the Río Aobamba begins its course to the Río Urubamba.

When you reach the first small group of houses below the pasture you will see the unimportant ruins of Palcay, about 3 hours from the pass. Little is left of these. The trail now continues down the valley, staying to the left of the Río Aobamba. You'll pass a waterfall and reach the village of Aobamba about 1½ hours from the ruins. The descent from the village to La Hidroeléctrica, on the Río Urubamba, takes about 8 hours through increasingly thick vegetation. Below the village cross a bridge to the right-hand side of the river where a wall of trees and bushes rises abruptly before you, the beginning of vegetation that will grow ever denser as you descend the valley.

Entering the forest, you can see the faint outlines and remains of an Inca road. After crossing a bridge to the left bank, the path is easily followed down through bamboo groves and into forests of increasingly tall trees providing some excellent birdwatching opportunities. There are no settlements until a short distance above the power station, and few camping places. On reaching the railway tracks, follow them up the Urubamba Valley to La Hidroeléctrica. To avoid confusion, make your presence known to the police who guard this area. From here you can catch the train to Machu Picchu, Cusco or Quillabamba.

VILCABAMBA HIKE

From information by Peter Frost and Kevin Haight

This hike is mainly for those with a serious interest in Inca history, and to get the most out of a visit to these important Inca ruins some background reading is essential (see *Further reading*). The brief history below is just to whet your appetite.

Although Inca ruins are the goal, the opportunity to walk through sparsely populated low-altitude rainforest gives this hike an added appeal to naturalists and birdwatchers.

History

One of the last Inca rulers, Manco, installed himself in this area around 1537 while fleeing from the Spaniards; he planned to regain control over Tawantinsuyo at a better moment. The Spaniards finally conquered the area in 1572, with a large and thoroughly prepared expedition, and killed the very last Inca ruler, Túpac Amaru. Thus ended the Inca Empire. Later the area was used for silver mining and the cultivation of sugar and coca, but there was little effort to settle this humid rainforest area and Vilcabamba became a memory until the 20th century when men of science began to take an interest in ancient Peru. Hiram Bingham, the 'discoverer' of Machu Picchu, found Vilcabamba in the same year: 1911. Gene Savoy organized large expeditions to this area in 1964 and 1965, and Vincent Lee became very interested in the region's large concentration of Inca remains. In 1976 a Lima historian claimed to have 'discovered' Bingham's ruins at Espíritu Pampa and suddenly the place was off limits. Appearances of terrorists around 1983 made it even worse, and the area became overrun with soldiers and police. Fortunately these problems are now over and hikers are again visiting the area without problems. Projects are planned for more research on these Inca remains. It is hoped that the area will receive more protection before the Inca roads disappear under modern road construction.

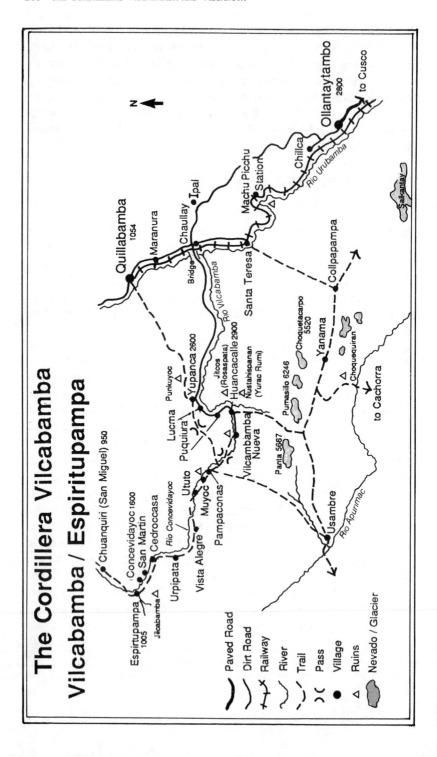

The Cordillera Vilcabamba
Vilcabamba / Espiritupampa

Legend:
- Paved Road
- Dirt Road
- Railway
- River
- Trail
- Pass
- Village
- Ruins
- Nevado / Glacier

N

to Cusco
Ollantaytambo 2800
Chilca
Station
Machu Picchu
Rio Urubamba
Salkantay
Ipal
Chaullay
Maranura
Quillabamba 1054
Bridge
Rio Vilcabamba
Santa Teresa
Collpapampa
Choquetacarpo 5520
Yanama
Choquequiran
to Cachorra
Punkuyoc
Yupanca 2600
Jitcos (Rosaspata)
Huancacalle 2900
Ñustahispanan (Yurac Rumi)
Pumasillo 6246
Lucma
Puquiura
Vilcambamba Nueva
Panta 5667
Chuanquiri (San Miguel) 950
Concevidayoc 1600
San Martin
Cedroccasa
Rio Concevidayoc
Urpipata
Ututo
Muyoc
Vista Alegre
Pampaconas
Usambre
Rio Apurimac
Espiritupampa 1005
Jicabamba
to Cachorra

Getting to the trailhead

The best and easiest way is to take the train from Cusco to Chaullay —
37km, 6½ hours, US$7-8. Chaullay has two stations: get off at the second
one (Chaullay Puente). Or if you come by truck/bus on the Cusco-
Quillabamba route over the Abra de Malaga, get off at Chaullay. Cross the
bridge to the road to pick up transport to Yupanca, Puquiura and
Huancacalle. The journey takes about 8 hours by truck, or if you are lucky
enough to get a ride by pick-up, about 6 hours. At Puquiura there is a
police checkpoint where you need to register and show your passport.

Huancacalle (2,900m) is the starting point of the hike to Vilcabamba
(Espíritu Pampa). You'll need a day to get organized. It's best to hire a
local guide in Huancacalle to show you the ruins, which are hard to find
and overgrown. Expect to pay a guide about US$5 per day, and the same
amount for a pack animal. Families will offer accommodation and meals
in Huancacalle.

Ruins near Huancacalle

Very interesting and important ruins are situated just outside Huancacalle:

Vitcos (also called Rosaspata), a huge fortress uphill from Huancacalle (1 hour).

Yurac Rumi, an enormous white rock, the showpiece of an entire complex
of ruins, including impressive baths, near the end of the valley (under an
hour from Vitcos or Huancacalle).

Los Andenes, a system of finely built terraces and rock shrines, in the
valley beyond Vitcos.

Hiking to Vilcabamba (Espíritu Pampa)

Practical information

Distance	About 60km
Altitude	Between 3,850m and 950m
Rating	Moderate, but the steep muddy paths can make hiking difficult
Timing	About 11 days, including transport there
In reverse	Possible
Maps	None available

Route description

The dirt road extends from Huancacalle to Vilcabamba Nueva, but is never
used by vehicles because of the very poor road conditions. Follow the road
out of the village for about 1km, where it forks. Stay to the right and pick
up the footpath about 100m farther along, climbing uphill, making short
cuts across the switchbacks. The trail splits and forks in several places, but

always rejoins itself. After about 2 hours you reach the small Spanish village of Vilcabamba Nueva. The trail continues from here up the left side of the drainage channel towards the pass of Kollpakasa at 3,850m, which you'll reach after about 2 hours. It descends into the valley of Concevidayoc along the south slope, over a fine Inca road, until you reach the bridge of Maucachaca over the Río Chalcha, about 1 hour from the pass. Take the route through the Pampaconas which forks uphill to the left. You will reach a clearing among low woods at a place called Muyoc, 1 hour later. Another hour of easy, level walking gets you from Muyoc to Ututo (3,000m), where there's a bridge to the north bank of the Río Concevidayoc.

Cross the bridge and hike down a forested ravine on sections of Inca road to Cedrochaca. There are several good campsites along the river. Recross to the south bank at Cedrochaca and traverse up a steep mountainous slope. After 1 hour you pass the hamlet of Tambo and 45 minutes later, descending, you cross the Río Zapatero which joins the Río Concevidayoc close by.

Continue along a stretch of broad floodplain to the tributary Río Sucsuchincana with good campsites, about 1 hour. The hamlet of Vista Alegre, also with good campsites, lies about 10 minutes downstream. From Vista Alegre to the village of Concevidayoc (1,600m) the trail is quite easy to follow, once you get used to ducking under overhanging vegetation. After passing the tiny clearing of San Guillermo, a deep-forest trail brings you to Urpipata. Here the trail follows a ridge-top among tall trees to Huaynapata, a cleared hill with a primitive sugar mill atop it and sugar cane growing nearby. The trail continues to Cedroccasa, where the forest gives way to scrub slope and cultivation until you reach the village of Concevidayoc. Altogether a 7-hour walk if you don't stop along the way.

The trail continues in the direction of Espíritu Pampa about 2 hours away. Avoid the right-hand trail fork, 20 minutes beyond Concevidayoc, which descends towards Chuanquiri. At Espíritu Pampa (1,005m) camping space is a few cramped square metres by the houses of the *campesinos*.

Visiting the ruins of Vilcabamba and Chuanquiri
The ruins are situated in the dense forest up the gentle slope beyond the settlement, between two small streams that merge below the settlement and in turn join the Concevidayoc a short distance downstream from their junction. You are recommended to hire a guide in Espíritu Pampa for about US$2, to make sure you don't miss the main parts; few ruins are visible, and unfortunately most are still overgrown with vegetation.

From Espíritu Pampa to Chuanquiri (also called San Miguel), take the trail leading down to a footbridge (not for mules) which crosses the gorge of the Río Chontabamba to the north bank. Then follow the trail downstream, high above the Río Chontabamba, to its intersection with the main valley trail, about 45 minutes from Espíritu Pampa. Mules must backtrack the long way round (1½ hours) to this river junction. About 3 hours from here you will come to a cable and concrete footbridge over the Río Concevidayoc. Cross it and begin a steep, twisting ascent of 1½ hours to a grassy height. Descend for another sinuous hour to the Río San Miguel. Cross the bridge here, and climb up again to Chuanquiri (San Miguel): 950m, about half an hour.

Getting back to Cusco
From Chuanquiri (San Miguel) you can only catch a truck to Kiteni on Saturdays — about 4 hours. Otherwise you'll have to hike this part, following the dirt road, taking 9-10 hours. There's a basic *hostal* and simple restaurants in Kiteni. Daily trucks do the route between Kiteni and Quillabamba in about 8 hours. In Quillabamba you can catch a bus or the train back to Cusco.

AUZANGATE HIKES

The Cordillera Vilcanota is named after the Vilcanota River lying to its west. This impressive range of mountains includes the massive Nevado Auzangate (6,372m). Hiking opportunities here are excellent, but the toughest in the region, so you need to be fit and acclimatized. The whole area lies above the treeline and is populated with traditionally dressed Quechua-speaking *campesinos* cultivating the barren *altiplano*. This is alpaca country. Enormous herds graze in the already eroded valleys. Typical Quechua festivals are popular in this region and you might find yourself drinking the local brew of *chicha* with the villagers. Their major fiesta is *Qoyoriti* ('The Ice Festival'), around the second week of June and — also in mid-June — is the fiesta of Raqchi. The most popular hike is the circuit around Nevado Auzangate, but there are many other interesting and spectacular hikes in the area to the south and it is an ideal region for finding your own route, with plenty of paths and local people to give you directions.

Conditions
This is a remote area, so prepare carefully, particularly if exploring off the main route. Always carry enough food and a compass. Plus some stones to fend off the dogs. Camp outside the villages and ask permission when possible. Be prepared for very cold nights (well below freezing) and strong sun during the day. It is dangerous to hike in this area during the rainy season when clouds and snow cover the passes and hide important landmarks.

Theft has been a problem near the villages on the Auzangate circuit, especially Tinqui and Upis. However, most of the time this happened when hikers made no contact with the villagers, or left things outside their tent.

The Auzangate circuit

This 5-6 day hike has everything: herds of llamas and alpacas, traditionally dressed Indians, hot springs, turquoise lakes, glaciers, ice caves, and even vicuñas. Not surprisingly, it is very popular with trekkers. The route takes you right round the massif of Auzangate and over three high passes before returning you to your starting point, the small village of Tinqui.

Getting to the trailhead

Tinqui is near Ocongate, southeast of Cusco. The easiest way to get there is to catch a bus to Urcos, leaving from the Coliseum in Cusco — and taking about 1 hour. From here catch a truck to Tinqui, leaving at around 11:00; the journey takes 5-6 hours.

Pack animals

There is an association of *arrieros* (about 50 members) at Tinqui, and prices are set: *arriero* about US$6 per day, and US$7 per day for his animal. Contact them in Tinqui, across the street from Hostal Tinqui.

Providing you have a map (and compass) you will not need a guide.

Practical information

Distance	About 80km
Altitude	Between 3,800m and 5,100m
Rating	Difficult
Timing	5 days
Maps	IGN *Ocongate* sheet 28-t, 1:100,000; *Auzangate Circuit* from the South American Explorers Club.
In reverse	Equally good

Route description

Take the broad track from the school in Tinqui and cross the river via a bridge behind the school. Cross a second smaller bridge and head up to houses on the right. Continue on a wide trail to open *puna* with house-sized boulders on the left. Continue on a deteriorating trail, cross a small stream and head south-southeast across the *pampa* towards Auzangate. There is no real trail here, just cattle paths. After about 2 hours, cross a small stream by a stone footbridge and ignore the track on the right immediately beyond the bridge. Instead, look for a wide track on the left which climbs gently beyond a group of houses, then crosses an irrigation ditch and soon drops down through a green, boggy valley to Upis. It takes about 5 hours from Tinqui to Upis. There are hot springs, a fantastic view of Auzangate and a great campsite (but beware of theft).

From Upis continue up the valley towards Auzangate, crossing the swampy area as soon as possible to the right of the valley where a faint narrow footpath is found. This continues to a grassy meadow. Cross the meadow and climb to the right to some stone corrals. Here two passes are visible, to the left and right of a yellow hill. Both go to the same place. The lower path is longer but easier, the higher route is more spectacular. It's about 2-3 hours to the top of the pass from Upis.

From the pass descend roughly south-southwest into the valley until you reach a lilac-coloured moraine. From here you can see Laguna Vinococha, with a waterfall. Head left (southeast) under the jagged and obvious rocky spires of Nevado Sorimani to the top of the waterfall cascading out of the turquoise lake. Hike over the top of a small hillock to the right of the lake and waterfall. From here continue to the right of another small hill on the far right of the lake, and continue roughly east to the base of an obvious red-coloured mountain by Laguna Pucacocha — about 5 hours away from Upis, and a possible campsite. It's worth climbing up the small ridge to the north of the campsite for the close-up views of Auzangate, and if it's clear, far off to the left (northwest) the pyramid of Salkantay can be seen.

Ten minutes from Pucacocha you reach some corrals (Pucapata). Head right around a small rocky hill, and continue roughly east on fairly good trails below red cliffs. After about 1½ hours you'll reach the top of a small pass with the main pass to the left (east) and Laguna Auzangatecocha below. Head down fairly steeply and for quite a long way to pasture at the right end of Laguna Auzangatecocha. When you've reached this lake, cross the small stream at the right end and then head northeast on trails behind the moraine, on the east side of the lake. You'll reach this spot about 2 hours after leaving Pucapata. The long, steep climb to the highest pass (5,100m — 17,000ft) is ahead of you. There are two choices: up a gully to the east (longer, but less steep), or continue northeast up a ridge (steeper, but more direct). Head roughly northeast to the pass of Palomani about 4-5 hours from Pucapata. From the pass to the next campsite you can go cross-country, or follow the trail roughly southeast for about 1 hour through a desert-like landscape, to the camping area under Cerro Puca Punta (which means 'Red Point').

From Cerro Puca Punta, continue east to a broad green valley (Pampa Jatunpata). Cross a stream near some houses and skirt the swampy green valley to the left (northeast), climbing over the hill to the left rather than dropping to the bogs below. Head northeast up Quebrada Jampamayo, a valley full of viscachas. You will hear these little animals whistling their alarm calls and they scurry for cover among the rocks. It's best to stay left of the river. At the small community of Jampa bear left (north-northwest) around the mountain and arrive at the very small Laguna Ticllacocha, which is not visible until you are there. There are some excellent camping places around here. It takes 4 hours from Cerro Puca Punta to the lake.

Cordillera Vilcanota North
Auzangate Hikes

to Cusco-Puno Road

to Puerto Maldonado

New road to Puerto Maldonado (not finished)

Ocongate 3533
Tinqui 3800
Quimsapuccio
Mojonpata
Vanama
Pacchanta
Upis
Cullpacata
Calachaca
Cullpacata
Colpa Ananta 6110
Colque Cruz 6093
Pico Tres
Puca Punta 5000
Maria Huamantilla
Santa Catalina
Yanajaja
Auzangate 6372
Alcamarinayoc 6102
Artaymarca 5456
Churrupa 6196
Jatunñaño Puma 5812
Jacurupuñta 5652
Yanamayo
Yanamayo
Jampa
Huayruru Punco
Murmurani
Condor Tres
Chuallani
Uchuy Tinaya
Uyani
Chillca
Jajatuni
Sorimani
Huasacocha 5435
Janchipacha
4700
Sbinacocha 4869
Sauma
Yanarun

Paved Road
Dirt Road
River
Lake
Trail
Pass
Village
Nevado / Glacier

N

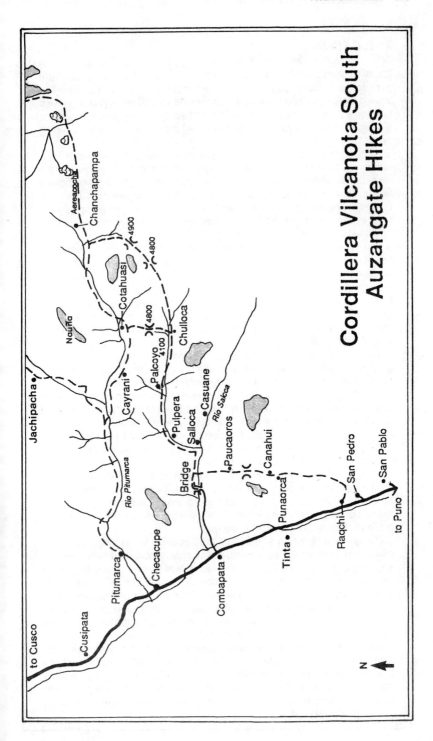

Cordillera Vilcanota South
Auzangate Hikes

THE *CASITA*

When leading a trek in the Auzangate region I had to evacuate a hiker because of altitude sickness. On reaching Ocongate I was anxious to get back to the group so Lynn agreed to return to Cuzco alone. Faustino, the *arriero*, agreed to lend me a horse so we could travel faster, but to spread the journey over two days instead of his customary one. He provided Sambo, a scrawny black pony hung about with flour sacks containing my sleeping bag, etc.

Faustino looked magnificent. Now that he was master, not servant, he'd changed into a splendid multicoloured poncho, and his bearing and the respect with which he was greeted as we trotted through the town showed that in Ocongate he was a man of considerable status. We trotted through the town, we trotted out of town, and we trotted off the road and along the track towards Pacchanta. I hadn't ridden for several years, and my bottom and knees were screaming for mercy.

I wondered where we were going to spend the night. Since it would be below freezing I hoped we'd be under cover. Yes, said Faustino, a friend of his had a *casita* in the next valley. Here we encountered the friend screaming Quechua curses at a herd of serene-looking llamas and alpacas. He and Faustino disappeared into a grass-thatched hut chattering volubly, and I decided to see if my legs still worked by climbing a nearby hill to watch the evening sun paint golden rings round the alpacas and touch the white bulk of Auzangate with pink.

It was almost dark when I returned to the *casita*. The interior was lit by one guttering candle and I ducked through the low door and groped my way to a seat by the wall — a remarkably comfortable and well-sprung seat, covered with a sheepskin. My host's daughter gave me a plate of tiny potatoes and I gave them some chocolate. Then I prepared myself for sleep. Father and daughter watched entranced as I laid out my requirements. I unrolled and inflated my Thermarest, stuffed a sweater into a T-shirt for a pillow, and pulled my sleeping bag from its stuff bag. In the background I could hear incredulous squeaks from the daughter punctuating the steady drone of man-of-the-world Faustino explaining what everything was for. When I actually climbed into the blue cocoon of a sleeping bag, it was too much for her. She burst into hysterical giggles and little explosions of laughter accompanied the rest of my preparations. When the show was over, she just curled up on a pile of sheepskins and went to sleep.

The girl was up again at 4:30 to start a cooking fire (inside) with llama dung, and to round up the horses. It was bitterly cold, and dark and eye-smartingly smoky in the hut, and I buried myself in my sleeping bag until it was light enough to see my surroundings. I was rather surprised at what I saw. To begin with, my comfortable seat of the previous evening turned out to be half a sheep carcass with a well-sprung rib cage. There was no furniture, and no windows, but Inca-style niches made useful shelves for more pieces of sheep, half spun wool, burnt out candles and a safety pin.

After a breakfast of potatoes we saddled up and set off for the final stretch. After labouring up the 5,000m pass, with Sambo equally breathless on the lead rope beside me, we stopped at a rocky knoll overlooking Ticclacocha. Rumbling glaciers and spiky snow peaks surrounded me on all sides, with ice-cream cornices bulging over the ridges. I was well content to wait there for the group's arrival.

Head approximately northwest out of Laguna Ticllacocha and soon you'll come to the pass of Campa at 5,000m. It takes about an hour. From some points the valley appears impassable because the glacier seems to stretch all the way across. There are glaciers to the right just before the pass and to the left just after. The glacier to the right has a spectacular ice cave. It's at the rounded point of the glacier nearest the trail; be prepared to spend some time looking for it, but it's very worthwhile. Sometimes the cave entrance is covered by icicles and is not easily seen. A torch is essential. The cave stretches back over 100m and has several chambers.

At the pass, which is adorned with several *apachetas*, the northwest trail heads through the long scree slope of Quebrada Caycohuayjo and emerges above and to the left of several lakes. At the final lake, Laguna Comercocha, head past a few houses and drop down into the valley below. There's a fairly clear trail to a river where crossing appears difficult. Don't do anything drastic: the trail runs along a ridge to the right of the river (you may have to backtrack for 50 to 100 metres from the river). Stay on top of this ridge on a narrow but obvious trail until you reach a small stone bridge which crosses the river. From here continue on a good and pleasant trail along the left bank of the river, past occasional pools and lakes, until you reach the small village of Pacchanta. There's a bridge over the river before here. Pacchanta has two hot springs and good campsites. It takes 5 hours from Laguna Ticllacocha to Pacchanta.

From Pacchanta you have to cross the river via a bridge and then follow the obvious trail northwest to Tinqui, about 3 hours away.

From Pitumarca to Laguna Sibinacocha

Route information from Apus and Incas *by Charles Brod*

This very long, rigorous, but infinitely rewarding trek visits the largest lake in the area (18km long), and can be done as a circular hike or joining up with the Auzangate circuit. One advantage is that it is much easier to get to the starting point of Checacupe. You start lower, walking up a lovely river valley of cultivated fields then climbing high to the *puna*. There are two passes over 5,000m so this is a tough hike.

Getting to the trailhead

Take a bus or *colectivo* which leave Cusco every half hour or so for Sicuani. Get off at Checacupe, about 1½ hours from Cusco. From here you can catch a truck or pick-up, or walk, to the small village of Pitumarca.

Before leaving Checacupe try to visit the church (which is often closed but you may find the *portero* who has the key). Unremarkable from the outside, its interior is a lovely example of colonial workmanship with some marvellous paintings, a fine altar and a beautifully carved pulpit.

Practical information

Distance	About 145km back to Pitumarca and 160km to Tinqui
Altitude	Between 3,440m and 5,300m
Rating	Very strenuous
Timing	7-10 days
Map	IGN *Ocongate* sheet 28-t, 1:100,000
In reverse	Equally good

Route description

From Pitumarca follow the trail up the valley along the left bank of the river until you reach the small village of Uchullucllo, about 4 hours from Pitumarca. Just before the village is an area of extraordinary eroded rocks. The village lies on the other (south) side of the river, so cross over the bridge. Above the village there are some rather unrewarding hot springs. The trail continues across the courtyard from the school, climbing up the slope and heading towards the village of Anaiso, about 3 hours away to the east. The trail drops down to the Río Pitumarca again, before reaching the village.

From above Anaiso, continue up the right-hand side of the broad valley to where it narrows. Cross a bridge to the left side, then follow the wide path through a narrow canyon, fording the river twice. The canyon opens on to a cultivated area. The path then crosses the river once again, climbing up the valley's right-hand slope, and finally arrives at a broad marshy plain, 4 hours from Anaiso. The Río Pitumarca changes its name: it is now the Río Yanamayu ('Black River'). Hike across the marshy plain to the upper end where there is a small settlement. Don't enter the settlement but cross the river to its left side. The trail then curves to the left, heading east over a spur in the valley. Coming off a steep slope, the trail splits and runs along both sides of the river. Stay on the left side and continue up the valley, remaining near the watercourse. The small village of Canchapampa lies 2-3 hours beyond the marshy plain.

From here the trail continues in an easterly direction, leaving the stream and crossing over hilly terrain to Laguna Aereacocha, about 2 hours from Canchapampa. From the lake continue across the plateau before descending on to a vast plain laced with rivers. Follow a path leading over the ridge that lies to the east. Once over the ridge, the path swings north and heads to the southern end of the enormous Laguna Sibinacocha (4,868m). It's 3-4 hours from Laguna Aereacocha to Laguna Sibinacocha. Vicuñas roam this highland region. Spend a day camped at the lake, exploring its shores and the nearby hills. The lake and its surroundings provide an ideal habitat for numerous species of birds.

When you are ready to leave, follow the shores of the lake to its northern end. The mountain ridge that borders the lake's left shore dips low, providing easy access to the village of Sallma on the other side. You are now heading south back towards Pitumarca. From Sallma, cross the nearby stream and make your way to the opposite side of the valley, a short distance below the village. Here the trail climbs the slope to a marshy pasture overlooking the valley. Continue to the left of the pasture before climbing to the right of a rocky crag. The pass lies just above 5,050m, and overlooks another broad valley. Laguna Chullumpina can be seen on the far side of the valley. Descend to the left of the open area before heading for the valley below.

Cross the Río Chumayu and climb towards Laguna Chua (4,900m); there are several houses nearby. Continue past the houses to a different trail that runs along the slope above the lake. Take this trail over the spur of Nevado Chuallani (5,300m) on your right. Standing on the spur, you look down into a basin of pasture-land with a small pond (Laguna Negromutayoc), dry most of the time. Above the pasture to the west you can see the pass leading out of the region around Sibinacocha. The trail crosses the pasture below the pond, then climbs steeply up the mountainside near Nevado Chuallani. This pass also lies at 5,050m and takes 1-2 hours to reach from the small lake. The trail comes down from the pass through Quebradas Lloclla and Misquiunuj, passing the small settlement of Jajatuni, until you reach the large valley of the Río Chillcamayu, some 3 hours from the pass. You have two possibilities here:

Hike back to Pitumarca in 2-3 days, passing through the small community of Chillca. Stay on the left-hand side of Quebrada Chillcamayo.

Join up with the Auzangate Circuit trail to Tinqui, taking 2-3 days. Cross to the right-hand side of Quebrada Chillcamayo to hike up to its northern end where it becomes the Quebrada Jampamayu, and part of the Auzangate Circuit — about 4 hours.

From Pitumarca to Tinqui, via Chillca

This is a variation on the hike above combined with the Auzangate Circuit. Starting in Pitumarca rather than Tinqui gives you the advantage of easier access, and a chance to get acclimatized as you walk gently uphill along a well-used trail trodden by countless *campesinos* and their laden llamas heading for Pitumarca.

Practical information

Distance	About 70km
Altitude	Between 3,440m and 5,000m
Rating	Moderate to difficult
Timing	5-6 days
Map	IGN *Ocongate* sheet 28-t, 1:100,000

In reverse   Possible, and less strenuous because you start
                              higher.

Route description

Follow the trail up the valley along the left bank of the Río Pitumarca,
passing the village of Uchullucllo on the other side of the river, about 4
hours from Pitumarca. Do not cross the river but stay on the left side until
you reach Quebrada Chillcamayo on your left (the third *quebrada* from
Pitumarca), about 1 hour from Uchullucllo. Go up this *quebrada*, following
the left bank of the Río Chillcamayo until you reach the village of Japua,
situated on the other side of the river. Cross by the bridge and follow the
path alongside the river, crossing it once more, to the community of Chillca
at 4,200m, about 5-6 hours from the start of the *quebrada*. Chillca lies at
the confluence of two rivers. Follow the right-hand branch, the Río
Chillcamayu, heading northeast, to the even smaller community of Uyuni
at 4,400m, about 2 hours away, and for another 4 hours up Quebrada
Jampamayo to the community of Jampa at 4,600m. You are now on the
Auzangate Circuit.

From Jampa you can take a side trip to Laguna Sibinacocha. Follow the
river valley to your right (northeast) to the community of Yanamayo, about
1 hour from Jampa. From here you start the climb to the pass of Huayruro
Punco at about 5,150m, passing Lagunas Osjollo and Ananía — about 3-4
hours. From the pass you get a spectacular view over the impressive Laguna
Sibinacocha and marvel at its size. Descend along Quebrada Huampunimayo
to the lake (no path) in about 2 hours. The camping by the lake is beautiful,
but cold and windy. An option from here is to follow the banks of the lake
south, and pick up the trail to Pitumarca described earlier or to hike back to
Chillca (also described earlier) to rejoin the trail towards Tinqui.

From Raqchi to Pitumarca or to Tinqui via Chillca

The southern loop was an accidental discovery during our first trip to the
Cordillera Vilcanota in 1979, so I have a special affection for it. We set off
on impulse from Raqchi without a map, so every pass was like approaching
a new world: we had no idea what lay the other side. The most dramatic
was our 'landing on Mars' when I slogged, exhausted, up the last few metres
of a pass just before sunset and found a landscape unlike any I had seen in
South America. It looked as though every hill was wearing a striped poncho
in green, lilac, ochre and a variety of rich reds and terracotta. There was
not a living soul, man or beast, as far as we could see in all directions. The
exhilaration of such a sight, especially when totally unexpected, is what
real backpacking is all about!

The extra bonus of this hike, and the one which enticed us to it in the first place, is the Inca temple of Viracocha at Raqchi. By combining the southern route with the extension to the Auzangate circuit you are giving yourself one of the most scenically varied, if strenuous, hikes in Peru. The full trek is a serious venture — about 110km or 8-10 days of hiking — and you need to be confident of your physical abilities.

Raqchi

The village is accessible by bus or truck, about 2½ hours from Cusco, or by train to San Pedro 2km away. Even without the astonishing Inca temple this would be a remarkable village. Centuries ago a violent volcanic eruption spewed black lava all over the area, and this has been put to good use by the resourceful villagers. Numerous walls and corrals have been built from it, and hunks of the stuff still litter the surrounding hillsides. The church in Raqchi is exceptionally attractive, as is the entire village. Perhaps civic pride has something to do with it: once a year, in mid-June, there is a fiesta here which is said to have some of the best costumed dancers to be seen anywhere in Peru.

The Inca temple of Viracocha

The bare facts do nothing to prepare you for the amazing spectacle that greets you as you pass through a little gate to the right of Raqchi church, nor for the legends surrounding the temple. A long single wall of magnificent Inca stonework is topped by an adobe extension bringing it to a height of 15m. The lower wall is nearly 1½m thick with typical trapezoid windows and doorways. The remains of a row of stone pillars run on each side of the wall, but only one has retained its adobe top. No other Inca building has pillars and none is as tall. The adobe wall is now protected with a little tile roof, but this is a recent addition. Beyond the temple are rows of identical buildings made from rough stone, and originally topped by adobe. These are arranged round six identical squares. In another area, towards the road, are the remains of 200 small circular constructions, arranged in lines of twelve.

These are the basic facts but what on earth was it all for? We asked at the archaeological museum in Cusco, and there we struck gold in the form of George Squier's fascinating account of his travels in Peru, published in 1877. In line with all 19th century explorers, Squier had a meticulous eye for detail and the patience to write it all down. I owe the following information to him, and to subsequent writings by Luis A. Pardo in the Revista del Instituto Arqueologico del Cuzco.

The most fascinating aspect of the Temple of Viracocha is the story of how it came to be built. Some people think it was to appease the god Viracocha, after a volcanic eruption. I suppose that's the most logical explanation but I prefer the account by the notoriously inaccurate Inca (he was mestizo, actually) chronicler, Garcilaso de la Vega, who described the building in all its glory.

This version is that the temple was built by Inca Viracocha, the son of Yahuar Huacac. The father was a mild, ineffectual man with little patience for his son's ambitions and impetuosity, so he sent the prince to the village of Chita, three leagues northeast of Cusco, in honourable exile, to supervise the royal herds pastured there.

After three years the Prince returned, saying he had had a vision. During a siesta in the fields, a white-bearded, celestial being appeared before him saying 'I am the son of the sun, brother of Manco Capac. My name is Viracocha and I am sent by my father to advise the Inca that the provinces of Chinchasuya are in revolt, and that large armies are advancing thence to destroy the sacred capital. The Inca must prepare. I will protect him and his empire.' Inca Yahua Huacac was unmoved by this warning, however, and took no precautions against the coming invasion. When the attack took place, as predicted, he fled to Muyna.

The people, abandoned by their Inca, scattered in all directions, but the prince (who had now assumed the name of Viracocha) arrived with some shepherds of Chita, and persuaded them to return and defend Cusco. Prince Viracocha fought valiantly, though his forces were greatly outnumbered. 'The very stones rose up, armed, white-bearded men, when the weight of the battle pressed hardly on the youthful Inca.' He won, of course, and deposed his father at the request of a grateful people.

The new Inca Viracocha ordered the construction of a marvellous temple, different from any preceding it, at Cacha (de la Vega glosses over the mystery of why the temple had to be built there, rather than at Chita where the vision had appeared, or on the battlesite).

The temple was to be roofless, with an elevated second storey. It would contain a chapel with the image of the God Viracocha, as he had

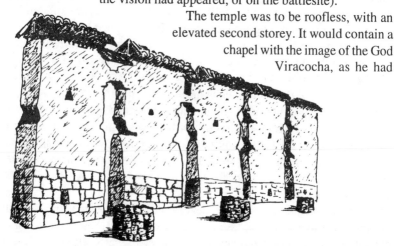

Temple of Viracocha at Raqchi

looked when he appeared to the prince. The floor was paved with lustrous black stones brought from afar.

De la Vega describes the temple in detail, but his descriptions don't fit with the present ruins, so it's likely that he relied on second hand reports. However, his sorrowful statement that the Spanish destroyed this magnificent temple in search of gold is certainly true. According to Squier, the churches of San Pedro and Tinta are built of stones from the temple walls, as is one of the bridges across the river Vilcanota.

Looking at the present ruins, you can see that the rows of pillars probably supported a slanting roof. The second floor could have been sustained on the columns, with ubeams running from them to holes in the centre wall.

De la Vega doesn't mention the other ruins, but it's probable that the identical houses were priests' dwellings, or perhaps barracks. The two hundred small circular buildings were thought by Squier to be pilgrims' lodgings, but it's more likely they were warehouses or granaries.

There is one other Inca site here, and that is the baths to the left of the temple. You will have to leave the Temple area by the gate you came in, and follow the path between stone walls. The baths have some fine water channels, and fresh running water can still be collected there. There is good camping nearby.

Practical information

Distance	About 50km/110km
Altitude	Between 3,440m and 4,900m/5,000m
Rating	Moderate to difficult
Timing	4-9 days
Maps	IGN sheets *Sicuani* 29-t, and *Ocongate* 28-t, 1:100,000.
In reverse	Possible for both routes

Route description

The trail starts northeast of the Inca temple, goes past the Inca baths and climbs steeply uphill to the main trail which snakes through the lava. Turn right and walk between stone walls until you reach an open area, then continue in the same direction to the foot of a stone-free hill. Turn left here and follow paths up the valley, above some houses sheltered by large trees. Go north up the valley on the right-hand side of the gorge, on a good trail which crosses the stream near the top and climbs over the pass. The path becomes fainter here, but you can follow it into the valley as it zig-zags down a scree shoulder towards the village of Paucaoros. There is good camping in the area or you can descend to the Río Salca through a eucalyptus plantation on the right-hand side of the stream. It takes about 5-6 hours from Raqchi to the river.

Turn left at the Réo Salca and follow it along a good track for about 2km until you see a village on the opposite bank. A kilometre further down you'll find a cable across the river with a small wooden platform dangling below it — and that's how you cross! Once on the other side walk back up the valley to the village of Salloca — 1-2 hours. From here, if you want to terminate the walk, you can hike out to the village of Combapata.

To continue the circuit to Pitumarca, when you reach the first houses of Salloca look for a well-marked path heading up the valley. It is exceptionally beautiful, crossing and recrossing the tumbling river over well-made bridges. There are flowers and flowering shrubs everywhere and plenty of hummingbirds. You'll reach some idyllic campsites about an hour after leaving the Salca valley.

The first community you come to is Pulpera, after about 3 hours. From here the path curves round to the right, up Quebrada Palcoyo, and after 2 hours of steady climbing you reach the compact small village of Palcoyo at 4,100m. Continue up the valley on a well-used path, probably together with a herd of llamas and/or alpacas, to the small community of Chulloca, about 3 hours from Palcoyo. Just before the village a path climbs up the valley to your left. Follow it to some corrals, and continue climbing steeply to the pass at 4,800m — about 2 hours. The landscape takes on a lunar quality and even the alpacas look extra-terrestial. At the top you may feel, as I did, that you've landed on Mars.

Two paths lead down the valley from the pass. One runs to the right (southwest) down the side of the mountain ridge into the valley; the other continues northeast. Take the latter and follow it to a village on the valley floor. The trail traverses a rather nasty scree slope so you may prefer to drop down to the village before this stretch. Continue up the valley past the houses, following any handy alpaca tracks you may find. There's no trail. The pass at 4,900m is on the right-hand side of the valley head. It's a hard slog and will take a discouraging 2 hours from the village. But an incredible view will greet you when you finally reach the top: Auzangate and the whole Vilcanota range stretches along the horizon. If you are finishing your trek at Pitumarca your climbing is over: it is downhill virtually all the way. Just descend to the Río Pitumarca, make a left turn (west) and follow the river until its junction with Quebrada Chillcamayu — about 2 hours — then continue to Pitumarca.

To continue your trek north to Tinqui, from the river junction (Pitumarca and Chillcamayu) continue west on the south side of the rivers until you reach the Uchullucllo bridge where you cross. From here follow the directions for the *From Pitumarca to Tinqui* hike.

TAMBOPATA: A RAINFOREST EXPERIENCE
By John Forrest

The Tambopata Reserved Zone (TRZ) was designated in 1977: 5,500 hectares of rainforest on the banks of the river Tambopata 3 hours upriver from the 'frontier' town of Puerto Maldonada. Over the ensuing years biologists from around the world, staying at the adjacent Explorer's Inn jungle lodge, established that the TRZ contained an incredible diversity of flora and fauna, including several world records. Over 580 bird species, 1,200 or so butterflies, 91 mammals, 127 amphibians/reptiles, 135 species of ant in the canopy alone and more than 600 leaf beetles amongst others were recorded as well as 165 species of tree recorded in just one hectare.

Lobbying by Conservation International, the Associacion por la Conservacion de la Selva Sur (ACSS) and the UK based Tambopata Reserve Society (TReeS) and others, led to the creation in 1990 of the Tambopata-Candamo Reserved Zone (TCRZ) covering 1,479m hectares. In addition to the luxuriant sub-tropical moist forest, swamp forest and bamboo thickets of the lower Tambopata drainage basin, the TCRZ now also encompasses tropical savanna and cloudforest ecosystems, through an increased altitudinal range (240-3,500m).

Two lodges, **Explorer's Inn** (Peruvian Safaris SA, PO Box 10088, Lima 1. Tel: (14) 316330; fax: (14) 328866) and **Tambopata Jungle Lodge** (Peruvian Andean Treks, PO Box 454, Cusco. Tel: (84) 225701; fax: (84) 238911) perched on raised ground above the river can be reached by air from Cusco in a few hours. Extensive trail systems run into the surrounding forest and allow the visitor to enter a beautiful and fascinating world, where patience and a quiet step are essential if wildlife is to be observed. The standard of the facilities at both lodges is good, with most guiding undertaken in English. On the upper Tambopata another more basic lodge, **Colpa Lodge** (Rainforest Expeditions, Galeon 120, Lima 41. Tel/fax: (14) 389325) is located close to one of the largest known 'Colpas' (macaw salt-licks). On most days this offers a fantastic display of colour and a cacophony of sound as the parrots assemble to nibble at the mud forming the river cliffs from which they derive important minerals.

TReeS was founded in 1986 to promote the conservation of the area on a sustainable basis in the long-term. The Society supports Peruvian biologists to enable them to undertake field research and applied investigations, works with the local native people to empower them to retain their traditional activities, especially with respect to health care, and provides advice to those visiting the area from abroad. A Resident Naturalist Programme offers a few places annually to foreign scientists, enabling them to undertake a study while guiding tourists to the lodges. Further details from **TReeS**, c/o 64 Belsize Park, London NW3 4EH, UK; or c/o 5455 Agostino Court, Concord, CA94521, USA.

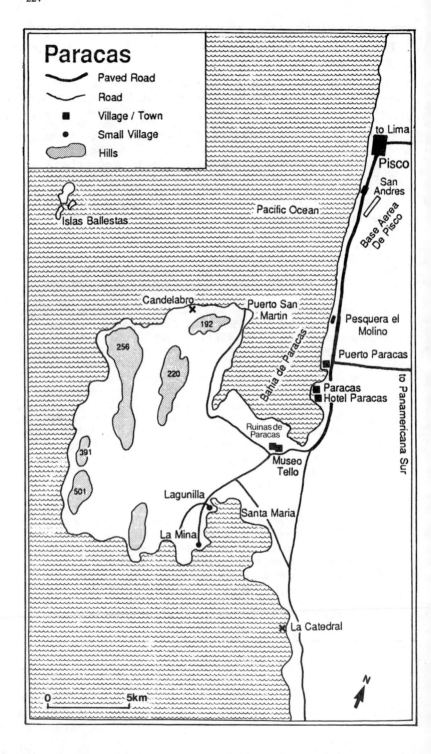

Chapter Fourteen

Paracas

Introduction

The focus of Paracas is the National Reserve of Paracas which is situated on a peninsula just south of the small town of Pisco about 266km south of Lima. Here you have the Peruvian desert with its incredible sand dunes, rock formations, and coastal cliffs. It is a fascinating area both for wildlife and history, and provides a nice change for the hiker who is satiated with snow peaks and green valleys.

THE PARACAS PENINSULA

Huge sand dunes behind steep rocky cliffs give this peninsula a stark grandeur. The protected area of 335,000 hectares (117,406 hectares of land and 217,594 of ocean) was established as a national reserve in 1975. A great variety of wildlife lives on and around the peninsula and its surrounding islands, with the Ballestas Islands the most important. There is no transport and only a few dirt roads; the only way to see it is on foot.

History

The archaeological riches of the Paracas peninsula were unknown before 1925 when the Peruvian archaeologist, J C Tello, discovered burial sites of the Paracas culture, which thrived in the area from approximately 1300BC until AD200. Little is known about the early years of this culture, called Paracas Antiguo, and not much more of the later years, divided into two periods: Paracas Cavernas (from 500BC to 300BC) and Paracas Necropolis (from 300BC to AD100). Both were named after the two main burial sites.

Numerous mummified remains have been found in the tombs, buried alongside funereal offerings, and wrapped in some of the most beautiful weavings produced anywhere in the world at any time. Perfectly preserved in the dry desert air, the woven llama wool and cotton tapestries are still vivid in colour, showing the most intricate designs of stylized marine creatures and human figures along with mythical beasts. They are one of the marvels of Peru. The average size of these weavings is one metre wide and 2½ metres long, but the largest measures four metres by an astounding 26 metres!

You can admire these texiles in the Tello museum at the entrance of the peninsula and in several museums in Lima.

Getting to the National Reserve
Daily buses leave from Lima to Pisco almost every hour, taking 3½ hours and costing US$4.

Lots of *colectivos* make the half hour journey from Pisco to Paracas, and some go on to the entrance of the reserve, 10 minutes from the town. If you walk it will take 1½ to 2 hours to the entrance from the village of Paracas along the bay. A taxi from Pisco will charge about US$10 to the entrance, and from Paracas to the entrance costs about US$5. Expect to pay a taxi about US$8 if you want to be dropped off at the village of Lagunillas on the peninsula.

Attractions
Places of interest in and around the reserve are divided more or less equally between archaeology and natural history.

The Tello Museum Be sure to visit this museum for the explanations about the Paracas culture which is continued in the information centre next door.

Flamingoes A good place to see these birds is behind the museum, as they walk down to the bay of Paracas.

El Sequion A lagoon which is a good place to see a variety of birds. It's situated along the road to Puerto San Martín, about half way up from the museum (7km).

Candelabro This is a candelabra-shaped pictogram scratched on to the highest point of a cliff overlooking the bay. You can see it from the beach, but it is best viewed from a boat. To get there, follow the dirt road to Puerto San Martín, and on to Puerto Pejerrey, the most northern point of the peninsula.

Lagunillas A little fishing village (only two restaurants, and nothing else), which lies to the south, about 1 or 1½ hours' walk from the museum (6km).

Sealions About 5km further south along the coast, you'll come to a cliff viewpoint above a sealion colony on the rocks below; plenty of seabirds can also be seen.

Viewpoint The highest hilltop of the peninsula, 501m, lies on the most westerly point of the coastline.

The Cathedral About 20km south of the peninsula along the coast is an impressive rock formation in the form of a cathedral.

Wildlife

The area is sometimes dubbed the 'poor man's Galapagos' but there is really no comparison. However, the Paracas peninsula and the nearby Ballestas Islands do certainly provide exceptional viewing of a large number and variety of marine mammals and birds: sealions, boobies, pelicans, penguins and flamingoes. It is also, surprisingly, one of the best places in Peru to see the Andean condor; this huge bird favours the area because of the thermals provided by the cliffs and the plentiful supply of carrion from dead sealions.

Harder to see but equally plentiful are the fish species. These include jellyfish, so beware!

The islands around the peninsula are part of the reserve and you are not allowed to go on shore as this will disturb the wildlife. Please repect this rule.

BALLESTAS ISLANDS

The islands (three in total) are a 2-hour boat ride from Puerto de Paracas. The most popular sight are the vast sealion colonies. The boats spend about an hour around the islands before they go back, passing the *Candelabro* along the way. The trip takes the whole morning and costs about US$5. Organized trips in a speedboat from the Paracas Hotel will cost about US$10, and last about 2 hours.

TOWNS

Paracas

This small village has little to offer: a few houses, some basic restaurants and a nice beach with camping possibilities. Boats leave from the port here for the trip to the Ballestas Islands.

Sleeping and eating

There are three or four mid-range hotels in the area around the village. There is nothing for budget travellers who have to stay in Pisco or camp on the peninsula.

Paracas Hotel On the beach outside the village. Bungalows with swimming pool and restaurant. About US$35.

Hostal Santa Elena 100m from the beach on the peninsula. About US$18

Hostería Paracas Close to the village. About US$18.

Hotel El Mirador At the entrance to the village. US$12.

Restaurants The speciality in this area is, of course, seafood. Almost all hotels have a restaurant. For cheaper meals try the restaurants in the village along the beach.

Pisco

Pisco is a traditional fishing village about 15km north of Paracas. The village is divided in two: Pisco Pueblo and Pisco Puerto. It is not a very exciting place, but has some charm in its own rather laid back way. There are *hostales*, restaurants, shops and a market. It is also the starting point for a trip to the Paracas peninsula, being the stopping place for long distance buses. There is frequent local transport from here to Paracas.

Sleeping and eating

Hostal Embassy One block from the Plaza. About US$10.

Hostal San Jorge Calle Juan Osores 267. About US$8.

Albergue Juvenil (youth hostel) Jr José Balta 639, Pisco Playa. About US$5.

BEACHES

There is a fish factory just outside Pisco so the beaches between Pisco and Paracas are polluted. Those along Paracas Bay are not bad, but are still not very clean. The best beaches are on the peninsula itself, and to the south:
The bay of Lagunilla (on the peninsula)
Playa Atenas (10km from the entrance of the peninsula)
Mendieta (21km to the south of the park)

Be very careful when choosing a place to swim; the ocean currents can be dangerous. Avoid beaches which face the open sea — it is better to look for a quiet bay. The most dangerous beaches are considered to be Yumaque, Arquillo, Supay and Playon. Also beware of jellyfish.

HIKING INFORMATION

The peninsula is an interesting area to hike around for a few days, providing a dramatic contrast to the highlands. Always bring a compass (it's very easy to get lost) and carry enough water.

Climate

The sun is very strong in the summer season (from December until April) so be prepared with good sun protection (sunscreen, a sun hat, and a shirt with a collar) and plenty of water. It never rains on the peninsula, and temperatures are usually high. In the winter season (from April to November) the famous *garua* blankets the coast and the temperature drops, which makes it chilly at night and sometimes even during the day.

Camping

Bring basic camping equipment, food and plenty of water (and something to carry it in) as there is nothing available on the peninsula except at Lagunillas where they serve fish and soft drinks at three basic restaurants.

The peninsula is a popular camping spot for the Limeños in the holiday months of December, January and February, especially around New Year's Eve when huge beach parties are organized.

Garbage is a big problem on the peninsula, since it does not decompose in the dry conditions. Set a good example and carry yours out.

Maps and books

A detailed map is available from the IGN in Lima; recommended if you are planning to hike on the peninsula.

Sadly, for such a fascinating area, there is little published information. The *Paracas Tourist Guide*, a little booklet sold in the bookstores of Lima is helpful with general information.

Safety

Robbery is a problem at the camping areas. It mostly happens when campsites are left unattended, and a few cases of armed robbery have been reported through the years. Never leave campsites unattended and try to camp in a group. Leave your valuables behind.

Chapter Fifteen

The Arequipa Area

Introduction

The fertile valley around Arequipa, 1,000km southeast of Lima and 320km from the Chilean border, is a sunny, fertile pocket tucked between the coastal desert and the high Andes. It has a lot to interest the hiker: snow-capped volcanoes, remote Quechua villages, the Colca Canyon, archaeological sites and the dazzling white colonial city of Arequipa.

This section is updated with the help of readers Linda Guinness and Renaye Upton.

AREQUIPA

Peru's second largest city lies at 2,380m and enjoys an almost idyllic climate: sunny and mostly dry, with a mild rainy season between December and April. Often called 'the White City' after the volcanic *sillar* from which its older buildings are built, it is overlooked by the snow-capped, perfectly shaped volcano, El Misti.

Arequipeños have never been able to agree on how their city got its name. Does it come from the Aymará 'Ariquipa', meaning 'the place behind the peak'? Or did it originate with the Inca, Mayta Kapac, who was so gripped by the beauty of this valley that he ordered his retinue to stop, calling out *'Ari quipay'* ('Yes, stay')?

Although an important settlement since pre-Inca times, Arequipa was refounded by the Spanish in 1545 and this gives *Arequipeños* an excuse to celebrate on and around 15 August every year. Unfortunately the valley is prone to earthquakes and volcanic eruptions. The city was totally destroyed in 1600, and as recently as 1991/92 the volcano Sabancaya erupted again, covering a huge area in volcanic lava and almost engulfing the village of Maca. Luckily several of Arequipa's 17th and 18th century buildings, including the Santa Catalina monastery, have escaped destruction and are now tourist attractions.

Getting there and away

To and from Lima

By air 70 minutes. All the domestic airlines serve this route. There are at least four flights daily.

By road 18 hours. Several bus companies operate on this route; Ormeño and Cruz del Sur have been recommended. Most companies have offices on Calle San Juan de Dios. Be warned that the bus station area has a bad reputation for theft. There is a new bus terminal for most buses a little way out of town.

To and from Cusco

By air 40 minutes. Many travellers take this flight as an alternative to the Arequipa to Cusco train, especially in the rainy season when the trains are often cancelled. There are daily flights.

By train 20-24 hours. A night train runs to Juliaca where it connects with the day train to Cusco. Daily trains in the dry season; fewer in the rainy season.

By road 18 hours (longer, and sometimes not even possible, in the rainy season). Buses and trucks daily. The road is in a very bad condition.

To and from Juliaca, Puno and Bolivia

By air Half an hour. Daily flights.

By train 10 hours. Night train to Juliaca as above; then a connection to Puno in 1 hour. Frequency as to Cusco.

By road 9 hours, depending on the weather and state of the road. Buses and *colectivos* daily. Most continue to Puno in a further ½ hour. Daily transport from Puno to La Paz, 8 hours.

To and from Tacna and the Chilean border

By air Half an hour. Two flights daily.

By road 5 hours. Several buses and *colectivos* daily.

Sleeping and eating

Readers have recommended **La Casa de mi Abuela** (Calle Jerusalén 606; about US$8 per person) and **Hostal Nuñez** (Calle Jerusalén 528; more basic at US$4 per person).

The popular Cusco vegetarian restaurant, **Govinda**, is here on Jerusalén 400.

Useful addresses

Tourist information office Plaza de Armas, opposite the cathedral. Helpful and friendly and they have a good city map.

Tourist police Calle Jerusalén 317. Tel: 239888. May be able to help if you have problems or complaints.

Ministry of Tourism (MITCI) Calle La Merced 117. Tel: 213116.

Touring y Automóvil Club del Perú Calle Sucre 209.

Travel agencies Several along Calle Jerusalén and around the Plaza de Armas, offering trips to the Colca Canyon and Toro Muerto. But be warned that some of these agencies are unreliable; make sure you understand what is on offer, and never pay in advance as your tour may be cancelled (possibly at the last minute) if not enough people turn up.

A recommended agency is *Expeandes* (Calle La Merced 408, Oficina 1. Tel: 212888), who organize adventure trips and may also have equipment to rent.

Club de Andinismo de Arequipa (Gimnasio los Dementones, Quinta Romaña 207. Tel: 233855) occasionally arranges hiking and climbing trips. Casual but helpful. Meets weekly.

Oficina de Guías (Calle Alameda Pardo 117. Tel: 231103) may be able to provide you not only with a guide but also with information and equipment to rent. Carlos Zarate, president of the Peruvian Mountaineering Club, can be contacted here. Recommended.

CLIMBING THE VOLCANOES

The dominant geographical feature of the area is the volcanoes, so these are the focus for most hikers. This is a dry area and little natural water is available: it must all be carried with you. You climb more for a sense of achievement than for the ever-changing views.

Practical information
Climate
Although enviably sunny for much of the year, the Arequipa area can be subject to heavy downpours between December and April, making the trails very muddy and dangerous.

Conditions/what to bring
Make sure you carry enough warm clothing and good camping equipment for those freezing nights! For much of the time you'll be hiking above 4,000m, so take time to acclimatize. Wear a hat and protect yourself from the sun. Take *plenty* of water.

Maps
The topographical maps of this area from the IGN are especially useful, as few others are available.

Guides and pack animals
You don't normally need a guide to hike in this area. Most trails are obvious, and there's usually someone to ask in case of doubt. On the volcanoes, however, routes can be confusing and weather conditions can change

quickly and dangerously. For these a guide is recommended, or at least someone who's done it before. Choose your guide with care; many are unreliable. Carlos Zarate or the Club de Andinismo will be able to put you in touch with one (see *Useful addresses* above). A trekking guide will charge US$30 per day; a climbing guide $40-50.

You can arrange for *burros* or mules if necessary, at one of the villages near the starting points of the hikes. *Burros* cost about US$8 per day; *arrieros* US$10.

Equipment
Very basic gear can be rented at some travel agencies, at the Club de Andinismo or from Carlos Zarate.

Food and supplies
Buy your main supplies in Arequipa, where there are several good supermarkets and a market. 'Govinda' has muesli and good bread.

Volcán el Misti (5,822m)
The volcano which provides Arequipa with its splendid backdrop is a popular climb, best done late in the season when there's less snow. Although not a difficult ascent, El Misti shouldn't be taken lightly. The weather can change without notice from extreme heat to snow, making it easy to get lost, cold and dispirited — a perfect recipe for disaster. If no-one in your party has done the climb before, you should consider taking a guide.

You need to carry a lot of water (there's none along the way), together with cold-weather clothing and camping equipment. The ascent doesn't, however, involve any technical climbing.

Getting to the trailhead
Buses for Chasqui leave Arequipa daily at 06:00. Ask to be let off at Aguadas Blancas, a hydroelectricity station where the Chivay and El Fraile roads meet.

Practical information
Altitude	Between 2,950m and 5,822m
Rating	Moderate
Timing	2 days
Maps	IGN sheet *Characato* 33-t, 1:100,000

Route description
Follow the El Fraile road to the far side of the first dam. (You may have some difficulty getting through the hydroelectricity station's security system.) Then continue for 5½ hours to Monte Blanco, a flat area with corrals where you should camp.

From Monte Blanco a zig-zag path will take you in 4 hours (rather more if there's a lot of snow) to the summit, which is marked by a 10m iron cross. On fine days the view is magnificent. From here you can continue to the edge of the inner crater where fumeroles can occasionally be seen.

Volcán Ubinas, 5,672m
Robin Eckhardt recommends this climb for 'its lonely position and the salt lake with flamingoes which you pass on the way to it'.

Getting to the trailhead
The starting point for this walk is Laguna Salinas Borax, 150km from Arequipa on the road to Puno. To get there from Arequipa, take a *colectivo* at 06:00 to the village of Ubinas from Sepúlveda 200. This street is reached by the yellow-white bus '5 de Agosto', and it's best to book a seat the day before. It's not clear from my information whether the *colectivo* goes all the way to Ubinas, or whether you have to get out at Laguna Salinas Borax. Either way, going via Salinas Borax, you reach the junction of the Puno-Ubinas road in about 4 hours, and after continuing towards Ubinas for another 1½ hours you come to the foot of the volcano.

Practical information
Altitude	Between about 4,000m and 5,672m
Rating	Moderate
Timing	2 days

Route description
From Laguna Salinas Borax it can be seen that the volcano has three peaks. The southern one to the right is the highest; for this you must ascend by the southwest route. There are many things to see from this peak: jets of steam, fumeroles and a turquoise crater lake 270m below. (If you go down to the lake, leave plenty of time to climb back or you'll be returning to Arequipa in darkness.)

Getting back
This can be a problem unless you've booked a *colectivo* in advance. 'If not, it is impossible to get a seat. The second possibility is a huge truck which travels by night and passes the volcano between 17:00 and 19:00. Extremely cold, and the drive lasts 6-7 hours.' (R Eckhardt)

Volcán Chachani, 6,076m
An impressive volcano about 20km north of Arequipa, this high and cold climb should be tackled only by experienced mountaineers with full snow- and ice-climbing equipment. Do not climb alone.

Getting to the trailhead

The starting point is on the road to the village of Chiva (4,700m), which you can reach by bus from Arequipa. The Chasqui bus company makes the trip three times a week, and there are others. Ask to be put down at the jeep track leading up towards the volcano.

Practical information

Altitude	Between 4,700m and 6,076m
Rating	Difficult
Timing	2-3 days
Maps	IGN sheets *Arequipa* 33-s, and *Characato* 33-t, 1:100,000

Route description

Walk 8km to the end of the jeep track, gaining 430m, and continue for another 1½ hours to a campsite in the shelter of some stone corrals, just below a saddle. After camping here (camping higher will expose you to fierce winds), turn left and drop 200m before starting the final ascent. The summit will be reached 10-12 hours after leaving the corrals.

THE COLCA CANYON

A hundred kilometres long, this incredible gorge is said to reach a maximum depth of 3,400m — twice that of the Grand Canyon. Although a mere 150km north of Arequipa, its full extent was recognized only as recently as 1954; the first explorations took place in 1978 and the first descent by raft and canoe in 1981. The Colca is a wild and dangerous river — not for the faint-hearted! (Expediciones Mayuc, Casilla 596, Cusco, are one of the few companies who offer white-water rafting on it.)

On both sides of the canyon you'll find picturesque villages whose inhabitants will help you with directions. Many still wear distinctive and colourful traditional costumes.

The agricultural terracing here must rival that of the Incas.

Cabanaconde to Andagua

This is justifiably the most popular of the Colca Canyon hikes. It takes you to the bottom of the canyon, up the other side, over a 5,000m pass and down to the village of Chacas, before going on to finish at Andagua in the so-called 'Valley of the Volcanoes'. This is a very strenuous trek because of the altitude gain and loss: 3,200m or nearly 10,500ft!

Getting to the trailhead

Cabanaconde — the best base for canyon excursions — can be reached in

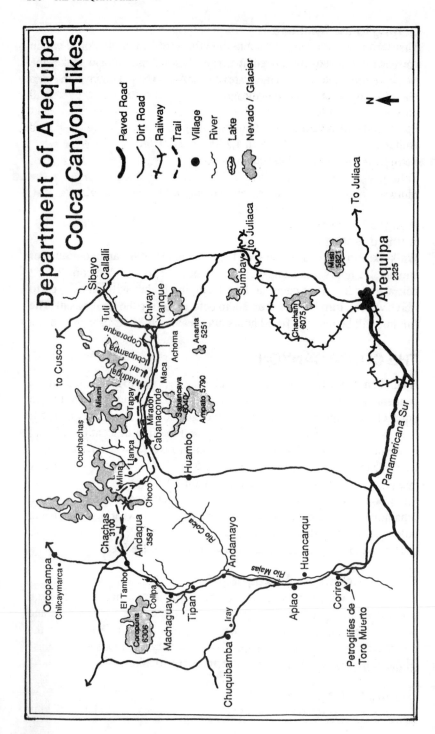

Department of Arequipa
Colca Canyon Hikes

10 hours by bus from Arequipa: a rough, dusty trip but with good views. Several buses leave daily at about 05:00 from Calle San Juan de Dios. En route you'll pass Chivay, a worthwhile stop (Hotel Colca, clean and friendly, single US$5), from where you can hike in half an hour to swim in hot pools at La Calera, or cross the canyon to the village of Sibayo on the one and only bridge built for vehicles. This 35km journey takes an hour by pick-up. From Sibayo you can continue to Cusco or to Andagua (also spelled Andahua).

An alternative route to Cabanaconde goes round the other side of Sabancaya via El Alto and Huambo — a 12-hour journey, longer in the rainy season.

Practical information

Altitude	Between 1,800m and 5,000m
Rating	Moderate to strenuous
Timing	6 days
Maps	IGN sheet *Chivay* 32-s, 1:100,000. Also a small picture book, *Arequipa and the Colca Canyon*, can be bought in Arequipa for US$10. It includes a map of the canyon.
Conditions	Water is scarce; carry as much as you can at all times. Protect yourself from the burning sun.

Route description

Cabanaconde is a sleepy village at 3,287m, where the road ends on the edge of the canyon. You'll find its friendly inhabitants dressed in beautiful hand-embroidered clothing. There are three very basic hotels on the plaza, with toilets but no showers and sometimes no water (single about US$2). Some basic restaurants offer meals, and there's a minuscule market. The hill 10 minutes' walk to the west of the village is an excellent place for viewing the canyon's much-publicized condors. The best times are around 06:00 and 18:00. (But Linda Guinness and Renaye Upton add that if you're unlucky here there's a stuffed one in a restaurant in the plaza that takes up an entire wall!)

Leaving Cabanaconde for the canyon is rather confusing, as there are many paths. Ask locals for the way to Choco and they'll point you in the right direction. A road has been built across the canyon, but apart from a short stretch you don't need to follow it; take the footpath instead.

After passing the hill just behind the village, the well-used stone path drops gradually into the canyon, keeping to the right, until it crosses a dry river at the bottom of a *pampa*. From here climb the hill to your left, passing a small house, and keeping left until you see the road. Now make a sharp right turn on a faint short cut to meet the road about 2 hours from Cabanaconde.

The road winds its way into the canyon and up to the village of Tapay on the other side. Follow it for half an hour until you see a well-marked trail climbing the hill to your left. This is your path to Choco. It drops gradually westward, with spectacular views of the canyon, to a footbridge over the Río Colca 5-6 hours from Cabanaconde. The first water of the day is found in a stream just before here. This bridge, Puente Colgado, lies at a mere 1,800m and until recently was one of Peru's last remaining Inca *manguey* fibre bridges. It became dangerous and has now been reconstructed, but the remains of the fibre bridge have been put on top of the new one. On the other side you'll find some small camping places between the rocks.

From Puente Colgado the path climbs steeply up the other side to the village of Choco (2,473m), taking about 3 hours. It gets hot in this valley so it's important to make an early start from the bridge.

Choco is one of those increasingly rare Andean villages — beautiful, friendly and so far unspoiled! Resting in the plaza, you'll soon attract an audience, and if you ask around one of the *señoras* may be willing to prepare you a meal.

From Choco a long and steep climb begins. The well-marked stone path starts on the left-hand side of the plaza (facing the mountains) and follows the river for about an hour, then goes up the mountain to the right, heading for an elusive 5,000m pass. There are some possible camping spots, but if they show signs of cultivation be sure to ask permission first. The first stream is 4-5 hours from Choco.

Continue climbing towards the pass, banishing feelings of despair (it seems to get no nearer) and filling your water bottles wherever possible as the valley is dry higher up. There are good campsites before the pass, but it will be freezing cold and there is no water. From Choco to the pass will take 10-13 hours.

As it approaches the summit the path becomes very faint, but always picks up again. At last you reach a moraine, and a final steep climb will bring you to the top of the pass. Incredible views! From here it's all downhill to the village of Chachas: a steep descent at first, but then easing off into meadows. Stay on the left side of the valley. About 2 hours from the pass you'll be able to take a well-deserved shower! From this point to Chachas will take another 3 hours.

Overlooking a huge lake and surrounded by rich farming land, Chachas (3,100m) is another beauty of the Andes. As in Choco, its people aren't used to strangers and you may find yourself the centre of attention, but the stares are friendly. The village has no shops, but if you ask around you may be able to get a meal and even accommodation. It might be better, however, to camp across the river. Ask the villagers where.

Occasional trucks make the journey from Chachas to Andagua, but really the walk is too good to be missed. (Don't forget to fill your water bottles.) Begin by climbing to the pass on your right, almost at the end of the mountain range, taking a footpath which short cuts the road. The summit is about an hour from the village, giving breathtaking views of the 'Valley of the Volcanoes' on the other side.

Follow the road from the pass down to the river, taking short cuts when they appear, then, leaving the lake on your right, take the footpath up the hill directly opposite for the final climb to Andagua. From the pass to Andagua is 4-5 hours.

Andagua is a small, mountain village at 3,587m where the road from Chachas joins the Arequipa-Orcapampa road. Basic food and meals can be found in the plaza, and you could probably get accommodation if needed. Or camp outside the village. The villagers here are very friendly, more acquainted with gringos, and happy to chat.

Buses leave for Chivay and Arequipa about 3-4 times a week, and trucks almost daily. The 12-hour trip passes the beautiful snowy peak of Corapuno (6,306m). You could stop at Corire in the valley of Majes (basic accommodation at the Hostal Manuelito) and visit the interesting Toro Muerto ('Dead Bull') petroglyphs.

Detour via Hacienda Tauca

If you want to spend an extra night in this area, take the path to the right from the highest pass (between Choco and Chachas), and follow the ridge down into the next valley. There are great views and it's a nice hike, but make sure you have enough water as it will be hot in the valley. The path drops down to the river where you'll find some houses which are known as Hacienda Tauca. Ask the way to the bridge (up the hill behind the *hacienda*). Just before the bridge, a short way to your right, are some good camping spots by a waterfall and pool. From the pass to the bridge will take about 7 hours. From the bridge a well-marked path climbs upwards, steeply at first, through rich farmland to Andagua.

Pinchollo to Cabanaconde
By Linda Guinness and Renaye Upton

This hike offers spectacular Inca stonework, fine village churches, ancient terracing, more condors and, near the Choquetico viewpoint, tombs and crude paintings high on sandstone cliffs.

NOTE: Hikers doing this route will need the spirit of adventure since these directions are for guidance only. An IGN map of the area would be useful.

Getting to the trailhead

Pinchollo is a small, cold village on the Chivay-Cabanaconde road. You can walk along the road from Chivay in a long day, passing the villages of Yanque and Achoma with their Inca carvings and huge churches, or you can take the bus. In Pinchollo very basic accommodation and simple meals are available.

Practical information

Rating   Moderate
Timing   2 days
Conditions   Hot sun and little water

Route description

From the church in Pinchollo, take the lower of two stone-walled paths through maize fields, and follow it for 20 minutes to a wooden bridge over a stream. Climb up the other side to an edge, and follow this for 10 minutes to join a road at a point where a water pipe crosses. Look here for a path to the right, and follow this past some houses, veering left downhill to a small lake. Go to the right of this and climb to join some animal tracks which lead through giant cactus gardens, parallel to the road.

Between here and the viewpoint called El Cruz del Condor, reached in 1½ hours from Pinchollo, there are plenty of places to camp, but no water. The cross is easy to see, standing out against the horizon. It's where the buses from Chivay stop to let passengers see the canyon. From the road beyond, animal tracks lead off in the direction of Cabanaconde, which is reached in 2-3 hours (longer if you follow the road).

When you're ready to leave Cabanaconde, take the path which leads past the Restaurante Colca, and once outside the village bear left at each fork until, after 10-15 minutes, you come to the canyon edge. The 2-3 hour descent is hard on the knees, but at the bottom you will find the lovely Sangaye tropical gardens where you may be permitted to camp. There is bathing in the tepid springs.

(Linda and Renaye returned by the same route, a climb of 3-4 hours, but were told that you can cross the river and climb up to Tapay on the other side in 1-1½ hours.)

Part three

BOLIVIA

Chapter Sixteen

Bolivia:
General Information

Introduction
Bolivia gets its name from the great Venezuelan liberator of so much of South America, Simón Bolívar, but it was probably discovered by Europeans even before Pizarro set foot in Peru. In 1520 a Portuguese explorer called Aleixo García journeyed west from Brazil, but was prevented from making the first transcontinental crossing by Inca warriors and the formidable barrier of the Andes.

Physical and social geography
The Western Cordillera of the Andes forms a natural border with Chile. To its east lies the high, barren Altiplano bounded by the Eastern Cordillera before the Andes drop down to the Amazon basin to their northeast. The Cordillera Real, which provides the best hiking and climbing in Bolivia, is part of the Eastern Cordillera.

Rising moist air from the Amazon rainforest is trapped as it heads towards the Andes, so the eastern slopes are thickly forested, and the rainfall is high. Northeast of La Paz this eastern region is known as the Yungas, divided into Nor and Sud Yungas. Being warm and wet, the Yungas produces large amounts of coffee, cocoa and all sorts of fruit. This is also the main area for coca production.

The people of present-day Bolivia are nearly three-quarters Indian, and 70% of the population lives on the unproductive Altiplano which comprises 10% of the country. The largest body of water in the Altiplano is Lake Titicaca which, for this landlocked country of people clinging to their ancient beliefs, has a spiritual significance far greater than its economic importance.

Climate
Bolivia shares Peru's highland climate, with a dry, sunny season from April to the end of October and a rainy season from November to April. On the Altiplano during the dry winter season it is bitterly cold (around or below

freezing) at night and in the early morning and evening, and cool on cloudy days, although these are rare at this time of year. Daytime temperatures range from about 10°C to 18°C.

The Yungas shares the same dry/wet months but varies from quite wet to very wet depending on whether it is the 'dry' or rainy season.

BOLIVIA'S CHANGING CLIMATE
By Jim Conrad

Western Bolivia's *altiplano* region once was covered by a huge lake extending from north of Titicaca to southwestern Bolivia: Titicaca, Poopo and other of the region's high-elevation lakes, marshes and salt-plains are remnants of that vanishing lake. In fact the whole region seems to be drying up, possibly as a reaction to man's influence. In 1993 a resident of the deep valleys in the Bolivian Yungas told me this: 'Forty years ago, before they began clearing even the steep slopes for coca and other crops, this valley stayed so moist and misty that you never saw the sun until 9.30. Now as soon as the sun rises above the peaks its rays are bright and hot. Moreover, new plants are invading the valley, especially weeds. Some of the prettiest wild flowers we used to wait for at certain times of the year don't even flower any more, or maybe they flower, but at the wrong times. Everything is all messed up nowadays....'

This conversation took place at the foot of a landslide probably resulting from a new clearing up the slope: natural trees succumbing to man's taste for cocaine.

A brief history
Pre-conquest

Unlike Peru, where various civilizations rose and fell before the advent of the Incas, in Bolivia one culture dominated: Tiahuanaco or Tiwanaku, by Lake Titicaca. Their beginnings are dated around 1000BC and their achievements in stone masonry and grandiose religious structures rival those of the Incas. However, they were not conquered by the Incas but collapsed through some natural disaster around AD900. Archaeologists believe that Lake Titicaca was once much larger than its present size and that whatever forces caused its diminishing spelled the end of Tiwanaku, which is now some way from the lake.

For some 300 years the people of Tiwanaku shared aspects of their culture such as road-building, land terracing and irrigation with the Huari of central Peru, with whom they probably had commercial links. Unlike the Huari, the descendants of the Tiwanacans, the Aymará, resisted the Incas who never really achieved domination over these fiercely independent people.

Post-conquest

Bolivia was conquered by the Spanish in 1538, its vast resources of silver making it a very valuable possession. It became part of the Viceroyalty of Peru, but there were revolts as early as 1661. By 1824 a series of uprisings had prepared the way for independence. Bolívar's general, Sucre, invaded Bolivia after winning the Battle of Ayacucho in Peru, and the Spaniards were defeated in the Battle of Tumusla in 1825. Later that year Bolívar named the country after himself.

Bolivia has become progressively smaller since independence, losing a series of territorial wars. The most painful loss was that of its Pacific coast to Chile in the War of the Pacific from 1879 to 1883. Both Brazil and Argentina followed suit by annexing Bolivian territory, and the greatest loss in terms of size came when Paraguay seized a vast chunk of Chaco in the first half of this century. Bolivia's aggressive neighbours usually built a railway in compensation, which explains why this country has one of the most extensive railway networks in South America.

When it was not under attack from across its borders, Bolivia suffered internal strife, and in modern times has become infamous as the country which has had more political coups than years of independence. By the mid-1980s the country was in economic chaos, with inflation running at 20,000%. Drastic measures taken by the newly elected President Paz Estenssoro to stabilize the economy have succeeded in bringing inflation down to a very respectable 10% or so. In recent years there has been steady economic growth and, although it is still the poorest country in South America, Bolivia is, at last, politically stable.

EXITS AND ENTRANCES

At present citizens of the European Union need only a passport to enter Bolivia for a stay of 90 days, and those from the USA can get a 30-day entry. Tourist cards are available at the airport and at frontier crossings and are valid for only 30 days, but are easily renewed at the Ministry of Immigration (see *Useful addresses* on page 259). Canadians, South Africans, Australians and New Zealanders need a visa. At land frontiers there's no insistence on a return ticket although in theory this is required, along with 'sufficient funds' for your stay.

When you leave Bolivia, even if only for a day, don't forget to ask for an exit stamp.

For onward travel you can get a visa for neighbouring South American countries from consulates in most large Bolivian cities and in many smaller towns near the frontiers.

Bear in mind that visa requirements for Bolivia seem particularly prone to change and you should check the current situation when buying your air ticket.

When arriving in Bolivia it is as well to heed Jon Derksen's advice: 'To avoid hassle — and I've seen many people hassled by officials — avoid wearing clothes that have "I might be the kind of person to buy or sell drugs" written all over them, for example dirty jeans, well-worn alpaca ponchos, T-shirts with holes, sneakers beyond their prime. And unfortunately long, unkempt hair is sometimes a sure way to prompt the "fickle finger", a rather uncomfortable sort of body search. Being rude is also a fine way to complicate your entrance into or out of the country. Although this may sound prudish, it is best to present yourself respectably.'

CURRENCY

During the 1980s Bolivia's economic problems were legendary. Inflation percentages were measured in thousands, people went around with neat newspaper parcels of banknotes, and beggars didn't even bother to pick up low value notes. Today the economy is stable and inflation is down to an acceptable level, but at considerable cost: Bolivia's wage levels are the lowest in South America and its cost of living among the highest.

The currency is the *boliviano*. Occasionally you'll hear these being referred to as pesos. But anyone quoting you a price with 'mil' on the end is either still thinking in *old* pesos (1,000,000 = 1 *boliviano*) or else trying to rip you off on a consummate scale!

The rate of exchange is now remarkably stable at about Bs4.80 to the US$.

USEFUL INFORMATION
Transport between Cusco and La Paz
AeroPeru flies three times a week between Cusco and La Paz. Transturin runs comfortable buses between the two cities and also boats across Lake Titicaca.

Telephones
Public telephone booths are easily recognizable in their bright orange paint. To operate them you need a token, *ficha*, which are sold by shoeshine boys, street vendors or small shops in the vicinity. Long distance calls within Bolivia can be made without an operator (area codes: Santa Cruz 03, La Paz 02, Cochabamba 046) and likewise overseas calls from a touch-tone phone. If you need an overseas operator dial 0713113.

Holidays
The ones that are likely to catch you out are Labour Day (May 1), the La Paz municipal holiday (July 16) and Independence Day (August 5 to 7).

These days are marked by military parades and closed shops and businesses.

In villages, fiestas are frequent and fabulous (see page 50). The tourist office in La Paz (see *Useful addresses* on page 259) will confirm the date and place of the best fiestas.

Business hours
Weekdays: 10:30-12:30, 15:00-18:00 or 19:00. Saturdays 10:00-14:00.

Mail
The mail system is efficient. Each town and city has its *centro de correos* (usually situated near the main plaza) but secondary post offices are starting to appear, making mailing a letter an almost enjoyable experience. In the main post offices you will find a large bin at the back of the post office where you post your letter according to the continent to which you are sending it.

As in Peru, letters should be sent to the *Lista de Correo* or c/o American Express. When writing to businesses, always use their *casilla* (PO Box) number. It will take up to three weeks for your letter to arrive in Bolivia from North America or Europe.

Newspaper
The English language *Bolivian Times* is published on Fridays and often has articles on hiking as well as other subjects of interest to travellers.

At the airport
El Alto is the highest commercial airport in the world and surely the most beautiful. You step out into bright morning sunshine, your heart fluttering through lack of oxygen, and see the entire Cordillera Real ranged in front of your admiring eyes. It could not be a better welcome for mountain lovers! The good impression is maintained in the airport itself which is calm and efficient, and even provides trolleys for your luggage.

It is only a short drive into La Paz and since most international flights arrive in the early morning you will probably prefer to take a taxi for around US$8. There are sometimes buses, however, and if the little tourist office at the airport is open they will advise you.

On leaving you must pay a departure tax. This is Bs10 for national flights, but US$20 — in hard currency—*plus* Bs150 to North America or Europe, and almost the same for Chile and Argentina (US$20 plus Bs100).

Laundry
As in Peru there are *lavanderías* where you can take your washing, but most hotels will do it for you and the cheaper the hotel, the cheaper the laundry charges. Make sure you know what the cost will be, however.

THE COCAINE TRADE
By Clare Hargreaves

Cocaine took off in the West in the 1970s; seen as glamorous, harmless and socially acceptable, it was the rich man's drug. Then in the 80s came crack, which is far more harmful. In the United States, where most cocaine and crack were consumed, drugs became a political issue and the government launched a 'War on Drugs'. Bolivia and Peru, which produce virtually all the raw coca leaves used to make cocaine became, together with Colombia, the main targets of the 'war'. Their governments came under strong US pressure to eradicate coca fields and put the drug barons out of business.

In Peru, coca is grown mainly in the northern Amazonas Department and in Bolivia it is produced in the Chapare, between Cochabamba and Santa Cruz, and the Yungas. In 1990 an estimated 51,000 hectares in the Chapare were planted with coca. The first stages of processing are also carried out here in primitive 'pits' in the jungle. The leaves are mashed with chemicals by barefooted men known as 'stompers'. The last of the three stages of processing is carried out in sophisticated laboratories in northeastern Bolivia, in the Beni. You are unlikely to see one, as they are well hidden (and if you do, make yourself scarce as quickly as possible).

In Santa Cruz you can see the luxurious houses inhabited by many of Bolivia's drug barons, and the businesses like discos and car dealerships where they recycle drug cash.

If you are travelling in the drug-producing areas, you should be very careful. Remember that if you have a white skin, drug dealers will assume you work for the CIA or the DEA (US Drug Enforcement Administration) and will not want you around. On the occasions that Westerners have run into trouble it has almost always been because they were in the wrong place at the wrong time. Don't be!

Many of the *campesinos* who grow coca for cocaine would prefer to grow a legal crop, but find that coca is the only product that pays. Attempts to grow alternative crops such as coffee, tea, cocoa and citrus fruits have failed because of the difficulties of penetrating the western markets. You can help by buying products like Cafe Direct which cut out the middle person and give a better return to the producer.

Clare Hargreaves is author of Snowfields: The War on Cocaine in the Andes, *see* Further Reading.

Handicrafts

Good quality tourist items are not particularly cheap, but on the whole the quality is better than in Peru and there is more variety and ingenuity. Machine-knitted alpaca sweaters are a good buy, and there are some 'designer label' sweaters that are almost the same price as you'd pay at home but gorgeous! Drool over them in the shops up Calle Sagárnaga.

Guitar players will probably fall for a *charango*, a small twelve-stringed instrument with an armadillo shell as a sound box. If you buy one, be sure to get an instruction book as well.

Bolivia's traditional weavings — ponchos and *mantas* — are second to none. The most beautiful are undoubtedly those made in the Potosí and Sucre areas. Designs on the ponchos and *mantas* woven here incorporate all sorts of mythical animals, and are unique. There is usually a good selection in La Paz, especially from street vendors up Calle Sagárnaga, although, inevitably, prices are higher than for those bought direct from the makers.

Leather goods are excellent and inexpensive; gold and silver jewellery is good value and often beautiful; and the tin cutlery and other tableware sold on Calle Sagárnaga, above the church of San Francisco, is attractive and cheap, although it tarnishes easily.

You can buy just about anything at low cost in the *Mercado Negro*, black market, in the Calle Maximiliano Paredes area.

Strikes

General strikes, *paros cívicos*, are now rare rather than commonplace. When they do occur, public transport is usually affected. More worrying for foreigners are the marches by coca workers in protest against the US anti-drug policy of eradicating the coca crops.

Hot baths

La Paz and other Altiplano towns are freezing at night, and a hotel without hot water is a real misery. If circumstances or economy force you to sleep cold, go to the public baths (*baños públicos*) which exist in most towns. They are usually very good value with lots of hot water.

For a real treat in La Paz, spend an afternoon in the sauna at the Plaza Hotel, and follow it up with a massage. Bliss!

Security

Jon Derksen writes: 'My wife and I feel very safe in Bolivia. We have never met such friendly and generous people as in the Bolivian countryside. But many have deep-rooted traditions and suspicions. Simple foresight and respect will help you to avoid most undesirable situations. For example, always ask before taking a picture — many native people truly do believe that a camera steals their souls. While visiting the town of Tarabuco, I tried to photograph a lady in the market. She called out to me, "If you take my picture I'll throw this bag of food at you!" My brother Craig, who was with me, called back jokingly, "If you do, we'll eat it!" At that moment a local passer-by, who had overheard the exchange, whipped out a knife and held it to my throat. "Take the picture and I'll cut you!" he said. Now, this may sound frightening, but the man was right; I'd overstepped my bounds. Luckily for me he put the knife away and smiled victoriously.

'Don't assume that if country people are dancing and having fun they want you to be part of it. On the other hand, if you are cornered or approached by one or more festive, drunk or perhaps belligerent individuals, don't panic and try not to look afraid. Use whatever Spanish you have to offer to buy a round of beers, or share a few coca leaves with them. I've won more than a few friends in the *campo* this way. Every so often you might run into a truly dangerous situation. As in any other country, racism is alive and well in Bolivia, and whatever you do or say, the colour of your skin may sometimes serve as an unspoken provocation. Try to read the situation as best you can.

'Use your common sense. People in remote areas are understandably wary or curious about you. If wary don't approach them too openly. In many parts of Bolivia backpackers are still a novelty. If the people are curious, invite them over, but be prepared to talk for a couple of hours about everything under the sun.'

When the inevitable question comes up of how much everything you own cost you, it may be prudent to say it was a gift rather than revealing its price tag.

PROTECTED AREAS OF BOLIVIA

By Jonathan Derksen

The national parks and reserves in Bolivia were created for the protection, preservation and survival of Bolivia's diverse wildlife. Only the native population may live within the national parks and reserves, although some non-native populations have been given consent to open up reserve lands in the jungle lowlands. In theory, the rainforest and cloud forest reserves were established to ensure that rare species of plants and animals would not be destroyed by human encroachment. However, in practice the decimation of forest lands and uncontrolled hunting have led to the tragic and rapid decline of rare natural habitat.

Since the late 1980s and early 1990s certain groups, both local and international, have been struggling to conserve endangered areas. Fundación Amigos de la Naturaleza (FAN) in Bolivia and Conservation International and Nature Conservancy in the USA, are just three organizations that have helped establish new protected areas. Some organizations have attempted debt-for-nature exchanges where part of Bolivia's external debt is cancelled in return for greater local commitment to financing conservation projects.

In 1992 the United Nations organized ECO-92, a massive meeting held in Brazil to discuss the more serious global environmental issues, especially the fate of the Amazon Basin. Since then, Bolivians seem to be more cognizant of the threat to their precious resources, but finding ways to put thoughts into action has proved difficult, given the lack of direct government involvement and funding, and given the conflicting interests of loggers, agro-industries and peasants eager to exploit new lands.

Is there an answer to these problems? Groups blamed for the irresponsible development of resources must be shown viable alternatives. Long-term sustainable development programmes must be effectively publicized so that those in positions of power feel the need for change and, at the same time, realize that such schemes can procure a profit. Stephen Schmidheiny, Swiss billionaire and chairman of UNOTEC, who has funded several sustainable development projects in Bolivia, states the following in his executive summary of *Changing Course: A Global Business Perspective on Development and the Environment*:

> Clean and equitable economic growth, which is integral to sustainable development, requires more efficient use of resources... such growth... requires open and competitive markets. It also requires a break with conventional wisdom that sidelines environmental and human concerns.

For example, by logging selectively, timber prices may rise, but there would not be the complete devastation caused by clear-cut logging. 'Extractive reserves' are an alternative. These try to use the forest as a renewable resource, harvesting such things as brazil nuts and rubber, thus avoiding deforestation. In the Pando, Bolivia's northernmost province, it is illegal to cut down a brazil nut or rubber tree, and as a result, huge tracts of land have, to a large extent, been spared.

National parks and reserves
These are listed according to their number on the map overleaf taken from *Bolivia Mágica* by Hugo Boero.

1 **Reserva Nacional Manuripi-Heath (1978)** Located in the northeast of the country, this reserve is dedicated to preserving the true Amazon rainforest found between the Heath and Manuripi Rivers. The reserve boasts an abundance of rubber and brazil nut trees, smaller areas of natural savanna and a wide variety of jungle life.

2 **Refugio de Vida Silvestre Estancias Elsner (1978)** This reserve was established primarily to protect savanna life in the Beni lowlands, especially along the Yacumo River basin.

3 **Estación Biológica del Beni (1982)** This research station was established in the Moxos region of the Beni Department to study and protect both upper Amazon basin wildlife and communities of Chimane Indians, who continue to live a hunter-gatherer existence. The 334,200 hectare

Protected Areas of Bolivia

PANDO
Cobija
1

PERU

BRAZIL

BENI
2
3   Trinidad
8

Lake Titicaca
4
LA PAZ
5
La Paz
6
7
10   11
COCHABAMBA
Cochabamba
13   12   9
14   Oruro   15
ORURO   SANTA CRUZ
Santa Cruz

Sucre
16   Potosi
17
POTOSI   CHUQUISACA
PARAGUAY
19   20   TARIJA
Tarija
18   21
ARGENTINA

CHILE

1 Manuripi - Heath	8 Noel Kempff Mercado	15 Torotoro
2 Estancias Elsner	9 Amboró	16 Yura
3 Estacion Biologica Beni	10 Isiboro-Sécure	17 Tapilla
4 Ulla Ulla	11 Repechon	18 Eduardo Avaroa
5 Condoriri	12 Tunari	19 Sama
6 Mallasa	13 Huancaroma	20 Las Barrancas
7 Makiri de Comanche	14 Sajama	2 Tariquia

territory is comprised mostly of forest, intermixed with savanna and swamp. Deer, jaguars, alligators and other animals are currently threatened by unregulated hunting. Contact: Conservación Internacional, tel: 341230 (La Paz).

4   **Reserva Nacional de Fauna Andina Ulla Ulla (1972)** This reserve is located in the remote Apolobamba mountain range near Bolivia's western border with Peru. The 200,000 hectare park spans three major zones: glacial highlands, tundra (*altiplano*) and sub-tropical Yungas. The tundra portion of the park not only harbours Bolivia's largest concentration of vicuñas, but its numerous shallow lakes also provide safe haven for waterfowl like the Andean goose and Chilean flamingo. Contact: INFOL, tel: 379048 (La Paz).

5   **Parque Nacional del Condoriri a Yungas (1942)** It includes the chain of mountains approximately 60km east of La Paz. The area is best known for the snow-capped peak, Chacaltaya, and the subtropical Zongo Valley. Andean condors, foxes and highland deer frequent the area. Contact: Señor Alfredo Martinez Delgado or Dr Hugo Berrios of Club Andino Boliviano, tel: 324682.

6   **Parque Nacional Mallasa (1955)** It includes lands bordering the river beds just below La Paz, and covers the eco-region of dry inter-Andean valleys characterized by bizarre, eroded sedimentary deposits, locally known as 'Valleys of the Moon'. Viscachas (a rodent related to the chinchilla) are commonly seen.

7   **Parque Nacional Cerro Makiri de Comanche (1946)**, recently renamed **Santuario de Vida Silvestre Flavio Machicado Viscarra** An area south of Lake Titicaca known for its gently rolling hills and extensive meadows. Guanacos may be seen here.

8   **Parque Nacional Noel Kempff Mercado (1979)** This 541,000 hectare park, previously known as Serrania de Huanchaca o Capurus is situated on Bolivia's northeastern border with Brazil (see page 313). It is best known for its impressive escarpments that rise majestically from an unbroken sea of forest, and several picturesque waterfalls. Rare animals like maned wolves and giant river otters may be spotted. The conservation group Fundacion Amigos de la Naturaleza are now running trips into the park during the May to October dry season. Contact: Miriam Melgar (Ecotourism Assistant), Fundación Amigos de La Naturaleza (FAN), tel/fax 533389 or 333806 (Santa Cruz).

9   **Parque Nacional Amboró-Carrasco (1973)** This park dominates 630,000 hectares on the east side of the Andes between Cochabamba and Santa Cruz (see page 309). It offers the widest variety of landscapes and life zones as it is situated where the Chaco, Amazon Basin and Andean foothills meet. The park is in danger of encroachment by loggers and peasants seeking to exploit its vast reserves. Contact: Jon Derksen, tel: 795903 (La Paz), and FAN (see above).

10 **Parque Nacional Isiboro-Sécure (1965)** This park covers an area of approximately 1.2 million hectares between the Isiboro and Sécure Rivers and the Serranías Sejerruma, Yanakaka and Mosetenes. Despite recent infiltration of loggers and peasant farmers, the more remote regions of the park are still home to prolific Amazonic wildlife. Contact: Fremen Tours, tel: 327073 (Cochabamba), fax: 48500.

11 **Santuario de Vida Silvestre Cavernas de Repechon/San Rafael (1986)** These little-visited caves are found in the Chapáre region of the Cochabamba Department. The caves are home to the *guácharos* or oilbirds (*Steatornis caripensis*), a rare species of nocturnal bird which navigates by echo-location. The young were once hunted for their fat content.

12 **Parque Nacional Tunari (1962)** The name refers to the protected mountain slopes surrounding the city of Cochabamba. Although the park's wildlife has been decimated due to poor management, it still offers several worthwhile hikes, including the trip to the El Pirámide summit.

13 **Refugio de Vida Silvestre Huancaroma (1975)** Privately owned lands 200km south of La Paz along the Desaguadero River. Although used as grazing lands for livestock, it protects a large area of dry *puna*.

14 **Parque Nacional Sajama (1945)** This remote park on Bolivia's southwestern border with Chile occupies an area of about 80,000 hectares, and includes Mount Sajama, an extinct volcano, arguably Bolivia's highest mountain at 6,542m. Attractions include the world's highest forest (*queñoa* trees), vicuñas, rheas, armadillos, flamingoes and Andean condors.

15 **Parque Nacional de Torotoro (1992)** This recently established park, like all parks in Bolivia, offers sights unique to the region, among them an extensive cave system, also called Torotoro, petrified dinosaur tracks and sea fossils.

16 **Reserva Nacional Fauna Yura (1974)** This reserve in Potosí

Department protects fauna of the high Andes, especially the vicuña. The area is seldom mentioned in studies on Bolivia's protected areas.

17 Reserva Fiscal Cerro Tapilla (1940) This is one of the oldest reserves in the country, originally set aside for breeding chinchillas (*Chinchilla brevicaudata*), which may now be extinct in the area, if not in all of Bolivia.

18 Reserva Nacional de Fauna Andina Eduardo Avaroa (1981) This reserve is found in the extreme south of the country, in the dry *altiplano*. The area originally only included Laguna Colorada (a high altitude lake, tinted a striking red by algae and home to over 21,000 James flamingoes and numerous rheas) and the 10km² surrounding it, but was later expanded to its present size.

19 Estacion Biológica Sama This research station located outside of Tarija in Bolivia's far south is dedicated to the study of the flora and fauna of the high Andean plains. Unfortunately, very little information on this area is available.

20 Parque Nacional Las Barrancas (1966) This park was set up to stop the severe erosion around the city of Tarija. Large tree- and herb-planting projects have been undertaken here.

21 Reserva Nacional de Flora y Fauna Tariquia (1989) This national park, also near Tarija, protects wildlife of the dry tropical valleys of the surrounding mountains.

22 Reserva de Vida Salvaje Ríos Blanco y Negro (1990) This 1.4 million hectare reserve, also known as Perseverancia and located 350km north of Santa Cruz, still contains huge areas of unbroken wilderness. The region is profuse in wildlife and boasts significant numbers of giant anteaters, monkeys, bush dogs, deer, peccaries, jaguars, river otters and other Amazon basin fauna. Access to this reserve is possible only by chartered plane in the dry season (March to October). Contact: Amazonas Adventure Tours, tel: 324099, fax: 337587 in Santa Cruz.

PACHAMAMA IN BOLIVIA

In Bolivia, people of all classes make the traditional *Pago a Pachamama* or sacrifice to Mother Earth to ensure good luck (or rather to prevent bad luck) when building a new house. A Bolivian friend described an elaborate affair which she attended to inaugurate a glass factory. One llama was sacrificed for the sales department and one for the plant itself. First a pit was dug, oriented east to west, and prepared with coca leaves, herbs and incense. Bottles of beer and sweet wine were placed at each corner of the pit, which was then blessed by the priest. A *brujo* (sorcerer) was called in to 'read' the coca leaves to see what colour the sacrificial llama should be.

The beast arrived, washed and groomed and wearing a silk coat decorated with gold and silver 'coins' and paper money. It was made to drink three bottles of beer and one of *aguardiente* (apparently it offered no resistance throughout the ceremony), then to kneel first towards the sun and then towards Illimani before its throat was cut. Even then it did not struggle; it did not even blink.

The blood was sprinkled around the perimeter of the factory and in the pit, which then became the llama's grave.

On a less lavish scale, but still symbolizing an offering to Mother Earth, is the *mesa con sullo*. This is what the dried llama foetuses and strange herbs and objects that are sold at the 'witches' market' near Calle Sagárnaga in La Paz are for. If Pachamama can't have a live llama, she'll settle for a dried foetus, rubbed with fat to simulate the real thing. This must be laid on a bed of wool (white for purity), along with sweets in the shapes of different animals and devils, nuts and seeds, and gold and silver trinkets. All this is by way of returning to Mother Earth what has been taken from her. The foetus may be dressed in a coat, like a real sacrificial llama, and little bottles of sweets may take the place of the beer in the full sacrifice. The whole thing may be topped with a piece of cat's skin to represent the untameable, which still succumbs to the power of Pachamama.

When complete, the objects will be blessed, then parcelled up and buried, to the accompaniment of incantations and sprinkles of alcohol, either under the foundations of a new house, or in the countryside in view of the major snow peaks and their *achachilas* (mountain spirits)

To ensure that vegetables and fruit are safe to eat in Bolivia, use locally bought DG-6 germicide. Squeeze 30 or so drops into a litre of water. Immerse the food into the solution for 10-15 minutes before eating. Most households in La Paz use DG-6 in preference to iodine since there is less aftertaste in the food.

Chapter Seventeen

La Paz

Introduction

The city huddles in a bowl-like valley with the Altiplano forming the rim. Whether you arrive by air or by bus, you won't forget your first sight of the city lying below you surrounded by the high peaks of the Cordillera Real. It's the highest capital in the world, at a cool 3,632m, and you'll soon find out if you're a *soroche* sufferer. Altitude sickness hits most people flying here, and the problem is compounded by this being one of the hilliest capitals in the world. Except for the Prado, the main street down the centre of the valley, everything of interest seems to be at the top of a steep hill. At least it's difficult to get lost in La Paz, which is like a giant funnel: walk downhill from anywhere and you'll arrive at the Prado.

The Prado, whose official name is Avenida 16 de Julio, is broad and lined with modern shops and offices, but the old city, up on the hill around the government palace, is full of character. The Indian market in the San Sebastián district (above the church of San Francisco), is a fascinating place. Here you can buy a llama foetus to bury under the foundations of your new house for luck, or more mundane things like an aluminium saucepan for your next hike.

When you are tired of sightseeing, sit on the steps of the San Francisco church and do some people-watching.

City transport

The most convenient way for tourists to get around is by taxi. Radio taxis are efficient and their numbers are posted everywhere. Short trips cost Bs5 (about US$1) and longer trips Bs10. In La Paz *colectivos* are called *trufis* and run along set routes. Microbuses and minibuses run along the major routes; they are crowded but cheap.

Sleeping and eating
Accommodation

Libertador The best value mid- to upper-range hotel, Obispo Cárdenas 1421. Tel: 327263 or 343362; fax: 351792.

Hotels recommended by readers include:

Hotel Italia, Av Manco Kapac 303; rather noisy, but hot showers.

Hotel Andes, Av Manco Kapac 364; similar to the Italia but cleaner.

Residencial Rosario, Calle Illampu 704; clean, with a nice restaurant — popular with travellers.

Hotel Torino, Calle Socabaya 457; central and friendly, slightly more expensive but good rooms at the back.

In addition to these popular gringo hangouts, Jon Derksen recommends: **Hostal La Republica**, Calle Comercio. Tel: 356617.

Hotel Eldorado, Ave Villazon. Tel: 326952-329652.

Hotel Bolívar, Ave Manco Kapac. Tel: 375030.

Hotel Gloria, Calle Potosí. Tel: 370010.

Hotel Calacoto, Calle 13 in Calacoto.

Calacoto is at the bottom of La Paz valley. To get there you follow the Kantutani highway down through Obrajes until you round a curve and cross a bridge. La Florida and Calacoto are just past the bridge. In addition to the hotel mentioned above, this is a good area for restaurants and bars.

Restaurants
Some favourites with expatriates:

New Tokio (Japanese), Ave 16 de Agosto.

Eli's Coffee Shop, Av 16 de Julio.

Restaurant La Suisse, Av Arce, across from the Radisson Hotel.

Restaurant Naira, Calle Sagárnaga, for traditional Bolivian food and music.

Restaurant Puerta del Sol, Av Ballivian, Calacoto.

Chifa Emy (Chinese), Av J Aguirre Acha, Los Pinos.

There is a British pub run by Tom Clough which is deservedly very popular: **The Britannia**, on the corner of Calle 16 and Av Ballivian in Calacoto. Next door is the **Abracadabra Restaurant** which will happily send a pizza or hamburger over to the Britannia. In the same neighbourhood, try the outdoor **Las Cholas** on Calle 7. The specialities are cheap local and imported beer, pickled onions and Chola sandwiches. The latter are snacks prepared by *cholitas* (local girls) consisting of a bun filled with pork, tomato, onion and *escaveche* (pickled this and that).

El Príncipe Morada provides a set Bolivian meal, including llama meat, and good live music for a reasonable price. Calle Simón Aguirre 150, off Av Tito Yupanqui in Villa Copacabana. Tel: 230123.

For a treat go to one of the *Kuchen Stube* tea-rooms, either in Edifício

Guadelquivir on Calle Rosendo Gutiérrez (a few blocks up from the Sheraton Hotel) or in Edifício Mariscal Ballivián at Calle Mercado 1328 (the same building as the tourist office — see *Useful addresses* below). How better to prepare for a hike than by gorging yourself on German cakes?

Hiking maps

Bolivia used to produce some of the best topographical maps in South America, but sadly most of the popular ones are now out of print. The IGM sales office is in Edificio Murillo. It is easy enough to find the front entrance, but map purchasers must go to the *back* of the building: go up Calle Oruro by the main post office and you will see the blue and white Edificio Murillo to the right. Turn left, *away away* from the building, and after about 50m turn sharp right on to Calle Rodriguez which runs uphill at an acute angle, then take the first road (unpaved) to the right. This is Pasaje Juan XXIII. Edificio Murillo and the back entrance to the IGM will be visible once you turn the corner. Open Monday to Friday 09:00-12:00 and 15:00-19:00.

Imprenta Don Bosco publishes contour maps by Walter Guzman Cordova which are fairly accurate. The Choro-Takesi-Yunga Cruz map is especially good, showing altitude, vegetation, lakes, mines, water supplies, towns, roads, trails and camping sites. They are available at the Amigo de Libros bookshops in La Paz.

Mountain guides

There are several good guides living in La Paz. The best way to contact them is through Alfredo Martinez Delgado of the Club Andino Boliviano (see below). Sr Martinez is one of the most experienced mountaineers in the country.

Erik Nijland recommends the brothers Bernado and Eduardo Guarachi who run a trekking office in La Paz: Andes Expediciones, Plaza Alonso de Mendoza, Edificio Santa Anita, 3er piso, local 314; tel: 02 320901.

Useful addresses

Ministry of Immigration Calle Gosálvez, between Av Arce and Calle 6 de Agosto.

Club Andino Boliviano Calle México 1638 (Casilla 1346), La Paz. Tel: 324682. Open Monday to Friday 09:30-12:30 and 15:00-19:00 pm, Saturday/Sunday 08:30-21:30. Small library with maps and a meeting place for members. Some maps for sale and equipment for rent. Pretty casual — opening hours not guaranteed!

Club de Excursionismo, Andinismo y Camping (Contact via Catalina Ibáñez at Plaza Tours, Av 16 de Julio 1789, La Paz. Tel: 378322.) Meets Wednesdays, 19:30-21:00. Members may be able to offer information on hiking, climbing, skiing, mountain biking and even kayaking. Some equipment to rent.

Secretaría Nacional de Turismo 18th floor, Edifício Mariscal Ballivián, Calle Mercado 1328 (Casilla 1868), La Paz. Tel: 367411 and 367463/4. Open Monday to Friday 08:30-12:00 and 14:30-18:30. General tourist and travel information.

TAWA Calle Rosendo Gutiérrez 701, La Paz. Tel: 325796. A French-run tour operator with an extensive programme of treks, jeep expeditions and rainforest excursions. They also operate charter flights between Paris and South America. (Address in Peru: Av N. de Pierola 672, Oficina 502. Address in France: 135 rue Marcadet, 75018 Paris.)

Colibrí Calle Sagárnaga 309 (Casilla 442), La Paz. Tel: 371936. Can rent equipment such as camping stoves; also have jeeps which you can hire (with driver) to take you to the trailheads.

Paititi Calle Pedro Salazar 848 (Casilla 106), La Paz. Tel: 341018, 342759 and 353558. Climbing and trekking trips.

Transturin Edifício Alameda, Av 16 de Julio 1656. Two blocks below Plaza Venezuela, on the left.

Camera repair Rolando Calla is highly proficient and speaks perfect English. Av Sanchez Lima 2178. Tel: 373621. 15:00-19:30 weekdays.

EXCURSIONS AND DAY HIKES FROM LA PAZ
Tiwanaku (Tiahuanaco)

Don't miss Tiwanaku. In the last few years an excellent small visitors' centre has been built which, with the help of models, gives a detailed and understandable account of this culture (in the 1980s a visit without a competent guide could be unrewarding — it's a site that needs to be explained).

Travellers coming from Peru will note that the people of Tiwanacu were as expert at carving stone as the Incas, and added interest is provided by the enigmatic carved figures and the wonderful Sun Gate.

On the way to Tiwanaku you pass through the small town of **Laja** which was the original La Paz, founded in 1548 by Alonzo de Mendoza. The town is dominated by its church, across a large plaza with bizarre-looking giant cacti interrupting the view. The church is usually locked (it is said to have a solid silver altar) but there are some interesting stone carvings on the outside pillars, including a monkey.

Ask at the tourist office for information on public transport to Tiwanaku, or consider taking a tour.

A day hike near La Paz
By Erik Nijland

This hike will lead you through wonderful countryside with superb views both of the city and of all the major mountains around La Paz. The first part is steep but it becomes easier later. It is a good hike to get accustomed to the altitude if you have plans to do one of the longer ones in the region.

Getting to the trailhead
Take a microbus 'Ñ' to its terminus at Ovejuyo. Then take any minibus going to Chasquipampa, from where the walk begins down the road past the police checkpoint.

Route description

Immediately after passing the Chasquipampa checkpoint, take a path on your right that descends to a riverbank and then goes steeply upwards in the direction of Collana. On the way up you'll twice cross a road (this is the one on which you'll return later). After 1½ hours you'll find yourself at a minor pass, from where there are good views back to La Paz. At this point avoid the temptation to follow the rolling footpath ahead of you. Instead take the road immediately beneath the pass; this way you'll be able to enjoy the wonderful views of Illimani and the flat-topped Mururata.

Keep to this road (occasionally used by trucks loaded with *campesinos*), ignoring two side-tracks on your left and passing a hill with a radio antenna on your right. After 45 minutes take a track to the right. This is used by vehicles, but probably not more than about one a week, so your hike is unlikely to be spoiled by traffic. The track descends and after half an hour you come to a small village called Lloto at 3,900m — the lowest point on the hike. The track turns into a footpath here. As you enter the village, look out for a trail going up slightly to your right; this will take you back to the pass. There are side-tracks, but the main trail is always clear. You will have lovely views of the city of La Paz and Huayna Potosí, and away to your left the valley of the Río Abajo which drains the city, with Muela del Diablo ('Devil's Tooth') standing as a watchtower over it.

After about an hour on this track you'll come to the pass crossed previously, from where you can retrace your steps to Chasquipampa. The whole walk will take between 4 and 5 hours. It could also be done by mountain bike if you keep to the road.

CHALCATAYA

By Jonathan Derksen

Mount Chacaltaya, located only 1½ hours' drive from La Paz, is an ideal day hike for those wishing to acclimatize for higher hikes, like Huayna Potosí glacier or Illimani. The summit at 5,600m (18,300ft) is a suitable climb for people of varying experience.

Like most glaciers in the Andes, this one is receding rapidly. According to recent studies, the ice pack at Chacaltaya is galloping backwards at a rate of six metres a year. In 10 years alone, environmental change has lopped at least 60 metres off the length and 10 metres off the width of this glacier. See it while you can.

Getting there

Rides can be arranged through a number of touring agencies in La Paz including: TAWA (tel: 341018, fax: 391175) and Zingara Travel, tel:

320837, 326287 — ask for John, George or Myrna Villegas). The Club Andino, which has a new clubhouse at the first (false) summit, also offers a bus service to the slope on Saturdays and Sundays. Tel: 324682.

For those approaching on foot, you should make your way for 1.5km on a surfaced road in the direction of Lake Titicaca, then turn right at the Bolivian Air Force base (recognized by a long, drab, grey wall with castle-like lookout towers). A wide road, paved at first, later a dirt road (to Milluni and Zongo) will lead you directly towards Chacaltaya. After 14km of easy slogging over open tundra, bear right at the sign indicating the ski resort. The road takes you up the foot of the mountain, past several glacial lakes on the right, then zig-zags wildly up until a large white research building appears on the left. Just above this are the old and new lodges of the Club Andino, the entrance fee is Bs5.

Practical information

Although this climb is relatively easy, you should remember that you are well above 5,000m and *soroche* or altitude sickness, is a real hazard. Do not attempt this hike if you have recently arrived from lower altitudes. The key at this altitude is to take rests even if you don't feel you need them. Deep, controlled breathing also helps.

The lodge is a good place to see how you fare at higher altitudes during the night. Snacks and hot drinks are available, but if you want something more nourishing you should bring it with you from La Paz.

Beware of the weather, especially between March and June when the heaviest snows fall. Bring waterproof clothing that will keep you warm in sub-zero temperatures.

Route directions

The approach to the summit is by the ridge just behind the new lodge. On a clear day a spectacular view of Huayna Potosí will unfold at your left. On your right is the glacier and ski-slope, a bit anorexic by North American or European standards, but nevertheless a thrill for anyone willing to go to the trouble of donning skis, although at the time of writing the new rope tow had not yet been installed. It is only 20 minutes to the the first summit at 5,400m where the rubble of an old observatory offers some shelter from the wind. The summit proper is reached by another 200m push up the slope. The Chacaltaya summits offer a panorama of the southern Cordillera Real, the Altiplano as far as Sajama, Lake Titicaca and La Paz. An alternative descent is down the west face to the Milluni road, visible below.

It is interesting to explore the glacial lakes and abandoned mines just below the foot of the glacier. I was surprised to discover a large lizard living among some ruins.

Chapter Eighteen

Lake Titicaca

Few travellers will intentionally omit a visit to Lake Titicaca (Titikaka). It is not hard to understand why this huge lake became the focus for a religion; today's visitors feel exultation at their first sight of this great sapphire-blue body of water contrasting with the dried yellow grasslands which surround it, and the white peaks of the Cordillera Real against the sky.

Most people find the Bolivian side of the lake more appealing than the Peruvian, perhaps because Copacabana is so much nicer a town than Puno.

Getting there

The drive from La Paz to the lake is full of interest. You climb out of the bowl of La Paz to the dusty, bleak Altiplano where the traditional way of life is maintained. Indians herd their sheep and llamas or till the dry soil, and (assuming it's the dry season) the sun shines from a relentlessly blue sky.

The first lakeside village is Huarina. As you drive west along the lake shore towards Huatajata you'll see the upmarket **Hotel Titikaka**, near Puerto Perez. This is pretty good value considering it has a heated swimming pool and a sauna, and wonderful views over the lake from the dining room (even if the pedalo boats do sink from time to time). Bookings for this hotel can be made at the Hotel Libertador in La Paz or by phone: 374877.

To reach Copacabana you have to cross the narrow Strait of Tiquina by ferry, and then comes a spectacular drive along an arm of the the peninsula and over the headland on a newly surfaced, twisting road to arrive high above Copacabana. The views of the lake and of the town are stunning.

Copacabana

Copacabana has plenty of hotels (**Hotel Playa Azul** being the best) and eateries, and Religion. This has been a sacred place from earliest times. First the Tiwanaku culture had its sacred sites near here, then the Incas, and now Bolivia's patron saint, the Dark Lady of the Lake, is housed in the church. Her chapel (in the main church) is well worth a visit because of the devotions of the people, but even more rewarding is the Capilla de Velas, to the left-hand side of the church, where people burn candles in support of their prayers. They used to press home their requests to the virgin by writing or drawing on the walls with melted candle wax; much to my regret this practice has now been forbidden. A few years ago there was hardly a bare space left on the walls: houses and trucks were by far the most sought after gift when I was there, with one worshipper spelling out 'Volvo' to make sure the Virgin didn't make a mistake (after all, what do women know about such things?).

Copacabana's inhabitants and non-gringo visitors seem to spend most of their waking and praying hours thinking about trucks. There are drawings of trucks in the chapel and models of trucks that you can carry past the Stations of the Cross hoping they will be changed by divine intervention into something larger and more practical, and, when the miracle has come to pass, there is a ceremony to bless the new truck. On Sundays and holy days there is a *challa* or blessing of cars outside the church. A priest officiates, and large quantities of alcohol and smaller quantities of holy water are sloshed or sprinkled over the engine and other vital parts. The vehicles are wonderfully decorated with flowers for the occasion.

On the hill behind town are the **Stations of the Cross**; pilgrims climb up here not only with model trucks, but with model houses or animals, to pray for a little materialism. It's easy to mock this, but when you climb with them and witness the seriousness and yearning with which the poor pray for possessions which we would take for granted, it is no longer a laughing matter.

The Copacabana fiesta is August 5-8.

On the other side of the town, away from the lake, is the path leading to the **Horca de Inca**, an impressive site, genuinely Inca, which was more likely to have had an astronomical significance than to have been the gallows that the name implies. The structure appears to be aligned to the winter solstice. The view from here is splendid but don't expect a beautiful red sunset — the Titicaca air is too clear!

THE INCA ROAD TO YAMPUPATA AND THE ISLAND OF THE SUN

Yampupata lies at the end of the Copacabana Peninsula and is the nearest land to the Island of the Sun. The 4-5 hour walk there, along an old Inca road (mostly destroyed, however, for the construction of a seldom-used vehicular road), is highly enjoyable.

Follow the road out of town and along the lake; there are very occasional vehicles, but mostly other foot travellers and their animals. 1½ hours after Copacabana the main track goes up a hill but a lower path to the left crosses a meadow with a stream (bridged by logs), near a house and a shrine, to climb steeply up an obviously Inca road (stone paved) to rejoin the road

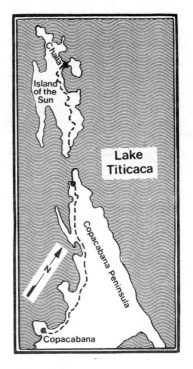

again. A tiring but scenically rewarding short cut. Yampupata is about 2½ hours after the log bridge. You can camp in Yampupata or probably find lodging in the small village. Ask here for a boat to Pilkokaina, on the Island of the Sun.

The Island of the Sun

The island supports a surprisingly large population so is networked with trails. You can walk and camp anywhere, and with fresh water readily available (providing you purify it) a few days on the Isla del Sol is a most rewarding experience. The most popular walk is to **Challa**.

From Pilkokaina walk along the terraces to the **Temple of the Virgins of the Sun**, which is Tiwanaku in style with early Inca influences. The stonework is crude, but there are some well-preserved and interesting adobe doorways moulded in the step-pattern that is typical Tiwanaku and also seen in Ollantaytambo in Peru. Illampu, a *nevado* sacred to the Incas, is framed by one of the trapezoid windows. You may be asked to pay a small entrance fee.

The walk continues by climbing higher up the terraces to pick up a trail running west with wonderful views over the blue lake. After some 3 hours you will reach an old *hacienda* which was owned by an ex-president and is said to have dungeons; below here, by the lake shore, are the **Inca Springs**. These have been 'modernized' to provide drinking water for the local populace (and for thirsty hikers). This is where the tour boats come in so where the handicraft sellers hang around.

Challa is a small village on the neck of a bulbous peninsula which now has a little gringo *pensión*, Posada del Inca, on the beach before you arrive at Challa village on the other side of the headland. You can also find lodgings in the village itself.

Continuing west along a good trail for about an hour you will come to the **Inca Labyrinth**. This is another of those sites given an explanatory name where no explanation is possible — or needed. It's enough to explore the many tiny rooms (for what purpose?) and admire dramatic views over the lake.

There are boats available in Challa to take you back to the mainland.

Chapter Nineteen

The Cordillera Real

The 150km of Bolivia's Cordillera Real stretch from the Sorata Valley to Río La Paz (Río Choqueyapu), providing a splendid backdrop for the world's highest capital city. There are six peaks over 6,000m, and many more above the 5,000m mark. This mountain range is perfect for backpacking, offering days of hiking above the treeline with snow-capped mountains appearing round almost every bend, and steep descents to the tropical vegetation of the Yungas. Here are two of the finest pre-Columbian highways in South America; the stone paving is even more impressive than in Peru.

All the trails described in this section start within a day's journey of La Paz, and a couple are only a few hours away. There is no problem acclimatizing for the hikes: a few days' sightseeing in La Paz will take care of that. All the trails can be done in reverse if you prefer going uphill to downhill (and it is a serious option for those getting fit and acclimatized for a mountaineering expedition).

THE CONDOR'S NEST: ILLIMANI BASE CAMP

By Erik Nijland

Many hikers who have just arrived in La Paz are tempted by the majestic sight of Illimani (6,440m), overlooking the city and shining in the evening sun. Although this is a challenging and technical climb, backpackers can enjoy an excursion to the base camp called El Nido de Condores (The Condors' Nest). This lies at 5,600m, giving you the chance to test your fitness and to check out your cold-weather gear, while watching the lights of La Paz twinkling below you as you listen to the cracking of the glaciers surrounding you.

Getting there

Follow directions for getting to the Takesi trail (see page 271). When you reach Ventilla look for transport as far as Cohoni, and get off at Estancia Una (3,330m), a settlement on the left side of the valley shortly after a low pass about 2 hours from Palca. The driver will know where this is.

There is one truck a day from Palca to Cohoni, leaving early in the morning.

Practical information

Altitude   Between 3,300m and 5,600m
Rating   Strenuous
Timing   3-4 days
Maps   *Cordillera Real o de La Paz (Sur)*, scale 1:50,000 by
                    Walter Guzman Cordova (available from Los Amigos
                    del Libro).

Route directions

The villagers of Estancia Una will want to rent you a pack animal. This is not a bad idea: you will need your energy for the final, steep climb to the base camp. From Estancia Una to a possible camping place, will take about 4 hours. It is a pleasant walk up the valley to the tiny village of Pinaya at the foot of Illimani. Just before you reach Pinaya, turn right and cross the river. From here head straight for Illimani, slowly climbing up through meadows and flat plains until you reach a broad, flat plain at an altitude of 4,500m. Any local person will point out the way. There are plenty of suitable camping places here. If you have hired pack animals they will leave you

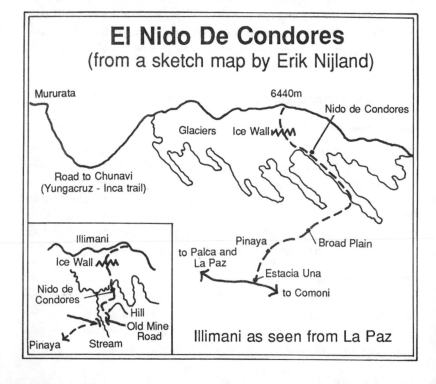

El Nido De Condores
(from a sketch map by Erik Nijland)

Mururata

6440m

Nido de Condores

Glaciers   Ice Wall

Road to Chunavi
(Yungacruz - Inca trail)

Illimani

Ice Wall

Nido de
Condores

Hill
Old Mine
Road

Pinaya   Stream

Pinaya

to Palca and
La Paz

Broad Plain

Estacia Una

to Comoni

Illimani as seen from La Paz

here — after this point the path is too steep for them!

It will take 5 very strenuous hours to reach the Nido de Condores from here. Shortly after the plain you will come to an old mining road. Follow this for about 15 minutes until you cross a bridge, and shortly afterwards a path leads steeply up a scree slope towards a ridge. Follow this to the Nido de Condores.

Warning

Illimani yearly claims the lives of climbers who are unprepared for the altitude, capricious weather and testing conditions. Do not climb the mountain without a local guide and full climbing gear.

THE TAKESI TRAIL

This is often called an Inca road, but was in fact almost certainly constructed before the Incas conquered the region. Whichever culture was responsible, we can admire the perfection of the work and its underlying engineering principles. The paved section covers half the trail, about 20km, and you'll see all the classic features of pre-Columbian road construction: stone paving, steps, drainage canals and retaining walls.

The walk takes only two days, but the variety of scenery is astonishing. From swirling snow on the 4,650m pass, you drop down to the treeline and through incredibly lush vegetation to the humid rainforest below the Chojlla mine. Above the trees the colours are soft and muted: green-ochre hills, grey stones, brown llamas. In the Yungas it's steamy-hot and bright with butterflies, flowers, green leaves and sparkling blue rivers.

The two main villages along the upper part of the trail, Choquekota and Takesi, pursue a way of life unchanged for centuries: men herding llamas, making rope or harvesting crops; women trampling *chuños* and preparing the next meal. Below the treeline, however, *mestizos* mix traditional customs with new innovations. Women still sit weaving outside their homes, but synthetic yarn is in vogue and bright cotton dresses replace the Indian homespun.

At its beginning and end the walk is served by two spectacular and contrasting bus journeys. To reach the trailhead you drive through a lunar landscape of eroded 'badlands' offering a display of brown, red, orange and yellow tones, unrelieved by any green. But the return trip from the Yungas is perhaps the most beautiful road of its kind in South America. It is cut into the mountainside and runs parallel to a river for much of the way. Luxuriant vegetation hangs from cliffs jutting over the road as it winds up to the bleak Altiplano.

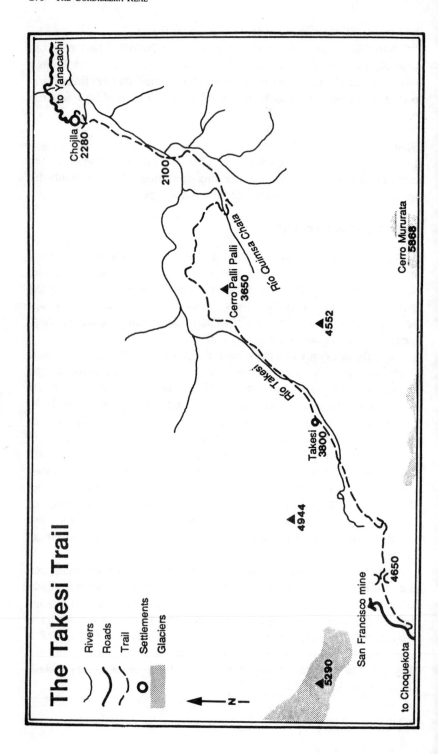

Practical information

Distance	About 40km
Altitude	Between 4,650m and 2,100m
Rating	Easy to moderate, but there is an altitude gain of 1,200m at the start and an altitude loss (over 2 days) of 2,550m.
Timing	2 to 3 days
Map	IGM *Chojlla* sheet, scale 1:50,000. But the trail is very clear.
Special requirements	A tent is not essential — lodging is usually available in Takesi — but you would be safer to carry one.

Getting to the trailhead

The access town is Ventilla. The easiest way of getting there is by taxi. Otherwise you must chance your luck with public transport. *Micros* go from Plaza Humboldt to Ovejuyo and then a minibus to Ventilla or, failing that, Chasquipampa. (Other vehicles also go to Chasquipampa from Plaza Belzú.) From the checkpoint at Chasquipampa trucks occasionally go to Ventilla. Alternatively make your way to Cota Cota on the outskirts of La Paz, from where there seems to be more frequent transport. Whichever way you go it's important to make a really early start. Climbing up to the pass in the midday heat is debilitating, and in the early afternoon clouds start to roll in, blotting out the views.

Route description

From Ventilla continue through the village and take a left fork towards the San Francisco mine. The track climbs steadily, passing through Choquekota after 1½ hours. Keep going up the track, which is the access road for the mine, past a derelict church and a graveyard full of cigar-shaped adobe burial mounds. The snowy flank of Mururata gradually comes into view on the right, with llamas providing a picturesque foreground.

About 2 hours from Choquekota, after a river crossing, the main track goes to the mine and the 'Inca' trail (rather indistinct at this point) branches off to the right and soon zig-zags steeply upwards to arrive at perhaps the most perfectly preserved stretch of stone paving in South America. This amazing road (one can hardly call it a trail) winds up the mountainside, easing the traveller's passing with a series of low steps. The top of the pass (4,650m) is reached in about 1½ hours, and if the weather is clear you'll have a fine view of the snowy peaks of the Cordillera Real and the Yungas far below. The first good (but bitterly cold) camping place is just below the pass by a small lake. The descent from the pass to Takesi takes about 3 hours. The path, if anything, is even more perfect; and the hillsides are dotted with grazing alpacas. There is camping by two lakes shortly before

Takesi, and lodging can be found in the village if you ask around.

Takesi is very attractive in its isolation and life goes on pretty much unchanged since the villagers' ancestors built the road. Shortly after the village the moist Yungas air asserts itself; boulders are covered in bright green moss and bushes and shrubs provide welcome relief from the stark mountain scene. The trail follows the course of the Río Takesi, hugging the cliff edge. This is a dry section and you should carry water. About 3 hours below Takesi the trail and the river make a long curve round Cerro Palli Palli ('It takes forever,' grumbled a hiker-reader: 1½ hours, at least) and eventually you'll see the ruins of a chapel and pass several houses surrounded by cultivated flowers. This is Kakapi; you can buy food and drink here, and pure water is available from a well just before the settlement. The trail then drops steeply down to Río Quimsa Chata which is crossed by a footbridge (just before the river the path splits into three; take the lowest one). Beyond the river you climb up and over a shoulder before crossing the Río Takesi at 2,100m. There's some lovely swimming in river pools here if you can stand the cold water. Half a kilometre further on, by the beginning of an aqueduct, is a good campsite. 'At dusk we were treated to a sky seemingly filled with bats; and then, in the night, to a myriad of fireflies.' (Jeremy Smith and Frédérique Thiriet)

Chojlla — the town which you could see from up on the shoulder — is reached 2 hours after crossing the river. 'A rough, dirty town, but friendly people.' (Helen O'Callaghan and Fiona Campbell)

If you want to avoid Chojlla take the left-hand higher track, through the mining area, to join the road about a kilometre beyond. Food and very basic lodging is available in Yanacachi, a further 5km down the road.

Getting back

A minibus leaves Chojlla for La Paz at 7:30. If you miss that, head for Yanacachi and hope to get a lift (via Unduavi). This is a very wet part of Bolivia; if it's not raining or misty when you get into the truck it will be later, and you may get snow on La Cumbre. Be prepared. As I've said earlier, this is one of the most stunningly beautiful rides in South America, so truck transport is recommended if you can stand it. It takes about 6 hours to get to La Paz, and a stop will be made at Unduavi where you can fill up on fried fish and other roadside goodies.

Choquecota to Tres Ríos
By Rick Ansell

This circuit involves two days' tough hiking, some of it cross-country, including a 4,850m pass. Be prepared! It finishes on the road to Tres Ríos and so could be combined with the Illimani to Chulumani hike.

Practical information

Altitude	Between 3,900m and 4,850m
Rating	Tough
Timing	2 days
Maps	(Essential). IGM *Palca* 6044-III, and *Chojlla* 6044-IV, 1:50,000.

Route description

From the ruined chapel at Choquekota head northeast up the hillside towards a house. From here continue traversing the hill, which is called Cerro Altipani, until you meet a river valley coming down from the southeast. Go up this valley, aiming for the obvious col (4,700m). The country is quite broken here, and you may find it easier to cross the ridge to the south of the col where the steep slope from the summit levels out.

Go down into the next valley, where there is camping, and follow this up into the basin below Mururata. Three streams come down to meet at the valley head. Take the first on the right, which comes from the southeast, and follow this up quite steeply to a pass at 4,850m, with Mururata on your left.

On the other side a narrow valley leads down to the southeast, and soon you'll pick up a path on the right-hand (south) side of the stream, leading to a *pampa* with abandoned houses. Improving all the time, the path keeps high above the river as it swings south. Follow it past some houses above the wet pastures of Totoral Pampa, eventually meeting the road from Ventilla to Tres Ríos at a hairpin. The trailhead for the Illimani to Chulumani (or Lambate) hike is only a couple of kilometres to your left.

ILLIMANI TO CHULUMANI

This is a rugged, but wonderfully varied trek of from 2 to 7 days (it can be ended or begun at various places) which takes you round the western flank of Bolivia's highest mountain, the triple-peaked Illimani (6,480m), then, like all the other Cordillera Real hikes, down into the tropical Yungas. And like the other trails, it provides contrasts of glaciers and citrus groves, goose-pimples and sweat, passing through some very remote areas where you are unlikely to meet anyone, only condors.

Practical information

Distance	About 100km
Altitude	Between 4,850m and 1,800m; altitude gains and losses of over 2,000m
Rating	Moderate to difficult
Timing	2, 5 or 7 days, depending on where you finish
Map	IGM *Palca* sheet, 6044III, scale 1:50,000, shows

the first part. Nos 6044II and 6044 I probably show the rest of the trail but are hard to obtain.

Special requirements   Pack for some very hot days and bitterly cold nights. Biting insects (not mosquitoes) can be a problem below the treeline. There's a small selection of provisions in Lambate. Pack animals and *arrieros* can be hired (with luck) in Tres Ríos and Lambate.

Getting to the trailhead

The trek begins at Tres Ríos, near the mining town of Bolsa Negra, about 37km (but 3 or 4 hours' drive!) beyond Ventilla. Transport is likely to be your biggest problem although there is a daily bus (the road continues to Lambate). Check bus information from the tourist office. If you go by truck dress warmly: there is a 4,700m pass before Tres Ríos. There is a good place to camp near the river, below the town and just below the bridge; take water from the standpipe in the village square, not from the polluted river.

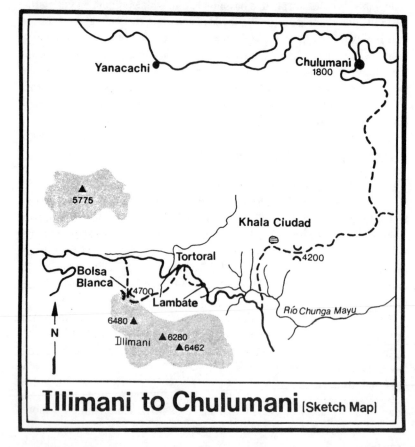

Illimani to Chulumani [Sketch Map]

Route description

From Tres Ríos look for a track that climbs the hill by the bridge above the campsite, to the right of the river. A road also goes up the valley but it is easier to keep to the path, with the river to your left, towards the head of the valley and Illimani. This will take 2 hours. You'll see the abandoned mining camp of Siberia across the valley. Then it's a steep climb, still on the right, up to a level *pampa* full of grazing horses and llamas, with lovely views of Illimani. Whatever time of day you arrive, camp at the end of the valley by some abandoned buildings (where there's some shelter from the cold wind). It's beautiful, freezing, and the last good campsite for several hours.

Looking up to the pass from your campsite your heart will sink. There is no obvious route up and the top seems vertically above you. In fact there *is* a trail: climb up behind the buildings to the right of the scree, to pick up the path which zig-zags to the top of the pass, 4,850m, and a very tough 1½ hour climb. Catch your breath before turning sharp right to make your way along a clear path along a rocky ledge towards a cleft in the rock. Beyond the cleft, head left down the valley, making your way down the steep slope, over grass and boulders, or sliding down a very slippery, dusty trail. A difficult descent. At the head of the valley make your way over to the right-hand side of the river and follow an improving path down that valley (always keep the river to your left) to the village of Totoral and the road to La Paz or Lambate. This is a long, tough descent from 4,700m to 3,400m, and is very steep towards the end.

Totoral is a friendly, cheerful village, seemingly involved in a continuous game of football. Beer is sold at one of the shops, and you can camp by the river. From Bolsa Blanca to here is about 7 hours. You can return to La Paz (there should be an early morning truck) or continue to Lambate (another day) or to Chulumani in 5 days.

Assuming you are continuing, your next destination is Lambate, which is quite a large town where refreshments (yes, beer!) can be bought. Cross the river by the bridge and follow the road for 20m. Just beyond the second bend in the road a steep track leads up to the right. It runs parallel to the road for a while, then forks right over a grassy hill from where you get good views of Illimani. Also, look in the opposite direction. See that far mountain range silhouetted like the Manhattan skyline? That's Khala Ciudad, 'rock city', and your destination in a couple of days' time.

After about 3 hours you descend, following steep gullies lined with foxgloves, to Lambate. As you approach the village take the left-hand path to the plaza. Lambate is an attractive town, full of character — and characters — and beautifully situated on a promontory. If you need pack animals to take you to the next pass, ask for Don Rosario. He lives in Lambate and generally works for the trekking company TAWA, but if he's available there is no better *arriero*.

Your next destination is the Chunga Mayu valley, way below you. From Lambate continue along the road, crossing a ford, and after about 1½ hours you'll reach a new road leading off to your left. Before that, keep an eye out for the clear trail running up the valley the other side of the river to a village. You'll be toiling up this tomorrow.

Follow the new road until you are just above a small house with a path leading towards it. Take this path, going to the right of the house (which had rather an endearing pig tied up outside when I was last there). The trail is clear, contouring the mountain through increasingly verdant vegetation (you start to see bromeliads and orchids and also parakeets), but don't be misled into following animal tracks. Keep an eye out for footprints. Five minutes before reaching the river you come to the remains of an old *hacienda*. Only some walls and two splendid conifers remain. Descend to the bridge and a welcome bath in the river (there are some reasonably private pools on the left). By this time your knees will be killing you — you have just descended 1,400m.

Finding a camping place is not easy. Groups camp at a deserted fruit farm 5 minutes along the trail (turn right after the bridge). Try to find someone of whom you can ask permission. Sometimes families in the next village, Ranchería or Quilcoma, will give hikers a place for their tent.

Now comes the toughest part of the trek. The Chunga Mayu is at a tropical 2,300m; the next pass is 4,300m! Even taking 2 days over the ascent this is hard work. The first part is very hot and there is no water for about 2½ hours so be sure to fill your water bottle at the river.

To reach Ranchería follow the path parallel to the river (ignore trails climbing up to your left) to the first building. Then turn left and climb steeply through the village to some eucalyptus trees and three conifers that you can see on the skyline. Continue climbing — hot and steep — for 2 hours until you come to a ridge and the beginning of the cloudforest.

Suddenly your efforts will seem worthwhile. The temperature drops, tree ferns and bromeliads adorn the trailside, and brightly coloured birds start to show themselves. Take your time to enjoy it. When you reach the campsite in about 4 hours from Ranchería you are amply rewarded. The river, which has been inaccessible as you sweated up the ridge to the left of its gorge, flows through meadows into pools and waterfalls, while at the head of the valley is the rock amphitheatre below Khala Ciudad. It's a magical place. Not as magical, however, as Khala Ciudad itself, which is my favourite mountain spot in Bolivia.

To reach it cast around for the path, which you pick up by climbing high above the campsite on the left. You will know when you're on the right trail — it's pretty clear, although sometimes confused by cow paths. It goes to the left of the sugarloaf that dominates the valley and then zig-zags up the right side of the next shallow valley, reaching the top through a V in the cliff wall. The focus of Khala Ciudad is the lake, or rather two lakes, which reflect the rock buttresses surrounding them; they seem as high as Illimani, once again visible across the valley.

If you are with a local *arriero* he will find an excuse not to camp by the lake. Several generations ago, so the story goes, the lake was dominated by an evil creature or spirit. The pilgrims heading for the Sanctuary of Irupana were not molested, but individuals and small groups disappeared. This was the only route to the Yungas and finally the locals became so desperate they asked the priest to perform an exorcism ceremony. The priest put a cordon of incense around the lake, whereupon a huge, three-headed serpent emerged from the water, broke through the cordon, and slithered away. The giant serpentine tracks can still be seen in the rock. The serpent still lives in the lake, they say, but these days it is subdued and causes no harm. The locals light fires around the lake to remind it to stay that way.

To continue the trek, traverse high on the rock to the right of the serpent's lake, and start the climb (1½-2 hours) to the final pass at 4,200m where you can add your stone to the large *apacheta*. The view here is magnificent: behind you is the Cordillera Real and ahead lie the steamy forests of the Amazon basin, stretching uninterrupted as far as the eye can see. It is not exactly downhill all the way, since the path skirts the mountains and climbs other small passes, but it is excitingly evident that you are now on an Inca (or pre-Inca) trail. From the pass the path goes to the left, contouring the mountain, and over a low pass to continue its contouring on the left side of the ridge.

Don't worry if you lose a bit of height but be careful not to descend too much. If you lose the path keep close to the crest of the ridge and you will pick it up when it joins the very clear trail (from the left) from Chuñavi, about an hour from the pass. This is the best 'Inca' section, with stone paving and steps. Three of the four times that I have done this trek I have seen condors; once four huge birds circled above us for some minutes, so close you could clearly see the white neck ruff.

From this point (the trail junction) to the next pass is about 4 hours. You should not lose your way (providing you take the upper path if faced with a choice) and with the walking easy and mainly level you can thoroughly enjoy the feeling of isolation and space. Everywhere you look are hills and forests — no sign of Man except in the far, far distance.

The final low pass faces you with a choice. Two trails lead through two notches in the mountain wall. Take the upper, left one. From there it is about 2 hours to the next — and last — campsite. You plunge dramatically into cloudforest, then out again. The campsite is at the second river crossing at about 3,300m. Beyond here there are very few camping possibilities.

The next day is a very tough one, so make an early start and keep the Band-Aids handy. You are going to descend about 1,500m (nearly 5,000ft). After the campsite the trail narrows, sometimes running along a stream-bed and past stands of bamboo — typical vegetation of this altitude. Once the trail starts descending it becomes very narrow, passing between steep banks and often through tunnels of vegetation, with great views when there's a gap in the trees which allows you the startling realization that you are skirting the edge of a 300m precipice. There's not much water, so fill up when you get the chance. About 3 hours after the campsite you'll emerge into a grassy clearing with a dome-shaped hill ahead. This is where everyone gets lost.

The correct trail leaves the clearing at the far end, heading towards the dome-shaped hill, and soon forks. Take the right-hand branch that runs *uphill* for a good 20 minutes, then through more forest (giving you your first views of Chulumani) for 1½ hours before emerging into a cleared, grassy area and views of Chulumani which looks temptingly near. It isn't. There's a final steep descent (watch out for snakes on this section, and fierce dogs guarding the coca plantations). Cultivation in the area has interfered with the trail so be careful not to get lost.

Finally you arrive at the elegant gates of Hacienda Siquilini with its private church, its fruit-bearing citrus trees and refreshing fresh water. It will have taken 6-7 hours from the campsite to here, and your knees and toes will be screaming for mercy. I'm afraid it's another 2 hours to Chulumani because the road has to skirt an immense gorge. There is a short cut (which you should take) through an orange grove down to the 'main' road and another short cut across the gorge but I'm not sure it's worth the effort of yet another steep descent and steep climb. Better, I think, to take your time walking along the road, help yourself to oranges and tangerines, view the coca plantations where the precious crop is grown on neat terraces, and enjoy your achievement. And hope for a lift.

Chulumani lies at only 1,800m, and is the capital of the Sud Yungas. It is a very attractive town with several hotels. If you feel that you deserve some luxury, the Prefectural and San Bartolomé are the best.

Getting back

Flota Yungueña buses take you back to La Paz (5 hours) up the dramatic 'Route of the Abysses'. Book well in advance, and remember to bring warm clothes with you: it's hard to believe as you board the bus in sultry Chulumani that 4 hours later you may be braving the snow on the break for refreshments in La Cumbre.

LA CUMBRE TO COROICO

This is another of those hikes which evoke a pleasing feeling of nostalgia. It was my first in Bolivia, and our information in 1973 was vague. An American told us that a drunk member of the Costa Rican National Orchestra had told him that if he went to a big 'Jesus cross' near La Paz and followed its outstretched left hand, he would find an Inca trail that led into the jungle. The tourist office staff were amused — and bemused — at the idea of anyone wanting to walk into the Yungas, and had never heard of an Inca trail — or any trail, come to that. However, they did know where there was a statue of Jesus. We had a wonderful and serendipitous hike, and beyond Achura (where I slept in a thatched building, under a poncho on a pile of potatoes because my sleeping bag had been stolen) we came across an 'Inca' road so amazing in its engineering that by the time we'd reached Coroico we'd decided to write a book and share this find with others.

The hike, now well-known, takes you from a snow-covered 4,850m pass down to sub-tropical river valleys full of parakeets, blue *morpho* butterflies, flowers and wild strawberries, and ends in hot citrus groves at just over 1,500m. The first part is easy, thanks to pre-Inca roadbuilders, but towards the end it may be overgrown and difficult to follow. Ten years ago readers' letters suggested that it had become almost impassable, but more recent reports indicate that it is being cleared on a regular basis to enable pack-carrying llamas and horses to get through. Tall backpackers may find that their pack keeps getting entangled in the vegetation. More seriously, be warned that the short cuts which have been forged between the switchbacks tend to be impossibly slippery and are best avoided.

You'll see plenty of llamas grazing on the first day, and will probably encounter them being used as pack animals on the trail. Theodore Hartman and Joanne Soto offer this advice after stopping to watch a caravan carrying carved wooden spoons up the trail on their way to the market in La Paz. 'Llamas are fascinated by onlookers; if you stop to watch them, they'll stop to watch you. This caused quite a bit of confusion for the animals and their herder was clearly annoyed. Best to walk slowly on.'

Practical information

Distance	About 70km
Altitude	Between 4,850m and 1,300m
Rating	Moderate
Timing	4 days
Maps	IGM topo sheets 5945 II *Milluni* and 6045 III *Unduavi*.

Conditions/what to bring

Prepare for one cold night and several warm ones. Theodore Hartman and Joanne Soto warn: 'Don't do this hike in the rainy season (November to May) unless you like water. You'll be thoroughly soaked every hour of the day and night. Prepare as if for a white-water expedition.' Betsy and Jeff Davies add: 'It's essential to have thin pants (trousers) for the last day, as it will be hot, the trail may be overgrown and there'll be prickly plants and biting insects.' At La Cumbre, on the other hand (whatever the season), you may encounter freezing rain, snow, hail and wind. To avoid a miserable start to your walk, dress up in preparation before leaving La Paz.

Stock up with provisions in La Paz; the first shops will not be found until Chairo. (Fresh bread can be bought in the street in Villa Fátima just before departure.) Theodore and Joanne suggest taking some extra food to share with the *campesinos*. 'They were some of the most welcoming, gracious hosts we've met in South America; and for the favour of being invited in out of the rain it's nice to split a pot of soup with them, or a *mate de coca*. Bread is much asked for. Most live outside the economic system and their stomachs matter more to them than their pockets.'

Another essential is insect repellent. Also a machete might be useful if the trail is overgrown. But only bring one if you know how to use it; accidentally cutting off your leg on this trail would be inconvenient.

Getting to the trailhead

Buses leave La Paz for the Yungas from 07:00 onwards from Avenida de las Américas 344, Villa Fátima. The short journey (about an hour) can also easily be done by one of the trucks which leave from a little higher up Avenida de las Américas throughout the day. It's best to make as early a start as possible, since mist tends to start billowing over the pass early in the afternoon, obscuring the view.

A special feature of this road is the dogs which stand like sentinels along it. I first noticed them in 1974, and have seen them (or their descendants) on every subsequent visit. I used to think they were just hanging around for scraps thrown from the trucks, but a Bolivian friend has since told me that they are the Guardians of the Cordillera Real. Locals placate the *achachilas* (mountain spirits) by feeding the dogs. Certainly when you see these patient figures, motionless but watchful in the swirling snow, it's easy to believe in the power of mountain spirits.

Route description

La Cumbre ('The Summit') is not a village, but simply the highest point (4,725m) on the bleak mountain road before it begins its descent to the Yungas. A statue of Christ the Redeemer faces north, his left hand helpfully pointing out the trail, which heads west towards some small lakes. After recent snow you should have no difficulty following the foot- and hoof-prints. If in doubt take the most obvious vehicle track, passing one largish lake and then passing between two small ones, before veering north up a scree slope to the pass. The climb to this point (4,850m) takes about an hour. When you reach an *apacheta* (stone cairn), you'll be rewarded with a spectacular view and the knowledge that it's downhill most of the rest of the way.

The trail is now very clear, dropping steeply down a *quebrada* (ravine) which broadens out after joining the main river (Río Phajchiri), allowing the path to continue more gently to the small village of Achura (also known as Chucura). There are plenty of campsites above and below the village, which is reached about 5 hours after the pass. The villagers certainly take an interest in backpackers; I've had reports of hostility and robbery but also of great friendliness. This may be something to do with the way hikers are beginning to distort the local economy. Readers have told of being asked for sweets, watches and money; and although handing over such things may assuage Western guilt it is destroying the good relationship that once existed.

One thing you *shouldn't* expect at Achura is much in the way of provisions for sale. Steve Newman warns: 'It took us 1½ hours to buy 2lbs of potatoes and three eggs!' It's difficult to avoid spending your first night in this area, because the next campsite (the only one before the next village, Choro) is a good 3 hours further on.

Beyond Achura the 'Inca' road really comes into its own, with some marvellous paving and low steps often arranged in a fan shape around a curve. After about 4km of paved track you reach the treeline and the path becomes narrower. Choro is some 5 hours beyond this point.

Many houses in Choro have been abandoned, and the original suspension bridge over the river has long since disappeared. In 1990 Dr Nizam Mamode wrote that 'a *campesino* grinned, told me it had been washed away three years ago, and pointed to a rather improbable strand of wire stretching across a cascade of white foam. I laughed, perhaps a little nervously, at the idea of my 12½ stones plus loaded rucksack crossing in this manner, but a few minutes later found myself wrapped in a piece of old cloth, hanging from a pulley and dragging myself over with white knuckles, to the amusement of the family watching from the bank.' By 1995 this arrangement had been replaced (perhaps disappointingly) by a sturdy wooden bridge.

From here on you should carry water, as the supply is erratic. The path climbs steeply up a series of switchbacks to a bluff, where there is a camping spot with water 20 minutes further on. Here the trail turns east to contour the hillside above the Río Huarinilla to Chairo, two hard days away, with plenty of climbing as well as descending. You'll encounter ravines, each

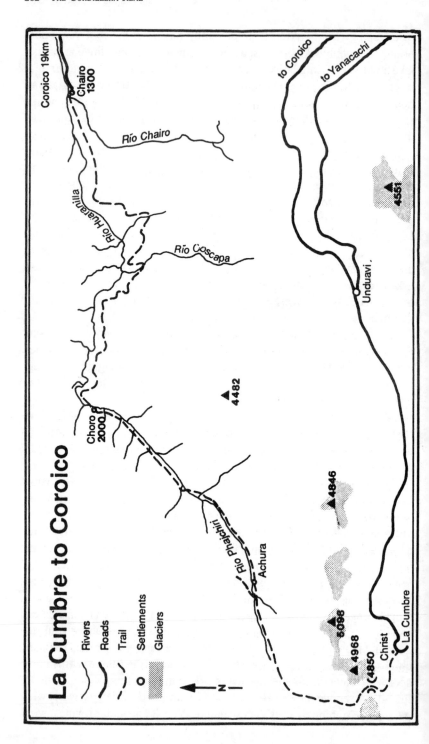

La Cumbre to Coroico

Rivers
Roads
Trail
o   Settlements
    Glaciers

N

Coroico 19km
Chairo 1300
Río Chairo
Río Huarauilla
Río Coscapa
to Coroico
to Yanacachi
▲ 4551
Unduavi
▲ 4482
Choro 2000
▲ 4846
Río Phajchiri
Achura
▲ 5098
▲ 4968
▲ 4850
Christ
La Cumbre

one containing a useful water supply, usually in the form of an icy torrent. The biggest of these, Río Coscapa, is crossed by an exciting suspension bridge set in a magnificent gorge.

About 7km before Chairo lives a Japanese man called Tamiji Hanamura who has become quite famous among backpackers. He made his home here many years ago, and you'll have no difficulty recognizing the rose-covered house, La Casa Sandillani. Tamiji has collected postcards from all over the world. The only fee he asks of campers is that you sign his visitors' book, but a postcard would no doubt be appreciated as well. He is also reported as selling beer!

The final stretch to Chairo (1,300m) is steep and badly eroded towards the end, but you'll find the villagers very friendly, and the two stores offer bread, canned goods and beer. There are occasional trucks to Coroico; otherwise it's a pleasant 4 or 5 hours' walk through coffee, citrus and banana plantations. After 3 hours the road fords the river. Just before this point, from a hairpin bend, you should be able to make out the remains of a brick bridge. Ten minutes further on, look for a path to the right which takes you down to the river, and cross here. (A new bridge of sorts has been reported alongside the old one.) Eventually you'll come to the La Paz-Caranavi road. An hour's walk to the right is the village of Yolosa and the road to Coroico. With luck you'll get a ride.

Coroico and getting back

If you are in a hurry you can skip Coroico altogether, and take a truck from Yolosa back to La Paz. That would be a pity, however, since Coroico is a very pretty sub-tropical town (1,525m), with several hotels (Don Hoyle recommends the Kory, which has a swimming pool) and nothing much to do except relax after your exertions. Hattie Lipton tells me that just below the Hotel Kory she found nuns selling peanut butter and wine (!) and honey is also sold next to the bank.

Flota Yungueña buses leave for La Paz at 07:00 most days, from the street to the right of the church. However, they are often booked up several days in advance. Trucks also make the journey; or you can take a small truck from just below the square to Yolosa, and then change to the (more frequent) trucks coming up from Caranavi.

The 96km road to La Paz meets the one from Chojlla at Unduavi. Until then it's little more than a track, winding under waterfalls (have your rain gear ready if you are travelling by truck!) and alongside vertical cliffs. Its impact on impressionable travellers is heightened by the many roadside crosses commemorating those who have gone over the edge.

MOUNTAIN CLIMBING

Huayna Potosí (6,094m)
By Sverre Aarseth, updated by Eleanor and Greg Neilson

Note: Only experienced mountaineers should attempt this peak, and full ice-climbing equipment must be carried. A guide is recommended; enquire at the Club Andino in La Paz (see *Accommodation*).

This is one of the easiest of Bolivia's 6,000m peaks, so it is popular with mountaineers. On reaching the dam from Milluni, cross it and follow an aqueduct to a small reservoir from where the route goes up the spine of a moraine, eventually joining a rocky ridge. Pick your way up this ridge to the snow plateau called Campamento Argentino at 5,500m, where you should make your base camp. A well-acclimatized party will have no difficulty reaching this point in one day. High winds are sometimes a problem here. Next morning an early start is essential. The route goes up the glacier towards the back wall of the basin ahead, then heads up towards the ridge on the right. Keep well to the right here to avoid crevasses. On reaching the ridge, follow it round to the left. The final part is steep.

Eleanor and Greg took 4 hours to reach the summit from Campamento Argentino, and 2 hours to return. On the glacier they strayed a little too far left and encountered crevasses, but found it possible to step over or walk round them. Dehydration, however, is a real danger at this altitude, you should carry more than a litre of water per person for the ascent from Campamento Argentino.

Japu Japuni (5,088m)
By Jeremy Smith and Frédérique Thiriet

We wanted to climb a 5,000m peak, and found that this was possible starting from the 4,880m pass on the first day of the Zongo-to-La Cumbre hike. Follow the rocky ridge north of the col, keeping slightly to the right, and about a third of the way up you'll find a large cairn. The summit (reached in about 1½ hours from the pass) affords an incredible view of the Cordillera beyond Huayna Potosí. The ascent doesn't require any special equipment or climbing skills, but we wouldn't recommend it in bad weather as there are cliffs below the ridge.

Huiata (5,092m)
By Kathrine Breistl and Ole Faye

We started from Achura, taking the steep path going north up the valley side past Waca Kunca and following the Zongo route in reverse up the wide, gentle llampu valley. There are several excellent camping sites along the river as far as the 4,100m contour below Jishka Telata; we made our 'base camp' here.

The next day we left the main trail, continuing southwestwards up the llampu, first on its north side, then crossing on a small footbridge before passing some big boulders and eventually climbing up the left-hand of two tributaries to a flat area southeast of Huiata at about 4,600m. From here we headed straight for the steep buttress of the lower, eastern part of the mountain. The path went to the right of this, giving a splendid view of the topaz-green waters of Laguna Chaco Kkota with the Telata glacier behind.

Keeping our elevation above the lake, we headed due west up the valley beyond, heading to the left (south) of the peak ahead, climbing a steep snowfield to a ridge, then gaining the summit from the rear (west) side.

Huiata gives excellent views of Huayna Potosí, the Telata massif, the Huarinilla valley towards the Yungas, and much more. It is easily climbed by 'ordinary' trekkers with no special equipment.

ZONGO TO LA CUMBRE OR COROICO

This is a high-altitude walk, partly along a good trail and partly cross-country, taking you parallel to the glaciers of Huayna Potosí (6,088m), past a series of lakes, and connecting with the La Cumbre-Coroico trail. Being so close to the peaks, you may feel an urge to climb one of them. I've included three possibilities in the Box opposite.

This was one of those happy hikes discovered accidentally when we were leafing through the topographical maps at the IGM while waiting for our order. The *Milluni* sheet caught our eye, covered in evocative blue contour lines, and we soon picked out a possible trail. As it turned out, this could only be followed part of the way, but the subsequent cross-country scramble was both exciting and beautiful.

Practical information

Altitude	Between 4,880m and 3,900m
Rating	Difficult, with cross-country stretches
Timing	3 to 5 days
Maps	IGM sheet 5945 II *Milluni*, 1:50,000.

Conditions/what to bring

The first two nights will be bitterly cold. Bring hat, gloves, and all the warm clothes you've got. You'll also need tough boots and a compass for the cross-country section. There is no habitation before Achura, and precious little to buy there, so stock up well with provisions.

Accommodation

A new *refugio* opened early in 1995 to provide mountain climbers and trekkers with a warm place to stay. There is hot water and a log fire. Refugio Huayna Potosí is situated to the east of Laguna Zongo, and should be booked in La Paz by phoning the Hotel Continental: 323538 or 795936. Fax: 378226. The warden can also arrange transport to the *refugio*.

Getting to the trailhead

If there's a group of you, a taxi is the easiest option. Alternatively, the Hotel Continental, La Paz, can arrange transport to the refugio most mornings during the peak season. The cost of transport is around US$15 per person, and leaves at around 11:00. A cheaper alternative is to catch the bus to Zongo which leaves at 06:00 every morning from Plaza Ballivián (El Alto).

Route description

Follow the Zongo road as it continues down the valley in a series of zig-zags. After 2km, just after the second hairpin bend, your trail leads off to

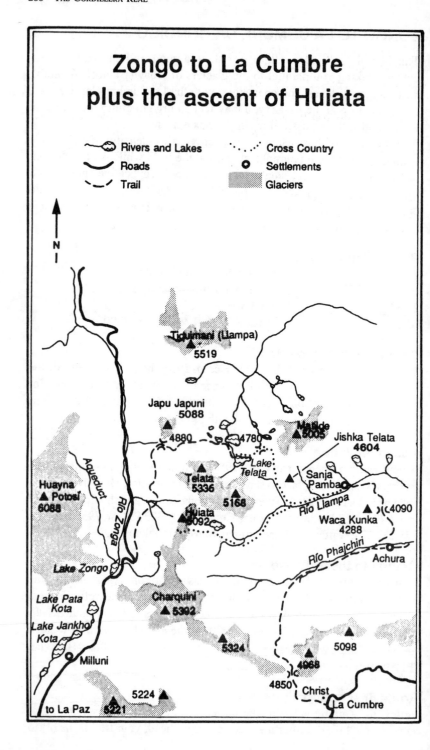

Zongo to La Cumbre plus the ascent of Huiata

Rivers and Lakes
Roads
Trail

Cross Country
Settlements
Glaciers

N

Tiquimani (Llampa)
▲ 5519

Japu Japuni
5088
▲
4880 4780

Matilde
▲ 5005
Jishka Telata
4604

Telata
▲ 5336
Lake
Telata

5168
▲

Sanja
Pamba
▲

Rio Llampa
Waca Kunka
4288

▲ 4090

Huayna
▲ Potosí
6088

Aqueduct

Río Zonga

Huiata
▲ 5092

Río Phajchiri
Achura

Lake Zongo

Charquini
▲ 5392

Lake Pata
Kota

Lake Jankho
Kota

Milluni

5324
▲

5098
▲

4968
▲

4850
Christ

5224 ▲
to La Paz 5221

La Cumbre

the right and across a small stream. The path is faint at times, disappearing altogether across open pasture, but you should have little difficulty following it along the contours of the mountain, above and parallel to the valley road. The views of Huayna Potosí are splendid, and soon the snowy peak of Telata comes into view.

After 1½ hours you'll pass a small lake, and 3 or 4 hours after leaving the road the path swings round a lower peak called Chekapa and heads towards an unnamed pass at 4,880m. Beyond the pass is a well-watered valley with a series of dammed lakes, part of another hydroelectric scheme. There's good camping all along this valley.

From the dam at the first lake, continue east to the second lake, taking a path along the south shore and uphill towards Laguna Telata, whose dam is just visible. There are marvellous views of the dramatic snow-covered peak called Ilampu on the IGM map, but better known as Tiquimani to avoid confusion with Illampu in another part of the Cordillera. The last possible camping places for several hours are near this lake, either below the dam or at the far shore. This is where the cross-country stretch begins. (For a poor-weather alternative, see next page.)

Walk across the dam and make your way over rocks and cliffs, guided by cairns, above the northern shore of the lake. This involves scrambling but no technical climbing. At the eastern end of the lake, start up the scree slope towards the lowest point on the shoulder above you to your left (northeast). This climb, again guided by cairns, isn't difficult and will take about an hour.

From the top you'll see three lakes and a shoulder to your right. From this shoulder you should make your way down towards the southeast and over a wall, then pick up a very faint path to the right of a stonefall. Continue steeply downhill to a swampy area studded with Andean gentians. Go down to the valley bottom and the river. As you veer east beneath the crags of Jishka Telata you'll pass a large cave beneath some monstrous fallen boulders — an excellent shelter if the weather is bad. Continue to follow the river on its left bank until the trail at last asserts itself and you can follow it easily to a *hacienda*, Sanja Pampa, and the bridge beyond.

After crossing the river you'll pass through a scatter of houses and up a steep but good path skirting round the end of a ridge called Waca Kunca. As it levels out, the trail passes several ponds, crosses a stream, then heads south, descending steeply before turning southwest to the village of Achura (Chucura). There's a bridge across the river and it is a short climb to reach the main trail just above the village.

Here you must make the decision either to go up to La Cumbre, about 6 hours away, or continue down to Coroico which will take you 2 more days.

Poor-weather alternative
By Rick Ansell

This is rather longer than my recommended route, with a bit more climbing, but may be preferable in bad conditions as it stays slightly lower.

After coming down from the first pass, follow the path which goes round the western shore of the first lake to the dam, and then descends very steeply to the lower lake which the IGM map describes as Laguna Kkota Khuchu. Should you lose the path, look for the bridge over the aqueduct before the steep part.

A well-used trail follows the northern shore of the lower lake before cutting down to join the river below the dam. Once beside this river, follow it for 10 minutes and where it starts to turn northeast strike out due east across the hillside below steep slabs until you gain the next valley.

A faint path will be found running south up the near side of this valley. Ascending steeply, it soon passes to the right (west) of a lake, and — more obvious now — climbs to a second lake where there are camping possibilities, surrounded by steep slopes. Continuing south, it climbs another 150m to cross a pass at about 4,700m, before descending to the west of Jishka Telata where you rejoin the route described above.

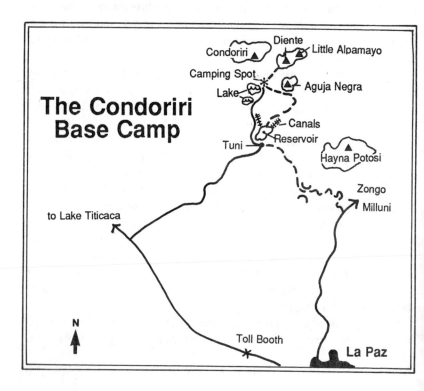

CONDORIRI CIRCUIT

By Erik Nijland

The Condoriri group of mountains are well-known to climbers as offering some of the best scenery in Bolivia and plenty of peaks to climb, varying from very easy to extremely difficult.

For hikers and backpackers there is a lovely natural lake where you can stay to enjoy the scenery, and a return route which takes you to the Zongo area and possible links with other treks.

Getting there

The base camp for Condoriri, 5,850m, is easily reached. Take any transport in the direction of Lake Titicaca and get off at the first village, some 10-15km beyond the *tranca* (toll-gate). You will see a dirt road leading off to the right.

Route directions

Follow the dirt road to the top rim of a broad river gorge. Ask the villagers for Tuni-Condoriri, the name of the lake at the foot of Condoriri mountain. You may get a lift but otherwise it is a dull, 21km walk along a jeep track towards Tuni, a small village where the road ends at a gate, just below the lake (reservoir). There are splendid views of Huayna Potosí from here. Climb the dike towards the house or follow the road after the fence and you will see an emerald green lake. Keeping the lake to your right, walk along its shores until you come to a high-water drainage system. Leave the lake at this point and follow the road until you come to a canal that feeds into the lake. The road follows this canal upwards, giving you beautiful views of Condoriri, which resembles a condor with outstretched wings.

One hour after the fence you will reach the end of the canal and of the road. Climb slightly uphill, following the left bank of the river, to a path some 100m above the stream. Condoriri will be ahead of you. The first lake you come to is small, with a tiny island in the middle of it. Continue to the big lake, Laguna Condoriri, which is about 1½ hours from the water project. This is an ideal base for exploring the area.

One of the 'easy' peaks is El Diente (5,600m) but this still needs proper equipment (crampons and rope) and glacier experience. The mountain lies at the far end of the valley, to the right of Condoriri.

Alternative routes back

Looking towards the mountain group, and the peak known as Ilusión, you will see a huge, rocky mountain, the Aguja Negra (Black Needle). Climb the hill to the right of this peak, crossing beneath the glacier at the foot of Aguja Negra, to climb to the top of the pass. From here you can see the reservoir you passed on your way up and can join the jeep track back to the main road.

A more scenic and adventurous route back is to take the old mining road from the village of Tuni and follow it for 24km to Milluni, between Huayna Potosí and Chacaltaya. The road is rarely used these days and offers spectacular views of Huayna Potosí and other peaks. There is a pass half way, but it is not a strenuous climb. At the main road turn left for Huayna Potosí (or its *refugio*) or right if you want to head back to La Paz.

By taking this route you are well placed to do a variety of treks or climbs in the Zongo area.

THE ZONGO VALLEY

By Jonathan Derksen

The Zongo Valley provides an alternative, yet not necessarily easy, route to the North and South Yungas. Like all journeys through these valleys east of the Andes, you experience rapid and surprising changes in climate and vegetation. Just below the pass you might see small herds of llamas grazing on *esparto* grass, glaciers spilling over high cliff edges, then slightly lower down you will notice a few shrubs and trees covered with moss, which will give way to forest and, eventually, sub-tropical broad-leaved plants and hardwood trees. It's hard to find a more dramatic change in scenery in such a short distance.

Another bonus of this easy walk is the well set-up boy scout camp which is available to backpackers (with a reservation).

Getting there

The approach to the valley is the same as going to Zongo Lake and the beginning of the trailhead to the Cumbre, except you continue along the well-reinforced and maintained road zigzagging dizzily down (you drop over 1,500m in a few kilometres) through a valley of waterfalls, rivers and hydroelectric stations.

Practical information

If transportation can be found to La Cumbre anyone in shape can walk down to the scout camp in a long day — it's downhill all the way, if your knees like that sort of thing. If you wish to continue on down to Bella Vista, you should tag on another 3-4 days from the last hydro station.

This area generally receives a lot of precipitation, so pack to stay dry. After the last station there are no villages, so be prepared with extra food. Water is available in abundance all the way down the valley.

Route directions

Simply follow the road, keeping right at any branches (I believe there are two) and continue steadily down past the hydroelectric stations including Zongo, Botijlaca and Cuticucho. After the Santa Rosa station you will pass by an outdoor cement football court on your right, then further down, a small school on your left. Just below these, to the right of the road, is a large open area of grass with a small building (bathrooms) and a thatched gazebo. This is the Scout Camp, established several years ago for the sole purpose of camping. Anyone is allowed to camp here as long as they have prior permission from the camp coordinator, John Osborne, of the American Cooperative School in La Paz (tel: 711663). There is a US$10.00 fee for any individual or group wishing to use the site for a weekend (two days). There are plenty of spots at the camp to pitch a tent, and a revitalizing river rushes past just metres away. Here you might try your luck at trout fishing. The caretaker will open the bathrooms for you (there's running water and showers) and chopped wood and barbecue pits are available for cooking.

The Zongo, like each of the Yungas valleys, is a micro-ecosystem and you have a good chance of sighting plant- or bird-life that can only be found in these valleys.

Perhaps one of the most interesting activities in the area is to explore the numerous maintenance trails that lead both east and west into the mountains from the River Zongo at the base of the valley. One of these trails begins after crossing a narrow iron bridge just opposite the Scout Camp and leads you up along a steep, forested hillside, then across a large steel pipe and up the spine from where you can catch glimpses of the jungle valleys far below. Be careful: when it is rainy the pipes are very slippery. If you don't mind heights and are sure-footed, it's a thrill to follow the aqueduct that runs from Planta Harca along the side of a cliff to a village beside the Río Yohuilaque. Higher up in the valley there are canals cutting through the rock in long tunnels that are worth a look.

After the last hydro station (Planta Huaji) a rough trail leads farther down the valley until it meets with the Río Coroico. This portion of the hike might take two to three days, depending on the weather. I'm told a machete is indispensable here. Once you arrive at the Río Coroico, follow the path going left for several kilometres until you come to the village of Bella Vista. Here you can cross over to the town of Alcoche where transportation back to La Paz, or deeper into the lowlands, can be found.

Tingling in the fingers is a common effect of altitude, and nothing to worry about.

Chapter Twenty

Sorata and the Tipuani Valley

Nestling at the foot of the Cordillera Real, Sorata has one of the finest settings in Bolivia. The second and third highest mountains in the country (Illampu, 6,362m and Ancohuma, 6,427m — although their heights, and therefore claims to eminence, are disputed) overlook the town, which lies at a mere 2,695m and has swanky palm trees in the plaza to demonstrate its mild climate. After a few days spent gasping and freezing in La Paz, it's a great relief to spend some time in Sorata, especially on a Sunday when the market is in full swing. Neighbouring Achacachi has an even better market; and between September 12 and 16 each year the two towns hold a wonderful fiesta.

Getting there
The road to Sorata is now paved and there is a good choice of transport. Buses make the 5 to 7-hour run from the main bus station in La Paz.

Sleeping and eating
Residencial Sorata has been recommended by many readers. It is a remnant of old Bolivia, with flowers in the courtyard and attentive service. Luís, the manager, has a wealth of information on hikes in the Sorata area, as does the manager of **Hotel Copacabana**, which, however, is slightly out of town. The **Club Sorata** (the local branch of the Club Andino) has its headquarters here.

'You'd be crazy not to try out Bolivia's most remote Italian restaurant, **Ristorante Italiano**, which serves some of the best food I've ever eaten — no exaggeration! The establishment sits on a steep hill, with a fantastic view of the surrounding mountains.' (J Derksen)

Short hikes in the Sorata area
San Pedro Cave
This is a large cave with a lake inside. You can explore it with the aid of the newly installed electric lights, for a fee, or by torch light for a rather smaller fee. The legends surrounding the cave are interesting: the

conquistadores are said to have buried a large treasure somewhere deep inside the cave and some say the cave was deliberately flooded to conceal the treasure. Probably the lake inside the cave is natural, but *El Dorado* is still in the minds of the local people. Divers have been discouraged from exploring the cave to its limits by a fatal accident (attributed to an Inca curse).

San Pedro is a small village some 3½ hours' walk from Sorata along a path down the valley (or rather along a ledge half way up the valley side). When you see San Pedro's church, climb uphill to reach the village and continue to its far side. The cave is 20m above the jeep track — which, incidentally, gives you an alternative route back to Sorata in about 2 hours.

In addition to the cave and its lake, there is a large population of bats.

Continuing down the valley

You can continue hiking down this beautiful valley to the towns of Quiabaya and Tacacoma. There may be transport, but most likely you will be walking so be sure to bring sufficient food. The way is easy (following the road), but for the truly adventurous, with a map, there are all sorts of possibilities in this area.

THE GOLD-DIGGERS' WAY

Written by John Pilkington and updated by various readers, most recently Richard Reiner, Sara Elliott and Paul Mosquin

This is a tough walk of about 6 days which takes you right across the northern Cordillera Real. From Sorata you'll climb over a 4,800m pass and then follow a roller-coaster course down the Tipuani Valley to the sub-tropical gold rush town of Llipi. During the walk and subsequent journey to Guanay you'll pass through a complete vegetational cross-section of South America, from the snows around Illampu through the Yungas to the rainforest and plantations (tea, coffee, bananas) of the upper Amazon basin. You'll see grazing llamas, *morpho* butterflies 15cm from wingtip to wingtip, and maybe a snake or two. For much of the way you'll be treading on stones laid by Inca or pre-Inca engineers, worn smooth and rounded by centuries of feet and hoofs. You'll use spectacular (but exhausting) staircases to overcome difficult obstacles and to climb and descend seemingly sheer hillsides, and you'll even walk through a tunnel hewn from solid rock. The trail ends in the heart of Bolivian gold-mining country, once the scene of Klondike-style activity, and now the centre of a feverish new gold rush.

History

For nearly 1,000 years this area has been a rich source of gold, and each generation of exploiters has left its mark on the landscape and on the traditions of its people. From the earliest years of the Inca Empire the inhabitants of the area had to deliver 40kg quarterly to the Sun King at Cusco. Then during the Spanish colonial period exploitation was intensified to satisfy the greed of the *conquistadores*, and new workings were opened up along the Río Tipuani and in nearby valleys. Later, when Bolivia regained her independence, gold production declined and today only in the Tipuani Valley is it carried out in any way seriously.

During all this time the search for gold was a haphazard affair; only when the Compañía Aramayo de Minas en Bolivia took over the work in 1932 were the first geological reports and maps made. Most of these were lost when the company was nationalized in 1952, and since then many prospectors have reverted to the old wildcat methods, breaking rocks on massive slopes of wet scree in the hope of a lucky strike.

Practical information

Distance	About 90km
Altitude	Between 4,800m and 2,695m
Rating	Difficult
Timing	4-6 days
Maps	IGM sheet 5846 I *Sorata* covers the first 2 days.

Conditions/what to bring

Be prepared for two cold nights and several warm ones. As you drop down into the Yungas mosquitoes and other bugs will become a problem, so bring a long-sleeved shirt in addition to insect repellent. In the rainy season (and possibly in the dry season too) you may get very wet from river crossings as well as from rain. For the first part of the walk — at least as far as Chusi — bring all the food you'll need. Top up your water bottle at every opportunity. The Tipuani Valley is a malarial area, so prophylactic pills should be taken.

Route description

With a climb of 2,100m out of Sorata, you may think it worthwhile to hire a jeep to take you to Ancoma (also known as Ancohuaya). From Sorata to the pass takes about 11 hours on foot, so if you are walking it's best to leave around midday and camp halfway up. Take the steps from the corner of the plaza past the Residencial Sorata and turn left at the top. You'll soon come to a cemetery, and here take the path leading up the hillside to the right. This leads eventually to an *estancia*, but the trail to Tipuani bears off to the right about 100m beyond the cemetery. Scramble up the slope as best you can; whichever path you take you'll soon find yourself following a stream which drops steeply down from the hillside ahead. Keeping the stream to your left, carry on uphill until, about an hour after leaving the plaza, you meet a trail coming up from your right. This will take you to the pass.

From this point the increasingly spectacular views of the Sorata Valley opening up behind you compensate for the uphill struggle. The trail follows the valley of the Río Challasuy, and after another 3 hours or so of climbing the intensively cultivated valley side you cross the river. From here on there's a series of excellent campsites, but with the pass still 7 hours away it might be better to get a bit more distance under your belt before calling it a day.

The next 3 to 4 hours are steeply uphill, but at last you'll pass a small lake and beyond that a false summit marked by a pile of stones. All round here is good camping, the last before the pass. Three trails lead from this spot; take the middle one, and in another half hour you'll find yourself climbing a magnificently engineered Inca staircase. The going gets easier for a while, but soon becomes steeper again as you approach the true summit. Coming up from below you'll see the jeep track built many years ago to link Sorata with the Challana valley.

From the summit, about 3 hours beyond the Inca staircase, take the jeep track to the right, or the trail which runs straight down the valley to rejoin it lower down. The jeep track is followed for about 4 hours. (About 1½ hours from the pass the valley bottom flattens out just enough to pitch a tent.) Eventually the track makes a wide detour and again a trail follows a shorter route, reached by a footbridge to the opposite riverbank. A short distance beyond is the village of Ancoma which has very basic supplies.

At Ancoma the jeep track bears off up the mountainside, but the trail to Guanay carries on down the river, closely following its right bank. In half an hour you'll pass a giant boulder with a cave underneath — there are camping possibilities here, and also in a large flat meadow another hour further on. Between this point and Tipuani the trail makes two digressions to the opposite bank: the first comes about 4 hours from Ancoma, bringing you back to the right bank via a footbridge after 45 minutes; the second is just after a scatter of houses, again returning via a bridge. Just beyond this second bridge is the settlement of Sumata, and an hour further on an enterprising *campesino* has set up a 'toll gate' where you must pay to pass! 'Carry a stick or a pocketful of stones here, as immediately beyond the toll are two *very* belligerent dogs.' (Richard Reiner, Sara Elliott and Paul Mosquin)

You'll find a good campsite by a small ruin in a meadow, 5 or 6 hours from Ancoma. Just over an hour further on is another excellent one, in a small clearing reached from a path that branches off to the left from a part of the trail that is particularly well built. Otherwise there's nothing suitable until Sumata, 8 hours from Ancoma. In another 2 or 3 hours you should reach Wainapata and, if you're lucky, a supply of fresh bread. This is the first real village along the trail, though it still consists of only a few houses.

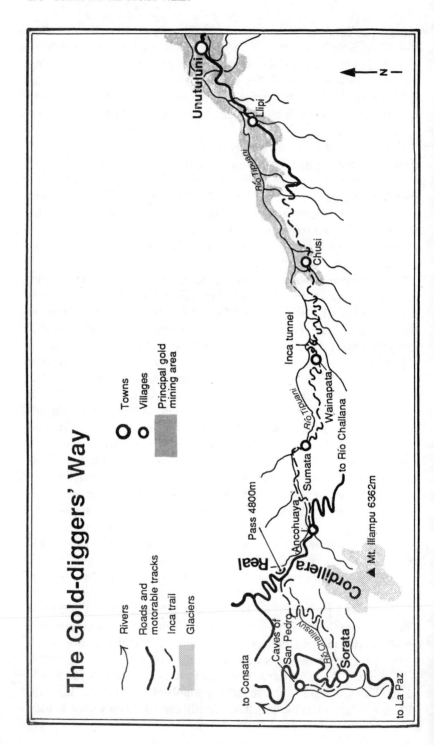

The Gold-diggers' Way

Rivers

Roads and motorable tracks

Inca trail

Glaciers

O Towns

o Villages

Principal gold mining area

— N —

to Consata

Caves of San Pedro

Sorata

to La Paz

Río Challasuyu

Cordillera Real

Pass 4800m

Ancohuaya

Sumata

Wainapata

Inca tunnel

Río Tipuani

to Río Challana

▲ Mt. Illampu 6362m

Chusi

Río Tipuani

Lipi

Unutuluini

Shortly after Wainapata you drop down to the river and what is perhaps the most spectacular part of the whole trail: amid orchids and flowering shrubs the path runs through an Inca tunnel. Continue on down to the Río Cooco where there is a camping spot (recently reported, unfortunately, to be covered with litter; a clean-up would be appreciated by all that follow).

Cross the river on a suspension bridge and climb the valley side again to those magnificent views. The village of Chusi is reached 8 or 9 hours after leaving Wainapata; but an hour before the village is a new settlement (on what used to be a campsite!) with a shop. This section of the trail has been much affected by mining activities, leaving mud-slopes which are difficult to negotiate after heavy rain or at dusk. Chusi is a proper village — the biggest on the trail — and has two shops and a school. You can usually get permission to sleep in the school, 'but the teacher and his friends made so much noise that we wished we hadn't.' (Ann and Frank Spowart Taylor)

If you continue for an hour you'll come to an almost perfect campsite. Quite suddenly, on a spur above the river, the trail opens out on to a large clearing with beautiful views in three directions. I say 'almost perfect', because the nearest water supply is a long way below. But there's another good place an hour further on, with water nearby. It's over the Río Grande de Yavia and up a stone staircase.

From Chusi to Llipi is 6 or 7 hours walking, but you won't do it in that time because of the bathing to be had in the streams along the way. It will be hot now and, the Incas having become ever more obsessional with their staircases (up and down), even those who are decidedly not cold-water lovers will want to cool off. Sadly this part of the valley is changing rapidly. Since 1980 the road has been extended progressively, and the Río Ticumbaya crossing 5 hours from Chusi, until recently a secluded bathing spot, is now just a muddy place beside the road. The only compensation for this is that where once you had to walk the final 15km to Unutuluni, you now have the choice of taking a truck to Llipi and then onwards. Such is progress.

Llipi is a mining settlement of plank houses with tin roofs, but it boasts plenty of shops, the people are friendly, and hikers are often invited to sleep in the school. You may find evidence of the mudslide which destroyed many buildings in 1992. This is definitely the end of the trail, since the rest of the valley has been so changed by mining activity that there is little point in trekking further. Early morning departures for Guanay and La Paz leave from the bottom of the town.

Getting back

The 4-hour trip to Guanay will take you through Unutuluni (dubbed 'You-too-are-loony' by tired trekkers), one of the bigger gold mining settlements,

which boasts several *pensiones* and a pool room. You then pass through
Gritado and Tipuani before crossing the Río Tipuani at Cangalli by ferry.

Guanay is a fair-sized town and an excellent place to relax for a few
days. It is the centre of trade in this part of the Yungas, and for a real taste
of the rainforest you can take canoe trips up or down the rivers. When you
are ready to return to civilization, you'd be well advised to take the bus
(book your seat as soon as you arrive). Flota Yungueña buses leave for
Caranavi, Coroico and La Paz at 05.00 daily from Calle 6 de Agosto 108.
The 230km journey to La Paz takes about 12 hours. Trucks loaded with
tropical produce also make the trip, but be warned: a reader reported that
he hopped on a nearly empty truck wearing his tropical clothes, hoping to
reach La Paz that night. He arrived 48 hours later! If you must take a truck
it would be sensible to break the journey in Coroico. From here, if you
were crazy enough, you could hike up to La Cumbre.

THE MAPIRI TRAIL

This begins at Sorata and crosses the *cordillera*, running parallel to the
Gold-diggers' Way and dropping down to Mapiri on the river of the same
name. The British explorer Colonel Fawcett reported using it in 1906. It
was last used by traders in 1953, after when it became overgrown and
impassable until 1990 when members of Club Sorata succeeded in reopening
it as a feasible hiking route.

That said, you should be warned that this is the most difficult hike in this
book. It is longer and much harder than the Gold-diggers' Way. Several
long stretches are without water, and depending on how recently others
have gone before you, the trail could be clear or completely overgrown.
The slightest fall of rain can turn it into a nightmare.

For these reasons you should not attempt to hike the Mapiri Trail without
a guide and full expedition gear, food for a week, and preferably mules.
Further information from Club Sorata.

Chapter Twenty-one

The Cordillera Apolobamba

Less known and less accessible than the Cordillera Real, the Apolobamba lies to the north and west of that range, rising abruptly from the Altiplano and straddling the Peruvian frontier at the northern tip of Lake Titicaca.

This is the place for truly adventurous hikers with lots of time. The beauty of the mountain scenery equals or even exceeds that of the Cordillera Real, and the glimpses of Indian life and wildlife (there is a vicuña reserve in the foothills) are even more interesting than to the south.

The Apolobamba owes its network of good trails to the Spanish lust for gold. This has been a gold mining area since the conquest, and ruined mines can be visited in remote valleys.

One of the biggest problems confronting the Apolobamba explorer is the lack of maps. Mine is drawn from a variety of sources and is only approximate. I am indebted to Pamela Holt, Pete Lawrence, Rachel Scott, Ken Valentine and Paul Hudson for information on areas that I haven't visited myself.

Getting there

For those without their own transport, just getting to the Cordillera Apolobamba is challenging enough. It may be as easy to approach from Peru via the northern side of Lake Titicaca as from La Paz.

Pete Lawrence and Rachel Scott report that there is a weekly bus and/or truck to Pelechuco, which usually leaves from Calle Reyes Cardona in the Cementerio district of La Paz on Wednesdays or Thursdays. The bus journey takes at least 12 hours and trucks even longer. 'Our truck took 19 hours, including a stop of 2-3 hours at night in the middle of nowhere.' The journey can be very cold — be prepared! Pete and Rachel add that there are several checkpoints along the way, so take some form of identification. The route goes via Escoma, close to Lake Titicaca, then north through barren, empty mountains towards the town of Ulla Ulla. 'There are settlements of sorts — mostly mudbrick shacks, seemingly deserted. Occasionally a figure emerges, or else someone jumps down from a truck and disappears through a silent doorway...'

Ken Valentine adds that in 1993 there were weekly buses from La Paz to both Pelechuco and Charazani (though not Curva). They departed from Calle Cancha Tejar in the Cementerio district. The Pelechuco bus left on Wednesdays at 10:00, returning on Friday (journey time 20-24 hours). The Charazani one was on Fridays at 05:30 returning on Sunday (12-16 hours). To Charazani there was also a weekly truck.

PELECHUCO TO CHARAZANI

I did this magnificent trek with TAWA (see *Useful addresses* on page 259), who solved the logistics of getting there and of carrying a pack over a 5,100m pass. It was a 6-day trek (including one rest day), and so spectacular and interesting that I wouldn't hesitate to recommend it to backpackers who are willing to face the transport difficulties or to groups looking for an exceptional trek. The clear trail runs along the eastern side of the Cordillera from Pelechuco, a village founded in 1560, which is at the crossroads of Amazon and Andean trade.

Apart from the breathtaking scenery, this trek was special because of the contact it allowed us with the Calahuaya Indians who are the traditional healers of the area. Highly respected throughout South America (they journey as far as Patagonia and Panama), they are expert in the use of herbal medicine and the art of making diagnoses by 'reading' a llama's entrails or scattered coca leaves. The Calahuayas were our *arrieros* and I am perfectly willing to believe that their acts of propitiation to the *achachilas* (mountain spirits) helped to make this the least problematic trek I have made in Bolivia. Bottles of the local *aguardiente*, Caiman, were opened at regular intervals, and the alcohol sprinkled around the wheels of the truck as we approached the trailhead, and on the hoofs of donkeys on the trail, amid muttered incantations. So accustomed did we become to the ritual that we felt uneasy without it when later we headed for a high pass in a truck. One of the group commented 'Shouldn't we Caiman the wheels?'

Practical information

Distance	About 70km
Altitude	Between 5,100m and 3,500m
Rating	Difficult
Timing	5 to 6 days

Guides and pack-animals

Ken Valentine recommends Alcides Imaño Pérez, a mule driver who knows the area well, who can be contacted through the Club Andino Boliviano (see *Useful addresses* on page 259).

Conditions/what to bring

Days will be cold and nights very cold, and you may encounter rain and snow even in the dry season. Around Pelechuco and Charazani however, it will be warm enough for T-shirts and shorts. Don't forget your sunglasses against the glare of the snow. Although provisions (including bread) may be available in Pelechuco, don't bank on it; stock up in La Paz.

Route description

By Ken Valentine, with additional material by Pamela Holt, Pete Lawrence and Rachel Scott

Pelechuco is quiet and pretty, with a strong Spanish flavour. There are cobbled streets, a fine church, colonial-style courtyards and a general air of decay. In the main plaza is Pensión México, run by friendly María de Alvarez. A few small shops sell basic provisions; and if you see a basket covered with a white cloth outside someone's front door it means they have fresh bread for sale.

To begin the walk, go up the steps by the church and turn left at the top. After crossing a small stream make a right turn and follow the path leading out of town towards the first pass. After about 2½ hours a small house will come into view. Bear right here and continue for an hour to an excellent campsite. The path is clear and well used, and one more hour will bring you to the top of the pass at 4,900m. A steep half hour descent follows to the Río Illo Illo and good camping.

Follow the river downstream past a number of small settlements. After an hour begin climbing again, first up the side of the main valley and then turning right into a side valley to reach the village of Illo Illo another hour further on. From above here a jeep track leads over the next pass towards the mining village of Viscachani. The path runs beneath the village and then climbs steeply to join this road after half an hour. Follow the road for an hour to the village of Piedra Grande, where camping is possible, then continue for another half hour, and after fording a stream, turn left up a steep path. A further 2½ hours of climbing, with ever-improving views of Yana Orko (5,500m), will bring you to a pleasant campsite. The Sunchulli Pass is now in view straight ahead, with the road leading down from it diagonally to the right.

The path heads straight for the pass, crossing a marsh before zig-zagging steeply up to the road. From the summit (reached 1½ hours after leaving the campsite) follow the road for 2½ hours to Viscachani. You may see condors on this stretch. The road loses much height before climbing again to Viscachani and you can avoid this by contouring round the side of the valley, although for most of the way there will be no path. You can camp below the village. There is a deserted gold mine here which may be fun to explore.

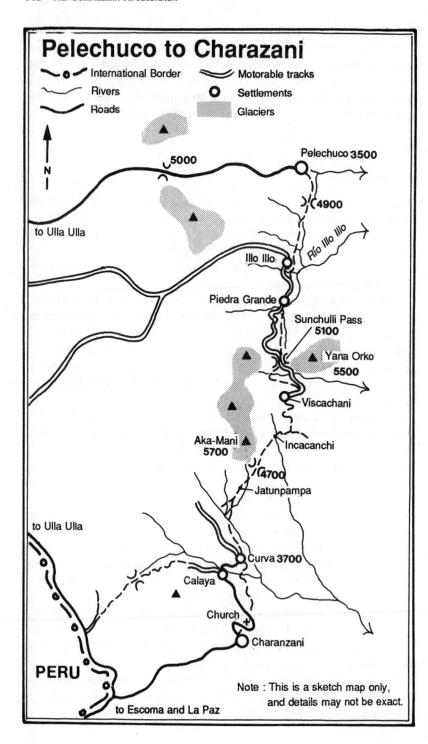

Pelechuco to Charazani

International Border — Motorable tracks

Rivers

Roads

○ Settlements

Glaciers

N

5000

Pelechuco 3500

4900

to Ulla Ulla

Río Illo Illo

Illo Illo

Piedra Grande

Sunchulli Pass
5100

Yana Orko
5500

Viscachani

Aka-Mani
5700

Incacanchi

4700

Jatunpampa

to Ulla Ulla

Curva 3700

Calaya

Church

Charanzani

PERU

Note : This is a sketch map only,
and details may not be exact.

to Escoma and La Paz

CLIMBING IN THE CORDILLERA APOLOBAMBA
By Paul Hudson and Ken Findlay, UK Apolobamba expedition, 1993

The attractions of the Cordillera Apolobamba for a climbing expedition were its feeling of remoteness, mostly good weather, Alpine-like peaks and high base camps.

The area has been visited by British climbers on various occasions and 47 of the 101 identified peaks had been conquered by British climbers. We climbed 13 peaks in the southern part of the range, 10 of which were first British ascents. Our first camp was at Paso Osipal, from where we climbed Sunchuli (5,306m), Cololo (5,916m) and Iscacuchu (5,650m). From the next camp, near the village of Sunchuli, we ascended Cuchillo 1 (5,655m), Corohuari (5,668m), Yanaorco (5,600m), Cavayani (5,700m) and Cuchillo 2 (5,450m) together with a number of unnamed summits. The best excursion was a two-day trip which started high up the valley west of Sunchuli, and saw us climbing on to the ridge via one of its side valleys. The trip west along its spine was excellent despite its difficulties and saw us bivying east of Cavayani itself.

Our equipment included snow stakes which were invaluable both as abseil anchors and running belays, the 3ft ones being better than the shorter ones. The glaciers we encountered were straightforward and the difficult and dangerous sections could easily be avoided. We employed only a few ice screws so there is no need to take too many; the rock gear remained unused mainly due to the poor rock. Our 9mm Cairngorm ropes were employed on a ratio of one to two people. We bivied out on two occasions without sleeping bags, our duvets and Phoenix bivy bags being adequate, although for real comfort extra layers and a Karrimat would have been good.

It is necessary to bring mountain food from home; this is essential if you are planning to stay up high on a multi-day route. We took multi-fuel stoves and bought paraffin from a garage in La Paz.

Maps are a problem, and a sketch map was drawn of the entire area by Paul Hudson. This, and a more detailed account of the ascents, is available by writing to P Hudson, 88 Ash Rd, Leeds, LS6 3HD (sae please).

From Viscachani your route heads up the right-hand side of the valley beneath the village and drops down into a neighbouring valley where you'll find a small lake. A short climb takes you into yet another valley, with a village away to the left. Go down to the right towards a gap between two crags, and about an hour from Viscachani you'll come to a magnificent viewpoint, from where the next and final pass can be seen. An hour of hair-raising descent from here will bring you to the river at a place called Incacanchi. This is an enchanting spot with a stone bridge, a waterfall nearby and a wonderful campsite from which you can contemplate the mountains all around.

The next climb takes some 2½ hours, and is bedevilled by false summits. Aka-Mani (5,700m) is in view to the right. From the true summit it's downhill — well, almost! — all the way (watch out for more condors).

Soon after leaving the summit, fork left at a cairn and descend to another good campsite, an hour from the top, called Jatunpampa. If it's late in the day you should consider stopping here, because the countryside ahead is intensively farmed and campsites harder to find. Otherwise continue descending through stone enclosures, cross the river and climb diagonally to the left on to a spur. Descend again to ford a second river (about an hour from the campsite) and follow the path up the valley side to meet a disused irrigation channel. Follow this for 15 minutes before turning off to the right, from where a further hour of gradual ascent will bring you to a road. Curva soon comes into view, on top of a small hill.

With no accommodation and very limited food supplies, Curva will offer little encouragement to stay. Luckily, an excellent 'Inca' path leads down from its main square, giving magnificent views of the terracing opposite, and after descending for an hour and climbing for a second hour you'll find yourself at a fork. The route to Charazani goes vertically up from here. When, after half an hour, you reach a church, look back for a final view of the Aka-Mani massif and forward for your first sight of Charazani. Go down to the road and follow this for a short distance before turning left towards a cross. The town is reached about 1½ hours after leaving the church.

Getting back

Sunday seems to be the best day for transport back to La Paz. The bus or truck will leave early in the morning and take 12-16 hours. Alternatively, you could walk to the junction with the Pelechuco road — a long day, but with plenty of good campsites and water en route in case you should decide to linger.

Pete Lawrence and Rachel Scott report that a vehicle track leads west from Calaya (the village in the valley below Curva) over a pass and then down to join the Ulla Ulla road. Details are sketchy, but Pete and Rachel had no trouble following this route in the opposite direction, and found lakes and potential campsites en route. This could be yet another way out of the area if transport can't be found. Again, allow at least a day, and preferably two.

ULLA ULLA NATIONAL PARK

By Jonathan Derksen

Some people ask for remoteness, others ask for nature in its undefiled state; Ulla Ulla National Park offers both. Located deep within the Apolobamba Mountains and approximately 100km north of Lake Titicaca, the park is not only a wonder to see but a true challenge to get to.

The park has a roughly defined area of just over 200,000 hectares, and was first established as a vicuña reserve in 1972. At that time, the vicuña count in the area had dropped to a mere 72 animals due to unrestrained poaching. In 1977, UNESCO managed to raise the park's status to Biosphere Reserve in the hope of protecting not only the native vicuña population, but the entire ecosystem. That same year, the Instituto Nacional de Fomento Lanero (INFOL) was created and put in charge of conducting vicuña research and safeguarding the reserve. Now Ulla Ulla boasts a swelling population of 2,500 vicuñas and healthy numbers of black ibises, Chilean flamingoes, Andean geese and viscachas.

The village of Ulla Ulla itself is located in the middle of a sprawling *bofedal* or ancient lake bed, that extends the length of the Apolobamba range. Most residents are alpaca farmers who share local water and other resources with adjacent villages.

There is much to see and do in the park. If you have your own transport, the wild vicuña herds can be observed at close range and followed cross-country, if one doesn't mind the rough ride. During the day, the vicuñas graze with the alpacas, but towards evening, when their domesticated brothers and sisters head home to their stone wall corrals, the vicuñas wander to more isolated pastures. It is especially beautiful to see these graceful cameloids grazing along the plains at dawn against a backdrop of snow-clad peaks.

In the Apolobamba foothills there are a number of lakes to visit including Katantira and Kanahuma, where you encounter flamingoes, ducks, Andean geese, black ibises and other waterfowl. Slightly further north, just east of the road to Pelechuco, are the Putina hot-springs, where you can wallow in steaming, sulphur-rich waters while witnessing isolated rainstorms sweep in over the broad plains.

Practical information

Travelling by car from La Paz follow the road to Lake Titicaca, then bear right at Huarina and follow the dirt highway to Achacachi and Escoma. In Escoma, the road turns north, traverses several passes, and then just after the turnoff to Charazani (stay left) descends into the Apolobamba valley. The total drive takes 8-12 hours. To reach Ulla Ulla by public transport see page 299.

Although Ulla Ulla offers no hotel accommodation, lodging may be found with local families. There are also plenty of campsites on the outskirts of the village. In fact, almost anywhere outside the village is a campsite. Supplies in the local store are limited but sufficient. Be sure to bring warm clothing as temperatures often drop below zero at night.

For further information contact INFOL (349048) at Calle Bueno 444, Casilla 732, La Paz.

HIKING THE ROAD TO APOLO

By Jonathan Derksen

One of the most thrilling, or perhaps terrifying, things about living in Bolivia is road travel. Some of the most spectacular drives might include the roads to Coroico, Sorata, the Zongo Valley or Illimani, or along the Carretera Cochabamba. A new, infrequently travelled, road has recently penetrated deep into the department of La Paz that rivals all of these: the road to Apolo. Apolo is a small jungle town that lies at the edge of the Amazon basin, several hundred kilometres north of Lake Titicaca.

Roads in the area were first built to access a number of mines (some of which date back to pre-Columbian times) just past the town of Charazani. Visitors without their own vehicle can derive just as much enjoyment from hiking this road, and exploring some of the side-trails, as can the car driver or mountain biker.

Practical information

Distance	About 90km
Altitude	Between about 3,800m and 1,500m
Rating	Moderate
Timing	7-10 days

Route description

From Charazani the dirt track winds down through a land of grassy mountains and running waters. Every bend offers breathtaking views of what were once heavily terraced hillsides (pre-Columbian), now often covered with thick forest. Waterfalls tumble down from the Andean heights to feed the many rivers that flow through the steep valleys.

At an altitude of 3,000m the valleys take on a distinctly tropical atmosphere streaked with white and yellow deposits from hot springs. Here butterflies, disturbed from puddles on the road, flit about in colourful clouds, small flocks of parakeets screech noisily overhead and orchids and other flowers adorn the roadside.

Lower down still, the road meanders along the foot of towering cliffs, streaked with white and yellow from hot springs, while massive boulders, that years ago tumbled from above, sit in their final resting place at the base of the valley.

Small green areas invite you to camp beside rushing streams and rivers, and for the more adventurous, there are mines to explore, trails to hike and ruins to discover. About 2 hours (driving) below Charazani a hot spring pours across the road. Bathing here by moonlight is an experience beyond words and, if you are lucky, you'll see the *guácharo*, a nocturnal bird, doing aerial acrobatics in small squadrons in the night sky.

Conditions/what to bring

The only towns between Charazani and Apolo are Camata, about half way between the two points, and Correo, about three-quarters of the way. In emergency there are several military/mining construction camps along the way where help may be sought. But remember, this place is remote, so prepare for the worst as well as the best. If you plan to hike down from the pass, make sure to bring clothing that will guard against freezing temperatures and precipitation. We had snow in November, when it's supposed to start warming up in that area. Bring extra water purification tablets, a well-stocked first-aid kit, sturdy boots, a tent, and surplus food.

AYMARÁ SPIRITUAL LIFE

The soul of the Aymará is the *Ajayu*, roughly translated as spiritual welfare. This is in two parts, *Ajayu mayor* and *Ajayu minor* (*Jacha Ajayu* and *Jisk'a Ajayu* in Aymará). *Ajayu mayor* is consciousness, movement, intellect — the humanity of a person. *Ajayu minor* is more subtle; it could be compared, perhaps, to the aura of New Age believers, or to an intangible fluid. Like the body it can become dirty, not through outside agents but through 'dirty deeds' — one's own actions or the actions of others. The *Ajayu minor* can also be lost, for instance if a child falls over or an adult receives a profound fright. The shock of such accidents can cause the *Ajayu minor* to leave the body.

If the *Ajayu minor* departs or becomes dirty, a *brujo* (wise man or witch-doctor) can clean and restore it with smoke and incense or with water. This is the significance of the quiet groups of people and the puffs of incense on the hill of the Seven Stations of the Cross, behind Copacabana. It hardly need be said that to take a photo of this ceremony would be seriously intrusive.

Our Aymará guide in Copacabana, Wenceslao, told us that his grandfather would take a cup of water from Lake Titicaca and tell his grandsons: 'This is only a tiny part of the lake, but an essential part of it; so are we in relation to all of Creation'. He taught them the ceremony of giving thanks to the sun, the rain and the earth for working together to produce crops. 'We need to thank them,' he said, 'and likewise we ourselves must work together in harmony.'

Wenceslao also told us that there are no Aymará words for rich and poor; just merit or no merit.

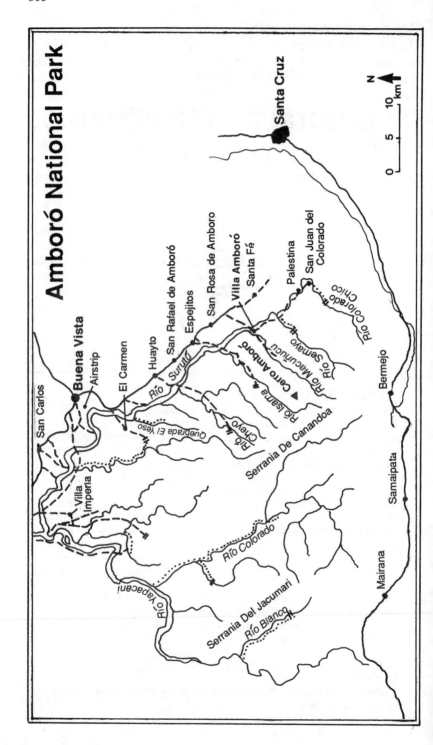

Chapter Twenty-two

Central and Northern Bolivia

The exceptional hiking in Bolivia is concentrated in the Cordillera Real so this range has been the focus of this section of the book. There are, however, plenty of other choices especially for those with an interest in natural history who wish to see the rainforest. Bolivia resident and wildlife enthusiast Jon Derksen sent these accounts of some little known lowland national parks, but first Connie Hickling suggests some Inca ruins near Santa Cruz.

THE SANTA CRUZ AREA
Samaipata
The easternmost Inca ruins in the empire can be reached by a pleasant walk. They are about 10km from the town of Samaipata, one of the access towns to the Amboró National Park, and reached by bus from Santa Cruz. First follow the road back towards Santa Cruz. In about 2km you'll see a kiosk on the left and a narrow road on the right. Follow this for 5km; cross a stream (upstream is a beautiful bathing spot so be sure to take your swimming things); then climb for the final 2km to the ruins on top of a hill. Overlooking rolling hills and mountains, the fortress protected the Inca highlands from incursions from lowland tribes.

Amboró National Park
By Jonathan Derksen, with additional information from Erik Nijland

Amboró National Park, covering an area of over 630,000 hectares, lies within three distinct ecosystems: the foothills of the Andes, the northern Chaco and the Amazon Basin. The park was originally established as the Reserva de Vida Silvestre German Busch in 1984, but, with the help of Bolivian biologist, Noel Kempff, British zoologist, Robin Clarke and others, the park was expanded to its present size. Because the park straddles different ecosystems, it has a diverse animal population, including jaguars, peccaries, several species of monkey, agouti, river otters, tapirs, capybara, raccoons and deer. And according to park zoologist, Robin Clarke, the bird species count has already passed the 700 mark.

Erik Nijland reports some tension in the area from the farmers who have worked the land here for generations and resent the new national park status. It would be as well to check on the situation in Santa Cruz or Buena Vista before visiting the park. There are several ways into the park, each approach offering something different. The northern approach is perhaps the most rewarding, many of the hikes following riverbeds bordered by dramatic red cliffs. Due to the temperamental nature of these rivers it is advisable to attempt these hikes between April and October. It is also advisable that a *guardaparque* or park guide, be hired (US$5/day or less) at the park headquarters in Buena Vista, since trails are often uncertain and in any case these rangers have a fascinating knowledge of the jungle.

Park administration

The park is administered by FAN (see page 253). Visit them in Santa Cruz to make a reservation to visit the park. The building is behind a large white wall on the left side of the old road to Cochabamba, at Km 5; tel/fax: 533389 or 333806. There is a small charge to enter the park. The park headquarters is in Buena Vista, tel: 2032.

Getting there

All treks into the northern portion of the park are accessible from Buena Vista. Buses bound for Buena Vista from Santa Cruz leave several times daily from the city's main bus terminal. The trip takes approximately 3 hours over very good roads, by Bolivian standards. Basic accommodation is easily found in Buena Vista.

From Buena Vista, a bus leaves daily to make the run along the Río Surutú, stopping near the mouths of its various tributaries including the Quebrada El Yeso, and rivers Cheyo, Isama, Macuñucú, Semayo and Colorado Chico, where dirt tracks take you deep into the jungle.

Conditions/what to bring

Backpacking in the lower jungled foothills of the Andes is different, of course, from packing the higher, generally clearer Inca trails. You do not experience the extremes in temperature that accompany changes in altitude. Perhaps the single greatest problem is how to prevent moisture from ruining everything you own. The best defence is to pack everything in plastic bags — and I mean everything. And remember, whatever is waterproof will also be bugproof. The best way to deal with the various dips in the river is to simply have a set of clothes (and sneakers) that will stay wet, then bag them when you get to the campsite. Unless you have a good fire, it is difficult to dry clothes in the high humidity of the forest. A rain poncho is useful, but more as an open covering — a rain-jacket is too hot. Anti-malaria pills should be taken, despite the negligible threat of contracting the parasite. Snakes are fairly common, so watch where you place your feet.

The Macuñucú
This is perhaps the best known of the jungle trails which follows the Macuñucú riverbed.

Practical information

Rating	The full trek is only for the fit and adventurous, requiring some jungle-bashing and a machete. The lower part of the river is easier.
Timing	4 to 7 days
Maps	IGM sheet SE 20-6, 1:250,000, gives a good overview of the area.

Route description
At Las Cruces, about an hour's drive (35km) from Buena Vista (ask the bus driver to let you know when to get off), stands a sign indicating the unofficial boundary of Parque Nacional Amboró. A rough road winds through fields and patches of jungle for 8km until it runs into the Surutu River. In the dry season the waters are low and the crossing easy. It is a good idea to keep clothes on as there are myriads of tiny *marigui* (midges), which love to feast on human blood. We found biting insects to be a problem only here. It is often easier to stick to the river's course (and resign yourself to wet feet) rather than the bordering jungle trail.

Not far beyond the river is Villa Amboró, a seasonal town, and your last chance for provisions. We bought some beer here and a live chicken for later consumption. Horses are available for hire as far as the first camp, if you are in need of a rest.

Beyond Villa Amboró you have to pass through a number of gates, designed to contain errant cattle. From here the trail tends to stick more to the forest. You will come to the confluence of a freshwater stream and the Río Macuñucú, a good place to rest. Beyond this point there is another small village of several thatched huts and a football field and then the forest closes in. An hour or so further along a good trail is the Campamento Macuñucú, a park station comprised of several thatched huts, a toilet and some crude showers fed by a pump at the river below. The camp also boasts numerous fruit trees.

Beyond Camp Macuñucú there is only jungle and the going gradually becomes more difficult. Sometimes the trail will seem to disappear, especially as it meanders in and out of the Macuñucú, but by following the course of the river, you will not get lost. The jungle along this portion of the route is awe-inspiring. Great liana vines hang from branches as large as trees themselves. There's a good chance you might see spider or howler monkeys, agouti, squirrels and toucans. Early morning is the best time for spotting wildlife. Eventually the trail narrows, and after a few more dips in the river, you should keep a careful lookout on the left side for a overhang of red rock, partially hidden by vegetation. This is a great place to spend the first or second night, and has some interesting graffiti dating back to 1933. The overhang will shelter two two-people tents quite comfortably. There's lots of dead wood to be found for a fire, and just downstream is the mouth of a freshwater stream. Beware of army ants. We had a column 12ft wide and a 100 yards long march through our campground!

Another half hour's trudge up the river will take you between steep canyon walls. If the waters are not too high you should be able to wade through the canyon without much trouble, but take time to feel around for the safest passage. Sometimes the waters of the Macuñucú are silty, especially if there has been a landslide farther up stream (which is common), and deeper pools are not easily anticipated. Remember, *never* have backpack chest or waist straps fastened when wading through deeper waters, particularly when there is a current of any kind. The weight of your pack could easily pull you under. Just beyond this narrow point, the canyon walls draw back. On the left side is another overhang/cave large enough to shelter six tents, and a sandy beach. Although I never witnessed the animals themselves, I identified the tracks of a tapir, peccary, capybara, coati-mundi and river otters. River otters seemed by far the most prolific mammals in the area.

The farther upstream you go from here the more spectacular the scenery becomes. On either side of the river tower the red cliffs, fresh water streams tumbling down their sheer faces in crystal cascades. In places, huge chunks of rock have fallen to leave great gaping holes. *Tojos* (weaver birds or, more specifically, yellow-rumped caciques), suspend their meticulously made nests from frail trees clinging to narrow ledges. A few twists in the river will bring you to a place where slides have intermittently blocked the river. In some places it is necessary to climb up through the jungle in order to circumvent the slides. From here the going is much tougher. The trail basically disappears, although you might pick up traces of it farther upstream. A machete would be helpful. You might want to try fishing in the larger pools.

The stream continues to narrow, and you will find yourself scrambling over beautiful red and grey sandstone formations caused by the eroding effects of water spilling down from the Andes. It was in this area that I saw jaguar tracks. It is a good idea to bring one or two heavy duty plastic bags or an airmattress so that, if you get tired of always climbing the banks of the river, you could swim, trailing your floating pack behind you.

After a couple of hours of hard going you will stumble upon a larger waterfall. This is a good place to try to make camp, as sandy areas are few and far between after this point. Just below the falls you might find a good site, and there is always driftwood for a fire. Beware: in heavy rain flash floods are common; when you set up camp, make sure you have an escape route planned just in case the waters start to rise. Stingless sweat bees are common here; irritating but harmless.

For the truly adventurous, a climb higher up the riverbed will take you to the headwaters which have rarely been explored. A guide might also be able to take you up over the backside of Mount Amboró and down along the Isama River back to the Surutú, but this is extremely hard going and you would have to be very well equipped.

Other hikes in the park

It should be noted that the hike outlined here is just one of the many in this portion of the park. The Isama River, I'm told, is equally beautiful, as is Chico Colorado.

For those without a lot of time, it might be more worthwhile to attempt the Mataracú River, farther north. The jungle in this area is incredible, but the access is easier. Of course, this means there is more evidence of human encroachment. There is a good campground with basic facilities. For the more experienced, and for those who want more jungle, you can hike from the Mataracú over the mountains to the Río Colorado. The wildlife on this route is less fearful of people, and you get a good cross section of flora.

The southern part of the park
By Erik Nijland

The villages of Samaipata and Mairana are about 3 hours by bus from Santa Cruz over a paved road. In Samaipata you can visit the ruins of an Inca fortress (see page 309).

From Mirana you can walk to the village of La Yunga in 4 hours. Here the organization FAN, Fundación Amigos de la Naturaleza, runs a guest house and can provide guides to take you into the park.

There is a fern-lined trail into the park from La Yunga. Otherwise you will need to follow the river gorges, entering and leaving along the same route.

NORTHEAST BOLIVIA

Noel Kempff Mercado National Park

This 541,000 hectare park previously known as Serrania de Huanchaca o Capurus, is situated on Bolivia's northeastern border with Brazil. It is characterized by near vertical cliffs that rise to meet a broad plateau, where dense forests, rolling hills and countless freshwater streams broken intermittently by sparkling cascades dominate the scene. In this geographically isolated area, flora and fauna have evolved separately, and many species are unique. In 1908 British explorer Colonel PH Fawcett ventured into this unknown territory — supposedly inhabited by ferocious cannibalistic tribes and dangerous beasts. In his published diaries, Fawcett describes his first impressions of this magnificent place:

> Above us towered the Ricardo Franco Hills, flat-topped and mysterious, their flanks scarred by deep *quebradas*. Time and the foot of man had not touched those summits. They stood like a lost world, forested to their tops, and the imagination could picture the last vestiges of an age long vanished. Isolated from the battle with changing conditions, monsters from the dawn of man's existence might still roam those heights unchallenged, imprisoned and protected by unscalable cliffs.

Fawcett's enthusiasm could have been the inspiration for Arthur Conan Doyle's novel *Lost World* published four years later (although Venezuela claims its *tepuis* for this honour).

The Nature Conservancy has included Noel Kempff Mercado National Park in its 'Park in Peril' programme, initiated to protect vulnerable ecological sites throughout Latin America. The park has also been classified by organizations such as the United Nations Development Programme as a vital area for the conservation of Amazon wildlife.

The impressive birdlife includes the giant rhea, jabiru stork, chachalaca, harpy eagle and hyacinth macaw (one of the rarest and most beautiful of parrots). The giant armadillo and otter, jaguarundi, maned wolf, bush dog, prehensile-tailed porcupine and dusky titi monkey are some of the rare mammals of this astonishing ecosystem.

Access
(Information by Miriam Melgar from Fundacion Amigos de la Naturaleza)

Getting to the park depends on how much time you have and of course your budget — because it is such a remote area it can get quite expensive. There are two ways to reach Flor de Oro (the main station in the park): by small plane (Cessna 206 carrying 4-5 passengers); or by driving 19 hours to Piso Firme (just outside the extreme northwestern corner of the park) and then by boat to Flor de Oro. The only way to visit the Serrania (escarpments) is by small plane. To reach Los Fierros from Flor de Oro you must also fly (roughly 30 minutes one way). The Ahlfeld waterfall is accessible from Flor de Oro, taking roughly 5 hours by boat. To reach Los Fierros from Santa Cruz is about an 18-hour drive. These roads are practically unusable during the rainy season (December -April), but should be all right during June — just very dusty. The overland route is tiring but worth the discomfort.

The camps

Visitors can stay at the camps located within the park, but to visit Flor de Oro you should first contact FAN to check availability. To visit Los Fierros and the waterfalls you must first contact the Centro Regional para la Conservación de la Naturaleza (CERCONA): Esteban Cardona, tel: 462173 (Santa Cruz). Flor de Oro is under the administration of FAN and is both an ecotourism/research site as well as the main protection and management camp for the northeastern section of the park. If anyone wished to visit the other camps (outside Flor de Oro) or any other location within the Park (ie. Huanchaca) FAN must first check and coordinate with CERCONA, which administers these other camps. By first coordinating with these organizations people can backpack and camp in the park. Reservations are necessary if you plan to stay at the camp itself, where basic accommodation is available.

Anyone who wishes to visit the park must be accompanied by a park guard, *guardeparque*, to ensure the safety of the individual as well as to check that they don't harm the flora and fauna.

Although this may all sound complicated, such regulations help maintain the pristine nature of the area. The people at FAN are friendly and helpful, and they will do what they can to ensure your trip into the park is unforgettable.

Conditions/what to bring

This region can be suffocatingly hot, even during the winter months, unless the *surazo* (south wind) is blowing when the temperatures can drop to almost freezing. It is best to be prepared for hot, cool and rainy conditions. Ticks can be a problem, especially the little ones (seedticks or *garapatillas*) which caused extreme discomfort to both Colonel Fawcett and me. Guard against these mischievous members of nature by sprinkling sulphur powder on your socks and around your ankles and make sure your trousers (pants) are stuffed into your boots. Ticks are best removed with masking tape before they become lodged in your skin. Avoid wearing shorts, except when in camp, and wear boots not sneakers. Many types of grass are razor sharp and can cause serious cuts.

Hiking

Backpacking possibilities into the interior of the park are many and varied. Speaking with FAN and the park guards will help you to decide which of these trips you would like to undertake.

You can view the most picturesque areas in the park in several days, but to really do it justice, two weeks would be needed. Noel Kempff is the kind of place where you will see something new with each day, especially since wildlife, with the exception of birds, tends to be elusive and shy.

THE PANDO AND THE BOLIVIAN AMAZON

By Jonathan Derksen

The Pando is Bolivia's northernmost department and the best place to experience true Amazon rainforest. There are many possible hikes that would make a visit to this department worthwhile.

The history of the Bolivian Amazon is generally one of exploitation and extraction — what was needed was taken from the forest with little thought of sustainability. Jonathan Kendall states in his *Passage Through El Dorado*:

> The conquistadors and *bandeirantes* searched for gold, precious stones and Indian slaves. The missionary settlements for Indians, with their riverside agricultural plots, came closest to breaking the extractive mould. But they depended for their economic survival on hunting and fishing, and a modest commerce in wild animal hides, nuts, cinnamon and medicinal herbs — all extractive enterprises. The rubber trade, entirely linked to the milking of wild trees, was the extractive industry par excellence...

Evidence of this extractive exploitation is still visible throughout the Bolivian Amazon. In abandoned boom towns old mansions, once belonging to the great rubber barons, now stand empty, slowly being reclaimed by the encroaching jungle. In some places overgrown railway tracks hint of some of the more ambitious dreams of frontiersmen hoping to open up the territory. Deeper in the jungle you might come across brazil nut (previously rubber) collection sites established in the first decade of this century. You will encounter the *siringa* or rubber tree, scarred by many long years of tapping, now left to heal, until, perhaps, the arrival of a new era of exploitation.

Getting there

Most people use Riberalta as their gateway to the Pando.

Aerosur and Lloyd Aero Boliviano fly from La Paz to Trinidad and Riberalta several times a week — the round trip costs about US$180. For you hardy types, Flota Yungueña buses run from La Paz to Rurrenabaque and then on to Riberalta — the cost one-way is about Bs150. River transportation is also possible, but unreliable. Inquiries can be made at the *Capitania del Puerto* (Port Captain's Office) on Calle Guachalla in La Paz.

Riberalta

The town sits on the banks of the Río Beni, several kilometres from its confluence with the Madre de Dios. Its location made it a perfect centre for trade during the rubber boom (1890s-1914) and some of the old charm from that era still lingers in the architecture. Riberalta has recently become a major stop along the La Paz - Guayaramerin - Cojiba highway. A large percentage of the population works in brazil nut processing plants. In fact, so many brazil nuts are produced here that the husks are commonly used as fill in road construction. The smell of dust and nuts fills your nostrils at all times. For a tour of one of the plants, you might try contacting the Hecker establishment, the oldest brazil nut producing family in the region (tel: 0852 8232 or 8154, fax: 0852 8559).

Conditions/what to bring

This portion of the Amazon is very flat. You will not find yourself scrambling up muddy ridges or caught in deep ravines, but the heat and humidity punish the spirit at times, and you will drink huge quantities of liquid. Bring purification tablets. Even if the numerous streams you encounter look clean, don't drink from them without purifying the water; all kinds of bacteria are found here. Wear shoes at all times, as worms could infest your feet. In places mosquitoes may be a problem; the Brazilian brands of insecticide available in Riberalta work the best (but I'm not sure they'd be legal in North America or Europe!). Take anti-malaria pills. Snakes are numerous but rarely seen. In the unlikely event of a bite, sites like Río Negro have emergency radios, and a light plane can be called to pick up the victim.

Be sure to pack everything in plastic bags to prevent moisture and insects from infiltrating your belongings.

There are no topographical maps available of the area at present.

Guided hikes

All of the most interesting hikes in the Pando involve venturing into the dense Amazon rainforest. You are advised to hire a guide who knows the jungle and area well. Gianni Zenari currently operates Amazonas Tours out of Guayaramerin, a town located on the Brazil-Bolivia border (tel: 0855 2246, or contact him through the Hotel Litoral, tel: 0855 2017). Mr Zenari speaks English and can take you deep into the forest for about US$50 per day including meals, accommodation and transport. He is fascinated by the history and wildlife of the Pando, making a guided tour with him all the more worthwhile.

One tiring, but unforgettable hike takes you from the port of Loma Alta to the brazil nut collection site of Río Negro. To get to the port, a boat can be hired at the docks in Riberalta to make the 3-hour trip downstream, or Gianni Zenari can arrange it for you. From Loma Alta it is about 35km to Río Negro. The road, which is really a glorified trail, passes through some of the most beautiful jungle I have ever seen. Brazil nut trees tower on all sides, some of them 200ft tall with trunks 8ft thick. Huge palm trees called *motacú* fan out like giant peacocks all along the overgrown track; thinner trees shoot up through openings in the canopy to secure their piece of light. If you're lucky you'll see howler or spider monkeys in the trees. Large lizards often lounge about in patches of sunlight, and in the mornings you might spy agouti or coati mundi feeding alongside the road. En route are small settlements and collection huts where life has remained relatively unchanged for 100 years, with most inhabitants still sheltered from the influence of larger towns like Riberalta. Electricity is scarce.

Río Negro is a paradise. Just below the town the river snakes its way through the thick foliage, and swimming is possible despite the presence of piranhas and electric eels.

Walking the wild brazil nut and rubber tree *estradas* or circuits is a must in order to get a feel for what the collectors go through on a daily basis. You might be able to hire a boat to take you up or down the river to explore further.

If you are interested in visiting this area, it is suggested that you contact the Hecker family (see *Riberalta*) as they own the Río Negro collection site and the surrounding lands.

One other hike which Mr Zenari introduced me to started not far from the abandoned boom town of Cachuela Esperanza, 95km north of Riberalta. A boat was hired to take us across the Beni River, just below the Esperanza cataracts (a sight in itself!) and we disembarked several kilometres downstream. I was then led into the jungle along questionable paths to a small rubber collection site, comprising five *pahuichis*, or thatched huts, where we set up camp. The best way to see the area and its wildlife is to do day or overnight hikes from the collection site, although Zenari would be willing to take you five days or longer into the forest, if you so wished.

DINOSAUR TRACKS IN SUCRE
Footprints of dinosaurs have recently been found on the grounds of a cement factory by workers clearing the land. They are on a high, exposed wall and are said to be those of *Tyrannosaurus rex*. The factory, which lies some 15 minutes by taxi from Sucre city centre, allows visitors to view the dinosaur footprints on Saturdays. Enquire at the tourist office.
From information by Erik Nijland

Appendices

FURTHER READING

I once asked an impressively fit woman how she had prepared for the trek. 'I did a lot of reading' she responded.

Background reading and a companion guidebook will help you get the most out of your trip. Here are a few suggestions, with subjective comments on those I particularly liked, but I would welcome further recommendations.

Readers wanting a complete bibliography of Peru and Bolivia should get hold of a copy of the *World Bibliographic Series* published by Clio Press (UK) and ABC-Clio (USA): *Peru* by John Ridley, with 705 entries and *Bolivia* by Gertrude M Yeager, with 816 entries.

The Hispanic and Luso-Brazilian Council at Canning House, 2 Belgrave Square, London SWIX 8PJ provides Londoners with an excellent library of books pertaining to South America, and publishes informed (and therefore often helpfully critical) reviews in *The British Bulletin of Publications on Latin America, the Carribbean, Portugal and Spain.*

Background reading: travel narratives

Murphy, Dervla; *Eight feet in the Andes.* John Murray 1983.
An entertaining and insightful account of the author's trek from Cajamarca to Cusco, accompanied by her ten-year-old daughter.

Parris, Matthew; *Inca Cola.* Weidenfeld & Nicolson, 1990/Phoenix 1993.
One of the best modern travelogues about Peru and Bolivia. Much of the narrative covers a hiking trip to the Cordillera Huayhuash. Witty, evocative and accurate.

Pow, Tom; *In the Palace of Serpents: an Experience of Peru.* Canongate Press, 1992.
A description of a Peru journey praised by the Canning House *Bulletin* as being perceptive, honest and accurate (I have not read it).

Simpson, Joe; *Touching the Void.* Jonathan Cape, 1988.
An award-winning description of a climbing accident in the Cordillera Huayhuash. An extraordinarily vivid and moving book.

Background reading: history

Burger, Richard; *Chavín and the origin of the Andean civilization.* Thames & Hudson, 1993.
The definitive book on a fascinating subject.

Hemming, John; *Conquest of the Incas.* Macmillan, 1970. The outstanding book on the Incas and their conquest by the Spanish. A hefty 640 pages but eminently readable.

Hemming, John & Ranney, Edward; *Monuments of the Incas*. Univ. of New Mexico Press, 1990.
Studies of the better known Inca sites, beautifully illustrated with black and white photographs. Highly recommended.

de la Vega, Garcilaso; *Royal Commentaries of the Incas*. Fascinating because it was originally written in 1609 by the son of a *conquistador* and an Inca princess.

Background reading: drugs and terrorism

Hargreaves, Clare; *Snowfields: The War on Cocaine in the Andes*. Zed Books/ Holmes and Meier, 1992.
The background to one of the most serious problems affecting Peru and Bolivia.

Strong, Simon; *Shining Path*. Harper Collins, 1992.
A powerful and first-hand account of the terrorist movement which vividly evokes life in Peru in the early part of this decade.

Practical guides

Box, Ben (ed); *The South American Handbook*. Trade and Travel.
Still the most up to date and practical guide to the two
countries, updated annually in August.

Mesili, Alain; *La Cordillera Real de los Andes — Bolivia*. Los Amigos de Libro, Bolivia, 1984.
Descriptions of all the routes up the peaks of the Cordillera Real (Spanish).

Neate, Jill; *Mountaineering in the Andes: A Sourcebook for Climbers*. Expedition Advisory Centre, Royal Geographical Society, London. 1994.
An extremely thorough and accurate survey of all the Andean Cordilleras. Includes mountaineering history and a comprehensive bibliography. An essential book for those planning a mountaineering expedition.

Rachowiecki, Rob; *Peru: A Travel Survival Kit*. Lonely Planet.
A thorough, practical and frequently updated guide by one of LP's award-winning authors.

Swaney, Deanna & Strauss, Robert; *Bolivia: A Travel Survival Kit*.
Provides thorough travel information for all Bolivia.

Health

Darvill, Fred; *Mountaineering Medicine*. Wilderness Press, USA, 1992.
A compact, 100 page booklet which should be carried by all North American backpackers.

Steele, Peter; *Medical Handbook for Mountaineers*. Constable, London.
The best pocket guide on the subject for British readers.

Wilson Howarth, Jane; *Healthy Travel: Bugs, Bites & Bowels*. Cadogan, 1995.
A super book! Practical, sensible and entertaining, written by a doctor who has lived and travelled extensively in the developing countries.

OTHER BRADT GUIDES TO LATIN AMERICA

South America

Backcountry Brazil by Alex Bradbury.
Three areas are covered in depth: Amazonia, the Pantanal, and the north-east coast.

Venezuela by Hilary Dunsterville Branch.
A guide for eco-tourists emphasising the mountains, jungles and national parks with several sections specifically on hiking.

Climbing and Hiking in Ecuador by R Rachowiecki & B Wagenhauser.
The definitive guide to the volcanoes, mountains and cloudforests of Ecuador, by two former residents.

Backpacking in Chile and Argentina by Hilary Bradt and others.
Hikes throughout the 'southern cone' of the continent, from the tropical northwest of Argentina to Tierra del Fuego.

Central and South America by Road by Pam Ascanio.
A guide to driving or cycling throughout the continent with all the necessary information on red-tape and route planning (due end of 1995).

South American Ski Guide by Chris Lizza.
Details of 35 ski centres mostly in Chile and Argentina, with ski history and trail maps.

Central America

No Frills Guide to Hiking in Mexico by Jim Conrad.
From the deserts of Baja California to the volcanoes of Popocatepetl and Ixtaccihuati.

The Maya Road by Jim Conrad.
Eastern Mexico, Belize and lowland Guatemala for ecotourists.

Guide to Belize by Alex Bradbury.
A detailed guide for lovers of the natural world written by a professional biologist and diver.

Backpacking and Hiking in Central America by Tim Burford.
All the main hiking routes from Guatemala to Panama, including the Darien Gap (due end of 1995).

This is just a selection of our books for adventurous travellers. Send for our latest catalogue.

Bradt Publications, 41 Nortoft Rd, Chalfont St Peter, Bucks SL9 0LA, England. Tel/fax: 01494 873478

Bradt Publications

Travel Guides

41 Nortoft Road • Chalfont St Peter • Bucks • SL9 0LA • England Fax/Telephone: 01494 873478

November 1996

Dear readers,

By contributing to the next edition of this guide you will be continuing a 21 year tradition! Do write to me with your updates, corrections (including the maps) and - above all - your new hikes and ideas. A new edition is scheduled for 1998, and I love hearing from other backpackers and trekkers.

Enjoy Peru and Bolivia and do let me hear from you. Don't forget to add your name and address (legibly) so you can be properly thanked and if sending a hand-written letter please print names so I can read them.

¡Vaya bien!

Hilary Bradt

MEASUREMENTS AND CONVERSIONS

Latin America uses metric measurements and so have I throughout this book. These conversion formulae and tables should help you.

Many people will want to convert metres to the more familiar feet. If you remember that 3 metres is 9.84 feet, or just under 10 feet, you can do an approximate conversion quickly: to convert heights shown in metres to feet, divide by 3 and add a zero, e.g. 6,000 m = 20,000 feet.

The error is only 1.5%.

CONVERSION FORMULAE

To convert	Multiply by
Inches to centimetres	2.54
Centimetres to inches	0.3937
Feet to metres	0.3048
Metres to feet	3.281
Yards to metres	0.9144
Metres to yards	1.094
Miles to kilometres	1.609
Kilometres to miles	0.6214
Acres to hectares	0.4047
Hectares to acres	2.471
Imperial gallons to litres	4.546
Litres to imperial gallons	0.22
US gallons to litres	3.785
Litres to US gallons	0.264
Ounces to grams	28.35
Grams to ounces	0.03527
Pounds to grams	453.6
Grams to pounds	0.002205
Pounds to kilograms	0.4536
Kilograms to pounds	2.205
British tons to kilograms	1016.0
Kilograms to British tons	0.0009842
US tons to kilograms	907.0
Kilograms to US tons	0.000907

TEMPERATURE CONVERSION TABLE

The bold figures in the central columns can be read as either centigrade or fahrenheit

Centigrade		Fahrenheit
-18	**0**	32
-15	**5**	41
-12	**10**	50
- 9	**15**	59
- 7	**20**	68
- 4	**25**	77
- 1	**30**	86
2	**35**	95
4	**40**	104
7	**45**	113
10	**50**	122
13	**55**	131
16	**60**	140
18	**65**	149
21	**70**	158
24	**75**	167
27	**80**	176
32	**90**	194
38	**100**	212
40	**104**	

(5 imperial gallons are equal to 6 US gallons.
A British ton is 2,240 lbs. A US ton is 2,000 lbs.)

INDEX

Abancay 176
acclimatization 24, 177
accommodation (general) 37-38
Achacachi 52, 292
airpass 4
airport, La Paz 247
airport, Lima 102, 107
alpaca 73-74, 209
Amazon (Bolivia)
   see Pando
Amazon (Peru)
   see Tambopata
Amboró-Carrasco (Nat. Park) 254, 309-313
Andagua 235, 239
Apolo 306-307
Arequipa 10, 176, **230-232**
arrieros
   see pack animals
Atahualpa 113
Auzangate (area) 209-222
Ayacucho 96, 169, 176
Aymará (language) 55-56
Aymará (people) 43-44, 244

backpacking (general) 79, 82-84
Ballestas Islands 227
begging 48, 87
Beni (biolog. station) 251
birds 65-71, 314
Bolívar, Simón 243, 245
Bolivia 243-318
brazil nuts 317-318

Cabanaconde 235-237, 240
Cajamarca 88-89, **113-117**
Calahuaya (culture) 300
Calca 185
Callejon de Huaylas 53, **127**, 128
camping 38, 83
Caraz 134
Carhuaz 134, 147
Cashapampa 138-139, 143-144
Cavernas de Repechon/San Rafael
   (wildlife santuary) 254
Cerro de Pasco 168
Cerro Tapilla (reserve) 255
Chacas 51, 134, 147, 149-152
Chachani (volcano) 234-235

Chachapoyas 119-126
Chachas (Colca Canyon) 238
Chairo 281-282
Chalcataya 253, 261-262
Challa 265
Challay 207
Charazani 304, 306
Chavín 129, 134, 135, **159**
Chavín de Huantar 95, 116, 119, **159**
Checacupe 215
Chinchero 186, 187, 188
Chiquián 134, 161-162
Choco (Colca Canyon) 238
Chojlla 272
Chulumani 272, 278
climate
   see seasons
coca 29, 49, 300
cocaine 248
Colca Canyon 235-240
Colcabamba 145, 146
condor, Andean 65, 146, 150, 227, 237, 277
Condoríri 253, 289
conservation 103-106, 314, 250-251
Copacabana 263-264
Cordillera Apolobamba 78, **299-307**
Cordillera Blanca 77, **127-159**
Cordillera Huayhuash 77, 78, 129, **161-165**
Cordillera Real 78, **267-290**
Cordillera Vilcabamba 77, 78, **191-209**
Cordillera Vilcanota 77, 78, **209-222**
Coroico 279-283, 285
culture, local 47-49
Cumbe Mayo 88-89, **116-117**
Cusco 10, 52, **171-189**, 246

diarrhoea 14-16
dogs 32, 53, 83
drugs 27, 246

El Misti (volcano) 230, 233-234
El niño 95
equipment (recommendations) 6-8
equipment (renting) 2, 136, 178, 233
Espíritu Pampa
   see Vilcabamba

festivals 50-53, 172, 209
fiestas
  see festivals
fitness 15
Flavio Machicado (Nat. Park) 253
flights 3, 36
flora 57-64
food 38-42
Fujimori, Alberto 98, 104

geology 75
Gold-diggers' Way 293-298
guanaco 73, 75
Guanay 297-298
guinea pig 26, 39, 40, 73

handicrafts 102-103, 248-249
health 15-28
high altitude sickness 24-26
hitchhiking 36
Huancaroma (wildlife reserve) 254
Huancavelica 52, 169
Huancayo 52, 53, 168
Huánuco 168
Huánuco Viejo 167
Huaraz 10, 52, **131-135**
Huari (culture) 95, 150, 151
Huascarán Mt 127, 131-135, 144
Huascarán NP 129-130
Huayllabamba (Inca Trail) 195, 198
Huayna Potosí 284, 290
Huiata (Mt) 284, 286
Huiñay Huayna 196
hummingbirds 70, 71
hypothermia 23

Illimani (Mt) 273-275, 267-269
Inca Road
  see Takesi Trail
Inca roads 44-45
Inca Trail, the 192-198
Incas 43-45, 97, 113, 171-172, 205,
  262, 265, 309
inoculations 15
insects 21-22, 84
Isiboro-Sécure (Nat. Park) 254
Island of the Sun 171, **265**

Juliaca 176

Khala Ciudad 277

Kuelap 121, 123-124
Kuntur Wasi 119

La Cumbre 279-280
La Paz 3, 52, **257-262**
Lachay de Lomas Nat. Park 112
Laja 260
Lambate 275
Lamud 126
Lares 189
Las Barrancas (Nat. Park) 255
Leimebamba 126
Levanto 125
Lima 3, 53, **107-112**, 133-134,
Limatambo 199
llama 73-74, 83, 279
Llamac 163
Llanganuco valley 134, 143-144, 145-
  146
Llanganuco to Santa Cruz hike 143-
  145
Llipi 297

Machu Picchu 177, 196-197, 203, 204
mail 101, 247
Mallasa (Nat. Park) 253
mammals **71-75**, 309, 312, 314
Manuripi-Heath (Reserve) 251
Mapiri 298
maps (Bolivia) 259
maps (Peru) 110, 137
Maras 187-189
minimum impact 86-87
Moche (culture) 95
Mollepata 199-200
money 10, 11, 99, 246
Mother Earth
  see Pachamama
mountain climbing (Bolivia) 284, 303

national parks
  see protected areas
natural history 57-72
Nazca (culture) 95
Noel Kempff Mercado (Nat. Park) 253,
  313-315

Ollantaytambo 197
Olleros 135, 157

Pachamama 46, 256

pack animals **85**, 133, 136, 178, 199, 210, 233, 275, 300
Pando 316-318
Paracas 95, **225-229**
Pastorurí (glacier) 79, 130
Paucartambo 51
Pelechuco 300-301
Persverancia (reserve)
    see Rios Blanco & Negro
Peru 93-240
photography 11-12
Pisac 181-182
Pisco 228
Pitumarca 215, 216, 217-218, 222
Pizarro, Francisco 93, 97, 113
plants, medicinal 27
police (Peru) 28-29, 111, 132
Pomabamba 143, 150
porters 85
presents 9
protected areas (Bolivia) 250-255
protected areas (Peru) 103-105
Puno 52, 53
Puya raimondii 64, 130

Quebrada Cayesh 154
Quebrada Churup 154
Quebrada Honda 149
Quebrada Ishinca 153
Quebrada Quilcayhuanca 154
Quebrada Santa Cruz 143-144
Quebrada Ulta 146-147
Quechua (language) 43, 55-56
Quechua (people) 43-44
Quillabamba 177, 207, 209

rabies 15, 20, 46
Raqchi 219
Recuay 134
Riberalta 316-317
Ríos Blanco & Negro (reserve) 255

Sabinacocha, Laguna 215-217
Sacsayhuamán 179-180
safety 28-32, 130, 229, 249
Sajama (Nat. Park) 254
Salinas 187, 188
Salkantay (Mt) 199-203, 204
Sama (biological station) 255
Samaipata 309, 313
San Pablo (Cajamarca) 118

Santa Cruz (Bolivia) 309, 310
Santa Teresa 202
seasons 4, 94-95, 135, 243-244
Sendero Luminoso
    see Shining Path
Shallop, Laguna 156
Shining Path 28, 96, 130
snakebite 19
Sorata 52, 292-293
South American Explorers Club 10, 12, **110-111**
Spanish (language) 54-55

Takesi Trail 269-272
Tambomachay 181
Tambopata (reserve) 104, 223
Tarahuasi 199
Tariquia (Nat. Park) 255
Tarma 168
theft 30-32
Titicaca, Lake 44, 52, 53, 244, **263-265**
Tiwanaku 95, 244, **260**
Torotoro (Nat. Park) 254
Totoral 275
trains 35, 176-177, 231
transport 33-36
trekking (general) 79, 80-81
Tres Ríos 274, 275
Tunari (Nat. Park) 254

Ubinas (volcano) 234
Ulla Ulla (Nat. Park) 253, 304-305
Ulla Ulla 299, 305
Unutuluni 297
Urubamba 187
Urubamba valley 181, 182, 184, 185-189

vicuña 73-75
Vilcabamba 206-209
viscacha 72, 211
Vitcos 207

Yalape 125
Yampupata 264-265
Yánama 145-149
Yerupajá Mt 127, 162
Yungas 78, 243, 244, 272, 273, 277
Yura (Reserve) 254

Zongo 285-287, 290-291